ACADEMIC LEGAL WRITING:

LAW REVIEW ARTICLES, STUDENT NOTES, SEMINAR PAPERS, AND GETTING ON LAW REVIEW

by

EUGENE VOLOKH
Gary T. Schwartz Professor of Law
UCLA School of Law

with foreword by

CHIEF JUDGE ALEX KOZINSKI
U.S. Court of Appeals for the Ninth Circuit

FOUNDATION PRESS
NEW YORK, NEW YORK
Fourth Edition 2010

© 2003 FOUNDATION PRESS

© 2005, 2007 THOMSON REUTERS/FOUNDATION PRESS

© 2010 By THOMSON REUTERS/FOUNDATION PRESS
        195 Broadway, 9th Floor
        New York, NY 10007
        Phone Toll Free 1–877–888–1330
        Fax (212) 367–6799
        foundation–press.com
Printed in the United States of America

ISBN 978–1–59941–750–9

Mat #40881285

To my beloved wife and sons,

Leslie Pereira,
Benjamin Pereira Volokh, and
Samuel Pereira Volokh

*

ABOUT THE AUTHOR

Eugene Volokh is the Gary T. Schwartz Professor of Law at UCLA, where he teaches free speech law, Religion Clauses law, criminal law, tort law, and academic legal writing. Before going into teaching, he clerked for Ninth Circuit Judge Alex Kozinski and for Justice Sandra Day O'Connor.

Since starting teaching in 1994, he has written (or, in a few instances, co-written) over 65 law review articles, including two in the *Harvard Law Review*, two in the *Yale Law Journal*, and five in the *Stanford Law Review*. He has also written over 80 op-eds in publications such as the *Wall Street Journal, New York Times, Washington Post, New Republic*, and many others. He is the author of *The First Amendment and Related Statutes*, a textbook from Foundation Press, and the operator of a daily blog called *The Volokh Conspiracy* (*http://volokh.com*, founded 2002). He is a member of the American Heritage Dictionary Usage Panel and the American Law Institute.

The article he wrote while in law school, *Freedom of Speech and Workplace Harassment* (UCLA L. Rev. 1992), has been cited in over 190 academic works and in 14 court cases; this seems to make it the most-cited student article from the 1990s and 2000s. A 2002 survey by Prof. Brian Leiter listed Volokh as the third most cited professor among those who entered law teaching after 1992 (with 810 citations in law reviews at the time; today, the number is about 2100). Four of his law review articles have also been cited in the opinions of Supreme Court Justices.

In Spring 2006, he participated anonymously (and, he's glad to report, successfully) in the *UCLA Law Review* write-on competition, to better hone the advice that he gives in the "Getting on Law Review" chapter. His pain is your gain.

TABLE OF CONTENTS

ACADEMIC LEGAL WRITING:

LAW REVIEW ARTICLES, STUDENT NOTES, SEMINAR PAPERS, AND GETTING ON LAW REVIEW

FOREWORD, BY JUDGE ALEX KOZINSKI

A few years ago I interviewed a candidate for a clerkship. He had record-breaking grades from a name-brand law school and his recommenders sprinkled their letters with phrases like "Kozinski clone" and "better even than you." This kid was hot.

His interview went well, and I had pretty much made up my mind to hire him on the spot, when I popped a fateful question: "So, have you decided on the topic for your law review note?"

"It's done," the candidate replied. And, with a flourish, he pulled an inch-thick document from his briefcase and plopped it on my desk. Impressed, I picked it up and read the title page: "The Alienability and Devisability of Possibilities of Reverter and Rights of Entry."

After making sure this wasn't a joke, I started wondering why someone would write a piece on such an arcane topic. Maybe this kid wasn't so smart after all. I decided I had better read the piece before making a hiring decision.

After the applicant left, his article sat on the corner of my desk like a brick. Every so often, I'd pick it up, leaf through it and try to read it, but with no success. It was well-written enough; the sentences were easy to understand and followed one another in seemingly logical fashion. But the effort was pointless because the subject matter was of absolutely no interest to me. Instead, my mind wandered to doubts about the author. How did he come to write on such a desiccated topic? Under that veneer of brilliance, was there a kook trying to get out? Could I really trust his judgment as to the countless sensitive issues he would have to confront during his clerkship? Would he constantly aim for the capillary and miss the jugular?

It is difficult to overstate the importance of a written paper for a young lawyer's career, especially if the piece is published. Grades, of necessity, are somewhat grainy and subjective; is an A- that much better than a B+? Letters of recommendation can be more useful, but they still rely on someone else's judgment, and they often have a stale booster quality about them. Words like "fabulous" and "extraordinary" lose their force by dint of repetition—though "Kozinski clone" is still pretty rare.

A paper is very different. It is the applicant's raw work product, unfiltered through a third-party evaluator. By reading it, you can personally evaluate the student's writing, research, logic and judgment. Are the sentences sleek and lithe or ponderous and convoluted? Does he lay out his argument in a logical fashion, and does he anticipate and refute objections? Is the topic broad enough to be useful, yet narrow enough to be adequately covered? Is it persuasive? Is it fun to read? Writing a paper engages so much of the lawyer's art that no other predictor of likely success on the job comes close. A well-written, well-researched, thoughtful paper can clinch that law firm job or clerkship. It is indispensable if you aim to teach.

Published student papers can also be quite useful and influential in the development of the law. A few law review notes and comments become classics cited widely by lawyers, courts and academics. Many more provide a useful service, such as a solid body of research or an important insight into a developing area. Most, however, are read by no one beyond the student's immediate family and cause hardly an eddy among the currents of the law.

Why do so many published student papers fail in their essential purpose? (The same question might well be asked about non-student academic writing.) The simple answer is that most students have no clue what to write about, or how to go about writing it. Finding a useful and interesting topic; determining the scope of the paper; developing a thesis and testing its viability; avoiding sudden death through preemption; and getting it placed in the best possible journal—these are among the tasks that most students aren't trained to perform. My applicant, smart though he was, went off track because no one showed him where the track was or how to stay on it. Many students make the same mistake every year.

This book fills a void in the legal literature: It teaches students how to go about finding a topic and developing it into a useful, interesting, publishable piece. It gives detailed and very helpful instructions for every aspect of the writing, research and publication process. And it comes from the keyboard of someone who has authored articles on a dizzying variety of legal topics and is widely regarded as one of the brightest lights in legal academia.

But I digress.

I pondered the fate of my applicant for some weeks and never did get myself to read more than a few lines of his dreary paper. Finally I called and offered him a clerkship with a strong hint—not quite a condition—that he drop the paper in the nearest trash can and start from scratch. I explained to him what was wrong with it, and what a successful paper should look like. "You can do whatever you want," I told him, "but if you should have the misfortune of getting this dog published, it will only drag you down when you apply for a Supreme Court clerkship or a position as a law professor."

The applicant gratefully accepted the advice. He chucked the "Possibilities of Reverter" paper and went about developing a new topic. Some months later, he produced a dynamite piece that became one of the seminal published articles in a developing area of the law. Eventually, he did clerk for the Supreme Court and has since become a widely respected and often quoted legal academic. His name is Eugene Volokh.

INTRODUCTION

A good student article can get you a high grade, a good law review editorial board position, and a publication credit. These credentials can in turn help get you jobs, clerkships, and—if you're so inclined—teaching positions. The experience will hone your writing, which is probably a lawyer's most important skill. Likewise, a good article written while you're clerking or in your early years as a practicing lawyer can impress employers (academic and otherwise) and clients.

And your article may influence judges, lawyers, and legislators. Law is one of the few disciplines where second-year graduate students write (not just cowrite) scholarly articles; and these articles are often taken seriously by others in the profession. Lawyers read them, scholars discuss them, and courts—including the U.S. Supreme Court—cite them.

Occasionally, student articles and articles by young practicing lawyers have a huge impact. Here are a few examples, limited to student articles published since 1990 (there are many others from the 1980s and before):

- Janet Hoeffel's student article, *The Dark Side of DNA Profiling: Unreliable Scientific Evidence Meets the Criminal Defendant* (Stan. L. Rev. 1990), has been cited by over 95 academic works, 27 cases, and at least 12 briefs. (Since Westlaw's BRIEFS-ALL database is quite limited in its coverage, the brief counts in this list are likely to be substantial underestimates.)

- Victor J. Cosentino's student article, *Strategic Lawsuits Against Public Participation: An Analysis of the Solutions* (Cal. Western L. Rev. 1990), has been cited by over 15 academic works, 19 cases, and 32 briefs.

- Kevin Werbach's student article, *Looking It Up: Dictionaries and Statutory Interpretation* (Harv. L. Rev. 1994), has been cited by over 125 academic works, 13 cases, and 16 briefs.

- Mark Filip's student article, *Why Learned Hand Would Never Consult Legislative History Today* (Harv. L. Rev. 1992), has been cited by over 90 academic works, 10 cases, and 23 briefs.

- Rachel Godsil's student article, *Remedying Environmental Racism* (Mich. L. Rev. 1991), has been cited by over 150 academic works and 2 cases.

- Bradley Karkkainen's student article, *"Plain Meaning": Justice Scalia's Jurisprudence of Strict Statutory Construction* (Harv.

J.L. & Pub. Pol'y 1994), has been cited by over 120 academic works, 2 cases, and 2 briefs.

- Jim Ryan's student article, *Smith and the Religious Freedom Restoration Act: An Iconoclastic Assessment* (Va. L. Rev. 1992), has been cited by over 120 academic works, 1 case, and 9 briefs.

- Chris Ford's student article, *Administering Identity: The Determination of "Race" in Race-Conscious Law* (Cal. L. Rev. 1994), published by the *California Law Review* (a top 10 journal) while Ford was a student at a different law school, has been cited by 105 academic works, 1 case, and 2 briefs.

- Craig A. Bowman & Blake M. Cornish's article, *A More Perfect Union: A Legal and Social Analysis of Domestic Partnership Ordinances* (Colum. L. Rev. 1992), has been cited by over 115 academic works, 4 cases, and 4 briefs.

- Your author's student article, *Freedom of Speech and Workplace Harassment* (UCLA L. Rev. 1992), has been cited by over 190 academic works, 14 cases, and 31 briefs.

As you can see, influential pieces aren't limited to general-purpose journals; consider the *Harvard Journal of Law and Public Policy* piece. Nor are they limited to articles written by students at top 10 law schools—consider the *California Western Law Review* article, which is the second most-cited-by-courts article on the list.

And the influence of student law review articles isn't limited to a few high-impact pieces. Courts cite student articles at the rate of at least about 500 citations per year. This means that over 1/8 of all court citations to law review articles are to student-written articles, and a typical student article is about 40% as likely to get cited as a typical non-student article—an excellent rate for student work. Law review articles appear to cite student articles at the rate of about 15,000 per year.

Top 10 journals do get a disproportionate share of the cites—but over 70% of the court citations in a sample that I've examined (the approximately 500 citations in 2006) came from non-top-10 journals, over 50% came from non-top-25 journals, and over 10% came from specialty journals (including those at many schools below the top 10). The sample included at least five cites each to the general journals at American, Arizona, Baylor, Georgia, Indiana, North Carolina, St. John's, Temple, the University of Washington, and Wisconsin.

Writing an article is also one of the hardest things you will do, whether you write it as a law review note, as an independent study project, or as a side project in your first years in practice. Your pre-law-school writing experience and your first-year writing class will help prepare you for it, but only partly. It's not easy to create an original scholarly work that contributes to our understanding of the law.

Seminar papers tend to be less ambitious and less time-consuming, in part because they don't have to be publishable. But they too help improve your writing—and if you invest enough effort into writing them, you can then easily make them publishable, and get extra benefit from your hard work.

In this book, I try to give some advice, based on my own writing experience and on discussions with others, for you to combine with other advice you get. These ideas have worked for me, and I hope they work for you.

Different parts of this book relate to different stages of your project. If you're just trying to get on law review, I suggest that you read Part XXV, about getting on law review, Part VII, about getting the first draft done, and Parts IX through XVI, about writing and editing. If you're writing a Note, seminar paper, or article, I suggest that you:

1. Skim the Table of Contents, to see the various topics that the book covers.

2. Start by reading Part I, on choosing a claim, Part II, on test suites, and Part XXVI, on academic ethics.

3. If you can, read Part XIX, which reprints and analyzes a very successful student article. Closely examining this successful article may help you succeed with your own article.

4. Read the short Part XXI as well, if you're writing a seminar term paper.

5. Once you identify a potential topic, read Part VIII, on research, and Part XVII, on using evidence correctly. (Read Parts XVII.G–XVII.I only if you plan to use social science evidence.)

6. When you're ready to start writing—which I hope you will be, soon—read Parts III through VII, on structuring your article.

7. As you get close to the end of your first draft, consider rereading Part I again, to see how you can improve your article in light of what you've learned while you were writing it.

8. Once you're done with the first draft, focus on editing it; read Parts IX through XVI, on writing and editing.

9. If you're a law journal staffer or editor, read Parts XVII and XXII to help you understand how to better cite-check others' articles, as well as how to better write your own.

10. When you're ready to publish the article, or publish the seminar paper that you've turned into a publishable article, read Parts XXIII and XXIV.

For more advice, read Elizabeth Fajans & Mary R. Falk, *Scholarly Writing for Law Students: Seminar Papers, Law Review Notes, and Law Review Competition Papers* (2000); Pamela Samuelson, *Good Legal Writing: Of Orwell and Window Panes*, 46 U. Pitt. L. Rev. 149 (1984); and Richard Delgado, *How to Write a Law Review Article*, 20 U.S.F. L. Rev. 445 (1986).

ACKNOWLEDGMENTS

Many thanks to Laurence Abraham, Bruce Adelstein, Alison Anderson, Stuart Banner, David Behar, Stuart Benjamin, Paul Bergman, David Binder, Julie Marie Blake, Andrew Brady, Dan Bussel, Stephen Calkins, Dennis Callahan, Paul Cassell, Michael Cernovich, Chris Cherry, Larry Dougherty, Jason Dreibelbis, Joseph Fishman, Cassandra Franklin, Eric Freedman, Dana Gardner, Jim Gardner, Bryan Garner, Ken Graham, Sharon Gold, Kendall Hannon, Justin Hughes, Sera Hwang, Alan Kabat, Brian Kalt, Pam Karlan, Orin Kerr, Ken Klee, Kris Knaplund, Adam Kolber, Mae Kuykendall, Terri LeClercq, Sandy Levinson, Nancy Levit, Jacob Levy, Jim Lindgren, Dan Lowenstein, Elaine Mandel, Jonathan Miller, Michael Mulvania, Steve Munzer, Michael O'Donnell, Steve Postrel, Deborah Rhode, Stephen Rynerson, Greg Schwinghammer, David Sklansky, Bill Somerfeld, Clyde Spillenger, Chris Stone, Lauren Teukolsky, Suja Thomas, Martin Totaro, Rebecca Tushnet, Hanah Metchis Volokh, Sasha Volokh, Vladimir Volokh, Alysa Wakin, Bruce Wessel, Ziggy Williamson, Neal Wilson, Virginia Wise, Steve Yeazell, Tung Yin, and Amy Zegart for their advice; to the UCLA Law Library staff—especially Laura Cadra, Xia Chen, Maureen Dunnigan, Kevin Gerson, June Kim, Jennifer Lentz, Cynthia Lewis, Linda Karr O'Connor, and John Wilson—for all their help; and to Sara Cames, Michael Devine, and Leib Lerner for their thoughtful and thorough editing, proofreading, and cite-checking. And, of course, my deepest thanks to Judge Alex Kozinski, who taught me most of what I know about legal writing.

I. FINDING WHAT TO WRITE ABOUT (THE CLAIM)

Good legal scholarship should make (1) a claim that is (2) novel, (3) nonobvious, (4) useful, (5) sound, and (6) seen by the reader to be novel, nonobvious, useful, and sound.[*]

This is true whether the author is a student, a young lawyer, a seasoned expert, or an academic. I will sometimes allude below to student authors (since I expect that most readers of this book will be students), for instance by discussing grades or faculty advisors. But nearly all of this book should apply equally to other aspiring academic writers.

A. The Claim

1. Your basic thesis

Most good works of original scholarship have a basic thesis—a claim they are making about the world. This could be a *descriptive* claim about the world as it is or as it was (such as a historical assertion, a claim about a law's effects, or a statement about how courts are interpreting a law). It could be a *prescriptive* claim about what should be done (such as how a law or a constitutional provision should be interpreted, what new statute should be enacted, or how a statute or a common-law rule should be changed). It could also be a combination of both a descriptive claim and a prescriptive one. In any case, you should be able to condense that claim into one sentence, for instance:

1. "Law X is unconstitutional because ...."

2. "The legislature ought to enact the following statute: ...."

3. "Properly interpreted, this statute means ...."

4. "This law is likely to have the following side effects ...."

5. "This law is likely to have the following side effects ..., and therefore should be rejected or modified to say ...."

6. "Courts have interpreted the statute in the following ways ..., and therefore the statute should be amended as follows ...."

7. "Several different legal rules are actually inconsistent in certain ways, and this inconsistency should lead us to ...."

---

[*] I am indebted for much of this formulation to Stephen L. Carter, *Academic Tenure and "White Male" Standards: Some Lessons from the Patent Law*, 100 Yale L.J. 2065, 2083 (1991).

8. "My empirical research shows that this legal rule has unexpectedly led to ..., and it should therefore be changed this way ...."

9. "My empirical research shows that this law has had the following good effects ..., and should therefore be kept, or extended to other jurisdictions."

10. "Viewing this law from a [feminist/Catholic/economic] perspective leads us to conclude that the law is flawed, and should be changed this way ...."

11. "Conventional wisdom that ... is wrong, because ...."

So a few examples:

1. "The ban on paying for organs to be transplanted violates patients' constitutional rights to defend their lives." This fits in category #1 discussed above.

2. "Punishing citizens for failing to report crimes that they observe may sometimes discourage reporting, because people who fail to report promptly will realize they've committed a crime and will thus be reluctant to talk to the police later." Category #4.

3. "Courts often favor the more religious parent over the less religious parent in child custody decisions, and this violates the Establishment Clause." Category #8, because it contains a potentially novel descriptive claim (about what courts do) as well as a prescriptive claim.

4. "Though many people assume that liberal Justices have broader views of free speech than conservative Justices, it turns out that Justice Kennedy has the broadest view of free speech, Justice Breyer has the narrowest, and the other Justices fall in between without a clear liberal-conservative pattern." Category #11.

Capturing your point in a single sentence helps you focus your discussion, and helps you communicate your core point to the readers. Moreover, many readers will remember only one sentence about your article (especially if they only read the Abstract or the Introduction, as many readers do). You need to understand what you want that sentence to be, so you can frame your article in a way that will help readers absorb your main point.

2. The descriptive and the prescriptive parts of the thesis

The most interesting claims are often ones that combine the descriptive and the prescriptive, telling readers something they didn't know about the world—whether it's about what courts have done, how a legal rule changes people's behavior, or why a rule has developed in a particular way—but also suggesting what should be done. The descriptive is valuable because many people are more persuadable by novel facts than by novel moral or legal arguments. The prescriptive is valuable because it answers the inevitable "so what?" question that many practical-minded readers will ask whenever they hear a factual description, even an interesting one.

You can certainly write an article that's purely prescriptive or purely descriptive (though see Part I.I.4, p. 36 for a discussion of one sort of descriptive piece that you might want to avoid). Combining the prescriptive and the descriptive, however, tends to yield a more interesting and impressive article. So, as you're developing your claim, try to look both for novel, nonobvious, useful, and sound descriptive assertions and for novel, nonobvious, useful, and sound prescriptions.

Thus, for instance, say that you are writing about freedom of speech and hostile public accommodation harassment law, under which courts and administrative agencies award damages when proprietors of public accommodations allow speech that creates a racially, ethnically, religiously, or sexually hostile environment for some patrons. You could just use First Amendment precedents and First Amendment theory to analyze the hostile public accommodation environment rules, and explain why they should be preserved, changed, or repealed (the prescriptive dimension).

But if you could find cases, including perhaps hard-to-discover administrative agency decisions, that show that there's a real problem, and that hostile public accommodations environment law is indeed restricting potentially valuable speech (the descriptive dimension), your argument would be stronger. It would better persuade readers that your proposal is useful, since many readers might otherwise be skeptical that there's a problem to be solved. It would help you more concretely present your prescriptive argument. And even if the readers disagree with, skim over, or forget your prescriptive argument, they might still find value in your novel descriptive observations—and give you credit for making these discoveries.

B. Finding a Claim

1. Finding a problem

To find a claim, you must first identify a problem, whether a doctrinal, empirical, or historical one, in a general area that interests you. The claim will then be your proposed solution to that problem.

Here are some tips, together with some quotes (in the footnotes) from people who have found their topics this way. These quotes might help you envision the suggestions more concretely. I also note in some of the quotes the rough ranking of the school to which the sender went, so readers can see that they can publish successful articles even if they don't attend one of the very top schools.

For more tips, read Heather Meeker's *Stalking the Golden Topic: A Guide to Locating and Selecting Topics for Legal Research Papers*, 1996 Utah L. Rev. 917.

2. ... in cases you've read for class, or in class discussions

Think back on cases you've read for class that led you to think "this leaves an important question unresolved" or "the reasoning here is unpersuasive."* But try to avoid the questions that excite everyone, since those are likely to have already been heavily written about. Look for something that interests you more than it interests others. "[R]un in the opposite direction from the crowd, in order ... to have something new to say."†

---

* From a graduate of a roughly #50-ranked law school, who is now clerking for a federal district judge: "I wrote my note on university liability for failure to prevent rampage killings on campus. We read *Tarasoff* in my first year torts class, and I found the idea of liability for failing to predict someone else's actions really fascinating. I would advise students to find something they're really interested in, and figure out a way to use a recent event (like the [Virginia Tech] shooting) as an excuse to discuss their interests.... [T]he judge told me the note played a factor in her decision to hire me."

† A quote from a lawyer, who also writes: "I took a Privacy Law course ... back in 1997 and at that time the 'big hot issue' was whether websites should be collecting information about children who sign up to play online games, etc.—so in that class, about 5 or 10 people all said they were going to write about that narrow topic. Needless to say, I went running in the opposite direction, and picked a topic that almost nobody was writing about at the time—the online databases of sex offenders, and the privacy consequences. That ended up being a published note in the *American Criminal Law Review* and when I last looked several years ago, it was cited by the Ninth Circuit."

13

Also think back on class discussions that intrigued you but didn't yield a well-settled answer.

3. ... in casebook questions

Read the questions that many casebooks include after each case; these questions often identify interesting unsolved problems.* Look not just at the casebook that you used yourself, but also at other casebooks in the field.

4. ... in issues left over or created by recent Supreme Court cases

Read recent Supreme Court cases in fields that interest you, and see whether they leave open major issues or create new ambiguities or uncertainties.†

5. ... in your work as a research assistant

If you're working as a research assistant for a professor, keep an eye out for topics that might be useful to you. Not only might you find a topic, but you'll have learned a lot about the surrounding area of the law,

---

"Also took a copyright law seminar .... It seemed like the majority of the seminar participants were writing about infringement, so again I ran in the opposite direction, and instead wrote about licensing, including a proposal for various forms of compulsory licensing in circumstances where the copyright holder did not otherwise want any use made of his works. Not only did I get an A, but also I submitted it to the Burkan Memorial competition, won a modest cash prize, and ended up having the paper published in the *Journal of the Copyright Society*, and it was even excerpted into a copyright law casebook."

* From a recent graduate, who went on to clerk for a federal circuit court judge: "I thought of the topic while reading through author commentary in my first-year Torts casebook. Good commentary sections in casebooks will often pose unsettled legal questions."

† From a student at a roughly #25-ranked law school who is clerking for a federal judge: "I knew I wanted to write a student note on [a recent Supreme Court case], since the decision had come down 3 months before. My first stop was to read the early literature on the decision, and I noticed the disagreement over what the opinion actually did. That got me thinking about doing a statistical study on the decision, by looking at every district court that had applied [the decision in a particular context] (and comparing it to a similar control group of cases from the year prior applying the 'old' standard). From there I read a number of similar statistical studies from the likes of Prof. Lee Epstein, Prof. Kevin Clermont, etc.... My note was well received (20 Law Review citations in 2 years, a court of appeals cite, and a couple of case books) and I think [it contributed to my] getting elected Editor in Chief and my subsequent clerkship."

and created a contact with a professor who may be inclined to help you.*
The possibility of finding such topics might even be a reason to take a
job as a research assistant.

6. ... by asking faculty members

Ask faculty members which parts of their fields have been unduly
neglected by scholars. Some of the professors you ask may even suggest
specific problems.† Not all take this view: some think it's the student's
job to find a problem. But it doesn't hurt to ask several professors, in
case some of them are indeed willing to suggest topics.

7. ... by asking practicing lawyers

Ask practicing lawyers which important unsettled questions they
find themselves facing. To the extent you can, focus on asking academi-

---

* From a graduate of a roughly #75-ranked law school: "I got the idea for my law review article, which was about proposals to reform the so-called 'bilateral regime' governing international air travel, based on information I learned while working as a research
assistant for one of my professors. The subject was tangential to what I was researching
for him (European Union aviation regulations), but I really wanted to explore the topic
further and it tied in well with my law journal's focus. I asked my professor for permission
to recycle part of the research materials I had gathered for him and he said that was fine
.... I used the article as a writing sample with my job applications and was uniformly
complimented on how it took a very obscure subject and explained it in a manner understandable to a lay reader."

A similar response from a graduate of a roughly #50-ranked law school: "I got my
note idea while doing research during 1L summer for my civ pro/antitrust professor, who
generously let me run with a new issue of personal jurisdiction that I'd researched for
him. I ended up winning the ABA Antitrust Section's annual writing prize, which was a
huge honor and thrill."

† From a graduate of a roughly #70-ranked law school who is now clerking for a federal administrative law judge: "My note was published and was one of the deciding factors
in acquiring my current clerkship, so I consider myself very fortunate that I was turned
on to a good topic. In the summer after my 1L year I interned with the local public defender's office, mostly working with juveniles accused of crimes. I found the work very interesting so figured it would be good to write my note on something relevant to juve-
nile/criminal law, but had no idea of how to come up with a topic. I e-mailed my first year
criminal procedure professor (who also happened to have written a treatise on our state's
Juvenile Act) and asked him about current issues/cases in juvenile law that might be ap-
propriate to research for a note. He gave me a list of a few suggestions, one of which was
the applicability of new 'sexual predator' laws to juveniles adjudicated delinquent for sexual crimes. The topic of my note ended up being the conflict between the Adam Walsh Act
and Pennsylvania's Juvenile Act, and I don't think I would have been able to come up
with that completely on my own."

cally-minded lawyers, for instance ones who had written law review articles, treatises, or practitioner articles. In particular, ask lawyers with whom you've worked, since they may feel especially willing to help you.

Ask the lawyers to suggest a specific problem, and not just to highlight a potentially fruitful area. As I mentioned, some (not all) faculty members may be reluctant to suggest such problems, since they may think that it's the students' job to find their topics themselves. But practicing lawyers should have no such qualms.*

8. ... by checking Westlaw summaries of important recent cases

Check the *Westlaw Bulletin* (WLB), *Westlaw State Bulletin* (WSB-CA, WSB-NY, and such), and *Westlaw Topical Highlights* (WTH-CJ, WTH-IP, and such) databases. These databases summarize noteworthy recent cases, in one paragraph each; many such cases contain legal developments that might prove worth analyzing.

9. ... by paying attention to interesting newspaper articles

When you read newspaper articles, keep an eye out for interesting legal questions.† This seems to be especially useful for international law articles, as one professor reports: "In the international law journal context, which is different from the general law review, a lot of good stu-

---

* From a law professor: "I called a public interest lawyer for whom I had worked in my first legal job, which was during my last year in college. He had been on law review when in law school and knew what made a good note. He told me about a constitutional issue surrounding some new mortgage programs about which the organization was concerned. I was able to write a good note and receive feedback from lawyers at the organization. The note garnered me a few awards in law school, a few citations, and helped me land a teaching position."

† From a graduate of a roughly #25-ranked law school who nonetheless got a federal circuit clerkship, possibly in part because of his Note: "I got the idea from a page 11 (or so) newspaper article. The article discussed a pending lawsuit against an energy company alleging human rights abuse in Indonesia, and mentioned that the district judge had solicited the State Department's view of the impact of the case on U.S./Indonesia foreign relations. I thought that was interesting, and did a little research to see if it was a common practice. It had occurred several times in similar cases, so I explored those cases in a Note." Likewise, from a law professor and former federal judge: "I got my student note from reading the editorial page of the *Wall Street Journal*. It highlighted a pressing legal issue. I researched the issue, discovered little had been written on it, and took things from there."

dent notes come out of issues raised in trade publications and newspapers." But it can also be helpful in other fields.

10. ... by reading legal blogs

Read legal blogs that specialize in fields in which you're interested. Bloggers often post about interesting new cases that pose thorny, unresolved problems.*

11. ... by finding articles that aim to identify unanswered problems

Look for articles that aim to identify unanswered problems in some field. Some of them have subtitles such as "A Research Agenda," which signal that they're trying to identify problems for others to solve. Others might not have such a tell-tale name, but might be known to professors who work in the field. Search for the "research agenda" articles, and ask professors whether they know of such articles.†

12. ... by looking back at your experience as an extern or summer associate

Think back on any experience you might have from summer jobs at a law firm,‡ a judge's chambers, or a public interest organization.* (See

---

* From a law student: "My note—which describes how a Ninth Circuit opinion exposes advertisers to additional liability for sending text messages—is accepted for publication. I discovered the topic by periodically reviewing law and technology blog postings. First, I used the blog postings to evaluate the decision's importance. Second, I searched SSRN and Google Scholar to determine whether anyone had forthcoming papers on the topic. Third, I searched for published articles through commercial databases including Lexis, West, and HeinOnline. I concluded the topic was important, but lacked published analysis. I decided to fill the void."

† From a law student: "I found my note topic as part of your suggested research agenda in your recent UCLA Law Review Article, *Implementing the Right to Keep and Bear Arms [for Self-Defense: An Analytical Framework and a Research Agenda]*. I'm writing about the Walsh Act mandatory release conditions, which you suggested as part of your research agenda. For me, this research agenda provided a number of very narrow, focused topics. I think this has been an advantage relative to my peers on ... Law Review."

‡ From a law professor: "My second law review comment—on insurance coverage disputes—has been cited in the Witkin California law treatise twice, in 13 law review articles, 2 federal district court opinions, 2 state court opinions, and at least 2 trial court memoranda and 6 appellate court briefs. It arose from a long research assignment from

Part XX below on turning practical work into articles, and on asking your employer for permission to do this.)

13. ... by thinking back on your pre-law-school experiences

Think back on your pre-law-school experiences, whether academic, professional, or personal. Can you tie interesting things you learned there to a legal question?

For instance, did your undergraduate history classes teach you about some fascinating but underdiscussed past legal controversies? Do you know something about a foreign country that can help you do comparative law work dealing with the law of that country? Did you get to know people in some past job who might give you useful suggestions?†

---

my second year summer associate gig, something that took me about three weeks of time to canvass the relevant case law from all jurisdictions on when events 'trigger' comprehensive general liability insurance policies. I got permission from the law firm to use the research memo (without using client information, of course) as basically the background section and then added my own normative analysis when converting it into a comment.

"I think this comment has garnered the court opinion citations (and briefs, etc.) because it was on a subject that had spawned different rules in various jurisdictions, and that arose with surprising frequency in modern litigation, and being somewhat 'unsexy' had not attracted much scholarly attention."

* From a law professor: "I got the idea for my note when I was volunteering at a public interest organization. A knotty legal problem came up and I was sent off to research it. That experience not only generated my note, but launched a career-long engagement with the topic that has produced numerous articles and a book."

Likewise from a recent graduate, who's now clerking for a federal appellate judge: "During my 1L summer with a prominent civil rights group, my boss asked me for a memo on 'whether corporations have the right to religious speech.' I found almost nothing on the subject, as the boss expected, because the group was considering it for potential impact litigation in an underdeveloped area. Many lawyers give 1L interns similarly broad and unexplored topics, not because the topics [are] unimportant, but because a boss can afford to expend limitless 1L summer hours on lengthy research about the unknown. I picked mine for a note topic because it would (1) fill a void in literature, (2) meet real needs of litigants, (3) consider theory and law at a reasonably challenging level in an emerging area, (4) avoid the fact-bound limited utility of the case note, and (5) be something I already knew about and could handle writing about during the busiest two months of law school. My note won three awards and was on SSRN's top ten download list."

† From a recent graduate: "The year before law school, I had worked at an onshore mutual fund in Moscow, run by Americans. My former boss there was a lawyer (albeit much more of an entrepreneur) and very much into legal reform and institution building issues; he suggested I look into the topic of privatization auctions in Russia. Two years later, the resulting piece of work was published as a full-fledged article."

14. ... by attending symposia or panels

Attend law school symposia or panels on subjects that you find generally interesting. These will often give you a sense of the hot and unresolved questions in the field. Try doing the same for symposia or panels at other law schools in town; you might be able to get on each school's mailing list, if you ask.*

Look for a problem that's big enough to be important and interesting but small enough to be manageable.

15. Looking for future claims when you're in class

If you're thinking ahead about writing an article a semester or two from now, look for claims when you're in class, especially a class you really enjoy. The key here is to face class like a scholar rather than like a normal law student.

Your course work will often bring you up against ambiguity, vagueness, and contradiction, whether in cases, statutes, or constitutional provisions. You'll also often read arguments that you realize are shallow, circular, or speculative.

The natural reaction for many lawyers and law students is to try to evade these problems. We pretend that a case announces a clear rule even though it's full of mushy terms that are often indeterminate in application. We learn the standard arguments, however conclusory they might be, so we can repeat them on the exam. We ignore the five different approaches courts have taken and instead just assume they fit in the "majority" and "minority" rules that the casebook gives you.

This approach may actually be good enough for succeeding (most of the time) in class, and even for succeeding in many tasks as a lawyer. Many cases that you'll face as a lawyer will involve only one of several competing rules—the one that's well-settled in your jurisdiction—or will trigger a rule's clear core rather than its vague periphery. And even

---

* From a recent graduate: "I ended up publishing my student research as an article in another school's journal [an international law journal at Yale] rather than a note in my own (I submitted it the summer after my graduation from law school).... I got my basic idea by attending an academic symposium in the general area in which I was interested... [S]eeing in person what others in the field were excited about or struggling with ... was an efficient way to determine the questions that were fertile for deeper exploration.... [I]f you have the opportunity to attend a conference on a topic you're interested in (mine, luckily, was right on my own law school campus), I'd certainly recommend it."

when a governing precedent is based on a circular argument, it's still the governing precedent, so the flaws in its justification often won't need to detain you.

But if you are a would-be scholar, even a temporary scholar who just wants to write an article or two while in law school, you should take a different approach. You should seek out ambiguity, vagueness, contradiction, glibness, circularity, and unsupported assumptions. They give you the opportunity to shine by doing better.

So if you find these flaws in the materials you're studying, look more closely. Check the notes following the case to see if they point to articles discussing the flaws. Maybe those articles cover the field, but maybe they themselves are inadequate, and just give you more to think about (or more bad arguments to rebut). Ask the professor whether he thinks the topic seems worth writing about, or whether it has already been well covered by others. And focus closely on those discussions that other students view as most unsatisfying: They are the natural foundation for your own work.

16. Checking with your law school's faculty

Once you've tentatively chosen a problem, run it by your faculty advisor. Your advisor will probably know better than you do whether there's already too much written on the subject, or whether there's less substance to the problem than you might think.

Also talk to other faculty members at your school who teach in the field, even if you don't know them. Most are happy to spend a few minutes helping a student.

Even if you're no longer a student, you should still be able to draw on your law school's faculty: Professors feel some obligation to help alumni, especially those who they think will eventually try to go into teaching. If you feel uncomfortable approaching a faculty member whom you don't know, ask another professor whom you do know to introduce you (in person or electronically).

17. Keeping an open mind

Do your research with an open mind. Be willing to make whatever claims your reading and thinking lead you to.

Also be willing to change or refine the problem itself. Remember that your goal is to find whatever problem will yield the best article.

Don't feel locked into a particular problem or solution just because it's the first one you thought of.

18. Identifying a tentative solution

Decide what seems to be the best solution to the problem. For the descriptive part of your claim, the best solution is the most plausible explanation of the facts that you've uncovered, such as facts about history, about the way the law has been applied, or about the way people behave.

For the prescriptive part, the best solution could be a new statute, a new constitutional rule, a new common law rule, a new interpretation of a statute, a new enforcement practice, a novel application of a general principle to a certain kind of case, or the like. This will be your *claim*: "State legislatures should enact the following statute ...." "Courts should interpret this constitutional provision this way ...." "This law should be seen as unconstitutional in these cases ..., but constitutional in those ...."

Test your solution against several factual scenarios you've found in the cases, and against several other hypotheticals you can think up. Does the solution yield the results that you think are right? Does it seem determinate enough to be consistently applied by judges, juries, or executive officials? If the answer to either question is "no," change your solution to make it more correct and more clear. (I discuss this "test suite" process further in Part II.)

The solution doesn't have to be perfect: It's fine to propose a rule even when you have misgivings about the results it will produce in a few unusual cases. But candidly testing your solution against the factual scenarios will tell you whether even you yourself find the solution plausible. If you don't, your readers won't, either.

C. Novelty

1. Adding to the body of professional knowledge

To be valuable, your article must be novel: It must say something that others haven't said before. It's not enough for your ideas to be original to you, in the sense that you came up with them on your own—the article must add something to the state of expert knowledge about the field.

21

In practice, the best bet is to find a topic that has not been much written on. The second best option is to at least find a claim that hasn't been made before, even if many others have made other claims related to the topic. But if you really want to reach a conclusion that others have already covered (e.g., race-based affirmative action is or is not constitutional, the death penalty is or is not proper, and the like), that too could work: You just need to make sure that your claim coupled with your basic rationale is novel.

For instance, say you want to criticize obscenity law. Many people have already argued that obscenity law is unconstitutional because it interferes with self-expression, or because it's too vague. You shouldn't write yet another article that makes the same point.

But a new test for what should constitute unprotected obscenity might be a novel proposal (and might even be useful, if you argue that state supreme courts should adopt it even if the U.S. Supreme Court doesn't, see Part I.E.2, p. 24). So would a proposal that obscenity law should be entirely unconstitutional, if you've come up with a novel *justification* for your claim: For instance, the claim that "obscenity laws are unsound because, as a study I've done shows, such laws are usually enforced primarily against gay pornography" may well be novel. (This claim and the others I mention below are just examples. I don't vouch for their correctness, or recommend that you write about them.)

What if you've chosen your topic and your basic rationale, and, four weeks into your research, you find that someone else has said the same thing? No need to despair yet.

2. Making novelty through nuance

Often you can make your claim novel by making it more nuanced. For instance, don't just say, "bans on nonmisleading commercial advertising should be unconstitutional," but say (perhaps) "bans on nonmisleading commercial advertising should be unconstitutional unless minors form a majority of the intended audience for the advertising." The more complex your claim, the more likely it is that no one has made it before. Of course, you should make sure that the claim is still (a) useful and (b) correct.

Some tips for making your claim more nuanced:

1. Think about what special factors—for instance, government interests or individual rights—are present in some situations covered by your claim but not in others. Could you modify your

claim to consider these factors?

2. Think about your arguments in support of your claim. Do they work well in some cases but badly in others? Perhaps you should limit your claim accordingly.

3. For most legal questions, both the simple "yes" answer and the simple "no" tend to attract a lot of writing. See if you can come up with a plausible answer that's somewhere in between—"yes" in some cases, "no" in others.

D. Nonobviousness

Say Congress is considering a proposed federal cause of action for libel on the Internet. You want to argue that such a law wouldn't violate the First Amendment.

Your claim would be novel, but pretty obvious. Most people you discuss it with will say, "you're right, but I could have told you that myself." Libel law, if properly limited, has repeatedly been held to be constitutional, and many people have already argued that libel law should be the same in cyberspace as outside it. Unless you can explain how federal cyber-libel law differs from state libel law applied to cyberspace, your point will seem banal.

Claims such as that one, which just apply settled law or well-established arguments to slightly new fact patterns, tend to look obvious. Keep in mind that your article will generally be read by smart and often slightly arrogant readers (your professor, the law review editors, other people working in the field) who will be tempted to say "well, I could have thought of that if I'd only taken fifteen minutes"—even when that's not quite true.

You can avoid obviousness by adding some twist that most observers would not have thought of. For example, might a federal cyber-libel law be not just constitutional, but also more efficient, because it sets a uniform nationwide standard? Could it be more efficient in some situations but not others? Could it interact unexpectedly with some other federal laws? Making your claim more nuanced can make it less obvious as well as more novel.

If you can, describe your claim to a faculty member who works in the field (besides your advisor), an honest classmate who's willing to criticize your ideas, and a lawyer who works in the field. If they think it's obvious, either refine your claim, or, if you're confident that the claim is in fact not obvious, refine your presentation to better show the claim's unexpected aspects.

E. Utility

You'll be investing a lot of time in your article. You'll also want readers to invest time in reading it. It helps if the article is useful—if at least some readers can come away from it with something that they'll find professionally valuable. And the more readers can benefit from it, the better.

1. Focus on issues left open

Say you think the U.S. Supreme Court's *Doe v. Roe* decision is wrong. You can write a brilliant piece about how the Court erred, and such an article might be useful to some academics. But *Doe* is the law, and unless the Court revisits the issue, few people will practically benefit from your insight.

You should ask yourself: How can I make my article more useful not just to radically minded scholars, but also to lawyers, judges, and scholars who aren't interested in challenging the existing Supreme Court caselaw here? One possibility is to identify questions that *Doe* left unresolved—or questions that it created—and explain how they should be resolved in light of *Doe*'s reasoning, along with the reasoning of several other Supreme Court cases in the field. Such an article would be useful to any lawyer, scholar, or judge who's considering a matter that involves one of these questions.

2. Apply your argument to other jurisdictions

Say *Doe* holds that a certain kind of police conduct doesn't violate the Fourth Amendment. This makes *Doe* binding precedent as to the Fourth Amendment, but only persuasive authority as to state constitutions, because courts can interpret state constitutions as providing more protection from state government actors than the federal constitution does.

The claim "state courts interpreting their own state constitutional protections should reach a different result" is therefore more useful than just "the Court got it wrong." Judges are more likely to accept the revised claim, lawyers are more likely to argue it, and academics are more likely to build on it. Your article will still be valuable to scholars who are willing to challenge the Court's case law, but it will also be valuable to many others.

3. Incorporate prescriptive implications of your descriptive findings

You can make a valuable contribution to knowledge just by uncovering some important facts: historical facts, facts about how judges or other government officials are applying a law, facts about how people or organizations react to certain laws, and so on. But your contribution would be still more valuable, and more impressive, if your claim also said something about how these findings are relevant to modern debates. You could come up with your own prescription based on the findings, or you could just explain how your findings might be relevant to others' prescriptive arguments, even if you don't endorse those arguments yourself.

Practical-minded people who read a purely descriptive piece will often ask "so what?" If you answer this question for them, you'll increase the chances that they'll see your work as useful. Don't do this if it's too much of a stretch: If there are no clear modern implications of your findings about 14th century English property law, you're better off sticking just with your persuasive historical claims rather than adding an unpersuasive prescriptive claim. But if you see some possible prescriptive implications, work them in.

4. Consider making a more politically feasible proposal

Say your claim is quite radical, and you're sure that few people will accept it, no matter how effectively you argue. For instance, imagine you want to urge courts to apply strict scrutiny to restrictions on economic liberty—a step beyond *Lochner v. New York*. You may have a great argument for that, but courts probably won't be willing to adopt your theory.

Think about switching to a more modest claim. You might argue, for instance, that courts should apply strict scrutiny to restrictions on entering certain professions or businesses. This would be a less radical change, and you can also support it by using particular arguments that wouldn't work as well for the broader claim.

Maybe courts will still be unlikely to go that far. Can you argue for a lower (but still significant) level of scrutiny? Can you find precedents, perhaps under state constitutions, that support your theory, thus showing your critics that your theory is more workable than they might at first think?

Or perhaps you could limit your proposal to strict scrutiny for laws that interfere with the obligation of contracts, rather than for all economic restrictions. Here you have more support from the constitutional text, a narrower (and thus less radical-seeming) claim, and perhaps even some more support from state cases: It turns out that state courts have interpreted the contracts clauses of many state constitutions more strictly than the federal clause.

If you really want to make the radical claim, go ahead—you might start a valuable academic debate, and perhaps might even eventually prevail. But, on balance, claims that call for modest changes to current doctrine tend to be more useful than radical claims, especially in articles by students or by junior practitioners. By making a more moderate claim, you can remain true to your basic moral judgment while producing something that's much more likely to influence people. Many legal campaigns are most effectively fought through small, incremental steps.

5. Avoid unnecessarily alienating your audience

You should try to make your argument as appealing as possible to as many readers as possible. You can't please everyone, but you should avoid using rhetoric, examples, or jargon that unnecessarily alienates readers who might otherwise be persuadable.

For instance, say that you're writing an article on free speech, and in passing give anti-abortion speech as an example. If you call this "anti-choice" speech, your readers will likely assume that you bitterly oppose the anti-abortion position. Some pro-life readers might therefore become less receptive to your other, more important, arguments; and even some pro-choice readers may bristle at the term "anti-choice" because they see it as an attempt to make a political point through labeling rather than through argument. If you're pro-choice, imagine your reaction to an article that in passing calls your position "anti-life"— would this make you more or less open to the article's other messages?

Avoid this by using language that's as neutral as possible. Right now, for instance, "pro-choice" and "pro-life" seem to cause the fewest visceral reactions; most terms have some political message embedded in them, but these seem to have the least, perhaps because repeated use has largely drained them of their emotional content. But in any case, find something that is acceptable both to you and to most of your readers.

The same goes for terms like "gun lobby," "gun-grabber," "abortionist," "fanatic," and the like. You may feel these terms are accurate, but that's not enough. Many readers will condemn these terms as attempts to resolve the issue through emotion rather than logic, and will therefore become less open to your substantive arguments. Likewise, if you're analogizing some views or actions to those of Nazis, Stalinists, the Taliban, and the like, you're asking for trouble unless the analogy is extremely close.

Try also to avoid using jargon that will confuse those who are unfamiliar with it, or that will unnecessarily label your work (fairly or unfairly) as belonging to some controversial school of analysis. If you have to use the jargon because you need it to clearly explain your theory, that's fine. But if you're writing an article on a topic that doesn't really require you to use a specialized method such as law and economics, literary criticism, or feminist legal theory, then stay away from the terms characteristic of those disciplines. Replacing such terms with plain English will probably make your article clearer and more accessible, and will avoid bringing in the ideological connotations that some people associate with these terms.

Likewise, try to include some arguments or examples that broaden your article's political appeal. If you are making a seemingly conservative proposal, but you can persuasively argue that the proposal will help poor people, say so. If you are making a seemingly liberal proposal, but you can persuasively argue that the proposal fits with tradition or with the original meaning of the Constitution, say that.

You should of course be willing to make unpopular arguments, if you need them to support your claim; that's part of the scholar's job. And if you really want to engage in a particular side battle, you might choose to bring it up even if you don't strictly have to. But in general, don't weaken your core claim by picking unnecessary fights.

F. Soundness: Prescriptive Claims

Part II will tell you more about *test suites*, an important tool for making your claim sounder—so important that it merits a separate section. Here, though, are some other suggestions.

1. Avoid excessive mushiness

Be willing to take a middle path, but beware of proposals that are so middle-of-the-road that they are indeterminate. For instance, if you're arguing that single-sex educational programs should be neither categorically legal nor categorically illegal, it might be a mistake to claim that such programs should be legal if they're "reasonable and fair, and promote the cause of equality." Such a test means only what the judge who applies it wants it to mean.

Few legal tests can produce mathematical certainty, but a test should be rigorous enough to give at least some guidance to decision-makers. Three tips for making tests clearer:

   a.   Whenever you use terms such as "reasonable" or "fair," ask yourself what you think defines "reasonableness" or "fairness" in this particular context. Then try to substitute those specific definitions in place of the more general words.

   b.   When you want to counsel "balancing," or urge courts to consider the "totality of the circumstances," ask yourself exactly what you mean. What should people look for when they're considering all the circumstances? How should they balance the various factors you identify? Making your recommendation more specific will probably make it more credible.

   c.   If possible, tie your test to an existing body of doctrine by using terms of art that have already been elaborated by prior cases (though this approach has its limits, as the next subsection discusses).

Thus, "single-sex educational programs should be legal if they have been shown in controlled studies to be more effective than co-ed programs" is probably a more defensible claim than "single-sex educational programs should be legal if they're reasonable." Instead of an abstract appeal to "reasonableness," the revised proposal refers to one specific definition of reasonableness—educational effectiveness—that seems to be particularly apt for decisions about education. It's still not a model of predictability, but it's better than just a "reasonableness" standard.*

---

* Some people argue that very flexible tests are actually better than seemingly more rigid ones; if you share this view, you might reject my approach here. Remember, though, that many readers will rightly worry about how your vague test will actually work out in practice. For your article to be convincing, you must either make the test more determinate or persuade these readers to accept its indeterminacy.

Part II will show how test suites can help you find and fix this problem. If you apply a proposal to your test cases, and find that it often doesn't give you any definite answer, you'll know the proposal is too vague. Once you discover this, you can ask yourself "what do I think the results in these cases should be, and why?" Answer this question, incorporate the answer into your original proposal, and you'll have a more concrete claim.

2. Avoid reliance on legal abstractions

"Reasonableness" at least sounds as vague as it is; other terms, such as "intermediate scrutiny," "strict scrutiny," "narrowly tailored," and "compelling state interest," seem clear but in reality have little meaning by themselves. To the extent that, say, strict scrutiny of content-based speech restrictions provides a relatively predictable test, the predictability comes from the body of caselaw that tells you which interests are compelling and what narrow tailoring means, and not from the phrase "narrowly tailored to a compelling state interest." The terms "strict scrutiny" and "narrowly tailored to a compelling state interest" aren't the test—they are just the names of the test.

Thus, a proposal such as "gun control laws should be examined to see if they are substantially related to an important government interest [i.e., intermediate scrutiny]" doesn't really mean much by itself. To be helpful, the proposal must explain which interests qualify as important and what constitutes a substantial relationship.

Nor is it enough just to say "the courts should borrow the intermediate scrutiny caselaw from other contexts." The intermediate scrutiny tests differ in different contexts, both on their face and as applied. Intermediate scrutiny in sex classification cases, for instance, has a reputation for being a very demanding test, while intermediate scrutiny of restrictions on expressive conduct has generally proven to be deferential; and if you look closely at the elements of the two tests, you'll find that they differ significantly, and for good reasons (since the underlying constitutional concerns animating the tests are different). Similarly, intermediate scrutiny in commercial speech cases was fairly deferential in the mid–1980s, but became much more demanding in the 1990s and early 2000s, all the while being called "intermediate scrutiny."

The solution is, in Justice Holmes's phrase, to "think things not words."[1]* Rather than relying on words such as "substantially," "important," or "intermediate," explain which interests may justify the restriction and which may not. Explain when restrictions should be allowed to be overinclusive or underinclusive and when they should not be. Explain when courts should demand empirical evidence that the law serves its goals and when they can rely on intuition. Of course, you may not be able to cover all possible situations, and in some cases where the question is close, your test may properly leave things ambiguous. But the more concrete your proposal, the better.

Again, test suites (see Part II) can help you identify this problem and refine your claim: Just as in the previous subsection, applying your proposed test to a set of concrete problems can help you see whether it has substance or is just words.

3. Avoid procedural proposals that don't explain what substantive standards are to be applied

Procedural proposals can be useful: It's often impossible or politically impractical to design the right substantive rule up front, so the best we can do is set up the procedures that will make it more likely that the right rule will eventually emerge. The Constitution itself, for instance, was intended to protect liberty largely through procedural structures, such as bicameralism, separation of powers, and the like. If you genuinely think that the right answer to your problem is better procedures, you should propose that.

But remember that courts and administrative judges, unlike legislatures, are generally required to apply a substantive rule, even if a vague one. It's not enough just to set forth procedures through which these bodies act—if your proposal asks such entities to review something, it has to tell them what rule they should apply.

Thus, say that you want to limit speech restrictions imposed on students by K–12 school officials; but because you recognize that it's hard to have a clear rule establishing which restrictions are good and which are bad, you propose a statute that requires that any such restrictions be reviewed by administrative law judges. This might be a good solution, but you need to ask: What substantive test should these judges apply?

---

* The numbered notes in this book are endnotes, which start at p. 377. They generally contain supporting evidence for assertions in the text, or citations to other sources.

Your answer might be "the judges must make sure any restriction is constitutional"; but if that's so then (1) you should make that clear, (2) you should explain why you think including administrative law judges as well as traditional judges will make much of a difference, and (3) you should discuss whether such a proposal will indeed materially constrain school officials, given that the Constitution leaves them pretty broad authority over student speech (see *Tinker v. Des Moines Indep. Comm. School Dist.* (1969)). Alternatively, your answer might be "the administrative law judges should independently decide whether the restriction, on balance, is a good idea." Again, if that's your answer, you should make it clear, and discuss whether administrative judges will be good at making such educational policy decisions.

Or you might recognize that there *is* some implicit substantive rule that you want the administrative judges to apply, for instance, "political speech by students must be protected unless there is concrete evidence that the speech has actually disrupted classes at this school." If that's so, you should make clear that your proposal isn't just about procedure but also about substance.

Likewise, it's often tempting to argue that courts should admit a certain class of evidence, for instance evidence about aspects of a person's cultural background that might have led him to act in a certain way. Why not let it in? Don't we trust jurors? Isn't more evidence better than less?

Well, maybe—but much depends on how we expect jurors to consider this evidence. Say that a defendant killed someone because the other person did something that the defendant's culture finds mortally insulting: the victim said something to the defendant, the victim pointed the soles of his feet at the defendant,[2] the victim made a homosexual advance to the defendant, or the victim, who was the defendant's wife, flirted with another man. And say that the defendant wants to introduce evidence of these cultural beliefs in his murder prosecution, seeking to have the jury convict him only of voluntary manslaughter, not murder.

Today, the presence of provocation can generally reduce the offense from murder to voluntary manslaughter only if the provocation is seen as reasonable by society at large. If this *substantive* rule is retained, then admitting the cultural evidence seems unwise, because jurors generally can't lawfully give effect to the evidence, and the evidence is thus more likely to be prejudicial or distracting rather than relevant.

Of course, if the substantive rule were changed to let murder be re-

31

duced to manslaughter whenever the defendant was provoked in a way that's seen as reasonable by the defendant's culture, then courts would have to admit evidence of what the defendant's culture actually believes. But this substantive proposal would be controversial, and should be defended explicitly. You can make your procedural proposal complete only by exposing the substantive assumptions behind it, or the substantive changes that would be required to make it work.

The same goes for proposals that:

a. "courts should take a hard look at X" (a hard look applying what test?),

b. "courts must carefully sift the facts" (what specific item will they be searching for in this sifting, and what role will this item play in what test?),

c. "executive officials must state their reasons for action on the record" (and then their reasons would be reviewed for compliance with what rule?), or

d. "there should be a hearing in which the affected parties may introduce evidence" (what legal rule would this evidence be relevant to?).

Focusing on procedure may often be good—but in such cases there's often an unexpressed substantive proposal lurking. Express it.

G. Soundness: Historical and Empirical Claims

1. Get advice from historians or empiricists

Say you are writing an article about the history of libel law, or an empirical analysis of prostitution laws. You might well choose a torts scholar or a criminal law scholar as your main advisor, either because you want substantive help on that area of that law, or because you know the professor well.

But you should also get some informal help from a professor who is a historian or an empirical researcher. Such a specialist can give you useful tips about research methods, sources to consult, pitfalls to avoid, and the like—subjects that your main advisor might not be as good at. This person need not take the main role in advising you, but it would be great if he could talk to you near the beginning of your research, and perhaps even read a draft.

If you don't know who the right specialist on your faculty might be, or you're afraid the person might be too busy to make time for you, ask your main advisor to pave the way for you. Your main advisor will probably be eager to help, since he will know his own methodological limitations, and will want you to get advice from someone who doesn't suffer from those limitations. And your main advisor could even get you help from historians or empiricists in other departments.

2. Look for books and non-law articles

Many law students (and even law professors) fall into the habit of doing nearly all their research on Westlaw and Lexis. It's convenient, and for purely legal issues it's usually not bad.

But this won't work for research on history, sociology, economics, and the like. For such research, you'll want to search for articles in the journals that serve the relevant fields. You'll also want to look for books, especially if you're writing about history; books play a much bigger role in historical scholarship than in legal scholarship. Ask your reference librarians for help figuring out how to find all these works (for instance, through resources such as JSTOR).

3. Watch out for the historian's "false friends"

Language teachers talk about translators' false friends—words in a foreign language that sound familiar, but are quite different. The classic example is the Spanish "embarazada," which means not embarrassed but pregnant. The Russian "magazin" means a shop, not a magazine. If you're not careful, the false friends can fool you into making an error.

Likewise, old sources speak a language that's usually very close to ours (at least if we go back only 200 years or so) but that sometimes includes false friends. To most readers today, "militia" means either the National Guard or some small quasi-private force. In late 1700s America, it generally meant the entire adult white male citizenry (possibly up to age 45 or 60) seen as a potential military force.[3] "Free state" today often means independent state, and in the early 1800s often meant a nonslave state. But in 1700s political works, it generally meant (more or less) a democracy, republic, or constitutional monarchy.[4]

The same is true in many other contexts: Words and phrases subtly change their meanings. Words that were once legal terms of art lose

33

their technical meaning and revert to their lay meaning, and vice versa. Grammatical and punctuation conventions change.

So before relying on your assumption that a term meant the same thing in 1830 or 1730 as it does today, do some investigation. Do some sources that use the term seem odd when the term is assigned its modern meaning? What do contemporaneous legal dictionaries say about the term? What does a faculty member who specializes in the era say about the term?

4. Consider whether you're limiting your dataset in ways that undermine your generalizations

Say that you are studying the effect of the Supreme Court's 1963–1990 Free Exercise Clause religious exemption doctrine. You want to figure out how lower courts actually applied the doctrine, which mandated strict scrutiny when religious exemption requirements were denied. Was this strict scrutiny really strict? Or was it, as some have argued, "strict in theory but feeble in fact"?[5] So you decide to go through all federal appellate cases from 1980 to 1990 that applied the Free Exercise Clause to religious exemption requests.

That would be an excellent project (and in fact such a project produced a superb student article, which is discussed in more detail in Part XIX)—but you should recognize an important limitation: By looking only at federal cases, you would be missing the possibility that some state courts have applied the federal Free Exercise Clause in a more demanding way than federal appellate courts have. That might seem like a counterintuitive possibility, but it turns out to be largely accurate. Yet your limiting your dataset to federal cases would lead you to miss this observation.

And missing this observation might lead you to make a less sound generalization than you might have if you had looked at a larger dataset. The federal cases, for instance, might lead you to conclude that the Court's Free Exercise Clause strict scrutiny test in practice offered no material help to religious claimants. But this conclusion might be in some measure mistaken or incomplete, if the Free Exercise Clause had helped many litigants in state courts.

Of course time is limited, and you can't cover everything. You must limit your dataset in some ways, if only to decisions that are actually available online. Perhaps you need to limit it in other ways, too. But think at the outset about how you are limiting your dataset, and whether this limitation might lead you to miss data and therefore reach a less sound result than you otherwise would have.

5. Pay especially close attention to the Using Evidence Correctly chapter below (Part XVII)

The Using Evidence Correctly chapter has material that's helpful even for traditional doctrinal articles; but some of its points—for instance, about reading, citing, and quoting original sources, or about being careful in using survey evidence or correlation evidence—are especially helpful for historical or empirical work. Read the chapter carefully before you start your research.

H. Selling Your Claim to Your Readers

Not only must your claim be novel, nonobvious, useful, and sound, but you must show your readers that this is so. More about this shortly (Part III.C, p. 48).

I. Topics and Structures You Should Generally Avoid

Here are some types of articles that you might want to avoid. These recommendations won't always apply: Sometimes, for instance, a journal may insist that you write a case note, or your article may deal with an important and interesting problem that arises only under one state's law. Nonetheless, I think you'll find the suggestions below to be helpful in most situations.

1. Articles that identify a problem but don't give a solution

Giving a solution makes your article more novel, nonobvious, and useful, and therefore more impressive. You want to show people that you have a creative legal mind that can identify solutions and not just criticize others' proposals. If you think there are several possible solutions, that's fine—just discuss all of them, and explain the strengths and weaknesses of each.

2. Case notes

An article that describes a single case and then critiques it is likely to be fairly obvious, even if it's novel. Also, because it focuses chiefly on only one already decided case, it's less likely to be useful. For instance, *Harvard Law Review* Recent Cases and Leading Cases items are cited more than 10 times less often by courts and nearly 4 times less often by law review articles than are *Harvard Law Review* Notes—even though Harvard publishes twice as many Recent Cases and Leading Cases items as Notes. Recent Cases and Leading Cases items are not quite the same as case notes in other journals (they're shorter than some), but my sense is that case notes in all journals tend to be on average less valuable than articles that focus on the issue rather than on the case.

A case note is also a less impressive calling card to prospective academic employers, and I suspect to law firms as well: It generally doesn't show off your skills at research and at tying together threads from different contexts.

If you got your topic from a particular case, that's fine. But don't focus on the case—focus on the problem, and bring to bear all the cases that deal with the problem.

3. Single-state articles

Articles focusing on a single state's law are generally useful only to people in that state. Such articles may still be valuable, especially if the state is big; but why limit yourself this way?

Other states probably have similar laws, or might at least be considering them. Frame your article as a general discussion of all the laws of this sort, even if it focuses primarily on two or three states as representative cases.

Of course, the various state laws will probably differ subtly from each other, which may require some extra discussion. But while this means some more work, considering these differences may make the article more useful, sophisticated, nuanced, and impressive.

4. Articles that just explain what the law is

These can be useful, and sometimes even novel, but they tend to seem obvious. The reader is likely to say, "true, I didn't know this, but I could have figured it out if I had only done a bit of research." This is just fine if your reader is a busy lawyer looking for a good summary of the law—but not so good if the reader is a professor, a law review editor, or a judge looking for a creative, original-thinking law clerk.

There are exceptions: For instance, showing that the law is actually applied quite differently from the way most people assume might well be nonobvious. But even there, adding a prescriptive component to your description would be helpful. Should the law be applied this way? If not, how can the law be amended to prevent such applications? If yes, should the law be clarified or broadened to make such applications easier?

5. Responses to other people's works

Framing your article as a response to Professor Smith's article will usually limit your readership to people who have already read Smith's article, and will tend to make people see you (fairly or not) as a reactive thinker rather than a creative one.

If your piece was stimulated by your disagreement with Smith, no problem—just assert and prove your own claim, while demolishing Smith's arguments in the process. Cite Smith in the footnotes; Smith's opposition will help show that your claim is important and nonobvious. But don't let Smith be the main figure in your story.

6. Topics that the Supreme Court or Congress is likely to visit shortly

You don't want to write an article that will be quickly preempted by a new federal statute or Supreme Court decision. At best, you'd then have to radically rework your article; at worst, you might have to throw it out altogether. If you're writing about the law of a particular state, then you likewise need to watch out for new statutes or high court decisions in that state.

Unfortunately, one common way that students find topics—by identifying circuit splits—involves a high risk of the article getting preempted. A circuit split happens when several federal circuit courts of appeals disagree on a particular question. That makes the question more worth writing about, because the split shows that there's an important problem with no obviously right answer. But a circuit split is also a signal to the Justices that it might be time for the Court to resolve the issue.

So if there's a circuit split on your problem, check to see how likely it is that the Court will consider the matter and thus preempt your work. First, make sure that, for each case involved in the split, the Court has denied certiorari or no petition has been filed and the time to file has run out. Second, ask the professors who work in the field whether they think it's likely that the Court will agree to hear a case on this subject soon. Third, ask the same question of the professors who specialize in the Supreme Court; they sometimes have a different perspective from those people who work on the particular subject area.

You might also do the same three things when there is no circuit split on the problem, but the problem seems likely to attract the Supreme Court's or Congress's interest for other reasons. Don't be paralyzed by the risk of preemption—the Court and Congress deal each year with only a small fraction of all the problems out there. But think a bit about how likely preemption seems to be.

Finally, do *not* write on a topic that you think the Court will resolve shortly, in the hope of getting your article published before the Court hears the case. True, it would be great if the litigants or the Justices read your article and relied on it—but that's highly unlikely. And once the Court acts, your article will be largely ignored, since scholars and lawyers will be looking for articles that consider the new decision, rather than articles that predate it.

J. If You Must Write a Case Note

As I mentioned on p. 35, I don't recommend case notes. Some journals, though, require you to write case notes, or give you an extra opportunity to publish if you're writing a case note. How can you make your case note as valuable and impressive as possible?

Remember that you still need a claim, and you need it to be novel, nonobvious, useful, and sound. For a case note, though, the claim can be a set of separate claims related to the case, for instance, "The majority opinion misconstrued these precedents in these ways, and the rule the court should have adopted is this-and-such, and the opinion leaves open these questions that should be answered in these ways." For a traditional article, it's often better to have one big claim than several little ones; but in a case note, the rules are different.

Here are several kinds of claims that often work well:

1. Most obviously, internal criticisms of the majority opinion—that it (i) misinterprets or misapplies precedents, (ii) misinterprets the statutory or constitutional text, (iii) makes an unjustified logical leap, (iv) fails to respond to certain counterarguments, and so on. You need not criticize the majority's result; you might, for instance, argue that the majority reached the right result, but

for the wrong reason. But you should probably disagree in some measure with the majority's reasoning, or else it will look like you aren't adding much value beyond what the majority said.

2. Criticisms that point to the bad results that the majority opinion may lead to. For this, you might want to create a test suite (see Part II) for the majority's proposed rule, and see which cases expose weaknesses in the majority result.

3. Criticisms of the vagueness or uncertainty of the majority's rule. Again, the test suite may be helpful here.

4. Criticisms of the concurring and dissenting opinions. You don't just want to limit yourself to this; but neither do you just want to criticize the majority, because then readers might wonder whether the other opinions might have made all the good points before you did.

5. Proposals for a better rule than that offered by any of the opinions.

6. If a case doesn't explicitly announce a rule, or announces a very vague one, syntheses of a clear rule from this case and previous cases, supplemented with your own suggestions.

7. Explanations of the unresolved questions left by the majority opinion, and proposals for resolving them.

8. Explanations of the unresolved questions created by the majority opinion, and proposals for resolving them.

II. Test Suites: Making Prescriptive Claims More Sound

A. What a Test Suite Is

When you're making a prescriptive proposal (whether it's a new statute, an interpretation of a statute, a constitutional rule, a common-law rule, a regulation, or an enforcement guideline), it's often easy to get tunnel vision: You focus on the one situation that prompted you to write the piece—usually a situation about which you feel deeply—and ignore other scenarios to which your proposal might apply. And this can lead you to make proposals that, on closer examination, prove to be unsound.

For instance, say you're outraged by the government's funding childbirths but not abortions. You might therefore propose a new rule that "if the government funds the decision not to exercise of a constitutional right, then the government must also fund the exercise of the right"; or you might simply propose that "if the government funds childbirth, it must fund abortions," and give the more general claim as a justification. But you might not think about the consequences of this general claim—when the government funds public school education, it would also have to fund private school education (since that's also a constitutional right), and when it funds anti-drug speech, it might also have to fund pro-drug speech.

Your argument, at least at its initial level of generality, is thus probably wrong or at least incomplete. But focusing solely on your one core case keeps you from seeing the error.

One way to fight these errors is a device borrowed from computer programming: the *test suite*. A test suite is a set of cases that programmers enter into their programs to see whether the results look right. A test suite for a calculator program, for instance, might contain the following test cases, among many others:

1. Check that 2+2 yields 4.

2. Check that 3-1 yields 2.

3. Check that 1-3 yields -2 (because the program might work differently with positive numbers than with negative ones).

4. Check that 1/0 yields an error message.

If all the test cases yield the correct result, then the programmer can have some confidence that the program works. If one test yields the wrong result, then the programmer sees the need to fix the program—

not throw it out, but improve it. Such test suites are a fundamental part of sound software design. Before going into law, for instance, I wrote a computer program that had 50,000 lines of test suites for its 140,000 lines of code.

You can use a similar approach for testing legal proposals. *Before* you commit yourself to a particular proposal, you should design a test suite containing various cases to which your proposal might apply.*

Assume, for instance, that you are upset by peyote bans that interfere with some American Indian religions. The government has no business, you want to argue, imposing such paternalistic laws on religious observers. You should design a set of test cases involving requests for religious exemptions from many different kinds of paternalistic laws, for instance:

1. requests for religious exemptions from assisted suicide bans, sought by doctors who want to help dying patients die, or by the patients who want a doctor's help;

2. requests for religious exemptions from assisted suicide bans, sought by physically healthy cult members who want help committing suicide;

3. requests for religious exemptions from bans on the drinking of strychnine (an example of extremely dangerous behavior);

4. requests for religious exemptions from bans on the handling of poisonous snakes (an example of less dangerous behavior);

5. requests for religious exemptions from bans on riding motorcycles without a helmet (an example of less dangerous behavior, but one that—unlike in examples 3 and 4—many nonreligious people want to engage in).[6]

Then, once you design a proposed rule, you should test it by applying it to all these cases and seeing what results the proposal reaches.

B. What You Might Find by Testing Your Proposal

What information can this testing provide?

---

* See, e.g., Jennifer E. Rothman, *Freedom of Speech and True Threats*, 25 Harv. J.L. & Pub. Pol'y 283, 336 (2001), for an example of one such test suite that the student used while writing her article, and eventually incorporated into the published version.

1. Identifying errors

You might find that the proposal reaches results that even you yourself think are wrong. For instance, suppose that your initial proposal is the one that we just discussed: that religious objectors should always get exemptions from paternalistic laws. Thinking about the assisted-suicide test case (case 2 in the list given above) might lead you to doubt that proposal, and conclude that people should not be allowed to help physically healthy people commit suicide. The proposed rule, then, would be unsound.

What can you do about this?

a. You might think that the proposal yielded the wrong result because it didn't take into account countervailing concerns that may be present in some cases—for instance, the special need to prevent a voluntarily assumed near-certainty of death or extremely grave injury, rather than just a remote risk of harm. If this is so, you could *modify* the proposed test, for instance by *limiting its scope* (for example, by including exception for harms that are likely to be immediate, grave, and irreversible).

b. Another possibility is that the insight that led you to suggest the proposal—in our example, the belief that there should be a religious exemption from peyote laws—is better explained by a *different rule*. For instance, as you think through the test cases, you might conclude that your real objection to the peyote ban is that it's factually unjustified (because peyote isn't that harmful), and not that it's paternalistic. You might then *substitute* a new rule: courts should allow religious exemptions from a law when they find that the religious practice doesn't cause any harm, whether or not the law is paternalistic.

2. Identifying vagueness

You might find that the proposal is unacceptably vague. Say that the proposal was that religious objectors should be exempted from paternalistic laws when "the objectors' interest in practicing their religion outweighs the government's interest in protecting people against themselves." In the peyote case, this proposal might have satisfied you, because it was clear to you that the government's interest in protecting people against peyote abuse was weak.

But as you apply the proposal to the other cases, you might find that the proposal provides far too little guidance to courts—and might therefore lead to results you think are wrong. This could be a signal for you to *clarify* the proposal.

3. Finding surprising results

You might find that the proposal reaches a result that you at first think is wrong, but then realize is right. For instance, before applying the proposal to the test suite, you might have assumed that religious objectors shouldn't get exemptions from assisted suicide bans. But after you think more about this test case in light of your proposal, you might conclude that your intuition about assisted suicide was mistaken.

You should keep this finding in mind, and *discuss it in the article*: It may help you show the value of your claim, because it shows that the proposal yields counterintuitive but sound results.

4. Confirming the value of your proposal

You might find that the proposal precisely fits the results that you think are proper. This should make you more confident of the proposal's soundness; and it would also provide some examples that you can *use in the article* to illustrate the proposal's soundness (as Part V.C, p. 67, discusses).

C. Developing the Test Suite

How can you identify good items for your test suites? Here are a few suggestions.

1. Identify what needs to be tested

The test suite is supposed to test the proposed legal principle on which the claim is based. Sometimes, the claim is itself the principle: For instance, if the proposal is that "the proper rule for evaluating requests for religious exemptions from paternalistic laws is [such-and-such]," you would need a set of several cases to which this rule can be applied.

But sometimes the claim is just an application of the principle: For instance, the claim that "religious objectors should get exemptions from peyote laws" probably rests on a broader implicit principle that describes which exemption requests should be granted. If that's so, then you should come up with a set of cases that test this underlying principle. One case should involve peyote bans but the others shouldn't.

2. Use plausible test cases

Each test case should be plausible: It should be the sort of situation that might actually happen. It's good to base it on a real incident, whether one drawn from a reported court decision or a newspaper article. You need not precisely follow the real incident, and you may assume slightly different facts if necessary—the goal is to have the reader acknowledge that the case *could* happen the way it's described, not that it necessarily has happened. But you should make sure that any alterations still leave the test case as realistic as possible.

3. Include the famous precedents

The test suite should include the famous precedents in this field. This can help confirm for you and the readers that the proposal is consistent with those cases—or can help explain which famous cases would have to be reversed under the proposal.

4. Include challenging cases

At least some of the cases should be challenging for the proposal. You should identify cases where the proposal might lead to possibly unappealing results, and include them in the test suite. Skeptical readers, including your advisor, will think of these cases eventually. Identifying the hard cases early—and, if necessary, revising the proposal in light of them—is better than having to confront them later, when changing the paper will require much more work.

5. Have a mix of cases

The test cases should differ from each other in relevant ways, since their role is to provide as broad a test for the claim as possible. If you are testing a claim about paternalistic laws, for instance, you shouldn't just focus on drug laws, or just on paternalistic laws aimed at protecting children. You should think of many different sorts of paternalistic laws, and choose one or two of each variety.

6. Include cases that yield different results

The cases should yield different results. For instance, if your proposed rule judges the constitutionality of a certain type of law, you should find some laws that you think should be found unconstitutional, some that you think should be found constitutional, and some whose constitutionality is a close question.

7. Include cases that appeal to different political perspectives

The cases should involve incidents or laws that appeal to as many different political perspectives as possible. Say that you are a liberal who wants to argue that the Free Speech Clause prohibits the government from funding viewpoint-based advocacy programs. You might have developed this view because you think the government shouldn't be allowed to fund anti-abortion advocacy, and your proposal will indeed reach the result you think is right in that case.

But what about advocacy programs that liberals might favor, such as pro-recycling advocacy, or advertising campaigns promoting tolerance of homosexuality? It would help if the test suite included such cases, plus generally popular programs such as anti-drug advertising, or programs that even small-government libertarians might like, such as advocacy of respect for property rights (for instance, anti-graffiti advocacy). This wide variety of test cases will help show you whether the proposal is indeed sound across the board, or whether even you yourself would, on reflection, oppose it.

8. Include cases that implicate different interests and policy arguments

In particular, think about the policy arguments and the private or government interests on both sides, and find cases in which different arguments or interests are more or less implicated. Say, for instance, you are writing about how state constitutional rights to bear arms should be interpreted. The obvious test cases would focus on situations in which citizens want to defend themselves, and the government wants to prevent criminal misuse of guns.

But what about laws aimed not at preventing crime but at preventing suicide or accidents? What about citizens who are concerned not just about access to guns, but about privacy—for instance, citizens who want to carry guns concealed rather than openly because they don't want to reveal their actions to everyone, or citizens who don't want their gun ownership or their concealed carry license disclosed in public records? Add test cases that involve laws which implicate these special concerns.

III. WRITING THE INTRODUCTION

A. *The Role of the Introduction*

A readable, interesting introduction is crucial to your article's success. Introductions have three important functions:

    a.   to persuade people to read further;

    b.   to summarize your basic claim for those who don't read further, so that they'll remember it and refer back to your piece when they run into a problem to which the claim may be relevant; and

    c.   to provide a frame through which those who do read further will interpret what follows.

To accomplish these goals, an introduction must do four things:

    1.   show that there's a problem, and do so concretely;

    2.   state the claim;

    3.   frame the issue; and

    4.   do all this quickly and forcefully.

B. *Show That There's a Problem, and Do So Concretely*

Your introduction should make the reader think, "wow, I need to read the rest of this." The best way to get that reaction is to show that there's an important, interesting problem that needs to be solved. This could be a descriptive problem (does this law work? how did this legal rule come about?) or a prescriptive one (what should be done in these situations?). But whatever it is, you need to persuade readers that they should spend their time reading about this problem.

And the most compelling problems are *concrete* ones. Don't just say that the law is unjust or oppressive, or ignores transaction costs or the plight of the subordinated. Give a specific example—a real scenario is good, but a plausible hypothetical is fine too—that shows how the law can fail. Make the reader say, "interesting, it looks like the law here is unsound" or "I wonder what the right answer is."

This, of course, is related to demonstrating your claim's utility (see below), but it's important in its own right: It makes people want to read what you wrote.

C. State the Claim

The Introduction should briefly state the claim, and briefly show its novelty, nonobviousness, and utility. This tells the readers what to expect, and persuades them that your article will make a valuable original contribution by solving the problem as well as identifying it.

Note the "briefly." The Introduction should be short, simple, and clear. It should make the reader want to read further, but it should also simply and memorably communicate your basic point—and the other interesting conclusions that you draw in the process of reaching it— even to those readers who will never read beyond the Introduction.

The best way to show novelty and nonobviousness is implicitly, by briefly explaining your claim and justification in a way that makes the reader say, "I'd never have thought of that." But if you think people might wrongly assume that your topic has already been heavily discussed, and that your claim has already been made by someone else, you might explicitly say something like "surprisingly, it turns out that few scholars have considered [the question]."

Utility is also best shown implicitly: Saying "this is a really useful point" will rarely add much to your argument. Instead, make sure that your introduction clearly summarizes your important findings, and their possible practical and theoretical implications.

D. Frame the Issue

Every law has many effects. In an ideal world, readers' judgments about the law would be the same no matter how the question is presented, because readers would consider all the effects. But in practice, the frame—the way you present the issue to the readers, and focus their attention on certain effects—is important.

Consider an article about gun control. Thinking seriously about gun control requires thinking about many things: The thousands of people who die each year from gunshots. The plight of people who need a weapon to defend themselves against criminal attacks when the police aren't there to help. The special concerns of women, who tend to be physically less capable of defending themselves without guns, and who are victimized in particular ways by crime. The Second Amendment and state constitutional provisions that guarantee a right to keep and bear arms. The uncertainty about how useful guns are for self-defense. The uncertainty about how effective gun controls would be.

Your article will have to confront all these subjects, whatever your bottom line will be; but it matters a lot how you frame the discussion. If you start by stressing that there were almost 13,000 firearms homicides in the U.S. in 2006,[7] and return to this throughout the piece, the reader will be more likely to look at all the evidence through this lens. If you start by stressing that the police are often far away, and that hundreds of thousands or perhaps even millions of people use guns to defend themselves against criminal attacks each year,[8] the reader may approach the evidence from a different perspective.

The Introduction is the place where you construct this basic frame—where you give a simple summary that puts the reader in the right mindset to absorb and agree with your point. Write with this in mind.

E. Do All This Quickly and Forcefully

The first few sentences of the Introduction can make the reader drop the article, or keep reading it. Don't start with platitudes or generalities that the reader already knows. Start with something that is concrete, and that quickly communicates your perspective.

Consider, for instance, a draft introduction I once ran across (I've numbered the sentences to more easily discuss them):

> [1] Campaign speech has long been a controversial topic among scholars and commentators. [2] Much attention has been devoted to the Supreme Court's treatment of individual expenditures, contributions and spending in *Buckley v. Valeo*. [3] Congress' recent consideration of campaign finance reform provides an ideal opportunity to revisit the 1976 Supreme Court decision that addressed the free speech implications of limits on federal campaign-related activities.

> [4] This essay briefly discusses the effects of such limits on individual speech, the disproportionate treatment of speech by the media and justifications presented by several members of the Court in the 2000 decision, *Nixon v. Shrink Missouri Government PAC*.

> [5] Let me begin by giving a concrete situation. [6] Imagine you are outraged about a particular candidate's stand on something. [More concrete details follow, aimed at showing that there's a basic First Amendment right to spend money to express your views about candidates.] ...

The first two sentences say something that's obvious to most readers, even those who barely know the field. The third and fourth sentences describe something less obvious—what the article's general topic

49

will be—but they're clunky and boring. The fifth sentence likewise adds little.

It's only the sixth sentence—"Imagine you are outraged"—that has the power to grab the listener. It provides a concrete scenario, which is usually more interesting than generalizations. It also quickly sets the stage for the core argument, which is that you have a right to spend your money to express your views.

Start the Introduction with this sentence, rather than hiding it after five sentences of generalities. If you need to make some general points, make them later, after you've gotten the reader hooked.

F. Some Ways to Start the Introduction

Finally, a few tips for good ways to start an Introduction. These are not at all the only options, but they often work, and they illustrate some of the guidelines mentioned above.

1. Start with the concrete questions you will try to answer

State with the concrete questions you will try to answer, for instance:

> What may government officials do to prevent speech that they think is evil and dangerous? What may businesses, organizations, or individuals do? ...

This says what the article will be about. It also shows the article will be useful, since most readers will quickly understand that these issues come up often. Later sentences should make this still more concrete, and make it still clearer that the article will be useful.

One possible problem: The reference to "evil and dangerous" speech is a little vague. You should make sure that subsequent sentences give examples, or maybe even work the examples into the opening question itself ("What may government officials do to prevent speech that they think is evil and dangerous, such as bigoted speech, speech that calls for revolution, or speech that advocates violence?").

Here's a worse way to start the same article:

> The freedom of speech is a vital part of the fabric of American democracy. Undoubtedly a wide range of speech cannot be barred by the government. In *Brandenburg v. Ohio*, the Court held that even advocacy of violence may not be restricted unless the advocacy is intended to and likely to provoke imminent violent conduct.

50

> Yet in certain situations some response to evil and dangerous speech may arguably be appropriate. It may be worth considering whether government officials and others may take some steps to prevent such speech....

The opening sentence is a platitude. The second sentence says something general and well-known. The third sentence summarizes a legal rule that most of your readers will know; and even readers who don't know it won't be reading your article to learn it.

The fourth sentence gets to the heart of the question, though indirectly and using a waffle word ("arguably," which I discuss on p. 116). The fifth sentence is when the Introduction first identifies the topic, and even then it doesn't signal that this is *the* topic. And it could be worse: I've seen articles in which the topic isn't identified until the fifth page.

You might hope that the reader will be willing to read on to the fifth sentence. But some readers will start skimming by then. Some won't recognize the fifth sentence as identifying your claim, even if they've read that far. And some will just be put off by early evidence of the article's tendency to meander. So avoid the generalities, and start early with something clear, concrete, and specific to your claim.

2. Start with concrete examples

Point to concrete scenarios that lead people to wonder, "How should these be resolved?" For instance,

> Some speech provides information that makes it easier for people to commit crimes or torts. Consider:
>
> (a) A textbook describes how people can make bombs. [Each example is followed by a footnote to cases or incidents that deal with the issue.]
>
> (b) A thriller or mystery novel does the same, for the sake of realism.
>
> (c) A Web site or computer science article explains how encrypted copyrighted material can be illegally decrypted.
>
> (d) A newspaper publishes the name of a witness to a crime, thus making it easier for the criminal to intimidate or kill the witness....
>
> These are not incitement cases: The speech isn't persuading or inspiring some readers to commit bad acts. Rather, the speech is giving people information that helps them commit bad acts—acts that they likely already want to commit. When should such speech be constitutionally unprotected?

51

This again quickly tells people what the article is about, and gives plausible and concrete examples that (a) help make the subject clearer and less abstract and (b) show that your article will be useful. It also helps that the examples at first seem different, but juxtaposing them under the rubric "information that makes it easier for people to commit crimes or torts" shows the similarity between them. Showing this similarity may itself be a novel, nonobvious, and useful contribution provided by the article.

3. Start with an engaging story

If you want to start with a story, make sure that it's a vivid story.

Percy Bysshe Shelley was a poet and a cad. He married his wife, Harriet Westbrooke, when she was 16, but left her for Mary Wollstonecraft Godwin three years later. When Shelley left Harriet, their daughter was a year old, and Harriet was pregnant with their son.

Two years later, in 1816, Harriet drowned herself. When Shelley decided to raise the children himself, Harriet's parents refused to turn them over, and Shelley went to court. Though fathers had nearly absolute rights under then-existing English law, Shelley became one of the first fathers in English history to lose custody of his children.

Percy Shelley was also an avowed atheist—and the Court of Chancery mostly relied on his views, not on his infidelity or unreliability, in denying him custody. Shelley shouldn't be put in charge of the children's education, the Lord Chancellor reasoned: Shelley endorsed atheism and sexual freedom, and would teach his children the same values. Twenty years later, Justice Joseph Story likewise wrote that a father could lose his rights for "atheistical[] or irreligious principles."

Shelley's case may look like something out of another time and place. That time and place, it turns out, is 2005 Michigan, where a modern Shelley might be denied custody based partly on his "not regularly attend[ing] church and present[ing] no evidence demonstrating any willingness or capacity to attend to religion with [his children]," or having a "lack of religious observation." It's 1992 South Dakota, where Shelley might have been given custody but only on condition that he "will agree to present a plan to the Court of how [he] is going to commence providing some sort of spiritual opportunity for the [children] to learn about God while in [his] custody."

It's also 2005 Arkansas, 2002 Georgia, 2005 Louisiana, 2004 Minnesota, 2005 Mississippi, 2006 New York, 2005 North Carolina, 1996 Pennsylvania, 2004 South Carolina, 1997 Tennessee, and 2000 Texas. In 2000, the Mississippi Supreme Court ordered a mother to take her child to church each week, reasoning that "it is certainly to the best interests of [the child] to receive regular and systematic spiritual train-ing"; in 1996, the Arkansas Supreme Court did the same, partly on the grounds that weekly church attendance, rather than just the once-every-two-weeks attendance that the child would have had if he went only with the other parent, provides superior "moral instruction."

This is risky: The first three paragraphs are a story from early 1800s England, introducing an article about modern American law. The item that shocks some readers and shows the relevance of the piece— that some American courts even today prefer more religious parents over less religious ones—begins in the fourth paragraph. A safer way of starting an article on this subject might be:

> Throughout the country, from Michigan to Mississippi to Pennsyl-vania, child custody decisions often prefer the more religious parent, or the more churchgoing parent. This, I will argue, generally violates the Establishment Clause and the Free Speech Clause. Courts generally ought not be allowed to consider a parent's religiosity even as part of the best interests analysis....

or maybe

> Throughout the country, from Michigan to Mississippi to Pennsyl-vania, child custody decisions often prefer the more religious parent, or the more churchgoing parent. Some, for instance, count against a par-ent his "not regularly attend[ing] church and present[ing] no evidence demonstrating any willingness or capacity to attend to religion with [his children]." Some order parents to go to church, for instance by giv-ing a parent custody only on condition that he "will agree to present a plan to the Court of how [he] is going to commence providing some sort of spiritual opportunity for the [children] to learn about God while in [his] custody."
>
> This, I will argue, generally violates the Establishment Clause and the Free Speech Clause. Courts generally ought not be allowed to con-sider a parent's religiosity even as part of the best interests analysis....

On the other hand, Shelley is a famous poet, and cases involving famous historical figures tend to be interesting. The story is dramatic— abandonment, suicide, an affair with the author of Frankenstein. And introducing the story helps persuade readers by leading them to think "what an unfortunate, archaic way of thinking" and then springing on them the continuing presence of this thinking. ("Shelley's case may look like something out of another time and place. That time and place, it turns out, is 2005 Michigan ....").

So the story is vivid enough that it will likely keep the reader's at-tention for three paragraphs. And it's relevant enough that it will likely help frame the problem and persuade the reader. If you have a story that is vivid, relevant, fairly short, and not yet cliché, it may be a good way to start the article.

4. Start with a concrete but vivid hypothetical that illustrates your point

You can also start with a concrete but vivid hypothetical, or a set of hypotheticals that you want to compare with each other.

> Four women are in deadly peril.
>
> Alice is seven months pregnant, and the pregnancy threatens her life; doctors estimate her chance of death at 20%. Her fetus has long been viable, so Alice no longer has the *Roe/Casey* right to abortion on demand. But because her life is in danger, she has a constitutional right to save her life by hiring a doctor to abort the viable fetus. She would have a right to a therapeutic abortion even if the pregnancy were only posing a serious threat to her health, rather than threatening her life.
>
> A man breaks into Katherine's home. She reasonably fears that he may kill her (or perhaps seriously injure, rape, or kidnap her). Just as Alice may protect her life by killing the fetus, Katherine may protect hers by killing the attacker, even if the attacker isn't morally culpable—for instance, if he is insane. And Katherine has a right to self-defense even though recognizing that right may let some people use false claims of self-defense to get away with murder.
>
> Ellen is terminally ill. No proven therapies offer help. An experimental drug therapy seems safe because it has passed Phase I FDA testing, yet federal law bars the therapy outside of clinical trials because it hasn't been demonstrated to be effective (and further checked for safety) through Phase II testing. Nonetheless, the 2006 D.C. Circuit panel decision in *Abigail Alliance for Better Access to Develop mental Drugs v. Von Eschenbach*—since vacated and now being reviewed en banc—would secure Ellen the constitutional right to try to save her life by hiring a doctor to administer the therapy.
>
> Olivia is dying of kidney failure. A kidney transplant would likely save her life, just as an abortion would save Alice's, lethal self-defense might save Katherine's, and an experimental treatment might save Ellen's. But the federal ban on payment for organs sharply limits the availability of kidneys, so Olivia must wait years for a donated kidney; she faces a 20% chance of dying before she can get one. Barring compensation for goods or services makes them scarce. Alice and Ellen would be in extra danger if doctors were only allowed to perform abortions or experimental treatments for free. Katherine likely wouldn't be able to defend herself with a gun or knife if weapons could only be do-

nated. Likewise, Olivia's ability to protect her life is undermined by the organ payment ban.

My claim is that all four cases involve the exercise of a person's presumptive right to self-defense—lethal self-defense in Katherine's case, and what I call "medical self-defense" in the others....

Here too there are risks. First, the claim itself is only described in the fifth paragraph (not counting the introductory sentence). Second, the first two paragraphs describe well-known and uncontroversial doctrines. That's their point: They are setting up two uncontroversial examples so the author can argue that the next two examples are analogous to the first two. But an impatient reader might just be annoyed that the first two paragraphs are restating the familiar.

Yet the claim is pretty clearly foreshadowed starting with the third paragraph, where the analogy between protecting life using pharmaceuticals and protecting life using abortion or lethal self-defense is drawn. And if the analogy set forth in the first four paragraphs is powerful, it may be the best way to frame the article's thesis, by getting readers to view things from the outset using the author's analogy.

Note, by the way, what this Introduction doesn't have: It doesn't have any warm-up language describing substantive due process, talking abstractly about courts and tragic choices, saying that courts must sometimes protect important fundamental rights against the democratic process, and the like.

Rather, it starts concretely, with the two hypotheticals that are necessary to understand the analogy at the heart of the article, and moves on quickly to the two specific controversies that the article will offer to resolve. General discussion about how all this fits within the broad debate about unenumerated rights has to be included somewhere in the article. But it shouldn't go at the start of the Introduction, where the goal is to quickly convey to the reader the specific value this particular article will add.

5. Start with an explanation of a controversy

If your article engages an existing controversy, you might want to start by outlining the controversy, in enough detail that your contribution will be clear. The disadvantage of this approach is that your contribution might not appear for several paragraphs. The potential advantage is that the significance of your contribution may then be especially clear, and your outlining of the controversy might set an evenhanded tone that will lead readers to respond better to your claim when it does come.

Here's an example:

"A well regulated Militia, being necessary to the security of a free State," the Second Amendment says, "the right of the people to keep and bear arms, shall not be infringed." But what did the Framing generation understand "free State" to mean?

Some say it meant "state of the union, free from federal oppression." As one D.C. Circuit judge put it, "The Amendment was drafted in response to the perceived threat to the 'free[dom]' of the 'State[s]' posed by a national standing army controlled by the federal government."

This reading would tend to support the states' rights view of the Second Amendment, and is probably among the strongest intuitive foundations for the view—after all, "State" appears right there in the text, seemingly referring to each State's needs and interests. The reading would suggest the right might cover only those whom each state explicitly chose as its defensive force, perhaps a state-selected National Guard. And it would suggest the Amendment doesn't apply outside states, for instance in the District of Columbia: "the District of Columbia is not a state within the meaning of the Second Amendment and therefore the Second Amendment's reach does not extend to it."

But if "free State" was understood to mean "free country, free of despotism," that would tend to support the individual rights view of the Amendment. "[T]he right of the people" would then more easily be read as referring to a right of the people as free individuals, even if a right justified by public interests, much as "the right of the people" is understood in the First and Fourth Amendments. The right would cover people regardless of whether they were selected for a state-chosen defensive force, since the right would not be focused on preserving the states' independence from the federal government. And it would apply to all Americans, in states or in D.C.

We see a similar controversy about the change from James Madison's original proposal, which spoke of "security of a free country," to the final "security of a free state." Some assume the change was a deliberate substantive shift towards a states' rights provision, and point in support to the Constitution's general use of "state" to mean state of the union (except where "foreign State" is used to mean "foreign country"). Others disagree, arguing that the change was purely stylistic, and sometimes pointing to the absence of recorded controversy about the change.

This Article makes a simple claim: There's no need to assume. There is ample evidence about the original meaning of the term "free state." "Free state" was used often in Framing-era and pre-Framing

56

writings, especially those writings that are known to have powerfully influenced the Framers: Blackstone's *Commentaries* (which I'll discuss in Parts II and III), Montesquieu's *Spirit of the Laws* (Part IV), Hume's essays (Part V), Trenchard and Gordon's *Cato's Letters* (Part VI), and works by many of the other European authors who are known to have been cited by Framing-era American writers (Part VII). It was also used by many leading American writers as well (Part VIII), including John Adams in 1787, James Madison in 1785, and the Continental Congress in 1774.

Those sources, which surprisingly have not been canvassed by the Second Amendment literature, give us a clear sense of what the phrase "free state" meant at the time. In 18th century political discourse, "free state" was a well-understood political term of art, meaning "free country," which is to say the opposite of a despotism. [More details follow.]

The Introduction starts by crisply articulating the issue (as in the example in subsection 1 above, p. 50). It then outlines the role the term "free State" has played in the Second Amendment debate (rather than just setting forth the Second Amendment debate more broadly). The hope is that by the time the sixth and seventh paragraphs arrive, and the reader sees the article's claim, the reader will want to hear how this dispute should be resolved. The fear is that the reader won't get to the sixth and seventh paragraphs, or will be skimming or bored by then.

Compare this to how the Introduction would look if the claim were brought to the first paragraph, and decide for yourself which would be more effective:

"A well regulated Militia, being necessary to the security of a free State," the Second Amendment says, "the right of the people to keep and bear arms, shall not be infringed." But what did the Framing generation understand "free State" to mean? This Article will argue that this phrase was consistently understood to mean "free country," which is to say the opposite of a despotism—not "state of the union, free from federal oppression."

Many have assumed that "state of the union, free from federal oppression" was the contemporaneously understood meaning. As one D.C. Circuit judge put it, "The Amendment was drafted in response to the perceived threat to the 'free[dom]' of the 'State[s]' posed by a national standing army controlled by the federal government."

This reading would tend to support the states' rights view of the Second Amendment, and is probably among the strongest intuitive foundations for the view—after all, "State" appears right there in the text, seemingly referring to each State's needs and interests. The reading would suggest the right might cover only those whom each state explicitly chose as its defensive force, perhaps a state-selected National

Guard. And it would suggest the Amendment doesn't apply outside states, for instance in the District of Columbia: "the District of Columbia is not a state within the meaning of the Second Amendment and therefore the Second Amendment's reach does not extend to it."

But, this Article concludes, such a meaning is inconsistent with how the phrase was used in writings that are known to have powerfully influenced the Framers: Blackstone's *Commentaries* (which I'll discuss in Parts II and III), Montesquieu's *Spirit of the Laws* (Part IV), Hume's essays (Part V), Trenchard and Gordon's *Cato's Letters* (Part VI), and works by many of the other European authors who are known to have been cited by Framing-era American writers (Part VII). It was also used by many leading American writers as well (Part VIII), including John Adams in 1787, James Madison in 1785, and the Continental Congress in 1774.

Those writings used the phrase to mean "free country, free of despotism," which tends to support the individual rights view of the Amendment. Such a reading makes it easier to read "the right of the people" as referring to a right of the people as free individuals, even if a right justified by public interests, much as "the right of the people" is understood in the First and Fourth Amendments. Such a right covers people regardless of whether they were selected for a state-chosen defensive force, since the right is not focused on preserving the states' independence from the federal government. And it applies to all Americans, in states or in D.C.

Likewise, the evidence that the article canvasses helps resolve the controversy about the change from James Madison's original proposal, which spoke of "security of a free country," to the final "security of a free state." Some assume the change was a deliberate substantive shift towards a states' rights provision, and point in support to the Constitution's general use of "state" to mean state of the union (except where "foreign State" is used to mean "foreign country"). Others assume the change was purely stylistic, sometimes pointing to the absence of recorded controversy about the change. This latter view, which cuts in favor of the individual rights view, seems to be correct. [More details follow.]

6. Start with an argument or conventional wisdom you want to rebut

If your article is an attempt to rebut some argument, or some conventional wisdom, you may want to start by quickly identifying what you're arguing against. But do it quickly; don't spend pages talking about others' arguments—quickly reveal to the reader what you are going to say. A short sample:

Which Justices generally take a broader view of the freedom of speech and which take a narrower view? Conventional wisdom still tells us that this should break down mostly along "liberal"/"conservative" lines, as it seemingly did during the 1970s and much of the 1980s. But it turns out that this is no longer true. [The article goes on to provide the evidence.]

Or another one—a very short articulation of the other side's argument in a short Introduction:

The Supreme Court has often held that content-based restrictions on fully protected speech are valid if they are "narrowly tailored to serve a compelling state interest." I believe this is wrong.

It is wrong descriptively: There are restrictions the Court would strike down—of which I'll give examples—even though they are narrowly tailored to serve a compelling state interest. It is wrong normatively: In striking these restrictions down, the Court would, in my view, be correct. And the official test is not just wrong but pernicious. It risks leading courts and legislators to the wrong conclusions, it causes courts to apply the test disingenuously, and it distracts us from looking for a better approach.

After briefly restating strict scrutiny doctrine (Part I), I'll give three examples of speech restrictions that in my view would pass muster if the strict scrutiny framework were taken seriously, but that nonetheless would and should be struck down (Part II). I'll then point to some of the costs of the Court's reliance on an unsound doctrinal structure (Part III), and finally (Parts IV and V) suggest the rough foundations—and, I concede, only the rough foundations—of two alternative approaches.

The first alternative is for the Court to acknowledge that there is a third prong to strict scrutiny, which I call "permissible tailoring." Rather than just asking about the strength of the government's interest, or about whether the means are narrowly drawn to accomplish the interest, it asks whether the means are nonetheless impermissible: Whether, no matter how narrow they are, and no matter how compelling an interest they serve, the means are still contrary to some basic prohibitions that the Free Speech Clause imposes. This, I'll argue, is an inquiry quite distinct from what the Court requires under the "narrow tailoring" prong.

The second alternative, which I prefer, is for the Court to shift away from means-ends scrutiny, and toward an approach that operates through categorical rules—such as a per se ban on content-based speech restrictions imposed by the government as sovereign—coupled with categorical exceptions, such as the exceptions for fighting words, obscenity and copyright. I think this framework would better direct the Court's analysis, and would avoid the erroneous results that strict

59

scrutiny seems to command.

This Introduction has its flaws. First, the second alternative proposal isn't defined precisely and concretely enough. (This reflects a flaw in the article more generally.) Second, it might have been better to mention a few concrete examples in the second paragraph, rather than just promising to get to them in Part I.

Still, the Introduction has the merit of being short and focused on exposing the article's value added. And while it begins with articulating the argument that the article is trying to rebut, it articulates that opposing argument as concisely as possible, and doesn't let the argument dominate the discussion.

G. Organize the Introduction as a Roadmap

Law reviews often ask for so-called "roadmap paragraphs" at the end of the Introduction. Here's an example:

> This Comment, in Part I, explains what speech harassment law restricts, and how it restricts it. Part II confronts the arguments, made by some courts and some commentators, that harassment law can already be justified under some of the existing First Amendment doctrines—for example, as a time, place, or manner restriction, or a legitimate attempt to protect a captive audience—but finds that none of the arguments has merit. Finally, Part III introduces the directed speech/undirected speech distinction, and argues that it is the most practical place to draw the line between harassing workplace speech that must be protected and harassing workplace speech that may be restricted.

Some sort of roadmap is good: Readers do find it useful to get a sense of how the article will flow, and of where to look for particular sections of the analysis. You as the writer may also find it helpful to lay out the roadmap at the outset, just to give yourself a better idea of how you want to write the article.

But roadmaps written as separate paragraphs tend to seem forced, boring, and hard to read. Instead, try organizing the Introduction itself as a roadmap. The Introduction is supposed to be a summary of the rest of the article; so summarize the article in a persuasive, well-flowing way, and note where your summary goes from Part to Part. That way the roadmap may take up many paragraphs, but it won't require any extra paragraphs, and it will seem more organically connected to the rest of the Introduction. Here's an entire introduction illustrating this (the Introduction is to a co-written article, which explains the "we"):

Say we think a new book is going to libel us, and we ask a court for a preliminary injunction against the book's publication. We argue that we're likely to succeed on the merits of our libel claim, and that failure to enjoin the speech would cause us irreparable harm.

Too bad, the court will certainly say; a content-based preliminary injunction of speech would be a blatantly unconstitutional prior restraint. Maybe after a trial on the merits and a judicial finding that the speech is in fact constitutionally unprotected libel, we could get a permanent injunction, though even that's not clear. But we definitely could not get a preliminary injunction, based on mere likelihood of success. Likewise for preliminary injunctions against obscenity and other kinds of speech, despite the fact that such speech, if ultimately found to be unprotected at trial, could be criminally or civilly punished.

In copyright cases, though, preliminary injunctions are granted pretty much as a matter of course, even when the defendant has engaged in creative adaptation, not just literal copying. How can this be?

True, the Supreme Court has held that copyright law is a constitutionally permissible speech restriction; though copyright law restricts what we can write or record or perform, the First Amendment doesn't protect copyright-infringing speech against such a restraint. But libel law and obscenity law are likewise constitutionally valid restrictions on speech, and yet courts refuse to allow preliminary injunctions there. The "First Amendment due process" rule against prior restraints applies even to speech that's alleged to be constitutionally unprotected. Why, then, not to allegedly infringing speech?

We explore this question below. In Part I, we discuss the history of preliminary injunctions in copyright cases and the current law relating to such injunctions. In Part II, we develop our central thesis by explaining why copyright law is a speech restriction; why preliminary injunctions of speech are generally unconstitutional; and why, at least as a doctrinal and conceptual matter, it's hard to see how copyright law could be treated differently for First Amendment purposes. What's more, we argue, giving copyright law a free ride from the normal First Amendment due process rules risks discrediting those rules in other contexts.

In Part III, we step back and ask whether this inquiry has cast some doubt on the prior restraint doctrine itself—whether copyright law's tolerance of preliminary injunctions might be right, and the free speech doctrine's condemnation of such injunctions might be wrong. In Part IV, we discuss the implications of the collision between copyright law principles and free speech principles, and propose some changes that are needed to bring copyright law into line with constitutional commands. We conclude that permanent injunctions in copyright cases should generally be constitutional, and the same should go for preliminary injunctions in cases that clearly involve literal copying, with no plausible claim of fair use or of copying mere idea rather than expression. Other preliminary injunctions, though, should generally be unconstitutional.

In Part V, we briefly explore these questions with regard to other kinds of intellectual property—trademarks, rights of publicity, trade secrets, and patents. We conclude that the problem is not limited to copyright, and that at least in trademark and right of publicity cases, preliminary injunctions may sometimes run afoul of the First Amendment. Finally, in Part VI we say a bit about the practical prospects for revising the law along the lines we suggest.

IV. WRITING THE "BACKGROUND" SECTION

A. *Focus on the Necessary Facts and Legal Rules*

The section after the Introduction is sometimes called the "background" section. Unfortunately, this tends to lead some authors into throwing in as much background as possible, and it obscures what aspects of the background are most important.

As a result, too many student articles spend eighty percent of their time setting forth the "background" and twenty percent explaining and proving their claims. And doing this is tempting: Describing the existing law, facts, or history is easier than articulating and defending an original claim. Plus, when you've spent many weeks doing research, it's hard to cut down the result to just a few pages.

Yet the purpose of your article is to state and prove your claim. That's where the action is, and you should be excited and impatient about getting there. Your claim and your proof are what you're adding to the field of knowledge; your achievement will be measured largely by this value added. You can't prove your claim without explaining certain facts and legal doctrines, but do this as tersely as possible.

So instead, think of this section as the section that explains those items that are *necessary* to understanding the problem. For instance, if you're writing about how the law should treat nonlethal weapons (such as stun guns and pepper sprays), you need to explain those facts about nonlethal weapons that are necessary to understanding such regulations. For instance, you should note what kinds of injuries these devices can inflict, how many times they can be used before reloading, in what circumstances they don't work well, and the like.

Do not explain the history of stun guns, except to the extent that it's necessary to understanding the regulatory regime. Do not explain the chemistry of pepper sprays. These are detours that will take the reader away from the heart of your article: how the law should treat nonlethal weapons.

Likewise, if you're writing about the First Amendment and restrictions on parent-child speech in child custody cases, you'll need to briefly explain the basic definitions, such as the differences between legal custody and physical custody, and between custody and visitation. You'll also need to briefly explain the family law rules that you're analyzing. You might also briefly summarize the First Amendment rules, though you might want to save that for the substantive analysis section, where

63

you can introduce the rules as you apply them.

But don't write a mini-treatise on the law. Don't even describe all the law and all the facts that you'll later use. All you must do in this section is give the reader the legal and factual framework necessary to generally understanding what follows. You'll have plenty of time to go into more detail later, as you set out your proof.

Also, don't talk in detail about how the rules have evolved over the centuries, again except to the extent that it's necessary to understanding the rules today. Don't discuss the leading cases related to the rules in detail, unless they are necessary to grasping the issue. Where possible, synthesize the precedents into a crisply stated rule (with the precedents cited in the footnotes, as needed) rather than discussing each case.

B. Synthesize the Precedents; Don't Summarize Each One

A bit more on the synthesizing I just mentioned: You should generally synthesize the precedents, not describe each one or explain how the law came to be the way it is. If the history is necessary to give a full picture of what the law means, you should of course mention it. But to the extent that the history doesn't really matter, cut it out. Your main mission is to prove your claim. Unnecessary tangents might seem interesting and colorful, but in practice they usually end up being distractions and excuses for the reader to stop reading.

Likewise, if there's a leading case that you need to compare and contrast in detail with the scenario about which you're writing, you'll need to discuss the case in detail in the proof section. Don't repeat all this detail in the background explanation section. And certainly don't go into the facts of the case if the facts are not really needed to understand the law.

Instead, briefly state the relevant rule, in whatever detail is needed, and cite your authorities in the footnotes. Imagine, for instance, that you're writing an article about how libel law should apply to false accusations of homosexuality (a surprisingly complex question), and that you want to set forth the basic First Amendment rules about what mental states must be proven for liability. You probably shouldn't write something like:

> In 1964, the Supreme Court handed down a landmark libel decision in *New York Times Co. v. Sullivan*. Police commissioner Sullivan

sued the *New York Times* for publishing allegedly false statements about him. Six Justices held that in a libel case brought by a public official, where the speech was on a matter of public concern, the plaintiff could not recover unless he showed that the defendant knew the statement was false, or was reckless about the statement's potential falsehood. The other three Justices would have categorically forbidden public officials from recovering libel damages when the statement was on a matter of public concern.

Three years later, in *Curtis Publishing Co. v. Butts*, the Supreme Court extended this rule to public figures who were not public officials. Butts was a state university football coach who was accused of leaking the team's playbook to an opposing team, but he was technically employed by a private organization, not by the state, and was thus not a public official. The Court concluded that his not being employed by the state should not change the constitutional analysis.

But in 1974, the Supreme court substantially cut back on protection for defendants. In *Gertz v. Robert Welch Co.*, lawyer Elmer Gertz sued the publisher of the anti-Communist John Birch Society's magazine for libel, based on an article that accused him of having a criminal record and of being a Communist. The Supreme Court held that when the statement was about a private figure, the plaintiff could recover compensatory damages if he showed that the defendant was negligent about whether the statement was false. Presumed and punitive damages could still be recovered only on a showing of knowing or reckless falsehood.

Finally, in the 1985 *Dun & Bradstreet v. Greenmoss Builders* case, the Court cut back protection still further. Greenmoss Builders sued credit rating company Dun & Bradstreet for falsely stating that Greenmoss had filed for bankruptcy. The Court held that where the statements were on matters of purely private concern, plaintiffs could recover compensatory, punitive, and presumed damages based merely on a showing of the defendant's negligence. The Court's opinion even left open the door for strict liability in such cases, though it didn't specifically confront this question.

In an article that's about modern libel law, the details of the past Supreme Court cases probably don't much matter; neither does the history of the law's evolution. Even if you do make arguments based on this history, or analogize to the facts of the past cases, you'll need to cite that history or those facts later in the article, where you make your arguments. You won't be able to rely on readers' remembering these points from the Background section.

Instead, synthesize the cases into a rule:

The First Amendment rule in libel cases turns on two main factors:

(1) whether the plaintiff is a public figure (a category that includes public officials but is not limited to them), and (2) whether the statement is on a matter of public concern.

Plaintiffs may recover in public figure / public concern cases only if the defendant knew the statement was false, or was reckless about the possibility of falsehood. In private figure / public concern cases, this same knowledge-or-recklessness standard applies for punitive and presumed damages, but the plaintiff may recover compensatory damages even if the defendant was merely negligent about the statement's falsehood. And in private concern cases, the plaintiff may recover all sorts of damages even when the defendant was merely negligent; and the Court has left open the possibility that defendants in such cases may even be held strictly liable.

Then just cite the relevant cases, with the proper parentheticals, in a footnote.

There are other ways to summarize the rule; you might, for instance, use a table or a numbered or bulleted list, devices that are often clearer than simple prose. But in any event, give the reader the background that he needs for understanding your article—don't waste his time with facts that are irrelevant to your claim.

V. Writing the Proof of the Claim

This part—basically everything after the Introduction and the "background" section, and before the Conclusion—is where you can shine, by showing that your claim is correct, and that it's the best way of solving the problem you've identified. Some tips:

A. Show Your Prescription Is Both Doctrinally Sound and Good Policy

Don't just show that your prescriptive proposal (if you have one) fits the case law; also persuade your reader that it's practically and normatively sound. Authors often come up with a neat logical argument that supposedly proves a law's unconstitutionality or explains how a law must be interpreted, but that leaves many readers unpersuaded. To the extent possible, show that your proposal makes practical sense as well as logical sense—that it is good policy as well as consistent with the doctrine.

B. Be Concrete

Illustrate your theoretical arguments with concrete examples, drawn from real cases or realistic hypotheticals. This will make your point clearer to your reader; it will show that you have a point and aren't just playing a theoretical shell game; and it will often make your point clearer to you, or lead you to rethink it.

C. Use the Test Suite

The test suite you used to show yourself that the prescriptive part of your claim is sound (see Part II) can prove the same to your readers. The test suite involves concrete test cases. It illustrates different aspects of your proposal. And if done right, it involves cases that come from a variety of political perspectives, and thus shows that you've thought through a broad range of implications that your proposal may have, not just those that seem to fit your politics.

At least in the first draft, try to mention every test case from your test suite.* Then, if necessary, you can remove the ones that prove re-

---

* For examples of using test cases in a published article, see Jennifer E. Rothman,

dundant.

D. Confront the Other Side's Arguments, but Focus on Your Own

Deal with all the counter-arguments, but take the offensive. Don't write "Some people say that this law fits within the captive audience doctrine, and this might at first seem plausible. Let me quote what they say: .... But on further reading it turns out that this isn't so, because ...."

Instead, write "the law can't be justified under the captive audience doctrine, because...." Cite your adversaries and rebut their assertions, but don't let them be the main characters in your discussion.

E. Turn Problems to Your Advantage

1. Improve your argument

Squarely confront the logical and practical difficulties with your argument; don't try to sweep them under the rug. Be honest with your reader—it's the right thing to do, it's more effective, and it'll make you feel better about your work.

To begin with, confronting the difficulties can turn a banal, straightforward argument into one that's more nuanced and interesting. Say that the leading precedent in the field doesn't support your claim as squarely as you'd like. Don't just ignore this; explain how some other precedents or policy arguments fill the gap.

For instance, suppose your argument rests partly on the claim that public single-sex junior high schools are unconstitutional. You could just cite *Mississippi University for Women v. Hogan* and *United States v. Virginia* for your proposition, as some people do.

But these cases don't actually stand for quite so broad a principle— they involve college education, and they stress the particular characteristics of the programs involved in each case. If you rely only on these cases, many readers will be unpersuaded, and you'll also have lost your chance to show off your reasoning skills. Rather, explain why the broad-

Freedom of Speech and True Threats, 25 Harv. J.L. & Pub. Pol'y 283, 336–66 (2001), and Eugene Volokh, *Freedom of Speech, Shielding Children, and Transcending Balancing*, 1997 Sup. Ct. Rev. 141, 183–87.

er policies embodied in the Court's equal protection jurisprudence fill the gap between the precedents and your proposed rule; or explain why, even if a gap remains, your case is factually close to the situations in the precedents.

Do the same when you see ambiguity in the facts, history, statutory or constitutional text, or policy arguments: Acknowledge the ambiguity and explain why your choice is better than the alternatives. You shine by showing how you deal with the tough questions, not by pretending that the tough questions are easy.

2. Refine your claim

The difficulties can also lead you to make your claim more moderate and nuanced. Say your argument proves your claim in most cases, but not in all: For instance, say that it persuasively shows that single-sex K–12 schools are usually unconstitutional, but that it doesn't really work for programs specially aimed at students who have been sexually abused or who are mentally disturbed.

Maybe you should change your claim from "single-sex public education is unconstitutional" to "single-sex public education is generally unconstitutional, but single-sex public education of certain kinds of hard-to-teach children is constitutional." This may be a sounder claim, and it's also more likely to be novel and nonobvious.

3. Acknowledge uncertainty

The difficulties with your argument can also require you to acknowledge some uncertainty, and to prove your argument as best you can in the face of that uncertainty.

This can help make your work look more sensible and thoughtful. After all, little in our lives or in the law can be logically proven. We must often make the best guess we can, given gaps in the evidence. It's no great loss to admit this, assuming you have enough evidence to make your point plausible, even if not formally proven.

Say the cases are best read as holding only that public single-sex K–12 education is unconstitutional unless there's strong evidence that such programs are educationally valuable; and say people disagree about the evidence. Use the evidence on your side as best you can, acknowledge that there's disagreement, and make the best pragmatic, logical, and doctrinal argument you can for your point—for instance, you might argue that, in the face of disagreements about the facts, courts should err on the side of nondiscrimination and thus coeducation.

This is especially true for historical or empirical claims. It's hard to be sure about what people really believed or did many decades or centuries ago, or about what's happening in thousands of courtrooms or workplaces today; and readers who think deeply about such matters realize this. Make your descriptive claims clearly and forcefully, and explain why your interpretation of the history or of the data is the best one. But also acknowledge what other interpretations there might be.

4. Acknowledge costs

Finally, the difficulties can make you acknowledge that your proposal is not cost-free—that it to some extent sacrifices important government interests, or causes some possibly harmful side effects, or may at times be hard to administer. Skeptical readers will see these problems on their own, even if you don't admit that they exist. If you ignore the problems, the readers may assume the worst about the problems' magnitude.

If, however, you acknowledge the costs of your proposal but explain why the benefits exceed the costs, you can persuade many readers. No one expects any new proposal to be perfect. Explaining the proposal's downside can actually make it more credible—and can make you look more forthright and realistic.

F. Connect to Broader, Parallel, and Subsidiary Issues

1. Make your article richer: Go beyond the basic claim

So far, we've focused on the core claim: The nugget of novelty, nonobviousness, and utility that will be your contribution to the state of legal knowledge. This is the heart of your article, and you should focus primarily on explaining and proving it.

Most claims, though, can provide insights that go beyond their narrowest boundaries; the claims have unexpected implications that flow naturally from them, even though these implications don't strictly need to be discussed. Exploring these matters can add nuance to your core claim that will make it more novel and nonobvious.

More broadly, it can make your article richer and more sophisticated—a thorough exploration of many facets of the problem, rather than just one narrow claim. Such an article will be more useful to people interested in the problem; and, if done right, these connections will make people think better of your article and therefore of you.

2. Connections: Importing from broader debates

Begin by asking yourself whether some of the issues you raise are special cases of broader matters on which there are already academic debates. For instance, if you are writing about a particular individual right, are there any theories of individual rights that you can draw on for your analysis? If you're interpreting one provision of a statute, is there a broader discussion going on in the law reviews about the statute's purpose or overall impact?

Say your work discusses whether a particular kind of statement should be admitted as evidence under some exception to the hearsay rule. There are many debates in the literature about hearsay generally—about whether hearsay should even be presumptively excluded in the first place, about whether there should be a single discretionary standard ("allow hearsay evidence if there are sufficient indicia of trustworthiness") or a rule that generally excludes hearsay but has many detailed exceptions, and so on. Do some points raised in these debates help you support your arguments? Do they provide counterarguments to which you ought to respond?

These connections to broader matters aren't always helpful. Sometimes, the broader, more theoretical arguments are notorious for not giving much of a concrete answer in any particular case. In other situations, the broader discussion may be too many levels of abstraction above your particular question: If you're talking about whether certain restrictions imposed on felons violate the Ex Post Facto Clause, and if you already have lots of doctrine and policy argument to draw on for your analysis, a discussion of the debates about whether courts should rely on natural law or original meaning may not be terribly useful.

But sometimes the theories might indeed provide valuable insights. Even if their application won't form the core of your argument, they may shed light on a particular aspect of the argument, or supply important counterarguments that you should rebut. Also, discussing the theories can help assure the reader (a) that you aren't missing some theoretical objections, and (b) that you are a sophisticated thinker who knows the important theoretical literature. You shouldn't overdo this— a weak, unnecessary, or unoriginal application of the theory can sometimes alienate readers more than impress them. Still, if you can do a good job with the theory, your article will be more impressive.

3. Connections: Exporting to broader debates

Just as broad debates can have applications to narrower problems, good solutions to the narrower problems can illuminate a broader issue. If you have persuasively shown that the right answer here is X, and some broader theory says that the answer should be Y, then your concrete point is evidence that the broader theory is mistaken (or at least is not applicable here), and that the theory's rivals may be more sound. For instance, if you show that certain speech should be protected under the First Amendment even though it would be unprotected under some free speech theory (the "marketplace of ideas," the "constitutional tension method," or what have you), then you might use your conclusion to cast doubt on the value of that theory more generally.

If done right, this sort of connection will make your piece deeper and more useful, and thus more impressive. People often accept or reject broad legal theories based not just on abstract legal arguments, but also on how well the theories fit with the results that seem proper in specific cases. Your article may provide powerful practical support or a powerful practical counterexample to some broad theoretical argument.

4. Connections: Importing from parallel areas

Sometimes, the best connections for your article come not from broader theories but from analogous issues in parallel areas. For instance, say that you are writing about whether waiting periods for buying a gun violate state constitutional right to keep and bear arms provisions.* Can you draw some analogies from the cases dealing with waiting periods for abortions, parade permits, or voting?

The analogies need not be perfect; you can often enrich your argument by pointing out the differences between your area and the other areas that at first might seem similar. Your reader might already have thought of these apparent similarities, and your discussion can dispel the reader's misconceptions. Likewise, the very process of pointing out the differences between, say, self-defense rights, abortion rights, speech

---

* *See, e.g.*, Wis. Const. art. I, § 25 (enacted 1998) ("The people have the right to keep and bear arms for security, defense, hunting, recreation or any other lawful purpose.").

rights, and voting rights might make the proof of your claim more persuasive. And sometimes, as with the importation from broader debates, the analogies may help you refine the claim itself.

5. Connections: Exporting to parallel areas

Again, once you're done seeing what light the analogies from parallel areas can shed on your problem, you should ask whether your solution sheds light on the parallel questions. If you conclude that waiting periods for buying guns don't unduly burden self-defense rights, can you generalize to a broader claim about waiting periods for the exercise of other constitutional rights? If you think that the answer should be different in different situations, can you come up with a general principle that distinguishes contexts where waiting periods are undue burdens from contexts where they aren't? Or can you at least draw a distinction that can help differentiate the two kinds of contexts, even if it can't do the entire job itself?

Even if there isn't yet any broader academic debate on your general subject, your claim might have possible consequences that would be worth noting. For instance, your argument about one provision of a statute might illuminate the interpretation of other provisions; you don't need to analyze those provisions fully, but it helps if you at least highlight your argument's implications. Perhaps you can start a broader academic discussion yourself.

6. Connections to subsidiary questions

Finally, consider what will happen if your claim is accepted. To begin with, ask what the people who would implement your proposed rule would have to do to make it work properly.

Would prosecutors enforcing your proposed law have to exercise their discretion in unexpected ways? Would your substantive proposal have nonobvious procedural applications? Would there be problems of proof that might require changes to certain evidentiary rules, or at least to trial tactics? Discussing such questions can make your article more useful and complete, and might generate new and interesting insights.

For instance, say you're arguing that speech revealing certain facts about someone's sex life should be seen as tortious, and that liability for such speech wouldn't violate the First Amendment. Your substantive constitutional point could have procedural implications for how such trials should be conducted. For instance, you might argue that though compensatory damages should be allowed in such cases, punitive damages should be restricted, by analogy to the rule in certain libel cases. Or you might explore whether such speech should lead only to damage awards, or whether courts should also be allowed to enjoin the speech, despite the ostensible rule against prior restraints.

You might also find that in some contexts your claim has unexpected substantive implications. For instance, does your broad point about revealing facts have particular consequences for publication of photographs, or of tape recordings? Even if the legal rule is the same, might it affect people's behavior differently in different situations?

Ask also what effect this rule will have on other tort rules. Will it make some of them unnecessary? Will it make others more important? For instance, in some recent cases the right of publicity has been used to bar the unauthorized distribution of nude photographs of celebrities. Would your proposed privacy right make such an extension of the right of publicity unnecessary or even undesirable?

7. A cautionary note

There are risks to exploring all of an article's implications:

1. If you explore them thoroughly, your article may become too long.

2. If you only sketch them lightly, the reader might find the discussion too cursory, too vague, or insufficiently supported; and this bad impression might undo some of the good impression that your core argument initially made.

3. If you don't structure the discussion well, some of the connections might become confusing tangents that distract your reader from the main point.

4. If you are too ambitious in looking for connections, you might find yourself drawing analogies that don't ring true.

The trick is to:

a. create a solid core argument;

b. incorporate into it those connections and implications that are necessary to a full understanding of your point;

c. discuss the other connections and implications in some detail— perhaps in a separate section—while making clear that your main point doesn't stand or fall with them; and

d. be cautious about the analogies you draw and the connections you make, and ruthlessly edit out those that on reflection don't seem persuasive enough.

Thus, first make sure that the readers understand your main point, and are impressed by it. Then, once they are already thinking well of you, they'll be more charitable towards any broader but tangential points that you might make.

But *be willing to cut those tangents*. Show readers—your faculty advisor, your trusted and thoughtful friends, your law review editor—a basically finished draft of your article. And if some of the readers tell you that some of the connections don't really work, be ready to edit them out.

Yes, it will be painful to jettison sections that you've worked hard to write, but you'll probably find that for every connection you cut, you'll be keeping two. And the connections that you keep will help make your article richer and more impressive than if you'd stuck only to the bare necessities.

VI. The Conclusion, and After the Conclusion

A. Write the Conclusion

The conclusion is where you remind people of the value that your article has added to the debate. Briefly summarize your claim, and the most important subsidiary conclusions. But keep it quick—the reader is looking forward to being done.

B. Rewrite the Introduction After the Draft Is Done

1. Rewrite the introduction in light of how your thinking has changed

When you're done with writing an entire draft of the article, rewrite the introduction. Since you wrote it, you might have:

    a. changed your claim,

    b. found better arguments for your claim,

    c. found better examples to illustrate your claim,

    d. found interesting and unexpected consequences of your claim,

or changed your thinking in other ways. Writing an article *should* change your thinking about the subject. Even if your bottom line remains pretty much the same, surely your understanding of the argument is now much deeper than when you started.

Rewrite the introduction using this newly acquired understanding. You'll find that the new introduction better fits the rest of the article, and that it better promotes the article to the reader. In particular, make sure that you briefly mention all the important conclusions that the reader should take away from the article—not just your claim, but also the implications of the claim, such as those discussed in the last few pages.

Many readers will read only your introduction. Make sure that they get as much out of it as possible, both so they absorb more of your ideas, and so they have a higher opinion of you as a possible law clerk, colleague, co-counsel, consultant, or scholar.

2. Note all your important and nonobvious discoveries

Your article may have started as a way to make and prove one novel, nonobvious, useful, and sound claim. But in the process of writing your article, you might have found several other novel, nonobvious, useful, and sound things that you needed to say to prove that core claim. (If you have a mathematics or computer programming background, think of them as reusable lemmas or subroutines.)

These subsidiary discoveries will probably be less important than the main claim, but they may still be valuable. And some readers who are unpersuaded by the main claim, or don't find it that useful to them, may nonetheless accept and use these subsidiary discoveries.

Make sure that your Introduction lists all these discoveries, so that a reader who reads only the Introduction will learn about them, and so that a reader who reads the whole article won't miss their importance. You might even expressly note that your article makes several different though related observations. For example:

> In Part III, I argue that these speech restrictions imposed in child custody cases are unconstitutional, except when they are narrowly focused on preventing one parent from undermining the child's relationship with the other; and the observations that lead to this proposal will, I hope, be useful even to readers who don't agree with the proposal itself. Here is a brief summary:
>
> 1. The best interests test leaves courts free to make custody decisions based on parents' speech, and to issue orders restricting their speech. Courts have taken advantage of this freedom and will surely do so again, as to a broad (and, to many, surprising) range of parental ideologies—depending on the time and place, atheist or fundamentalist, racist or pro-polygamist, pro-homosexual or anti-homosexual. The breadth of such restrictions should give pause to those who advocate exempting speech-based child custody decisions from constitutional scrutiny.
>
> 2. The First Amendment is implicated not only when courts issue orders restricting parents' speech, but also when courts make custody or visitation decisions because of what parents have said to the child, or are likely to say to the child. And just as the Equal Protection Clause bars child custody decisions that discriminate based on race, so the First Amendment presumptively bars child custody decisions that discriminate based on a parent's constitutionally protected speech.
>
> 3. Even when the parents' speech is religious, the Free Speech Clause is probably a more important protection for the speech than the Religion Clauses are, though nearly all the scholarship and most of the litigation has neglected the Free Speech Clause.
>
> 4. If parents in intact families have First Amendment rights to speak to their children, without legal prohibitions on speech that is

77

supposedly against the child's "best interests," then parents in split families generally deserve the same rights, except when the speech undermines the child's relationship with the other parent.

5. Parents in intact families should indeed be free to speak to their children—but not primarily because of the parents' self-expression rights, or their children's interests in hearing the parents' views. Rather, the main reason is that today's child listeners will grow up into the next generation's adult speakers. That next generation is entitled to hear a broad range of ideas, without government interference; restrictions on ideological parent-child speech are a powerful way for today's majorities or elites to entrench their ideas, and to block their ideological rivals from being heard in the future. The First Amendment is a necessary check on this entrenchment.

6. It may seem appealing to protect speech generally, but to withdraw that protection when the speech imminently threatens psychological harm to the child. But such an approach will likely prove unhelpful: It's hard for courts to reliably predict whether speech will cause harm, to reliably determine whether certain existing harm was indeed caused by speech (as opposed to by the breakup itself, or by the other parent's condemnation of the speech), and to weigh the present upset caused by certain teachings against the teachings' potential long-term benefits.

These points are related, and they help prove the article's overall claim. But some of them are also independently valuable.

The descriptive item 1 may be interesting even to people who aren't persuaded by the article's prescription. Item 5, which speaks more broadly about parental speech rights—even outside child custody decisions—may be useful to people who are writing articles on this broader theme. Item 6, which criticizes the "protect speech unless it's harmful" option, may be worth highlighting to people who quickly accept the notion that parental speech should be protected, but who assume that of course the speech may be restricted when it is harmful.

Your article likely has many subsidiary findings like this. Make sure that you properly highlight them.

C. Decide What to Set Aside

"A poem is never finished, only abandoned."* For many articles, there's no clear theoretical stopping point. You can always discuss other

---

* Usually attributed to French poet Paul Valery.

interesting legal issues that relate to your core claim—for instance, if you're writing on a substantive free speech issue (e.g., the tension between the First Amendment and hostile work environment harassment law), you might see some interesting procedural questions that this raises: Should injunctions barring harassing speech be treated as prior restraints? Should there be independent appellate review in harassment cases that are based on speech?

Sometimes your running out of time or patience makes the decision for you. But if it doesn't, how do you know when to set these interesting points aside?

There's no clear answer to this, but my suggestion is to (1) thoroughly discuss your main claim, and then (2) have a short section that identifies and broadly outlines the other points, but doesn't fully resolve them. Generally, if you discuss your main claim in enough depth, you'll have a nice, substantial piece. Adding a thorough investigation of the tangents is unnecessary.

But flagging these tangents as interesting avenues for future research, and briefly giving some tentative thoughts on them, can help enrich your article and make it more relevant and useful. The very fact that your main topic raises these related questions can help show that the topic is important.

Make especially sure that you flag the implications of your claim, or of your framework for resolving the claim. These help show the importance not just of your topic (which existed before you started writing), but also of your analysis, which is your own contribution. If, for instance, you develop a test, briefly discuss where else the test, or tests like it, might be applied. If you develop a categorization scheme, briefly flag where else it could be helpfully used.

How brief should these tentative discussions be? That's a judgment call; you want them to persuade the reader that there's something interesting there, but you don't want them to get long enough that they make your article unnecessarily bulky and take up too much of your time. Four tips:

1. Ask your faculty advisor for advice, but *after* you've handed in the rough draft of your main discussion. Before you deliver the draft, the advisor won't be sure that you're able to handle even the core claim, much less the tangents.

2. Make clear at the start of the section that these points are avenues for future research, and that you will be discussing them

only briefly. People's evaluations are related to their expectations: If they are warned that the discussion will be brief, they'll be less likely to be bothered by its brevity.

3. How substantive the digressions must be turns on how substantive your core argument is. If you deal thoroughly with your main claim, readers will be more likely to assume that your tangentially raised points are interesting, and that you would have dealt with them well if your article had been more focused on them.

4. Be prepared to delete these digressions—or to save them for a future article—if readers tell you that they're unpersuasive or distracting.

Finally, note that this has to do with how *broad* you make your article—how many related issues you choose to cover. If you have an opportunity to make your article *deeper*, by better justifying more of your arguments, do so (at least unless you think your justifications will be redundant). Inadequately supported assertions, or even assertions that are supported by the doctrine but not fully defended on policy grounds, make your argument weaker.

VII. Finishing the First Draft, and the Zeroth Draft

A. Defeat Writer's Block by Skipping Around

When you're writing the first draft, and get blocked on one section, go on to the next. If you need to leave a subsection for later, that's fine. If you feel that the best you can do is outline a section, or write a few unconnected paragraphs, do that.

Just keep going forward, and don't let your difficulties with one part interrupt the whole writing project. Usually, even if you're bored with one section or confused about what you want to say, you'll be invigorated by moving to another part of your argument. And once you have the first draft done, no matter how rough it is, revising it and filling the gaps will probably be much easier.

Your producing a first draft quickly, and then quickly improving and completing it, will also give your faculty advisor more time to give you useful feedback, and maybe to read through more drafts; and it will make you look industrious and disciplined—which is how you want the person who's grading your work to see you.

B. The Zeroth Draft

One way to get a first draft done is to begin with what I call a "zeroth draft"—something halfway between an outline and a first draft. Here's one way of doing this:

1. Start by writing a fairly complete Introduction, if you can. For the reasons mentioned in Part III.A (p. 47), the Introduction can help you get a better grasp of what you're trying to say.

2. Lay out in your document the structure that you anticipate for the rough draft, including the section and subsection headings.

3. For each subsection, start by writing a sentence or two summarizing the argument in the section. For instance, if you're writing about the First Amendment and workplace harassment law, one section might read:

A. Fighting Words

Workplace harassment law can't be justified using the "fighting words" exception because it isn't limited to speech that isn't face-to-face, and isn't likely to immediately start a fight.

4. Then, when you've filled in all the subsections that you can—or if you're blocked on what to write in some subsections—go back over the one-sentence summaries and expand them to a paragraph or two, for instance:

A. Fighting Words

Workplace harassment law can't be justified using the "fighting words" exception because it isn't limited to speech that isn't face-to-face, and isn't likely to immediately start a fight. The premise of the exception isn't that all offensive speech or all insults are punishable because they offend—it's that they (i) lack value, (ii) can be restricted without interfering with valuable speech, since one can still convey the same views in other ways, and (iii) are likely to cause an immediate fight. Nothing in harassment law limits itself to this narrow category; it can just as well cover [give examples of non-one-to-one-speech].

Discuss *Cohen v. California* as example of this limitation.

5. Repeat this expansion as much as you can. Expand each paragraph into a couple of paragraphs, each couple of paragraphs into a full subsection, and so on.

6. Don't worry about spelling, grammar, footnotes, and the like. Feel free to use bulleted and numbered lists. Use whatever shortcuts will help you express your substantive points in as much detail as possible.

7. Do worry a little about statements that seem too abstract or conclusory—see if you can, in the next pass, make them more concrete or provide more support for them. But worry only a little: The difference between a zeroth draft and a first draft is that you should expect some of the zeroth draft to lack concreteness or detailed argument.

C. As You Write, Use Subsection Headings

Readers find subsection headings helpful: Even if your article is well organized, readers might at times lose sight of the structure, and subsection headings can bring the reader back on track. Try to choose headings that refer to your specific argument—such as "Identifying Speech That Lacks Value When Communicated to Minors"—rather than generic ones such as "Background" or "Applying the Test."[9] Subsection breaks also provide extra white space on the page, which seems to make text more appealing to many readers.

But the main value of these subsection breaks is to help you organize your own thinking. If you break up a section into five subsections, giving each a topical heading, you'll be more likely to see organizational problems, such as shifts from one issue to another and then back to the first, or digressions that break up the article's logical flow.

Naturally, there will be some overlap among the subsections within each section. But to the extent possible, you should completely cover each detail within a few adjacent pages, rather than returning to it repeatedly throughout various parts of the article. Readers find it hard to grasp an argument that's made in five chunks in five parts of the paper. They'll need to do this for your broad argument, which will indeed pervade the whole article. Don't ask them to do the same for subordinate arguments.

Good places for subsection breaks are usually easy to spot. For instance, when you're dealing with a multi-prong test, it generally makes sense to have a subsection for each prong, even for a prong that takes only several paragraphs. Many multi-pronged tests actually have several subprongs contained within each prong; consider having a subsection for each of these subprongs. Be willing to have subsections that go four or five levels deep.

If you're discussing several factual scenarios, policy arguments, or statutory sections, consider having a separate subsection for each one. Err on the side of having more subsection breaks rather than fewer.

After you're finished, you might decide to delete some of the lower-level subsection headings, especially if the subsections are very short, and the structure of the broader section is clear. Still, the headings will have served the goal of helping you write the article, even if they won't be needed to help the reader read it.

D. Use a Table of Contents

Most word processors can easily produce a table of contents from your section headings. Use this feature, partly to help the reader, but mostly to give you an overview of the article's structure as the headers reflect it. The table of contents may help show you some missing steps, or some redundancies.

The table of contents can also point out inconsistencies in your headings. Check, for instance, that you consistently use upper and lower case, and that the headings in each section are grammatically parallel.

Make sure that you use the editing commands needed to make the automatic table of contents work: In Word, for instance, use the Heading 1 through Heading 5 styles to set up the headings—control-alt-1 to control-alt-3 are usually configured as keyboard shortcuts for Headings 1 to 3—and when you insert the table of contents, ask for it to show up to 5 levels, and not just the default 3.

E. Note Down All Your Ideas

As you write, you'll often get interesting ideas that you can't act on immediately, for instance because they relate to another section or to something that you should research.

Write down these ideas before you forget them. I prefer to record them in my main document—either in the computer or on the printout that I'm editing—tagged with some text, such as "**." You can put them into the section where they'll ultimately be discussed, in a master "to do" list at the top or bottom of the document, or even in whatever text you're currently working on. Because they're specially marked, you can easily find them later; and because they're written down, you won't lose what might be a great thought.

Likewise, at the end of a writing session, always write down what you plan to do next.[10] That way, you won't lose your train of thought, and you will find it easier to start the next session.

VIII. Tips on Researching

There are five basic things you need to find for an article:

1. the *legal rules* that govern your field, and the cases and statutes that can help you identify the basic policy arguments for refining the legal rules;

2. the *academic literature* about your topic, so that you can (a) figure out whether your contribution is really novel, (b) learn the important arguments that you could build on, or try to rebut, and (c) find those legal rules or sample cases that you couldn't find on your own;

3. *sample cases or incidents* that can help you concretely and vividly illustrate your problem and your solution;

4. *details on each especially important case or incident* that you plan on featuring in your article, including details that might not be present in the usual places (such as in the report of the appellate decision);

5. *empirical studies*, often from other disciplines, that can help support your arguments, to the extent that your arguments rely on factual questions.

You should come to your writing project generally understanding how to find cases, statutes, and law review articles that deal with a given topic; your first-year research class must surely have taken care of that. I'll therefore just provide some extra tips that I think are particularly useful when writing articles and seminar papers.

A. *Identifying Sample Cases and Incidents*

Part I.B, p. 13, discusses ways you can identify an interesting topic to write on. Some of these ways will themselves point you to one or two cases that show how the topic arises in real life.

Look closely at these cases, and find more like them. Such sample cases:

a. help you figure out what you think about the problem,

b. introduce you to the arguments that have been made by the judges and lawyers in those cases,

c. show you what related problems your topic might implicate,

d. help you make the topic concrete for readers,

85

e. help you persuade readers that there really is a problem that needs to be solved, and

f. form the kernel of the test suite that you'll use in designing your claim (see Part II).

Generally, the more different examples you have to start with, the better.

How do you find more examples? Here are a few tips:

1. Look for cases that your initial cases cite.

2. Look for cases that cite your initial cases.

3. Search for some of the keywords that are likely to be present in cases that implicate your topic. If those keywords are likely to find too many cases that are only tangentially related to your problem, limit your Westlaw search by using the *SYNOPSIS* field—for instance, *SY(copyright & parody)* will find all cases that have the words "copyright" and "parody" in the case's synopsis, not just anywhere in the text. *SY,DI(copyright & parody)* will find all cases that have those words either in the synopsis or the headings.

    Lexis's *OVERVIEW* feature will do something similar, though it seems to find fewer cases than *SY,DI*—both fewer false positives and fewer cases that you may indeed want to find.

4. Use West's key number system, which often lets you find cases on a particular topic even when the cases can't be consistently found using any specific full-text search terms. Look at West's *Analysis of American Law* volume for the general field in which you're doing research, and see what headnotes seem helpful. Also, see what headnotes are used in the on-point cases that you have found. Then search for the headnotes using on Westlaw, for instance using a search such as *92k1550* if you're looking for key number 1550 within category 92.

5. Look for administrative agency decisions that involve this issue. In many fields (for instance, public accommodation discrimination law), cases are often filed before federal, state, or local agencies, and then aren't appealed to a court. Some such agency decisions are available on Westlaw and Lexis, though you'll have to search each agency's decisions separately; there's no "all administrative agency" database that you can use. Find the relevant Westlaw and Lexis databases (in Westlaw, the IDEN database helps you find other databases), and look through them.

6. Look for trial court opinions that involve this issue. Westlaw includes some trial court opinions in the ALLCASES database, but there are more in the TRIALORDERS-ALL (civil cases) and CRORDERS-ALL (criminal cases) databases. LEXIS includes some in its CourtLink service.

7. Look for attorney general opinions (in Westlaw, AG and USAG, and in Lexis, STATES;ALLAG and GENFED;USAG) that deal with your topic.

8. Look for briefs and court filings that deal with your topic, for instance in Westlaw's BRIEFS-ALL and FILING-ALL databases, or in Lexis's CRTFLS;BRFMOT and CRTFLS;PLDNGS files.

9. Look for newspaper or magazine articles that discuss incidents that might never have turned into an electronically available court decision.

10. Do an Internet search (for instance, using Google) to find other incidents.

11. Look through legislative history databases to see whether any statutes might have been proposed to deal with your problem.

12. If you are looking for statutes that cover a particular topic, look also for municipal codes. Check with your research librarians to see the best places to search for municipal codes: Unfortunately many are strewn over various databases—Lexis Municipal Codes, MuniCode.com, AmLegal.com, SterlingCodifiers.com, ConwayGreene.com, and more—and some are on the cities' own sites.

B. Understanding the Law

1. Get the big picture

Once you've identified your general topic, figure out the general structure of the applicable legal regime. For instance, if you plan to write on free speech and captive audiences, learn the structure of free speech law. If you plan to write on the copyrightability of clothing designs, learn the structure of copyright law.

Start by *reading a short book* that's aimed at introducing students or lawyers to the field. Books in Foundation's Concepts and Insights series, West's Nutshell series, and Matthew Bender's Understanding series are often good for this. Ask both a reference librarian and the professors who teach in the field to recommend the book that they think is the best.

Do this reading even if you've done well in a class on the subject. First, you might have forgotten some important details. Second, few classes cover the whole field; they omit many topics, some of which may be important to your problem.

Much of the book, of course, won't directly relate to your particular question. But some of it will, and you might not know in advance which parts will and which won't.

For instance, if you're writing on free speech and captive audiences, you don't just need to understand the cases that have mentioned captive audiences. It turns out that you also need to know at least:

a. the distinction between content-based restrictions and content-neutral ones,

b. the distinction between the government acting as sovereign and the government acting as proprietor or K–12 educator,

c. the distinction between commercial speech restrictions and other restrictions,

d. the obscenity cases that discuss the risk that some people will inadvertently see the offensive material,

e. the cases elaborating the meaning of "strict scrutiny" in free speech law, many of which happen to be campaign finance cases,

f. the rules dealing with offensive speech generally, and

g. various free speech procedural rules, such as the void-for-vagueness doctrine and the overbreadth doctrine.

Moreover, to make the policy arguments needed to support your claim, you may have to draw on principles that arise even in doctrinally unrelated areas. Captive audience questions, for instance, have little to do with incitement law and libel law. But when you write about captive audiences, you'll probably need to discuss arguments about the marketplace of ideas, chilling effects, and the like—and you'll want to draw analogies to the way those arguments have been made in leading incitement and libel cases.

2. Get the details

After you broadly understand the general area in which you'll be writing, you need to learn about the specific topic in much more detail.

a. Start with *a treatise*. Read carefully the chapter that discusses your topic, plus any other chapters that you've identified as doctrinally connected to your topic. Pay close attention to the footnotes, pocket parts, and other updates.

If there are multiple treatises, find the best one by asking your librarian or the professors who teach in this field. In some fields, different treatises are known for having particular ideologies; if this is true of your field, read the best treatise on each side.

b. After you're done reading the treatise chapters, go back and see which cases and statutory sections seemed to be the most important; then *read each entire case and statutory provision carefully*, from beginning to end.

Treatises usually tersely summarize most cases, and often omit important policy arguments, implicit limitations, and even significant doctrinal details. And while a treatise will usually give you a good sense of the broader legal context, sometimes it will omit some context that is irrelevant to most lawyers but quite relevant to your argument. There's thus no substitute for reading the cases and statutes themselves.

3. Find other works on the topic (the literature search)

Once you get a sense of what the law is, you need to find the articles and books that touch on your particular topic. You should read them because (1) they might say something useful, and (2) you need a novel claim (or at least a novel argument for your claim), so you need to know what has already been said.

How can you find these works?

a. *Check the Index to Legal Periodicals and the Legal Resource Index* (available in Westlaw as the ILP and LRI databases), and of course the book catalog in your law library.

b. For many topics there are several cases that are so important that any serious article on the subject must discuss them. *Search for all the articles that mention those cases.* If that yields too many articles, try doing an ATLEAST search in Lexis, finding all articles that mention the cases at least a certain number of times. Do the ATLEAST search using the case's short-form name, since an article may cite a case fully only once and then use the short form.

c. Ask your professor and others who teach in the field for the titles of articles *or names of authors* that you should check out. People will often forget particular titles, but remember the authors who are working on the subject. Use professors' suggestions, though, only as starting points: Few scholars know everything written in the field, so you need to do your own research to make sure that you don't choose something that has been preempted.

d. Try to find even as yet unpublished pieces on the subject, by searching the Social Science Research Network database and the Bepress Legal Repository. These databases don't include all unpublished articles, and some of the articles in them have already been published. But the search will let you search through at least some unpublished articles on your subject.

Some of these articles might be useful in your research; and if one does indeed preempt the topic you're thinking about, better learn it now than when the article is published six months from now. Limit your search to the last year or two, though, so you won't find lots of articles that are already published and that you've already found using your Westlaw or Lexis search.

4. Identify how the articles you find are relevant

Here's a message from a then-law-student (my sister-in-law Hanah Metchis Volokh) that captures what many, including me, have suffered from:

> [N]ear the beginning of my research after getting an idea for a paper, I think that any published paper that has ever touched on the issue I want to discuss is preempting me.
>
> So, for example, I got the idea for the paper I'm currently writing: The congressional immunity statute violates separation of powers. I went to Westlaw and ran a JLR search for "congressional investigation" & "separation of powers". Something like 20 papers popped up. PANIC! Everyone has written about this already! I'd better come up with a new topic.
>
> It wasn't until a few days later that I thought to print out some of those papers and see what they actually said. It turned out many were not very relevant to my idea at all. But then I came across one, this Sklamberg article, that had exactly the *Chadha/Bowsher* analysis I was going to do. PANIC! I've been scooped! I'd better come up with a new topic.
>
> It was probably a full week after reading the paper when I finally realized that since Sklamberg drew the *opposite* conclusion from me, I

could still write the paper—and in fact, that it's a lot easier to write a paper if you have someone to disagree with.

This panic is a perfectly understandable reaction. There are hundreds of thousands of law review articles out there. Most of us have a nagging fear that surely someone has already done what we're trying to do, and done it better. That's especially so when we're just starting our legal careers. We forget that nearly all the articles are about other topics; that articles touching on the topic often mention it only in passing; and that articles discussing the topic may have a different view than ours—or just may not be very good. So we panic.

There are also two reverse problems, though. First, we may so worry about preemption that we don't do a serious literature search, or do it too late. Bad idea. If you don't find the other literature on the subject at the outset, you're likely to run into it eventually, or your advisor will identify it, or the law review editors will.

Better find the other works on the subject at the outset. That's when it's easiest for you to shift your own claim to avoid the past articles (see Part I.C, pp. 21-23 above, for more on that). And that's when it's easier to incorporate the arguments from the past articles as counterarguments for your own work to deal with.

Second, we may under- or overestimate the importance of the articles we're reading, or even just misunderstand their thrust, because we're afraid and aren't reading as calmly and thoughtfully as possible.

So set aside your worries. See the literature search as primarily a device for *refining your claim*, not for deciding whether to throw out your claim and shift to something else. (In some cases, such a total shift is required, but pretty rarely, especially if you've already refined your claim using what's suggested in Part I.) Do the literature search early. And go through it with confidence and genuine interest, not panic.

C. Knowing When to Start Writing

When exactly are you done with your research? It's impossible to tell for sure: There's always the risk that you haven't found some key case or some perfect example.

Realize, though, that starting writing doesn't mean stopping your research—it just means shifting your primary energies to writing. While you're writing, you'll find yourself supplementing your initial research as you realize that your original searches didn't address some important aspects of the problem. And this extra research might well have been impossible at the outset, because you didn't know that it was needed until you really thought through the question, and you couldn't really think through the question until you had to write down your answer. Your understanding of the caselaw and the factual background doesn't have to be perfect when you start writing. It's enough if you understand the basics, and fill in the gaps later.

As Pam Samuelson has pointed out, the trick here is to know yourself.[11] Many of us (including me) use research as a device for procrastinating, because research is more manageable and less daunting than writing. If you fall into this category, force yourself to shift to the writing phase earlier than you normally would. Conversely, if you've found that you tend to breeze through the research, then do a bit more than you usually do.

D. Digging Deeper into the Key Sources

So far, we've talked about researching *legal rules* and *sample incidents*. But once you've identified the key cases, statutes, and incidents, you might also want to research deeper into each of these sources. For instance, you might:

1. Track down earlier drafts of the statute you're writing about, precursor statutes, committee reports on the statute, and debates about the statute.

2. Track down lower court decisions, including unpublished ones, in some of the key cases that present the problem you discuss.

3. Track down complaints, indictments, trial transcripts, documentary evidence, and briefs in those cases.

4. Investigate why a case was brought: Was it part of an advocacy group's litigation strategy? Did it flow from unusual local conditions?

Often the results can give you extra perspective on why the court didn't deal with a certain argument (maybe it just wasn't raised in the briefs), why a court reached an unexpected result, what a statute was intended to do, and more. And sometimes lower court decisions, and especially the briefs, can point you to extra arguments or counterarguments that you hadn't considered—though keep in mind that some of those arguments might not be sound.

Sometimes the results will also give you a more detailed picture of what happened in the case, a picture that can help you illustrate the problem more concretely and persuasively. Thus, for instance, a published appellate case may say that it upholds an order "restricting the father from discussing any issues pertaining to his religion or philosophy with the subject children." But the unpublished trial court opinion, which no-one other than the parties has read, may explain that the father is a jihadist who named his children Mujahid David and Mujahid Daniel, and the mother was trying to keep him from teaching them his jihadist ideology. That makes the story more interesting, more complex, and likely a better vehicle for your discussion.

And looking at the documents could help you avoid embarrassing errors. One casenote I know about, for instance, concluded that a reviewing court should remand a particular case for further fact-finding. (The casenote was in an online law review supplement, so it came out while the case was under review.) But it turns out the fact that supposedly had to be found was already known to the court; there was no uncertainty about it. Looking at either the record or the briefs would have made this clear.

How can you track down some of the sources?

1. Some of them are available on Westlaw or Lexis, for instance in Westlaw's ALLCASES, TRIALORDERS-ALL (civil cases), CRORDERS-ALL (criminal cases), BRIEFS-ALL, and FILING-ALL databases, or Lexis's CourtLink service and CRTFLS; BRFMOT and CRTFLS;PLDNGS files.

2. Recent federal court documents can be quickly retrieved from PACER by your law library's research librarians. Librarians probably won't give you direct access to PACER, because it costs the library 8 cents per page. But they will probably be happy to do a modest amount of PACER lookup on your behalf.

3. More broadly, your law librarians will likely be happy to help even with the more difficult document retrieval tasks, so long as you ask them politely and explain to them why the document is important to your scholarship. (For more on getting the help of your law librarians, see the material starting at p. 95 below.)

4. Lawyers who worked on the cases will often be glad to send you public documents in the case, if you ask them nicely and make clear that you're working hard on a serious law review article. If one side's lawyer doesn't help, the other side's might. And sometimes lawyers will even talk generally to you about non-public information: For instance, they could tell you whether the case

settled, and sometimes give you a general sense of the size of the settlement.

E. Digging Deeper into the Subject of the Legal Rules

You should also learn as much as you can (given time constraints) about the subject that is being regulated by the legal doctrines you describe.

Thus, for instance, say you're writing about whether the Equal Protection Clause forbids sheriff's departments from releasing more men than women when the men's jails are more overcrowded, and vice versa. You may have thought of the project because you read an article about such a policy in one jail. But call other jails in other places and ask them whether they have the same policy. Do some jails find sex-neutral policies feasible even when others insist that such policies can't possibly work? Do different jails have different sex-based policies, some of which may be less discriminatory than others?

Also try to find out how jails are designed, and whether they can be designed in ways that minimize the need for sex-based releases. For instance, are all jails set up so that there is one building for men and one for women, so that when there's a surge of male inmates there won't be room for them until a new building is built? Or are some jails built in a way that easily lets jailers shift some cells from one gender to the other, so empty women's cells can be used when the men's cells overflow—or at least in a way that lets jailers make sure that both sides are equally overcrowded, and require an equal degree of early release?

These questions might at first not seem directly relevant to the constitutional question, which might in theory be answerable in the abstract. But in practice few legal issues can be answered purely abstractly: There are often doctrines (such as the least restrictive means requirement in Equal Protection Clause law) that require courts to look closely at the facts. And more importantly, you never know what you're going to uncover when you make some calls like this. You might not even know which questions to ask until you talk to a few people.

So call those who have personal knowledge of the subject. Also feel free to call scholars who work in the field—in this examples, criminologists who study jail policies—or even lawyers who work in the field. People are often flattered to be asked for their expert opinion, and while some may be too busy to help, others might be glad to give you a little time.

Do some research yourself, though, before calling on others for help. First, this will help you know what questions to ask. Second, it will make others more willing to help you. You want to show people that their help will supplement your own hard work, rather than that you're trying to use their help as a substitute for working.

F. Talking to Your School's Reference Librarians

Most law schools' reference librarians are happy to help students with their research. They can help with specific research questions, such as "How can I get this unpublished source?" or "How can I gather this sort of data?" They can also help you craft a general research strategy—including the literature search, the search for relevant cases and statutes, the search for relevant newspaper articles, and even the search for a topic within some general field.

Don't be bashful about consulting the librarians. They are busy, but at most schools helping you is part of their job, and a part they often enjoy. They also tend to be trained lawyers themselves, often lawyers with great credentials but with no desire to work in a law firm. And research is what they do, so they've often seen tasks like yours and can quickly see what you might miss.

1. If you've selected a topic

Once you've selected a topic, make an appointment with a reference librarian near the start of your research, and see what advice the librarian can give you.

Do some research beforehand: Think about your research plan first, record in a file whatever searches come to mind, and run them to see what you get. It's always good to do some work of your own before asking someone else for advice—the advice will be more helpful, and the advisor will take you more seriously if you've shown a willingness to put in some effort yourself. But don't wait until you've done months' worth of research. Ask a professional for help near the beginning.

When you go to the meeting, bring *a list of the research you've done*, preferably in a nicely formatted printout. Also, be ready to *explain clearly what your article is about.* You don't have to be completely certain, but the more precise you are, the more helpful the librarians can be. Write your topic down beforehand, to make sure that it has jelled in your mind.

2. If you're looking for a topic

If you're looking for a topic, the librarians can help point you where to look—they know the best treatises in the field, the best loose-leaf legal news services, and the like. Again, look around a bit yourself, and make clear to the librarian that you've looked and where you've looked. But if you've tried hard yourself and haven't found something, don't hesitate to ask for help.

Librarians can also point you to areas that are related to your current target area, areas that you might find interesting but might not otherwise have thought about. Ask them specifically about this, to see if the question jogs their memories.

One point to keep in mind, though: Librarians can point you to helpful places to look, and can help you do a literature search—but they can't tell you themselves whether a claim you're considering is novel, nonobvious, useful, and sound.

For advice on that, you should talk to a professor who works in the field. Even professors will tell you that there's no substitute for a full literature search, coupled with careful and critical thought; but at least scholars who write in the field can give you a somewhat better sense of which claims and topics are likely to be more successful and which are likely to be duds. Knowing what makes for good scholarship in a particular field is the professors' job; it is not the librarians'.

3. If you have questions about a specific task

You should also ask librarians when you have questions about a specific task—for instance, how best to formulate a particular Westlaw or Lexis query, how to find unusual sources (for instance, administrative agency decisions that may not be on Westlaw or Lexis), and the like.

These questions may best be asked by e-mail, because that helps you precisely identify the question. Mention in the e-mail what you've already tried and where you've already looked, so that librarians can help you better and so that they'll see you're not asking them as a first resort. And proofread the e-mail, so it is clearer, more precise, and more professional-looking.

4. If you want bluebooking help

If you have a bluebooking question, look the matter up yourself in the Bluebook or ask law review editors for advice. That's not part of the research librarians' job, especially since you can do it (once you've learned the Bluebook) as well as anyone else.

5. Talk to the librarians with the right attitude

I stress that you shouldn't hesitate to ask librarians for help—but remember that you're asking them for help. Be suitably polite, both in making your request and in thanking them.

Don't be impatient. It may take the librarian a while to find what you need, especially given the other tasks the librarian may have.

And help the librarians help you: Come with as well-articulated a question as you can, and provide as much in writing as possible (for instance, all the details on the court proceeding you're looking for, a list of all the searches you've already done, and the like).

And finally, if a librarian asks you a question about your research (e.g., "Is the case you're looking for state or federal?" or "When you searched for ___, what did you get?"), don't be embarrassed to say "I don't know." Tempting as it may be to pretend you know the answer, neither you nor the librarian will be happy if your false claim of certainty sends the librarian down the wrong path.

G. Use Books and Treatises

Don't forget books and treatises, including those that are available only in print, and not just on Westlaw or Google Books. It's easy to miss them these days, when people are so focused on online searching. But they often go far beyond the articles you can find.

H. Use the Most Readable Printout Formats

When printing cases, try using Westlaw's "West Reporter Image" printing feature. I find that this output is easier to read than the usual two-column Westlaw or Lexis output.

Likewise, when printing articles, use HeinOnline, to which your library probably subscribes. This lets you see the article the way it was printed in the law review.

I. Search for Older Articles on HeinOnline

Westlaw's and Lexis's powerful search engines are generally the best tools for finding recent law review articles. But for most journals, Westlaw and Lexis generally go back only to the 1980s and 1990s. To search articles from earlier decades, you should use HeinOnline, which has a much more complete collection of older articles.

J. Use ATLEAST, NOT W/, and SY,DI() Searches

If your queries are returning too many false positives, try Lexis's *ATLEAST* and *NOT W/* searches, or Westlaw's *SY,DI()* feature.

1. Lexis searches for *ATLEAST3(copyright)*—just to give an example—will find all documents that mention the word copyright at least three times. This excludes most documents that mention copyright in passing (for instance, court cases that use the word in a parenthetical describing an earlier case) without excluding many that do focus on copyright.

2. Lexis searches for *rico NOT W/2 puerto* will look for *rico* but not within two words of *puerto*, thus finding references to the RICO statute but excluding documents that just discuss Puerto Rico. This is not the same as *rico AND NOT puerto*, since the latter would miss cases that mention both Puerto Rico and RICO by itself. You can generalize this in obvious ways.

3. As I mentioned above, Westlaw searches for *SY,DI(search terms)* find all cases that contain the search terms in the Synopsis—usually a West-written paragraph at the start of the case—and in the Digest entries for the case. This will thus focus on what West sees as the heart of the case's holdings, and skips casual mentions in the facts or in a parenthetical briefly discussing some other case.

Note that *SY,DI()* searching will exclude many unpublished cases, for which West often doesn't prepare synopses and digests—but excluding unpublished cases may be part of your goal.

K. Researching Older Anglo-American Law

Here are some suggestions for researching Anglo-American law from the 1700s and 1800s.

1. Old treatises

Look up all the treatises you can find from that era—or from the following few decades—relating to your subject matter. Also look up the relevant sections of broader treatises, such as Blackstone's *Commentaries* and American editions of the *Commentaries*. These treatises will

a. give you a big picture of the legal rules as they were then understood,

b. point you to cases (both American and English) that you might otherwise have missed, and

c. alert you to what terms were used during that era, so you'll know what to search for electronically.

2. Old English cases

American courts of the early Republic routinely cited English cases. Much of the law of that era (tort law, contract law, property law, criminal law, evidence law, and more) was common law that was based on pre-Revolutionary English common law. English courts often faced the same legal questions that American courts were facing. There often wasn't yet much American law in many of the fields. Many American court decisions weren't published, so English law was sometimes more available than American law. And many influential treatises on common law subjects continued to heavily cite English cases.

So look for English cases as well as American cases. You'll find many cited in the treatises of the era, but you can also search for them in HeinOnline's English Reports database.

3. Modern history books and articles

Read some leading modern books and articles on the legal and political institutions of that era, even if they don't relate closely to your subject. These works can give you a feel for what political, legal, and economic life was like at the time, and a sense of which modern assumptions you need to discard. They can also point you to other sources that are more directly relevant to your work, and that you might not have been able to find through online searches.

4. Online databases

Don't rely just on Lexis and Westlaw searches. Though nearly all reported cases are now on Lexis and Westlaw, many early cases were never formally reported, and treatises and other sources were more important before 1900 than they are now. So talk to your research librarians about the various online databases of historical materials, and figure out how to search them. Some of the key sources are:

a. Pre-1700 English books (not just on law): Chadwyck-Healey's Early English Books Online (EEBO).

b. 1700s English books (not just on law, plus some from outside England): Gale's Eighteenth Century Collections Online.

c. 1700s and 1800s American books and pamphlets (not just on law), plus newspapers (which sometimes reported otherwise unreported legal decisions, jury charges, and the like): Readex's Archive of Americana.

d. 1800s and early 1900s English and American legal treatises and other law books: Gale's Making of Modern Law.

e. 1800s and early 1900s American legal treatises and other law books: HeinOnline's Legal Classics database.

f. 1800s American magazines (not just on law): ProQuest's American Periodical Series Online (1741-1900).

g. Some reports of English and American trials and other legal documents from the 1600s to the early 1900s: Galenet's Making of Modern Law—Trials.

h. English reported court cases from 1220 to 1865 (whether cited to Eng. Rep. or to the individual reporters): HeinOnline's English Reports database.

i. Some early books: Google Books.

5. Reporters that aren't on Westlaw and Lexis

As I mentioned, most American reporter volumes are now on Westlaw and Lexis. But not all: If you really want to thoroughly examine the late 1700s and early 1800s American sources, you should look through the indexes to reporters like *Addison's Reports* (Pennsylvania), the *New York City-Hall Record, Smith's Decisions of the Superior and Supreme Courts of New Hampshire,* and *Wright's Ohio Reports.* At *http://volokh.com/writing/research*, I've posted a longer list of some American reporter volumes that have not been uploaded to Lexis and Westlaw (though the list is likely incomplete).

There can be some gems in these early sources, as well as in the treatises, monographs, and books in the last few subsections. Thus, for instance, in writing an article on symbolic expression and the original meaning of the First Amendment, I relied on a couple of dozen late 1700s and early 1800s sources to support the conclusion. The sources included several Westlaw-findable cases, but also, among others:

a. a case reported in the *New York City-Hall Record*,

b. a grand jury charge reported in *Addison's Reports*,

c. passages from St. George Tucker's edition of *Blackstone's Commentaries*, Chancellor Kent's *Commentaries on American Law*, and a manual for Justices of the Peace,

d. an editor's note in an early collection of Pennsylvania statutes,

e. an argument, made by a legislator who later became a federal judge, published in the *Proceedings and Debates of the General Assembly of Pennsylvania*,

f. a prominent lawyer's essay on libel published in a newspaper,

g. a grand jury charge reproduced in Francis Wharton's *State Trials of the United States*, and

h. four trial judges' charges to juries, which were published in newspapers.

All these were important sources for showing what the law during that time actually was. And I wouldn't have seen them if I had limited myself to Lexis and Westlaw searches.

6. Watching out for past legal conventions

"The past is a foreign country: they do things differently there."[12] You need to watch out for these differences, especially the subtle ones. Today, for instance, we assume that anything published in a reporter, such as U.S. Reports, is either an opinion of the Justices or a headnote prepared by the publisher. But in the 1800s, published reports often began with a summary of the arguments of the lawyers—the great quote your Westlaw search found might well be an argument from an advocate, not a statement of the law from a Justice.

Likewise, we generally assume that cases in U.S. Reports come from the U.S. Supreme Court; but all the cases in volume 1 of U.S. Reports are actually Pennsylvania state court cases. Likewise, many cases from volumes 2, 3, and 4 came from Pennsylvania state courts, Delaware courts, lower federal courts, and the Federal Court of Appeals in Cases of Capture (established under the Articles of Confederation). Statements such as "The Supreme Court recited these requirements in the *The Amiable Isabella*[, 19 U.S. 1, 5 (1821)]. In *Purviance v. Angus*, 1 U.S. 180 (1786), the Supreme Court stated ....," are thus mistaken: *Purviance* was decided not by the U.S. Supreme Court but by the High Court of Errors and Appeals of Pennsylvania.

So read everything carefully. Make as few assumptions as you can, and keep your eyes open for signals that something is amiss. The date on this case is 1786—was there even a U.S. Supreme Court in 1786? The line about Justice so-and-so delivering the opinion of the Court is in the middle of the case report; might the preceding materials be something other than the court opinion?

7. Watching out for old citation formats

Old cases often used citation formats that are quite different from the ones you're used to. They often cited then-familiar treatises using abbreviations, such as "Bl. Com." for Blackstone's Commentaries. They also generally cited cases by using the name of the person who published the case report, so that *Marbury v. Madison* was generally cited as "1 Cranch 137," with no reference to the U.S. Reports (which didn't yet exist). Old English cases were likewise cited using what is now called the "nominative citation" system, such as "2 Wils. K.B. 203."

If you're not sure what a citation means, you can look it up in a reference work such as *Bieber's Dictionary of Legal Abbreviations*, which is largely searchable on Google Books. You can just go ahead and try to find a case using Westlaw and Lexis (which recognize many of the alternate reporter names) or HeinOnline (which lets you search English cases using the nominative citation format). Or if you've tried these things and failed, you can ask your law library's reference librarians.

8. Finding the right terms to search for

You can search through many more historical sources online than you could have just a few years ago. But you need to know what to search for.

Searching in Westlaw's ALLCASES-OLD database for *text("intellectual property") & date(< 1/1/1900)*, for instance, yields three cases; but this is not because nineteenth-century lawyers didn't see copyrights as property (as I've heard some suggest). Rather, they spoke of literary property, and a search for *text("literary property") & date(< 1/1/1900)* yields 58 cases. If you want to find early cases that deal with what we'd now call "symbolic expression" or "expressive conduct," you'd need to search for the term "signs" (often appearing in the phrase "signs or pictures"). If you're searching for "freedom of the press," you should also search for "liberty of the press."

Likewise, if you want to find early references to the right to trial by jury in civil cases, you should search for "Ninth Amendment" as well as "Seventh Amendment." The first Congress proposed twelve amendments to the states; what we call the Bill of Rights consists of amendments three through twelve of that set. The first two amendments were not ratified at the time, but some people included them in the numbering for at least about 25 years. Thus, for example, the 1815 case *Hunter v. Martin* speaks of the "9th article of the amendments" and the "ninth amendment" to refer to the civil jury trial right, "the twelfth amendment" to refer to what we now call the Tenth Amendment, and "the eighth amendment" to refer to the Sixth Amendment rights to speedy trial and jury trial.

Late 1700s and early 1800s documents also had one marked font difference from modern documents: Some "s" characters were printed in a way that looks much like modern "f"s, so that "Congress" might look like "Congrefs"—and electronic scanning software may scan it as "Congrefs."

Many electronic databases have corrected for this, but some have not. You should therefore take this into account in your searches, so that if you're trying to find (for instance) the phrase "free state," you might want to search for "free ftate" as well.

How can you find such translations from modern terms into the older ones?

First, keep your eyes open. If you read an old copyright case and see it talk about "literary property," recognize that this might be a search term that could find more cases for you.

Second, read the old treatises to see what terms they use.

Third, independently look up the cases that are cited by the cases and treatises you've found, and that cite them in turn, rather than counting on your electronic keyword searches to find all the cases you need.

IX. Editing: General Principles

A. Go Through Many Drafts

"Nothing is ever written," my high school journalism teacher taught us, "it is rewritten."* Aim to produce your first draft well before the deadline. This is hard, but critical.

Print the draft, edit it thoroughly, and enter the changes. Edit the draft on the printout, not on the computer; it's generally easier to spot errors that way. As you edit, ask yourselves these questions:

1. (For each sentence:) What information does this sentence communicate to readers that they *don't already know*?

2. (For each sentence:) Has this information—or even part of it— *already been communicated by a previous sentence*?

3. (For each sentence:) Are this sentence and the previous sentence *so closely related* that part of the first sentence is repeated in this one?

4. (For each word, phrase, or sentence:) Can I *eliminate this without changing the meaning*?†

5. (For each phrase in a sentence:) Is this how *normal people talk*?

6. (For each word:) Does this word communicate *exactly what I want it to*?

7. (For each noun:) *Should this noun be a verb, adjective, or adverb* instead?

For more tips, check out Bruce Ross–Larson's *Edit Yourself,* which focuses mostly on word and sentence edits; C. Edward Good's *Mightier Than the Sword* and *A Grammar Book for You and I*; Bryan Garner's *Elements of Legal Style*; and Strunk & White's *The Elements of Style,* the classic general writing guide.

Set the draft aside for a day if you have the time, or for a few hours if you don't have a day. Repeat often.

---

* Giles K. Chesterton, Beverly Hills High School.

† The careful reader may have noticed that these questions, aimed largely at finding redundancy, are themselves redundant. This is intentional: When you are looking for things that are often overlooked—such as redundancies or other writing problems—it's often useful to look for them using several slightly different approaches. This, though, is one of the rare situations where redundancy is helpful.

Even with my writing experience, I try to do about 10 complete edits before sending an article to the law reviews. When I clerked for Judge Kozinski, the norm was about 30 to 40 drafts for an opinion, which included 20 to 30 substantive edits (the others were primarily cite-checks). Balzac supposedly went through 27 drafts of one book—and without a word processor.[13]

This is painful and time-consuming, but necessary. Your first draft will be badly flawed, unless you're a great writer, in which case it will be merely mediocre. So will the second through the fifth. As you're editing, keep some old drafts, and compare the tenth draft against the first. You will notice a vast difference.

Words are the lawyer's most important tools. If you use the wrong word, or make a minor grammar, spelling, or punctuation error, you come across as a craftsman who doesn't know how to use his tools. You lose credibility, even if the substance of what you're saying is sound.

B. If You See No Red Marks on a Paragraph, Edit It Again

At least during the first few drafts, every paragraph—even every sentence—will likely need to be corrected, made clearer, and made more forceful. If you're not seeing at least one flaw in each paragraph, you're not looking hard enough.

C. If You Need to Reread Something to Understand It, Rewrite It

As you're reading your draft, watch for times when you find yourself rereading a sentence or a paragraph. If your writing confuses even you, won't your readers be still more confused? And a reader who finds it hard to understand your writing will often stop reading.

"But this is complicated material," you might say. That may be right—but your job is to make the material as clear and as simple as possible. And a clear explanation should be readable in one pass: Remember, your readers aren't lazy, but they are busy.

D. Ask "Why?"

As you read any assertion you make, ask yourself what a skeptical reader—not a sympathetic one—would say. The changes you make to satisfy this reader will enrich your argument for all readers.

So for every sentence in your argument, ask "why?" Say that your sentence is "this result would be undemocratic"; ask yourself "why is this so?" Either the sentence itself or the sentences that precede it or follow it must answer that question (unless the answer is obvious). If you don't see the answer there, put it in.

E. Ask "Why Not?"

For the same sentence, ask "why not?"—"why might a reasonable person think the opposite?" Might there be several possible definitions of what is "democratic"? Might there be reasons to doubt the accuracy of the assumptions that lead you to your conclusion? If you can think of a plausible counterargument, make sure you address it.

F. Use Your Imaginary Friend (and Adversary)

Imagine someone whom you respect but who takes the opposite view from you—a friend, a professor, a judge—and try to read the piece as if you were that person. What counterarguments would he come up with? Would he be impressed by your logic, or would he see some flaws with it?

G. Use a Trusted Classmate (or Two)

Get a classmate to read the draft. The classmate must be (a) smart, (b) willing to read the piece carefully, and (c) willing to give criticism, even harsh criticism. Of course, those who like you enough to satisfy criterion (b) may be less likely to satisfy criterion (c); people who satisfy all three criteria are rare and valuable. Buy them dinner as compensation.

Warning: Check first to make sure that your professor doesn't have any objection to others reading your draft. Most professors won't, at least for your articles and probably even for your seminar papers; but it's always good to check.

H. Read the Draft with "New Eyes"*

Read the draft with "new eyes": Try to imagine that you're a reader who doesn't know the subject, not the writer who knows it intimately.

If you have the time, put your latest draft away for a day or two before rereading it, so you can come back to it with a fresh perspective.

I. Conquer Your Fear

It's natural to be afraid of reading your own work critically. What if your claims are all wrong? What if you find the killer counterargument? What if you have to start over?

The fear is understandable, but nearly always unfounded. If your claim is flawed, you can correct it. Most counterarguments are answerable, and if you find one that isn't, you can amend your claim without throwing everything out. Your draft represents a lot of research and thinking. Even if you have to revise it dramatically, you'll still be able to use the bulk of what you've written.

And if you figure out that your claim is wrong, then your readers—including those who will grade your work—will too. Better fix the claim before you turn in the article.

J. There Are No Lazy Readers—Only Busy Readers

Many writing tips stress simplicity, clarity, and brevity. Avoid unnecessary long words and complex sentences. Get to the point quickly. Keep paragraphs short. Make things easier for your readers, and keep them from losing interest.

Some writers think this advice assumes that readers are lazy or stupid; those writers feel they're being told to "dumb down" their prose for dumb readers. After all, smart, industrious readers wouldn't mind long paragraphs filled with long sentences and long words—they would focus on the substance, not the form.

No. Your industrious and smart readers are busy people, precisely because they are so industrious and smart. They can spend only limited time and effort reading your article—not because they're lazy or dumb, but because they have other things to do.

---

* I owe this expression to Judge Kozinski.

They can parse complex words and sentences; but this parsing takes more work than reading simpler, clearer prose. Why waste my time wading through this morass, they'll ask themselves, when I could be working on something else? You can keep their precious attention only by making things as easy for them as possible.

X. Editing: Getting Help from Your Faculty Advisor

A. Ask Your Advisor for Especially Detailed Advice

Once you've gone through several drafts, your faculty advisor may be willing to read your work and give you advice. Different professors operate differently: Some may be reluctant to read any rough drafts, especially for seminar papers, while others will be willing to read at least one such draft, or even more. Some may give you only general comments about the substance, while others may also edit your writing, at least in one or two sections.

But whatever advisor you have, you're likely to get more if you ask for more. Ask the professor up front (1) whether he will read over a rough draft, and also (2) whether he will give you suggestions about your writing as well as about the substance. Sometimes, if you ask nicely enough—in a way that makes it clear that you really want to improve your writing—the professor will agree to more than he might have otherwise offered.

B. Give Your Advisor an Already Closely Proofread Draft

Don't ask your advisor to read a first draft, or even a third draft. Instead, proofread several times before handing in your rough draft (and many more times before handing in the final draft).

First, you want the professor to identify the problems that you wouldn't have found on your own—the problems that remain after several edits that you yourself did.

Second, badly written prose is hard to read, and the harder the draft is to read, the less closely the professor will read it.

Third, the professor may feel that you're wasting his time by asking for comments on material that you haven't already edited yourself. You don't want your editor, or your future grader, to think that.

C. Give Your Advisor a Rough Draft as Quickly as Possible

Give your advisor a rough draft as quickly as possible. This is in some tension with the preceding suggestion, but you need to keep both goals in mind.

It will take time for the professor to read your draft and give you thorough comments—and this won't be the only task on the professor's schedule. The earlier you hand in the draft, the earlier you'll get the feedback, the more time you'll have to react to it, and the easier it will be for you to persuade your professor to read another draft. And you don't want the professor to feel rushed, because that will yield less thorough comments.

D. Treat Each Editing Comment as a Global Suggestion

Treat each editing comment as a global suggestion, not just a local one. If the professor circles one "it's" and tells you that it should be an "its," check *all* the "it's" in your paper—you've probably made this mistake more than once.

Do the same for broader comments. Professors reasonably assume that once you see a few sentences marked "redundant" or a few paragraphs marked "too long," you'll understand that your prose needs trimming. They might not take the time to mark all the other instances of these problems.

So as you read the marked-up draft, keep a checklist of the kinds of problems that the professor found. Then, focus your next edit on identifying and correcting more examples of each problem.

XI. Writing: Logical Problems to Watch For

A. Categorical Assertions

Avoid "never" and "always," as in "this law would be completely un-enforceable" or "could never be enforced." Completely? Never? Really? Modest claims may sometimes seem less rhetorically effective, but they're more likely to be right.

B. Insistence on Perfection

People often criticize laws by arguing that they're imperfect: "The law is targeted at preventing children from accidentally killing them-selves or other children with a gun. However, the law itself would not adequately protect against all of the possible accidental handgun deaths."*

This is a weak criticism. No law can prevent *all* instances of a cer-tain kind of harm. The questions are usually whether the law does more harm than good, and whether other alternatives can do still better. You can't avoid these hard questions merely by showing that the law doesn't always do the good that it's meant to do.

More broadly, be careful when you implicitly assume that the world is neatly divided into two categories—for instance, perfect laws and pointless laws. Such divisions often ignore the existence of a third cate-gory, such as laws that do something but not everything.

C. False Alternatives

"Is pornography free speech or hate speech?" "Are race-conscious af-firmative action programs permissible or discriminatory?" "Was this speaker's motivation artistic or commercial?" "Should American foreign policy aim at making other countries fear us, or at getting them to work with us?"

The trouble with these either-or questions is that the answer may well be "both." Pornography might qualify as "hate speech" under some definition, but still be constitutionally protected. Race-conscious affir-mative action programs might be discriminatory and yet constitutional-

---

* This quote and most of the others in the writing and editing chapters are drawn from real papers and articles that I've read.

ly permissible. Speakers may want to both make art and make money from it. American foreign policy might aim at making some countries work with us by making them fear us.

Asking "X or Y?" tends to suggest that the answer must be one or the other. If this suggestion is incorrect, then asking the question will confuse the reader, and may make your argument unsound. And if you do think that X and Y should be mutually exclusive—that, for instance, hate speech should never be protected by the Free Speech Clause—you should demonstrate this mutual exclusiveness, rather than just assuming it by posing the "X or Y?" question.

D. Missing Pieces

A logical argument should consist of several steps that fit together, for instance: "All As are Bs. X is an A. Therefore, X is a B." Legal arguments aren't exercises in formal logic, but they must still fit logically, with no unproven connections.

Say your argument looks roughly like this:

1. Classifications based on sex are subject to the most exacting scrutiny.

2. Separate schools for boys and girls involve classifications based on sex.

3. Therefore, separate schools for boys and girls are unconstitutional.

The pieces don't quite fit: Points 2 and 3 prove only that separate schools are subject to the most exacting scrutiny, not that they are unconstitutional. You must fill in the missing piece, by showing that the classification fails the exacting scrutiny.

Before writing your proof section, and again after finishing it, summarize each significant assertion in one sentence, much like the list I've just given. Then see if the assertions fit each other. If they don't fit together on your list, they probably don't fit together in the paper.

E. Criticisms That Could Apply to Everything

It's not enough to say that a law "has a chilling effect," or "starts us down the slippery slope," or "imposes the majority's morality on the minority," or "intrudes on people's privacy." Most laws that constrain people's conduct—murder laws, antidiscrimination laws, bans on cruelty to animals—impose the majority's morality on the minority; sometimes that's good. Many laws have chilling effects or intrude on people's privacy; but we often tolerate this because these laws' good effects outweigh the bad. Almost every law potentially starts us down some slippery slope, but that's not reason enough to reject it.

Be specific. Explain why this chilling effect is worse than other chilling effects that we're willing to tolerate (and what exactly you mean by chilling effect). Explain why this slope is more slippery than others, or why it's wrong to impose this particular kind of moral principle on people, or why this intrusion on privacy is unjustified even though other intrusions are permissible.

Whenever you criticize a law, especially when you do it using generalities, *ask yourself whether the criticism could equally apply to laws that you endorse.* If it can, refine your criticism to make clear specifically why this law is bad when the others are good.

F. Metaphors

Metaphors can make your writing more vivid, but they can also hide logical error and incompleteness.

Metaphors are literally false. Societies do not literally slip down slopes. Laws do not literally chill speech. These terms have some truth to them, but only to the extent that they describe *concrete mechanisms* and not just abstract metaphors. When we say "slippery slope," that's shorthand for "this seemingly unobjectionable decision may cause other, much more troublesome decisions in the future."* When we say "this speech restriction has a chilling effect," that's shorthand for "this speech restriction may deter certain speech even though the restriction ostensibly doesn't cover that speech."

Once you unpack the metaphor this way, you can see that you need to support it with a more concrete explanation. Why would this decision lead to other decisions in the future? What speech would be deterred by this restriction, and how?

Many people omit these explanations, perhaps because the metaphors sound self-explanatory. In the physical world, we can say "Watch out for that driveway—the slope there is slippery" without further ex-

---

* For more on slippery slope arguments, see Eugene Volokh, *The Mechanisms of the Slippery Slope*, 116 Harv. L. Rev. 1026 (2003).

planation, because we know the mechanism that underlies the slippery slope: It's gravity coupled with inadequate friction.

But these physical mechanisms obviously don't carry over to slippery slopes in law; so when we use the term "slippery slope" metaphorically, *our argument is incomplete unless we give more details* about what the metaphor really means. Whenever you see a metaphor, ask yourself, "To what actual phenomenon does this figurative usage refer?," and describe this phenomenon. If you think the metaphor helps people understand your point, you can still keep the metaphor as well as the actual description. But remember that the heart of your argument should be the real, not the figurative.

G. Undefined Terms

Look skeptically at any abstraction that you mention but don't specifically define, such as "paternalism," "privacy," "democratic legitimacy," "fundamental fairness," "evolving standards of decency," "narrow tailoring," "good faith," or the like. These abstractions can be useful, but they are vague enough that (1) the reader might not clearly understand what you mean by them, (2) you yourself might not clearly understand what you mean by them, and (3) you risk using them to mean different things in different cases.

Make clear what you mean by each term: What constitutes paternalism (whether good paternalism or bad)? How do you decide what's democratically legitimate and what isn't? Does "fundamental fairness" refer to an existing body of law that defines the term, or just to your moral judgment? If it's the latter, what is that moral judgment, and why is it right? Are evolving standards of decency the standards of decency expressed in legislation throughout the states, or are they whatever standards the judges believe are decent? What is required to make a law narrowly tailored?

Many of these terms can't be defined precisely, and that may be fine. But if you find that they are too vague, you might ask yourself whether they really help your argument; and in any case, trying to give a clarifying definition can help you refine your argument, both for your own understanding and to make the argument easier for readers to follow.

H. Undefended Assertions, and "Arguably"/"Raises Concerns"

If you make an assertion, you need to be sure that it's adequately defended (unless it's obvious). Including "arguably" or "it can be argued that" isn't enough: It acknowledges that the statement is controversial, but it doesn't explain why the reader should accept your side of the controversy. If you think something is arguably true, then give the argument, and explain why it's better than the counterargument.

Likewise, it isn't enough to argue that some proposal "raises constitutional concerns" or "is troubling." If you think the proposal is actually unconstitutional, or actually unsound, explain why you think so.* It's not enough just to hint at the possibility, and to expect this hint to carry your argument.

I. Proofread, Proofread, Proofread

All these points reinforce the need to go through many drafts, looking at your arguments with new eyes. The only way you can catch problems like these—or the writing errors mentioned below—is by repeatedly and carefully reading your own work.

---

* Showing the existence of "serious questions about the statute's constitutionality" may suffice when you're applying the rule that statutes should, if possible, be construed to avoid such questions. But even there it's not enough to say that the statute raises constitutional concerns—you have to show that they are indeed "serious" concerns.

XII. Writing: Paragraph-Level Problems to Watch For

A. Paragraphs Without a Common Theme

Each paragraph should be about one main thought. The first sentence should usually express that thought; that's why it's often called the topic sentence. The other sentences should fit with that thought. If they don't, then they belong in a different paragraph.

B. Long Paragraphs

Avoid long paragraphs. People tend to digest one paragraph at a time, and if they see that they'll have to absorb twenty sentences, they may get intimidated and skip to the next paragraph.

Writers disagree to some extent about the best average paragraph length. I recommend two to four sentences; others like five or six. But I'm pretty sure that (1) one-sentence paragraphs are usually too choppy, though they're sometimes good when introducing several longer paragraphs, and (2) once you get past six medium-length sentences or four longish ones, you'll be taxing many readers' attention spans.

A paragraph that's about one big thought can often be easily split into several paragraphs, each one about a smaller thought. Try to make sure that the split follows the natural structure of the discussion, and that each of the new paragraphs starts with a topic sentence.

Occasionally, you might want to split a paragraph where there's no natural paragraph break. If, for instance, you have a topic sentence followed by half a dozen sentence-long illustrations, you could split the paragraph just to give the reader a breather. Look over the result, though, and make sure that it doesn't seem too disconnected.

C. Inadequate Connections Between Paragraphs

Each paragraph should be logically linked to the one before it. When the reader starts reading a paragraph, he should understand its relationship to the preceding one.

This doesn't mean that you must start each paragraph with a transition like "Moreover" or "On the other hand." Transitions are sometimes helpful, but not always, and sometimes they're distracting. For

117

instance, this paragraph is connected to the preceding one without an explicit transition—the pronoun "This" does the job.

Repeating a word or a concept from the previous paragraph, and especially from the paragraph's last sentence, is another connecting mechanism; so is the word "another." Feel free to change the part of speech when you repeat a word this way, for instance by using "connecting" in the first sentence of a paragraph to link back to "connected" in the last sentence of the previous one. Such links help you take the reader smoothly from thought to thought, making it clear how the thoughts fit.[14]

XIII. WRITING: SENTENCE/CLAUSE PROBLEMS TO WATCH FOR

A. Redundancy

When you see two sentences that express similar thoughts, try to eliminate one, or part of one. If you're intentionally restating a thought to make it clearer, try to make it clear the first time you say it.

The phrase "in other words," in particular, is a clue that the first words you used aren't that good. Repetition annoys busy readers who want to get to the point quickly, and it can also confuse readers: If the second sentence makes the same point as the first sentence but uses slightly different words to do it, some readers will assume that the two sentences must say something different, and spend time looking for this nonexistent difference.

Likewise, avoid phrases such as "any and all," "null and void," or "cease and desist," in which two words linked by an "and" or an "or" are, practically speaking, identical. Except when the redundant phrase has legal significance (for instance, "a cease-and-desist letter"), eliminate one of the components (making it "all," "void," or "cease," or, better yet, "stop").

These redundant couples are often clichés, but writers also often create their own, such as "the new nouns generally tend to be more abstract and conceptual than the concrete actions and attributes that they replace" (a phrase from an earlier draft of this book). "Abstract" and "conceptual" might sometimes mean subtly different things, but not here. "Abstract" alone will do fine, and will keep the reader from wondering which nouns are more abstract and which ones are more conceptual.

Repetition is sometimes rhetorically useful for stressing an important point, and sometimes actually clarifies things. The introduction and the conclusion of an article, for instance, necessarily repeat some of what the body of the article says. Usually, though, redundancy makes your writing less effective.

B. Unnecessary Introductory Clauses

"*It should be mentioned that* knowledgeable gun owners already know that ...." "*In having researched the implications of the act,* I would recommend that ...." The italicized phrases add nothing: They're throat-clearing—things people say before they start getting to the point. Delete them.

C. Other Unnecessary Phrases

More broadly, each sentence and each clause should make some specific point that's useful to your argument. Consider one example from a student paper: "The state legislature should reject this proposal because it is the wrong solution." What extra information does "because it is the wrong solution" convey to the reader?

Likewise, consider another example:

> Given the large number of accidental firearms injuries among young people that occur annually in this country, everyone would agree that firearms safety is a matter of great public concern.

On that level of generality, everyone does agree—to the point that the sentence adds nothing substantively, and is such an obvious platitude that it adds nothing rhetorically either.

Either delete the sentence or make it more concrete. For example, it turns out that in 2006, about 55 children age fourteen or under died in firearms accidents in the U.S., and about 2500 were nonfatally injured in such accidents (split roughly evenly between those who were treated and released, and those who were transferred or hospitalized).[15] If you replace the vague phrase "large number" with the specific number, you'll be saying something that might be news to many readers, and you'll be giving readers a better idea of just how concerned they should be about this.

Finally, consider these opening paragraphs of a draft article on campaign finance law (also mentioned on p. 49 above):

> Campaign speech has long been a controversial topic among scholars and commentators. Much attention has been devoted to the Supreme Court's treatment of individual expenditures, contributions and spending in *Buckley v. Valeo*. Congress' recent consideration of campaign finance reform provides an ideal opportunity to revisit the 1976 Supreme Court decision that addressed the free speech implications of limits on federal campaign-related activities.

> This essay briefly discusses the effects of such limits on individual speech, the disproportionate treatment of speech by the media and justifications presented by several members of the Court in the 2000 decision, *Nixon v. Shrink Missouri Government PAC*.

> Let me begin by giving a concrete situation. Imagine you are out-

> raged about a particular candidate's stand on something. [More concrete details follow, aimed at showing that there's a basic First Amendment right to spend money to express your views about candidates.] ...

What does the first sentence add? Very little: Virtually all readers will already know how controversial the subject is. The same goes for the second sentence. The third sentence says something nontrivial, by suggesting that this article is relevant to "Congress' recent consideration of campaign finance reform," but most of the rest of the sentence isn't helpful either.

That's a lot of unnecessary generalities—and at the very beginning of the article, which sets the tone for what follows. Here's an alternative, with the surplusage cut out:

> Imagine you are outraged about a particular candidate's stand on something. [More concrete details] ...
>
> May the law restrict this sort of speech, in the name of preventing corruption or equalizing people's voices? May the law allow the media to editorialize about elections while limiting speech by others? These questions are made especially relevant by the enactment of the new campaign finance bill. This essay will briefly discuss them, with a special focus on the Justices' arguments in *Nixon v. Shrink Missouri Government PAC*.

Not perfect—the last two sentences are clunkier than they should be—but at least each part adds something to the argument.

D. Needless Tangential Detail

Organize your narration around the needs of your argument, rather than around the internal structure of the facts that you've learned while doing your research.

When you've learned a lot about a subject in writing your paper, it's tempting to just put all the facts down on paper using whatever internal structure (for instance, chronological) the facts have. Say you read all the Supreme Court cases related to some doctrine that you'll apply; it's tempting to describe each of those cases. Or say you're writing about the legal regulation of nonlethal weapons, such as pepper sprays: It's tempting to explain in detail how the weapons work, the chemicals they use, the subtle differences between the chemicals, and the like.

But not all this detail will be important to your claim, and readers will see much of it as a needless (and often boring) tangent. First, focus on what the readers need to know, and cut the remainder.

Second, articulate what's left in ways that are most useful to readers. Thus, for instance, if a state law limits pepper sprays to 2½ ounces, don't focus on that—instead, figure out how many defensive uses that amounts to (one? five? ten?). The reader wants to know what the restriction will do in practice, not how it's defined as a matter of physics or chemistry.

XIV. WRITING: WORD/PHRASE PROBLEMS TO WATCH FOR

A. Legalese / Bureaucratese

Write like normal people speak, not like lawyers or bureaucrats tend to write. Don't write "Opposition to the bill is needed on the grounds that the means will produce little or no desirable ends." Saying "We should oppose the bill because it won't [fill in the goal, e.g., reduce violence]," "Legislators should oppose the bill because it won't reduce violence," "The proposal won't reduce violence," or even the "The proposal won't do what it's supposed to do" would make the same point in plain English.

Likewise, replace "Guns have a far greater utilitarian value than ..." with "Guns are far more useful than ...." Instead of "could negatively affect the accessibility of handguns," write "could make handguns less accessible." Replace "made through this form of behavior" with "made this way."

B. Nominalization

The three examples in the preceding paragraphs illustrate one common cause of legalese: "nominalization"—turning verbs, adjectives, and adverbs into nouns or noun phrases. The verb-heavy phrase "we *should oppose*" becomes the noun-focused "*opposition* to the bill is needed." The adverb phrase "are *far more useful than*" becomes the noun-focused "have a *far greater utilitarian value* than." The adjective phrase "could make handguns *less accessible*" becomes the noun-focused "could negatively affect *the accessibility* of handguns."

Nominalization tends to add words, which makes text longer, and to add prepositional or verb phrases, which makes text more complex. It also tends to make the writing less concrete and thus less lively, because the new nouns ("opposition," "value," and "accessibility") generally tend to be more abstract than the concrete actions ("should oppose") and attributes ("more useful" or "less accessible") that they replace. If you see an abstract noun, ask whether you can replace it with the concrete verb, adjective, or adverb that the noun phrase embodies.

123

C. Long Synonyms for Short Phrases (or for Single Words)

Legal writers also tend to use long phrases instead of their short synonyms. Instead of "many," lawyers often write "a large number of." "Near" becomes "in close proximity to." "The legislature" turns into "the legislative branch of government."

Sometimes the long phrases might seem to add some important nuance: For instance, a person may write "the legislative branch of government" to highlight the distinction between the legislature and other branches of government. But even then, simpler versions—such as "the executive," "the legislature," and "the judiciary"—can often express the nuance equally well. If you see a formal-sounding phrase that seems to represent just one basic concept, ask whether one word could do the job instead.

D. Appendix I

If you really learn to write in normal English, you'll be set. But in the meantime, Appendix I (p. 344) gives some tips on particular words and phrases you might want to avoid.

E. Misplaced Attempts at Dignity

Some argue that formal words and legal clichés add dignity to prose. And some prose does sound better when it's more formal—"Four score and seven years ago" sounds better in the Gettysburg Address than "Eighty-seven years ago" or "In 1776."

But the Gettysburg Address was an oration in honor of fallen soldiers; Lincoln had a captive audience that was disposed to agree with him; and the entire address was only three minutes long.[16] Most law review articles won't satisfy any of these criteria. For practical reasons, they should be clear and easy to read; and while you'd like them to seem intellectually hefty and sometimes even emotionally stirring, formal language isn't likely to give you that.

So as you read your draft, ask yourself for each sentence: Do ordinary people talk this way? Would I ever hear this from an articulate nonlawyer friend over dinner? "Opposition to the bill is needed on the grounds that the means will produce little or no desirable ends" flunks this test.

F. Unnecessary Abstractions

You should make your argument using words that concretely describe the real problems that people face, rather than talking about the problems in abstract terms (even if the abstract terms aren't especially legalese). Consider the following phrases:

... when law enforcement is unavailable.

Considering the amount of violence that is connected with guns ...

... will have a positive effect.

They are written in fairly plain English, and aren't hard to understand—but they make their points through abstract terms such as "unavailable," "violence," and "positive effect," and the circumlocution "law enforcement."

When you want someone to protect you, whom do you want? Your visceral, real-life answer will be "the police," not "law enforcement." What do you want them to do? Your normal answer will be "come in time," not "be available." "When the police can't come in time" quickly engages the reader's practical concerns; "when law enforcement is unavailable" doesn't. (I assume that the "[come in time] to prevent a killing, rape, or robbery" is implicit from context; if it isn't, then some such phrase should be included.)

Likewise, instead of "Considering the amount of violence that is connected with guns," try "Considering how many people are killed, injured, or threatened with guns." Killings, injuries, and threats are what people *really* worry about; "violence" is just the abstract term for that. Readers will intellectually understand what "violence" means, but they won't be as engaged by it as they would be by "killed, injured, or threatened."

Instead of "will have a positive effect," describe the actual effect, for instance "will prevent many murders and suicides." No one wants "positive effects" in the abstract; they want specific, concrete benefits, and if you explain the benefits, people will be more persuaded.

One more example:

The waiting period provides a vital time frame, which allows an individual the time to reconsider their actions and consequently, lives will be saved.

This sentence contains several writing glitches; "individual" is legalese for "person," "a vital time frame" is vague, and "their" is plural while "individual" is singular. But the deeper problem is that the sentence is written using unnecessary abstractions. A better formulation would be:

> The waiting period can prevent impulsive murders and suicides, by giving people time to calm down [optional: and reconsider their plans].

Instead of the general "time to reconsider their actions" and "lives will be saved," this explains concretely which actions (impulsive murders and suicides) will be reconsidered and which lives will be saved. It provides more substantive details, describes a concrete scenario for the reader (an impulsive person needs to calm down, or else he'll commit murder or suicide), and thus makes the argument more persuasive.

There are two situations in which the concrete is not as good as the abstract. First, sometimes you need to use a term that's more abstract but more precise. For instance, "murder" is usually a better, more concrete term than "homicide," but if you are talking about a study that measures all homicides (including manslaughter, justifiable homicide, and excusable homicide), you need to use the more accurate term.

Second, sometimes you intentionally want to soften the emotional force of a claim, either because you fear that the issue may be too viscerally engaging (part of the reason that some articles use "sexual assault" instead of "rape"), or because you're describing the other side's argument. This second reason is not entirely praiseworthy, but it may be tolerable; you have an obligation to describe the counterarguments honestly, thoroughly, and clearly, but you need not frame them in the most emotionally forceful way possible.

But these are exceptions. The rule is to talk about what actually matters to the reader (the police not coming in time) and not about abstractions (law enforcement being unavailable).

G. *Passive Voice*

Many people recommend that you turn the passive voice—"The action was done by this person" (the object was verbed by the subject) or just "The action was done"—into the active voice, "This person did this action" (the subject verbed the object).

This is generally good advice. Passive voice often makes writing less direct: "Passive voice should be avoided by you" is worse than "Avoid the passive voice." It also sometimes conceals responsibility, as in the famous "Mistakes were made" used as a substitute for "We made mistakes."

But if your discussion focuses more on the object than on the subject (the actor), you might want to use the passive voice, which has a similar focus. If you're writing about the USA Patriot Act, for instance, the passive sentence "The Act was adopted shortly after the September 11 attacks" may be better than the active "Congress adopted the Act shortly after the September 11 attacks." The passive voice properly focuses the discussion on the Act, rather than on Congress.

H. Simple Word Choice Mistakes

Poor word choice is especially dangerous, because it undermines your credibility. In some respects, it is worse even than redundant or abstract writing: Though using the wrong word might leave your meaning quite clear, it will lead some readers to think that you are ill-educated or inarticulate.

This reader reaction might be unfair, but it's the way of the world. You need to keep it in mind.

Many word choice mistakes will be obvious if you carefully and skeptically proofread your draft. Reread each sentence and ask yourself: Is this exactly what I want to say?

Take two sentences I read in student papers, "the police already have alternate counts to chase criminals," and "citizens' suspicions of intrusive gun control laws are at a height." If the writers had reread the sentences, they would almost certainly have seen the errors. ("At a height" might not be technically mistaken, but it's highly unidiomatic, and thus nearly as annoying to readers as an error.)

If you find yourself consistently missing such errors during your proofreading—one sign would be that your teachers keep marking word choice errors on your drafts—try reading the sentence aloud. As one law review editor told me, "Your ear will tell you if things are badly phrased much more quickly than your eyes will."

I. Inattentiveness to the Literal Meaning of a Word

Consider the sentence "Firearms are one of the most lethal forms of suicide." It's clear what this means, but if you look closely, it's not literally accurate, for two reasons. First, all *suicide* (as opposed to attempts to commit suicide) is by definition completely lethal. Second, firearms are a *means* to commit suicide, not a form of suicide. "Firearms are one of the most lethal means for committing suicide" would be better, though "Suicide attempts with guns are especially likely to succeed" might be more accurate still.

This sort of objection may be pedantic, but many readers will make it. Consciously or not, some people may see such logical errors as evidence of an illogical mind; and sometimes (though not in this example), the errors will make the sentence ambiguous or hard to understand.

True, English is full of illogical idioms: "Ice cream," for instance, isn't made of ice, and "iced cream" would have been more logical—but "ice cream" is standard and "iced cream" is not. Still, outside these established idioms, you're better off using words as logically as possible.

J. Errors Obscured by Intervening Words

Word choice errors are particularly likely if the two parts of the unidiomatic or illogical phrase are separated by other words. In "crimes done in the heat of passion," for example, the unidiomatic usage ("crimes done") is pretty clear; but in "crimes which would have been done in the heat of passion," it's less obvious. Again, you need to carefully and skeptically proofread your work, looking for such problems.

K. Inattentiveness to How Words Are Normally Used

A more subtle problem is inattentiveness to the way words are normally used. Consider the phrase "the crime is not that serious (it is only negligent)." There's no inherent reason that we can't say "negligent crimes"; after all, we say "negligent homicide" or "negligent misrepresentation." But people don't normally use this phrase.

Likewise, the phrase "crimes done in the heat of passion" is not logically wrong, but it is unidiomatic—crimes are generally "committed" rather than "done," and readers may find "crimes done" to be odd and jarring. Ask yourself, as you do when looking for legalese: "Do people actually talk this way?"

The Roman poet Horace spoke of "the will of custom, in whose power is the decision and right and standard of language." If you depart from customary usage, you risk alienating readers. At the very least you are likely to distract them. Stick with common idiom, and you can get readers to focus on your ideas and not be distracted by your words.

L. Failing to Listen to Your Doubts

Sometimes, as you're writing or editing, you realize that something might not be quite right. Don't ignore that reaction. Instead:

1. *Take a moment to look up the word in the dictionary.* Checking a dictionary is easier than ever before; just go to dictionary.com, or to Black's Law Dictionary on Westlaw. If you learn that you have been misunderstanding the word, you will avoid embarrassment, not just this once but also many times in the future.

2. *Look up the word in a usage dictionary.* If you can, buy a usage dictionary and keep it by your desk—*Merriam-Webster's Dictionary of English Usage, The New Fowler's Modern English Usage,* and Bryan Garner's *A Dictionary of Modern Legal Usage* are all good. These will tell you what controversies there are about particular words, and will help you avoid irritating readers who are prejudiced (whether reasonably or unreasonably) against particular usages.

If you don't own one of these dictionaries, you can search through *Merriam-Webster's Dictionary of English Usage* on Google Books.

3. *Search online to see which of several alternatives is more commonly used.* If you're not sure which word or phrase to use—"esthetic" or "aesthetic," "premier lawyer in the country" or "premiere lawyer in the country," "forbidden from carrying" or "forbidden to carry," "al-Qaeda" or "al-Qaida"—see how others are using it. Search through Westlaw's cases or journals database, or through prominent news sources on Lexis (such as the Major Papers database, NEWS;MAJPAP), or even Google, and see which gets more hits.

If one term gets many more hits than the other, use the more popular one. If both get roughly the same number of hits, that means both are standard (though you might still check a usage dictionary, in case one alternative is for some reason disliked by self-described purists).

4. *Ask a friend.* If you're still not sure whether something sounds wrong or unidiomatic, or which phrase sounds better, ask someone.

5. If you don't want to be distracted from the flow of your writing or editing, no need to look up the word or phrase right away; just *mark the possible error so you can check it later.*

M. Using Needlessly Fancy Words

There are two problems with using needlessly fancy words.

1. Simple words will rarely steer you wrong: You know what they mean, and you generally use them only because you think they're the right tools for the job. Fancy words are often less familiar, and people sometimes use those words precisely because they are fancy. This increases the risk of writer error.

Thus, for instance, I sometimes hear people say "fulsome" to mean "full" or "thorough," for instance in the phrase "a fulsome analysis." But as it happens, one common meaning of "fulsome" is "offensive to good taste, especially as being excessive" or "excessively or insincerely lavish."

Some people even claim that this pejorative meaning is the only correct definition, and "fulsome" in the sense of "thorough" is wrong. I think they themselves are wrong on that: Both definitions of "fulsome" are common in educated writing, and both are listed in dictionaries. But it's still unwise to use "fulsome" for "thorough"—it annoys some people, and distracts others. Why use in a positive sense a word that has a negative connotation to many readers?

Likewise, I sometimes hear people use "nonplussed" to mean "unfazed" or "unperturbed." But the dictionary definition is "utterly perplexed." Many people will assume this is what you mean, even if the "unfazed" meaning becomes common enough to be a standard alternative definition (and I don't think it has become that common yet). Much better to avoid "nonplussed" altogether, and certainly to avoid it when you mean "unfazed."

Of course, the question is how to avoid falling into these traps when you don't know that they are traps. One answer is to stick with simple and common words. If "thorough" had an inherently negative connotation, you'd know it by now. The fancier and rarer terms, such as "fulsome," are the ones likely to come with little-known dangers.

2. Even if you as a writer know the definition of a fancy word, your readers might not. However perfect the word might be in the abstract, it won't work well for you if many of your readers don't know it. Maybe that's their fault; maybe if our educational system worked better, they'd know the word. But that doesn't matter when you're choosing what words to use.

What matters is that using words that many of your readers don't know will not effectively communicate your point to them. At best it will merely distract them, as they try to deduce the meaning from context or (very rarely) look it up in a dictionary. At worst it will confuse them. In either case, it could alienate them, and make them less likely to keep reading, and to be open to your argument even if they do keep reading.

In particular, avoid using words that you have just learned. (The exception is when the words are legal terms that you're expected to learn in law school, and that nearly all lawyers do learn in law school.) If you hadn't learned the word during all your years of pre-law-school education, many of your readers—law students, lawyers, and even judges and academics—are probably in the same position you were in before you learned the word.

Nor should you worry that avoiding fancy words will make your prose look "dumbed down." In my experience, people notice misuse of fancy words. They notice use of fancy words, and often dislike such use even when it's technically proper.

But they don't notice the absence of fancy words, in a passage that consists entirely of simple words: They just notice what the simple words are saying, which is what you want readers to notice. What persuades and impresses readers is the quality of the argument, not the sophistication of the wording.

N. Tip: Read a Usage Guide

The best way to avoid usage traps is to get a good usage guide, and read it cover to cover. *Merriam-Webster's Dictionary of English Usage* is my favorite, but you can choose others as well.

These guides are quite readable, because they are more like mini-encyclopedias than like traditional dictionaries: Rather than just including a definition, they tend to briefly discuss each usage question they cover. These discussions are often interesting, and sometimes witty.

And reading them alerts you to where the landmines are buried. You might not know that there are controversies about the words "disinterested," "enormity," and "historic" (to give just a small sample); but the usage guides will tell you.

Reading such a guide takes time, but there's no need to read it in one sitting. If you can read a few entries a day, you'll learn how to avoid many potentially embarrassing problems, and you might have fun while you learn.

O. Clichés

Generally avoid overused phrases, such as (to borrow examples that I've cut from drafts of this book) "more than meets the eye," "law of the land," "flat wrong," "time and time again," "mix and match," "done to death," "abandon ship," "chock full," or "go back to square one."

These phrases may seem like colorful intensifiers that catch the reader's attention; and sometimes they indeed do that, which is why the advice "avoid clichés" sometimes seems overstated. But the advice is usually sound. These phrases were once (I almost wrote "once upon a time") novel and vivid, and added flair to people's writing. But overuse has drained most clichés of this capacity. And because authors tend to overestimate their own wittiness, they often think that a cliché will add color even when it really doesn't.

There is thus little advantage to using clichés, and there are disadvantages. Some clichés annoy some readers; and almost all clichés make sentences longer and more complex. Each one may not make much difference, but the extra mental translation that they require can add up. And clichés keep you from inventing your own original imagery, which would be helpful precisely because it's fresh to the reader.

P. Figurative Phrases

Most clichés and all metaphors (see p. 114) are figurative phrases: They use words and phrases that mean something other than their literal meaning (for instance, "like a bull in a china shop"). Figurative phrasing is sometimes helpful, but it's often dangerous precisely because it uses terms in their nonliteral sense. You should use figurative terms sparingly, and you should always be aware of the literal meaning as well as the figurative when you do use them.

1. Overrelying on the figure of speech instead of on a substantive argument

The first danger of the figurative was mentioned in the discussion of metaphors: Writers sometimes assume that the figurative usage will do the work of persuading people or explaining the proposal. But "allowing courts to decide this would be like putting a bull in a china shop" is not a complete argument; "courts should balance the freedom of speech and the need for individual privacy" is not a complete proposal. They become complete only when the writer answers the underlying questions: Exactly why are courts incompetent at deciding this? Exactly how should courts deal with speech that reveals private information about others?

If you had used literal language, e.g., "courts aren't going to do a good job of deciding questions like this," you'd have seen the need to flesh out the argument. But figurative language, by hiding the literal meaning, can also hide this need.

2. Forgetting the literal meaning of the figurative phrase

The second danger is forgetting that the figurative phrase has two different meanings, and using the figurative meaning without realizing that the literal meaning will distract or confuse the reader.

a. *Mixed metaphors*, such as "the political equation was thus saturated with kerosene," are one example of this.[17] Standing alone, "the political equation" and "saturated with kerosene" would just convey their figurative meanings, and their literal meanings would be largely ignored. But when you put them together, readers will notice their incompatible literal meanings, and be distracted (and unintentionally amused). My favorite, possibly apocryphal, example: "This field of research is so virginal that no human eye has ever set foot in it."[18]

b. Even a single figurative usage can have its literal meaning *unintentionally highlighted by surrounding concepts*: "The felony murder rule has been done to death in the literature" is either a weak (and macabre) intentional joke or a weak unintentional one. "Done to death" on its own just conveys its figurative meaning of "exhaustively covered," but when it's used while discussing felony murder, readers will think of the literal meaning as well, and be distracted. The distraction might be justified if you think the joke is funny enough, but usually it isn't.

c. Figurative usages that allude to some literary work or historical practice may *clash with their original meaning*. To "decimate," for instance, originally meant to kill every tenth person as a collective punishment (hence the joke that "You can tell the ancient Romans were tough—in their language, 'to kill every tenth person as a collective punishment' was one word"). The figurative meaning, which is "to dramatically reduce," is now well established, but some people are still reminded of the old usage, which can either distract or annoy them.

Likewise, "East is East and West is West, and never the twain shall meet" is sometimes used to suggest that two cultures are irreconcilable. But Kipling's poem continues with "but there is neither East nor West,

Border, nor Breed, nor Birth / When two strong men stand face to face, tho' they come from the ends of the earth." People who are familiar with the poem will thus be reminded of the exact opposite of what the person who is quoting the "East is East" phrase is asserting.

You might think that such objections are pedantic: After all, you're using the modern meaning, not the original one. But when a writer chooses to express the modern meaning using a literary or historical allusion, he brings the literary or historical origin to the minds of those readers who know the origin. And if that original meaning distracts the reader from the actual meaning that the writer wanted to evoke, that's the writer's fault.

3. Misusing the figurative phrase

Figurative usages are often misused, because people don't think about (or don't understand) the literal meaning. "Back to ground zero," for instance, is often used instead of "back to square one." "Ground zero" is the location where a bomb is detonated, not the first step of a long task. But the similarity of "ground zero" and "square one," coupled with writers' lack of attention to the terms' literal meanings, makes it easy to confuse the two.

Likewise, "free rein," "toe the line," and "tough row to hoe" are often miswritten as "free reign," "tow the line," and "tough road to hoe." Even writers who would rarely misspell a literally used word may fall into these traps for figurative phrases, because the phrases' literal origins—which provide an important clue about their spelling—are often forgotten.

4. Being tempted into using a figurative phrase that isn't exactly right

Finally, writers are often tempted into using figurative phrases even when the phrase isn't quite right for the occasion. Thus, "raises the question" often becomes "begs the question"; "begs the question" traditionally refers to the fallacy of assuming the very point that you're trying to prove, but because the phrase seems so colorful, many people use it in a broader, and incorrect, sense. Likewise, a person's changing his behavior, even incrementally, becomes "the leopard changing its spots," even though the latter phrase generally refers not to all changes but specifically to radical ones.

So if you think some figurative phrase can make a point more vivid, use it, but only after considering both (1) whether the phrase really adds something, and (2) whether the literal meaning of the phrase might weaken your point more than the figurative enhances it. And always second-guess yourself whenever you use a figurative term unintentionally; many such uses prove to be unhelpful.

Finally, never, ever use the word "literally" when you mean "figuratively," as in "[T]he number of lawyers in the United States has literally exploded over the last 53 years." *Literally* exploded?

Q. Cultural Allusions (High Culture or Pop Culture)

Allusions to pop songs, great literature, classical mythology, or other works pose some of the same risks as metaphors. They seem appealing, because they promise to make the work more lively, erudite, or amusing. But they often come across as forced and distracting. Sometimes they're counterproductive because they're not precisely on point, but the author was blinded to this by his joy in making a little joke. They're often cliché. And sometimes they are obscure enough that they may confuse or alienate readers, or else require an explanation that further distracts the reader with irrelevancies.

Some allusions are good, because they vividly—and often humorously—capture your point. You just need to look suspiciously at every allusion you use, to make sure you're using it for the right reason.

Alex Long's *[Insert Song Lyrics Here]: The Uses and Misuses of Popular Music Lyrics in Legal Writing* illustrates this well:

> Take ... the following passage from an unpublished federal opinion:
>
> > The Beatles once sang about the long and winding road. This 1992 case has definitely walked down it, but at the end of the day, the plaintiffs and their counsel were singing the Pink Floyd anthem "Another Brick in the Wall" after consistently banging their collective heads against a popular procedural wall—Northern District of Illinois Local Rule 12 governing the briefing and submission of summary judgment motions.
>
> The court's use of the "Long and Winding Road" and "procedural wall" metaphors coupled with the reference to Pink Floyd in this instance is counterproductive [because, among other things,] ... the court's use of metaphor does little to assist the reader in understanding the court's meaning in any meaningful way. If one of the purposes of metaphors is to allow people "to understand one phenomenon in relationship to another and to illuminate some salient details while shad-

ing others," the "Long and Winding Road" metaphor just barely serves this purpose.

Litigation often takes a lot of twists and turns and may take a long time. We get it. There is nothing particularly wrong with [t]he Beatles metaphor; however, if one assumes that one of the purposes of metaphors is to make a point in a more concise manner, then the inclusion of the metaphor fails this purpose....

Contrast that example with the California courts' use of the "you don't need a weatherman to know which way the wind blows" metaphor used to explain under what circumstances expert testimony is required. [This observation has become almost boilerplate included in the decisions of the California appellate courts when ruling on when ... expert testimony before a jury is required. According to a California appellate court, Dylan states "the correct rule," and the California courts are simply in harmony with his statement of the law.]

The metaphor is effective in that it serves the purpose of metaphors by "making abstract concepts more concrete" and aids in understanding; the court's use of it is also pretty darn funny. Both the inherent truthfulness and applicability of Dylan's statement are so spot-on that even one who dislikes or is ambivalent toward Dylan would be hard pressed to quibble about a court's use of the phrase.

This is precisely right: The "long and winding road" and "brick in the wall" allusions add no support to the argument. Maybe they'll amuse some readers, but they're probably more likely to annoy, precisely because they're needless distractions.

But the "you don't need a weatherman" line does support the argument. It crisply captures a truth (we can understand some things without calling on experts) that's closely connected to the legal question at hand. This makes the author's point more vivid, and more likely to come across as witty.

The same also applies to epigraphs: Use them only after you've thought hard about whether the quote is genuinely apt.

R. Abbreviations

Abbreviations (such as SSA, FIFO, DBA, TLA, and so on) tend to make a work less accessible, at least to readers who aren't already thoroughly familiar with the abbreviations. This is especially so if a reader sees several such abbreviations on the same page.

Some abbreviations are unavoidable, and are so standard that most readers won't really notice them; everyone knows about the EPA and the FCC, and most people who read about religious freedom law know about RFRA (the Religious Freedom Restoration Act). Calling these entities by something other than their abbreviations will be jarring and unnecessarily wordy.

But don't create your own abbreviations, and try to avoid using preexisting abbreviations that are relatively unfamiliar to most readers. For instance, if you're writing about the Gun Free School Zones Act, don't call it GFSZA—call it "the Act," since it's probably the only Act you'll be discussing in detail. If you're talking about slippery slope arguments, don't call them SSAs; spell out the phrase, or just say "such arguments" if your meaning is clear from context. Shorter is usually better, but not when you get brevity by making the article seem forbidding to casual readers.

XV. WRITING: RHETORICAL PROBLEMS TO WATCH FOR

A. *Unduly Harsh Criticism*

Be understated in your criticisms, even if they're well founded. Don't call your opponents' arguments "fraudulent," "nonsense," "ridiculous," "silly," or even "egregiously wrong." Use "mistaken," "unsound," "erroneous," or other mild criticisms instead. People will get your message, and will be more disposed to accept it precisely because it's understated.

Why?

1. Overstating your argument *raises your burden of proof*. Call an argument "fraudulent," and skeptical readers might say "Wait, is it really fraudulent, or could it just be an honest error?"; and this will distract them from your more important claim, which is that the argument is just wrong. Likewise, call the argument "irrational," and skeptical readers may try to find some reasonableness in it. You don't want to weaken your claims by making unproven and unnecessary allegations.

2. *No one likes a bully.* Excessive harshness may alienate readers and make them sympathize with your adversaries.

3. *Invective often hides lack of substance.* Readers realize this, and become suspicious when they hear overheated rhetoric.

4. *Readers are less likely to tolerate harsh criticism by juniors—* such as law students or young lawyers—than similar criticism by respected scholars. By all means, pick fights with the Big Guns; your professor and other readers will admire your pluck. But be scrupulously polite to the people you criticize: A polite upstart is more tolerated than a rude one.

5. There's *no need to make unnecessary enemies*. When you're applying for a job, and Justice X's former law clerk is reading your article, you'll be glad that you called Justice X's arguments "mistaken" rather than "stupid." This shouldn't stop you from expressing disagreement; people respect honest disagreement. But they don't respect rudeness, or even borderline rudeness, especially rudeness to people they know and like.

6. *If you're ultimately proven wrong*, even in part, it's much easier to gracefully backpedal from a mistaken assertion that some ar-

gument "seems unsound" than from a mistaken assertion that the argument is "idiotic."

Follow Prof. Dan Markel's advice: "Anytime I'm tempted to write out of rage that someone's argument is hopelessly misguided or fabulously wrong, I try to remember how much I cringe when my own work is criticized. I drop adverbs and instead use locutions such as [']the claims advanced in the article 'seem mistaken or inaccurate' for the following reasons.['] ... This helps focus on[] what Michael Walzer wisely described[as] the task of 'getting the arguments right.' [Scholarship should be about that, not] about making anyone look foolish or wicked."[19]

B. Personalized Criticism

Attack arguments, not people. Most readers will react better to "this argument is wrong because ..." than to "Volokh is wrong because ...." Likewise, when you're criticizing an argument, don't call it Volokh's argument. Label it by name ("the cost-lowering slippery slope argument") or just say "the argument," if it's clear from context which argument you're referring to. Of course, properly attribute your adversary's argument, but do it in the footnotes, or with no more than one named reference in the text.

This sort of circumlocution helps readers feel that your disagreements are substantive, not personal. There's nothing inherently *rude* about criticizing a person's argument using his name, but such criticism tends to come across as unduly combative, even when it's not intended that way. And the more substantively devastating your criticism is, the more you should keep the devastated author's name out of it.

C. Caricatured Criticism

Prof. Dan Markel puts it well:

> [Avoid] the drive-by characterization of or criticism against a "school of thought." One often reads something like: retributivists believe X, or utilitarians believe Y, or [critical legal studies scholars] think Q and originalists think R....
>
> [T]his is largely unhelpful, except in very introductory materials. Far better to name names and cite particular works of scholarship than to make vague generalizations that are more often accepted by critics of the particular school of thought but rarely accepted by adherents to the relevant school of thought.

Relatedly, avoid quoting a critic of X when trying to explain what X is. Better to find an adherent of X to cite and quote than someone who thinks X is wrong or inaccurate .... [T]he critic of X is less invested in actually describing X accurately than an adherent of X is.

And he offers a good bottom-line test as well: "Could I show [my work] to the objects of criticism and be assured that they will think I've acted fairly, if not charitably, toward their work[?]" Always ask yourself that.[20]

XVI. EDITING: THREE EXERCISES

A. Basic Editing

Practice these suggestions using three concrete examples. The first two are paragraphs from real seminar papers written in response to the following assignment:

> Your boss, Senator Elaine Mandel, is a member of the State Senate Committee on the Judiciary. The Committee will shortly consider the proposed Child Firearms Safety Act, which states that "Any person who lives in the same household as a minor and who possesses a handgun shall store the handgun unloaded and in a locked container." Please write a short memo advising the Senator whether she should vote for the law.

Here are the opening paragraphs from the two papers:

> The Child Firearm Safety Act as currently written is a well intentioned piece of legislation which will likely have little effect on the incidence of minors accidentally killed by handguns. However, with some critical modifications the act could play a significant role in lowering the number of minors lost to handgun accidents each year. These modifications should include: compelling either that the gun be kept in a locked container *or* unloaded; the inclusion of long guns in the Act; and making violation of the Act a felony offense.

and

> The proposed Child Firearms Safety Act (the "bill") is an inconsequential piece of legislation. Aside from the significant political impact of the bill, it carries little weight and makes little difference. Despite public misconceptions, the few benefits of the bill, notably the probable slight decrease in the number of childhood gun accidents, do not exceed the drawbacks, such as the inaccessibility of guns during a home invasion and loss of civil liberties. Therefore, unless some strong amendments are made to the bill, I recommend that you oppose the bill.

Try rewriting each to make it clearer and about 50% shorter; I give some possible answers in Appendix II.A.1, p. 352.

B. Editing for Concreteness

Consider also this paragraph; assume that it's the first paragraph in an article on laws prohibiting the wearing of masks in public:

> The existence of antimask laws poses difficult questions of constitutional law. We know that the freedom of speech is one of our most cherished rights, especially when there is a danger that the free ex-

pression of unpopular speakers would be deterred by the fear of negative consequences. And yet the prevention of crime, including crime facilitated by the wearing of masks, must surely be ranked as one of the more compelling of the possible government interests. The public understandably wants to avoid the harm to property, persons, and the social fabric that may flow from such crime.

The purpose of the antimask laws, as the paragraph suggests, is to prevent crime: Anonymity can make it easier for people to get away with crimes; masks facilitate anonymity; so therefore banning masks should (at least in some circumstances) help prevent crime. On the other hand, some people will be reluctant to express unpopular views unless they can do so anonymously, so antimask laws deter some unpopular speech.

This paragraph is much better written than the preceding two—and yet it's still too abstract, and too full of unhelpful generalities. Rewrite it to make it more concrete, clear, and vivid. Feel free to cut material and add material, if you think that the changes will improve the paragraph. A possible answer is in Appendix II.A.2, p. 357.

XVII. USING EVIDENCE CORRECTLY

In trying to prove your claim, you'll use a lot of evidence—cases, statutes, historical facts, social science data, and so on. You need to use this evidence correctly.

Part of the reason is honesty and professional responsibility, but another part is self-interest: Instructors don't like errors, and neither do other readers. A couple of mistakes, even on tangential matters, can undermine the credibility of all the sound arguments you make. An error, however small, can be like the proverbial thirteenth chime of a clock—not only wrong itself, but casting doubt on all that came before it.

If some evidence seemingly contradicts your claim, you can confront the problem and explain why your claim is nonetheless sound. But if you try to hide the problem by misdescribing the evidence, you'll damage your argument much more than if you had been candid about the issue. This Part offers tips for avoiding common errors in the use of evidence, together with some examples drawn from real cases and articles (though with the authors' names intentionally omitted).

The examples are ones that I've run across in my own research, so you'll find them skewed towards those areas in which I work. But you can find similar problems in any field of scholarship, coming from all perspectives, left, center, right, and beyond, and even in the work of otherwise careful writers.

A. Read, Quote, and Cite the Original Source

Whenever you make a claim about some source, you nearly always must read the original source. Do *not* rely on an intermediate source—whether a law review article or a case—that cites the original. You should generally also cite the intermediate source that pointed you to the original, to credit it for helping you. But also cite the original, and reason based on the original.

1. Legal evidence

If you're discussing a case or a statute, read, quote, and cite the case or statute itself. Do not rely on other cases, articles, treatises, or encyclopedias that mention the source.* Check the original. If you can't find the original, ask your librarians; they will usually be glad to help you.

Intermediate sources may seem authoritative, but they're often unreliable, whether because of bias or honest mistake. You can't let their mistakes become your mistakes.

Here's an example, from an interdisciplinary faculty-edited journal published by a leading university press:

> On the one occasion when such [gun control] legislation was overturned, in *Bliss v. Commonwealth* (1822), the Kentucky Supreme Court ruled that state regulation of firearms violated the state's militia amendment, which granted an explicitly individual right to bear arms (12 Ky. 90). In response, the legislature immediately amended the state constitution to allow such legislation, rewriting the militia amendment to more closely match the federal Constitution's Second Amendment (Kentucky 1835).[21]

Seems reliable, no? Well, it turns out that:

(a) *Bliss* did not involve "the state's militia amendment," but rather a constitutional provision that never mentioned the militia: "That the rights of the citizens to bear arms in defence of themselves and the State shall not be questioned."[22] The militia provisions were in a separate article of the constitution.[23] And the provision was technically not an amendment, since it was enacted together with the rest of the state constitution.

(b) The legislature did not immediately amend the state constitution. The constitution provided no mechanisms for amendment,[24] and the provision was changed only when a new constitution was adopted in 1850—28 years after *Bliss*.[25] The Kentucky 1835 source, which actually gives an 1834 publication date on its title page, does not show any change to the original provision.

(c) The 1850 revision did not make the right to bear arms provision "more closely match the federal Constitution's Second Amendment"—it added the clause "but the general assembly may pass laws to prevent persons from carrying concealed arms," which doesn't appear in the Second Amendment.

---

* One exception: Old sources are sometimes reprinted in authoritative compendia; because the purpose of these works is to be authoritative sources, they tend to be quite well-checked and reliable. If your librarian tells you that some such source has a good reputation, you can generally count on it. Francis N. Thorpe, *The Federal and State Constitutions* (1909), for instance, is a reliable reference for pre–1909 state constitutions.

Whoops! Pretty embarrassing for the author. But if you cited this as evidence of what *Bliss* said and what the Kentucky legislature did, then it would be embarrassing for *you*.

There are many other examples, some of which themselves arise from scholars' not checking the original source, and thus repeating the intermediate source's error. For instance, several articles claim that the common phrase "rule of thumb" originated in a "common law rule that a husband could beat his wife without legal sanction if he used a rod no thicker than his thumb." This etymological claim—like many interesting etymological claims—appears to be mythical.[26] But it has appeared in many reputable journals, and is poised to lead still more people into error.

Even Supreme Court opinions can contain mistakes; for instance, *Reno v. ACLU*, where the Court struck down the first Internet indecency ban (the Communications Decency Act), said the following to distinguish two earlier cases:

> The breadth of the CDA's coverage is wholly unprecedented. Unlike the regulations upheld in *Ginsberg* [*v. New York*, 390 U.S. 629 (1968),] and [*FCC v.*] *Pacifica* [*Foundation,* 438 U.S. 726 (1978)], the scope of the CDA is not limited to commercial speech or commercial entities.[27]

Sounds like you can confidently assert, citing *Reno*, that the restrictions in *Ginsberg* and *Pacifica* were limited to commercial speech or commercial entities.

Unfortunately, the *Reno* opinion was wrong. The *Ginsberg* law, which barred the sales of certain sexually themed magazines to minors, was not limited to commercial speech: Such magazines, even ones sold for money, do not qualify as commercial speech, a term that generally refers only to commercial advertising.[28] The *Pacifica* regulation was not limited either to commercial speech or to commercial entities; the broadcast in *Pacifica* itself was noncommercial speech carried by a nonprofit, noncommercial radio station.[29] Whoops.

If you want to cite *Reno* as evidence of how the *Reno* Court *treated* the precedents, that's fine, though from the context it doesn't look like the Court was intentionally trying to redefine the terms "commercial speech" and "commercial entities." But you shouldn't cite *Reno* as evidence of what actually happened in *Ginsberg* and *Pacifica*—read, quote, and cite the precedents directly.

One significant exception: Judges' discussions of the factual findings in the litigation itself tend to be fairly reliable. These discussions aren't perfect, but they're generally good enough for you to trust. Even in this context, though, consult the most thorough available version of the factual findings—if the trial court's finding of facts are available, read them, rather than just relying on the appellate court's account.

2. Historical, economic, or scientific evidence

If you're making a claim about:

- history (the Framing generation thought this-and-such),
- economics (demand for these sorts of goods operates this way),
- social or physical science (people in this experiment behaved this way),
- or any other specialized discipline,

you should read, quote, and cite a work in that discipline. Do not rely on law review articles that make this assertion.

People who write law review articles are usually not experts in history, economics, and science. Some are quite knowledgeable in those fields, but some have learned just enough to be dangerous.

If possible, you should go to the ultimate source, such as a historical document or a scientific study. Many of the ultimate sources are available in your university library—your law school reference librarians can help you find them, and possibly even borrow them for you from another library, if necessary. Law students often overestimate the difficulty of getting books from other libraries. Librarians tend to be quite ready to help students (or recent alumni) with this sort of research.

Sometimes, you might have to rely on an intermediate source. The ultimate source might be too technical for you to adequately understand. The authors of a book may be expressing their own expert judgment based on a wide range of materials, and no single ultimate source will directly support that judgment. Or you might just not have the time to go through a large body of original material.

Still, you should rely on such secondary sources as rarely as possible, because each time you rely on them, you risk inadvertently incorporating their errors or at least their selective quotations. And you particularly should not rely on secondary sources *outside the underlying discipline*, such as law review articles that cite history books; there, the risk of error is too high.

There's one important exception to this: In some fields, such as legal history or law and economics, the original scholarship is itself published in legal journals. So if you're making a claim about, for instance, the Framers' understanding of the Fourth Amendment (a historical question), citing a law review article may make sense, so long as the cited article is the original historical work, and so long as you read all the historical sources that you plan on citing.

But if you're making a claim about the demographics of the various states shortly after independence, don't cite a law review article for that proposition. Find the history books that the article cites (or, better yet, the sources on which the books rely), and read, quote, and cite them.

3. Newspapers

Newspaper articles often omit critical details, or err in the details they do include. This makes it risky to rely on them.

Most reporters are generalists, who write about subjects on which they aren't expert. They also tend to write under tight deadlines, and with strict word limits. Their work is then edited by editors who often know still less about the subject, and have even less time.

Reporters also rarely check the original sources; instead, they usually rely on some supposed expert's judgment. Moreover, in my experience, reporters rarely check back with the experts to make sure their quotes were accurately transcribed and edited. (One story, for instance, rendered my reference to a "marina operator's right to his property" as a "marina operator's right to hypocrisy."[30])

This unreliability may not be the reporters' fault; they might be doing the best they can, given their deadlines. But the result is that their work is much less reliable than even the imperfectly reliable law review articles, which at least are written by people who are relatively expert, who have time to check their sources, and who know that they must include footnotes that someone will check. Think back on how many errors or important omissions you've seen in newspaper articles about subjects you know, and you'll get a sense of how often newspaper accounts err about all things.

Here, then, are some guidelines.

a. Newspaper accounts of a published case, a statute, or other legal source

Never rely on a newspaper article's account of a published case, a statute, or other legal source. The articles are too often wrong, and it's easy enough for you to check the source yourself.

b. Newspaper accounts of legal documents or academic studies

Don't rely on newspaper descriptions of legal documents—such as complaints, briefs, or unpublished court decisions—or of historical or scientific studies, if the information is at all important to your claim. Instead, get, read, and cite the underlying document or study. Lawyers involved in the case are often good sources of legal documents. And your research librarians might also help you track down both the legal documents and the academic studies.

c. Identifying the original sources by looking at other newspaper articles

If the newspaper doesn't clearly identify the original source, do a Lexis NEWS;CURNWS,ARCNWS or Westlaw ALLNEWSPLUS search for stories that mention the same assertion. Some of the other stories may give more details that can help you track down the original document. For instance, if you did this for the famous claim that Vice President Dan Quayle once told Latin Americans that "I wish I'd studied Latin at school so I could talk to you in your own language," you'd find that the story was made up as a joke, and then repeated as if it were true.[31]

d. Contacting quoted speakers

Sometimes the newspaper is the original source, for instance when it repeats what someone told the reporter, or said at some event; you might then have to use the newspaper account. Keep in mind, though, the risk that the newspaper may have erred or quoted someone out of context. For instance, in early 2003, several op-eds ridiculed former Representative Cynthia McKinney for saying that "In no other country on the planet do so many people have so little as they do in this country"—a patently false claim. Listening to the CSPAN video of the speech, however, reveals that McKinney actually said "In no other *rich democracy* on this planet do so many people have so little" (emphasis added), a very different and more plausible assertion.[32]

Therefore, if you can, e-mail the quoted speaker to verify the quote. You can often find e-mail addresses through search engines, especially when you're looking for the address of an academic or a lawyer. You can also find many lawyers' phone numbers and e-mail addresses through the Westlaw WLD directory, the Lexis MARHUB library, or the Web sites of state bars. And if the quote was from a publicly broadcast speech, check whether a video of the program might exist online.

e. Acknowledging possible reliability problems

If your only source for a proposition is a newspaper article, or some person quoted (or misquoted) in the article, acknowledge in the text the possibility that this is not a highly reliable source (e.g., by using a phrase such as "press accounts report that"). And if there is reason to doubt the quoted source's accuracy, for instance if the source is an interested party, or is talking about something that he might have misperceived or misunderstood, you should note that explicitly.

f. Expressly describing the newspaper article's limitations

In any event, if you are citing a newspaper article for a proposition, make clear—either in the footnote, or, if this is important, in the text—

i.   the nature of the article (is it an opinion piece or supposedly objective reporting?),

ii. the nature of the source (whom does the article quote for the proposition, and what are the source's possible biases?), and

iii. any other reasons why the source might be inaccurate.

Here's an example: According to one history book,

> Supreme Court Justice Antonin Scalia agreed with this view that citizens have a constitutionally protected right to own machine guns.

Seems like a reliable claim, written by a history professor. We're all set to say "Justice Scalia takes the view that citizens have a constitutional right to own machine guns," citing the book.

But have a look at the source on which the book relies, the *Baltimore Sun*, April 30, 1999, at 27A. (The citation in the endnote contains only this, with no further information.) Here's how the article—which turns out to be an opinion column entitled *Scalia Is Wrong on Guns*—begins; all the relevant material is in these paragraphs:

> Five days before two teen-agers went on a murderous shooting rampage in a Colorado high school, U.S. Supreme Court Justice Antonin Scalia told a group of students at the Park School in Baltimore County that if he had his way, people would have more—not less—

access to deadly weapons.

At a small luncheon following his speech to 300 students there, Justice Scalia said that citizens have a right to own machine guns, said ... a 17-year-old Park senior.

Pressing the outer limits of his thinking on this matter, [the student]—who has earned early admission to Princeton University—said she asked Justice Scalia if he thought people should also "be allowed to have hand-held rockets that can bring down airplanes."

After a moment of contemplation, Justice Scalia told [the student] he didn't like that idea. Justice Scalia fancies himself an "originalist"— someone who thinks the Constitution means today exactly what it meant when it was adopted two centuries ago.

So not surprisingly, Justice Scalia says the language of the Second Amendment, which gives citizens the right to bear arms, is a license for people to amass a nearly limitless arsenal of weapons.

The book, then, was indirectly relying on a high school student's paraphrase of what she recalled Justice Scalia saying at a private lunch.

It's certainly possible that the student was right. It's also possible, though, that she may have misheard, misremembered, or misinterpreted Scalia's position (for instance, treating a devil's advocate argument as a sincere assertion), or omitted some explicit or implied qualifier. It's likewise possible that the student was correct, but the opinion writer who quoted the student misinterpreted or misdescribed the student's account. We can't tell for sure—but the book's author should have alerted us to these uncertainties, by providing more than an unqualified assertion that "Justice Antonin Scalia agreed with this view that citizens have a constitutionally protected right to own machine guns," with no explanation of the possible problems with the source.

So if you want to say something about Scalia's views in your own article, you certainly shouldn't just cite the book or the newspaper column. The source here seems so potentially unreliable that you might not want to use it at all. But if you do use it, you should at least make clear to the readers the possible accuracy problems—chiefly that the statement was made to a small audience, that there's only one source, and that the source's statement is itself being reported second-hand. For instance, you might say

Supreme Court Justice Antonin Scalia said at a private talk that citizens have a constitutionally protected right to own machine guns, according to a newspaper article that cites a high school student who was present at the talk. [Footnote: DeWayne Wickham, *Scalia Is Wrong on Guns*, Balt. Sun, Apr. 30, 1999, at 27A.]

150

(It's not necessary to say in the footnote that this is an opinion column, because the title makes this clear.)

4. Transcripts

Transcripts of news programs may seem more reliable than quotes in reporters' articles; you're supposedly getting the speaker's literal, unedited words. But be on guard for three problems:

a. *Transcribers make mistakes.* One NPR transcript, for instance, contains the puzzling assertion that courts will have to decide "whether a state even makes good religion."[33] What the speaker really said (the speaker was me) was "whether a state even may exclude religion." The *New York Times* likewise once had to run the following correction:

> Because of a transcription error, an article yesterday about Senator Alfonse M. D'Amato's remarks about Judge Lance A. Ito misquoted the Senator at one point in some editions. In his conversation with the radio host Don Imus, he said: "I mean, this is a disgrace. Judge Ito will be well known." He did not say, "Judge Ito with the wet nose."[34]

When a speaker sounds like he's saying something stupid, it might be the transcriber's fault.

b. In many radio and television shows, only a sentence or two from a long interview makes it into the program. The risk of being *quoted out of context* thus remains.

c. Even intelligent and articulate people sometimes misspeak. When writing, they can see their errors and correct them. When speaking, they might not have the airtime to correct themselves, or might not even notice the error, since they don't have a chance to proofread. Thus, even an accurate transcript *might not accurately reflect the speaker's considered judgment.*

So if you do want to quote a transcript as evidence of what the speaker believes or wants to communicate, be careful. If possible, e-mail the speaker to make sure that the quotes are accurate, especially if the quote seems surprising or damning.

5. Web sites

Web material, like printed material, is *no more reliable than its authors.* For instance, Web-based documents published by U.S. government agencies, such as the Census Bureau, are generally as reliable as these organizations' printed reports, and are generally more timely. A Web page containing a university's student conduct policies is likely to accurately state what the university's written policies actually are. A Web page maintained by an activist group is likely to reliably state the group's views—but it may not reliably describe the underlying facts, just as a pamphlet published by the group may provide a biased view of the facts.

A Web page *maintained by an individual should generally not be seen as reliable by itself,* even if the person is an expert. Individual authors of Web pages often check those pages less carefully than they would check published work. If you want to cite assertions made on a person's Web page, you should:

a. check the sources yourself and then both cite the sources and give credit to the Web page;

b. if the sources aren't given, ask the author for the sources; and

c. at least, if you can't check the statement yourself, confirm that the author still stands by the statement, and has not lost confidence in it.

Because Web pages change often, you should *keep printed copies* of all the pages on which you rely. That way, if the document changes, moves, or vanishes, you'll still have the copy in case someone asks for it.

6. Wikipedia

Over five hundred student articles cite the online Wikipedia encyclopedia. Unlike with most encyclopedias, anyone is allowed to create Wikipedia entries, and generally to update existing entries. This is an unorthodox approach for an encyclopedia, but the theory is that (a) those people who want to spend time writing entries tend to be knowledgeable, and (b) even when those people err, their errors end up getting corrected by others.

Perhaps surprisingly, the theory works most of the time. Wikipedia entries tend to be relatively accurate, probably no worse and possibly better than the typical newspaper article. (This is especially so given that many newspaper articles are written by generalist reporters who are relying on hastily assembled material from others.)

Nonetheless, while Wikipedia may sometimes be a good place to look, don't stop looking there. Instead, find the original sources that the

Wikipedia entry's author relied on—they'll often be cited in the entry—
and read, quote, and cite them.

First, that's the standard procedure you should use for intermediate
sources (including, as I said before, newspaper articles). Second, whether or not Wikipedia is more reliable than the typical newspaper article,
many readers—including law review editors who are deciding whether
to publish your article—will assume that it's less reliable; citing to it
may thus decrease your credibility.

7. Avoid falling into others' bad habits

Many law review articles don't follow these guidelines. My earliest
pieces didn't, either. But there is little safety in numbers: If relying on
an intermediate source leads to your making an error, you'll be faulted
for that error, even if lots of other people rely on intermediate sources.
Protect yourself by being more careful than others are.

B. Check the Studies on Which You Rely

Once you find the original study on which you ultimately want to
rely, *read it with a skeptical eye*. Pretend that you disagree with the political view that the study buttresses: For instance, if the study concludes that immigration is a net minus for the economy, pretend that
you support broad immigration, and try to read the study from that
perspective. Can you identify some possible problems, perhaps including the ones discussed later in this chapter? Does the study confound
terms that seem similar but are actually different (Part XVII.D.1, p.
155)? Does it confuse correlation with causation (Part XVII.H.1, p. 172)?

Then, *search for criticisms of the study*. Use Lexis or Westlaw to
find the law review articles that cite the study; search also for newspaper references; and search whatever indices are available within the
relevant field. (Your law school's or university's research librarians can
point you in the right direction.) You can often quickly find what an article's critics say about it, and get a sense for whether you agree with
the criticisms.

If you find flaws in the study, you might still be able to rely on it.
But you should ask yourself how serious the flaws are; and if you think
the study is still valuable, you should acknowledge the flaws and explain why you think the study is sound despite them.

Why do all this? Four reasons:

1. *Accuracy for its own sake.* You should want your article to be correct; honesty requires this, and it will make you feel better about your work.

2. *Persuasiveness.* Many people who read the article will know the flaws in the studies, or at least will know enough about the subject that they'll sense that there might be something wrong. If you acknowledge the flaws but explain why the studies are still basically sound, you might persuade these readers—but if you ignore the problems, you'll lose credibility.

3. *Depth.* Showing your awareness of the possible weaknesses in the data will make the article deeper and more thoughtful, and thus more impressive.

4. *Grade.* Your professor, who's giving you the grade, is probably one of those readers who knows the studies' flaws. Confronting the flaws will get you a better grade than you'd get if you ignored them.

C. Compromise Wisely

These suggestions—track down the original source, don't rely on newspaper accounts, e-mail people who are quoted to make sure that the quotes are accurate, check the studies that you cite—are time-consuming, and you might not have much time: Your seminar paper or law review article is due at the end of the semester, you have to study for other classes, and you have to actually write the article.

It's best if you follow all the suggestions given above, because they aren't as time-consuming as they may appear, and they help avoid embarrassing and grade-reducing errors. But if you do need to cut corners, here are a few items to consider in deciding when to do so:

1. *Importance.* If an assertion is one of the significant steps in your chain of reasoning, check it particularly well.

2. *Controversy.* If an assertion seems especially controversial or counterintuitive, make extra sure that it's right. First, such assertions are more likely to be wrong or exaggerated than the conventional wisdom tends to be. Second, your readers (including the person who is grading you) are more likely to pay close attention to these assertions.

3. *Personal accusation.* If you're claiming that some person or small group did something bad or foolish, make sure that you have solid proof. This is a matter both of fairness to the targets and of self-protection—readers are especially likely to scrutinize such accusations closely.

4. *Ease of finding the original source.* If the original source is easy to find—for instance, if it's a case or a statute—there's no good excuse for relying on a summary in an intermediate source.

5. *Bias.* Information in an opinion piece, in a law review article written by an advocate for a particular position, or on a site run by an advocacy group is more likely to be unreliable or incomplete than information in a more objective news story or treatise. And careful readers will be especially likely to notice the bias of such sources (especially when the sources are advocacy groups), and lose confidence in your own article as a result. So even if you have to save time by trusting someone, avoid cutting corners with sources like these: Track down the original study, and read, quote, and cite the study, not the advocacy group's summary of the study.

D. Be Careful with the Terms You Use

1. Avoid false synonyms

The law is full of terms that sound similar—for instance, murder, killing, and homicide—but that are actually different. These sorts of seeming synonyms can trip you up if you aren't careful.

Here's an example, from the article mentioned on p. 144:

> In 1905 [New York] ... outlaw[ed] the possession of firearms in any public place by the foreign born (New York State 1905). [footnote: Pennsylvania's law forbidding foreign born residents from killing any animal was upheld by the U.S. Supreme Court in [*Patsone*] v. *Pennsylvania*, 232 U.S. 138 (1914).]

The author also mentioned this two more times in the same article, and in three other articles and a book.

It turns out, though, that neither the New York State 1905 source (N.Y. Consolidated Laws, § 1897) nor the statute upheld in *Patsone* disarmed the *foreign born*; they restricted gun ownership by *noncitizens*. That's significantly different: Among males over 21, the only category for which I have seen the data properly broken down, there were over twice as many foreign-born people as noncitizens in 1900;[35] and disarming noncitizens likely reflects a different public attitude towards the right to bear arms (the subject that the author was discussing) than would disarming all the foreign born, citizens included.

This further reinforces the need to check the original sources rather than relying on articles that cite those sources. But it's also a reminder to consider carefully the distinctions between different terms. Under U.S. law, nearly all noncitizens are foreign-born; but not all the foreign born are noncitizens. The two terms are not synonymous, and can't be used interchangeably.

2. Include all necessary qualifiers

Legal rules often get compressed to short phrases that omit a lot of detail. Sometimes this is necessary, especially when the rule is tangential to your main point. But when the details of a rule are relevant, you should include all the qualifiers needed to make your discussion accurate.

For instance, is it correct to say that *Zacchini v. Scripps–Howard Broadcasting Co.* upheld the right of publicity against First Amendment challenge? Well, the Court did uphold a narrow version of that right— the right to stop others from rebroadcasting one's entire performance— but not the much more commonly invoked broader version, the right to stop others from using one's name or likeness for commercial purposes.[36] So saying that *Zacchini* held that the right of publicity is constitutional, as some do,[37] is a mistake: It fails to acknowledge that the Court considered only the narrower version of the right.

Likewise, if you want to use Justice Holmes' aphorism that the First Amendment doesn't protect people's right to shout fire in a crowded theater, do so correctly: Remember that the phrase is "The most stringent protection of free speech would not protect a man in *falsely* shouting fire in a theatre and causing a panic."[38] People quoting the phrase usually drop the "falsely,"[39] which changes the meaning substantially. (False statements of fact are often constitutionally unprotected; true ones, even if harmful, are generally protected.)

You could argue that even accurately shouting "fire" in a crowded theater is so dangerous that it should be prohibited. But if you want to make that argument, make it explicitly, rather than relying on the authority of a statement that says something quite different.[40]

Omitting necessary qualifiers is closely related to using false synonyms: "Foreign-born," for instance, is a false synonym for "noncitizen," because it omits the qualifier "unnaturalized." Likewise, "the right of publicity" is a false synonym for the right mentioned in *Zacchini*; the terms are used interchangeably in casual asides, but they are in fact quite different.

More broadly, these are instances of the careless use of language—

using terms without thinking hard about what exactly they mean.

3. Use precise terms rather than vague ones

"Almost 1,000 children," an article reports, "die each year from unintentional gunshot wounds."

Exactly what does this mean? At first, the phrase might not seem vague, but it is: Does "children" refer to minors—people younger than 18? This might seem plausible, but actually we rarely call 17–year-olds "children." I suspect that the connotation of "child" is mostly limited to younger people. Does it refer to 0–to–14–year-olds, a range that's commonly used in fatality statistics?[41] Does it refer to pre-teenagers?

In fact, it turns out that the article apparently refers to all 0–to–24–year-olds.[42] This is an outright error, since even the vague term "children" clearly can't mean that.

But even if "almost 1,000 children" referred to some more reasonable age range, the phrase is still vaguer than it should be. Instead of using the vague term "child," either use a more precise term (such as "minor") or indicate the age range, for instance "From 2004 to 2006, an average of 111 children age 0 to 17 per year died in the U.S. from unintentional gunshot wounds."[43] This is more informative, and thus more helpful to readers. It may help you yourself think through the matter more carefully. And it may make your article more credible, because it shows that you're a careful researcher who insists on precision.

Being more precise can also show you possible problems with your argument, and help you fix those problems. For instance, once you make explicit that you are talking about all people age 17 or younger, you should wonder: Why are you drawing the line at this age? Does this line fit with the general structure of your claim? For instance, if you're using the statistic as an argument for laws that require that guns be kept unloaded, would such a law affect accidents involving 17–year-olds the same way that it would affect accidents involving 7–year-olds? By using specific terms, you'll more clearly see the relationship between the evidence you're using and the argument you're making.

E. Try To Avoid Foreseeable Misunderstandings

Guns, one article says, "produce a toll of over 35,000 killed every year and hundreds of thousands more raped, robbed, and assaulted in firearms-related violence." Quick: About how many gun murders were there in 1995, the year that the author was likely talking about?

"Well," you might say, being a careful reader, "we don't know; the 35,000 might include manslaughter, too." You might even realize it includes accidents, though you may have been distracted from that by the context, which focuses on "violence" and crime. So how many gun murders, manslaughters, and accidental killings were there, put together?

The answer, it turns out, is 17,500. Why? Because 18,500 of the over 35,000 were suicides.[44]

Of course, some readers may believe that suicides should be considered on par with homicides or fatal accidents in determining the costs of gun possession—but others might not. The readers should make this decision for themselves, based on nonmisleading information. In the context of a sentence where the most explicit descriptions are of violent crime ("raped, robbed, and assaulted in firearms-related violence"), many readers will infer that the less explicitly defined term "killed" also refers to criminal killings. This is especially so because the typical reader will be reading the sentence quickly, rather than thinking closely about the various possible literal definitions of each word.

So when you write a sentence, think whether some readers may read it as making a different claim than the one you're trying to make. In particular, think about *what assumptions readers may make* based on the context, and make sure those aren't the wrong assumptions.

F. Understand Your Source

Carefully read the source on which you're relying, and understand how all its elements relate to each other. For instance, if you're relying on a statutory section, read the whole statute (or, for vast statutes like the Tax Code, at least all the related sections). Pay especially close attention to the sections containing the definitions, and to other generally applicable provisions that might shed light on the provision that you're considering.

Likewise, if you're looking at a statistical table, make sure you understand what the table discusses:

a.   what *time* the table covers (one year? ten?);

b.   what *geographical or jurisdictional areas* it covers (the whole country? some states? only those states that reported their results to the federal agency? only federal prosecutions?);

c.   what *events* the table covers (all homicides? only solved homicides? only murders?);

d. what *sources* the table relies on, and what inaccuracies there might be in those sources;

e. how various line items *relate to each other*.

Consider two examples:

1. Assume that an article says,

[T]he annual accidental death toll for handgun-related incidents is slightly under 200 ....

relying on National Safety Council's *Injury Facts* (2000) (1996 data), p. 17, which I reproduce below. (The actual article relied on an intermediate source.) What's wrong with the quote? The answer is on p. 360.

ALL DEATHS DUE TO INJURY, UNITED STATES, 1995–1997, Cont.

Type of Accident or Manner of Injury	1997a	1996	1995
Mechanical suffocation, E913	1,145	1,114	1,062
In bed or cradle, E913.0	236	219	207
By plastic bag, E913.1	44	40	37
Due to lack of air (in refrigerator, other enclosed space), E913.2	21	15	14
By falling earth (noncataclysmic cave-in), E913.3	54	57	59
Other and unspecified mechanical suffocation, E913.8, E913.9	790	783	745
Struck by falling object, E916	727	732	656
Struck against or by objects or persons, E917	247	171	198
Caught in or between objects, E918	85	71	90
Machinery, E919	1,055	926	986
Agricultural machines, E919.0	530	496	514
Lifting machines and appliances, E919.2	119	115	141
Earth moving, scraping, and other excavating machines, E919.7	85	73	106
Other, unspecified machinery, E919.1, E919.3–E919.6, E919.8, E919.9	321	242	225
Cutting or piercing instruments or objects, E920	104	97	118
Firearm missile, E922	981	1,134	1,225
Handgun, E922.0	161	187	233
Shotgun (automatic), E922.1	84	93	116
Hunting rifle, E922.2	65	50	64
Other and unspecified firearm missile, E922.3–E922.9	671	804	812
Explosive material, E923	149	130	170
Fireworks, E923.0	8	9	2
Explosive gases, E923.2	57	49	62
Other and unspecified explosive material, E923.1, E923.8, E923.9	84	72	106
Hot substance or object, corrosive material and steam, E924	111	104	97
Electric current, E925	488	482	559
Domestic wiring and appliances, E925.0	53	66	88
Generating plants, distribution stations, transmission lines, E925.1	139	135	158
Industrial wiring, appliances, and electrical machinery, E925.2	27	15	26
Other and unspecified electric current, E925.8, E925.9	269	266	287
Radiation, E926	0	0	0
Other and unspecified, E914, E915, E921, E927, E928	3,007	2,984	2,730
Late effects (deaths more than one year after accident), E929	1,204	1,126	1,091
Adverse effects of drugs in therapeutic use, E930–E949	248	253	206

2. The table on the next page, from the *Sourcebook of Criminal Justice Statistics*, seems to show that 69.4% of all sexual abuse offenses are committed by "Native Americans, Alaska Natives, Asians, and Pacific Islanders," who together make up 5% of the population.[45] What's the

explanation? The answer is on p. 360.

Table 5.25

Offenders sentenced in U.S. District Courts under the U.S. Sentencing Commission guidelines

By primary offense, sex, race, and ethnicity, fiscal year 1999

Primary offense	Sex					Race ethnicity							
	Total cases	Male		Female		Total cases	White		Black		Hispanic[a]		Other[b]	
		Number	Percent	Number	Percent		Number	Percent	Number	Percent	Number	Percent	Number	Percent
Total	55,388	46,841	84.6%	8,547	15.4%	54,394	16,728	30.8%	14,246	26.2%	21,231	39.0%	2,189	4.0%
Murder	108	95	88.0	13	12.0	103	29	28.2	18	17.5	17	16.5	39	37.9
Manslaughter	57	38	66.7	19	33.3	57	10	17.5	6	10.5	8	14.0	33	57.9
Kidnaping, hostage-taking	81	77	95.1	4	4.9	80	19	23.8	19	23.8	22	27.5	20	25.0
Sexual abuse	230	226	98.3	4	1.7	229	42	18.3	17	7.4	11	4.8	159	69.4
Assault	455	404	88.8	51	11.2	437	120	27.5	96	22.0	72	16.5	149	34.1
Robbery	1,790	1,638	91.5	152	8.5	1,771	732	41.3	852	48.1	138	7.8	49	2.8
Arson	82	79	96.3	3	3.7	82	60	73.2	10	12.2	3	3.7	9	11.0
Drug offenses														
Trafficking	21,993	18,992	86.4	3,001	13.6	21,780	5,311	24.4	6,743	31.0	9,345	42.9	381	1.7
Communication facility	397	320	80.6	77	19.4	395	120	30.4	137	34.7	130	32.9	8	2.0
Simple possession	689	565	82.0	124	18.0	612	275	44.9	171	27.9	146	23.9	20	3.3
Firearms	2,679	2,570	95.9	109	4.1	2,647	1,064	40.2	1,179	44.5	328	12.4	76	2.9
Burglary, breaking and entering	54	52	96.3	2	3.7	54	14	25.9	10	18.5	2	3.7	28	51.9
Auto theft	189	178	94.2	11	5.8	184	87	47.3	56	30.4	37	20.1	4	2.2
Larceny	2,082	1,322	63.5	760	36.5	1,977	981	49.6	705	35.7	170	8.6	121	6.1
Fraud	6,196	4,517	72.9	1,679	27.1	6,077	3,127	51.5	1,876	30.9	752	12.4	322	5.3
Embezzlement	959	386	40.3	573	59.8	939	519	55.3	272	29.0	80	8.5	68	7.2
Forgery, counterfeiting	1,295	1,008	77.8	287	22.2	1,287	526	40.9	533	41.4	167	13.0	61	4.7
Bribery	196	177	90.3	19	9.7	194	91	46.9	49	25.3	33	17.0	21	10.8
Tax	728	596	81.9	132	18.1	712	519	72.9	83	11.7	53	7.4	57	8.0
Money laundering	1,001	766	76.5	235	23.5	991	442	44.6	166	16.8	321	32.4	62	6.3
Racketeering, extortion	977	893	91.4	84	8.6	961	344	35.8	291	30.3	200	20.8	126	13.1
Gambling, lottery	136	124	91.2	12	8.8	136	112	82.4	6	4.4	5	3.7	13	9.6
Civil rights	81	73	90.1	8	9.9	78	52	66.7	16	20.5	10	12.8	0	X
Immigration	9,659	9,053	93.7	606	6.3	9,531	363	3.8	339	3.6	8,652	90.8	177	1.9
Pornography, prostitution	414	405	97.8	9	2.2	410	347	84.6	24	5.9	22	5.4	17	4.1
Prison offenses	299	270	90.3	29	9.7	289	101	34.9	107	37.0	75	26.0	6	2.1
Administration of justice offenses	866	631	72.9	235	27.1	840	350	41.7	182	21.7	271	32.3	37	4.4
Environmental, wildlife	211	195	92.4	16	7.8	205	160	78.0	6	2.9	24	11.7	15	7.3
National defense	20	17	85.0	3	15.0	20	15	75.0	0	X	2	10.0	3	15.0
Antitrust	44	42	95.5	2	4.5	43	37	86.0	2	4.7	1	2.3	3	7.0
Food and drug	78	67	85.9	11	14.1	76	48	63.2	12	15.8	9	11.8	7	9.2
Other	1,342	1,065	79.4	277	20.6	1,197	711	59.4	263	22.0	125	10.4	98	8.2

Note: The sentencing reform provisions of the Comprehensive Crime Control Act, Public Law No. 98-473 (1984), created the United States Sentencing Commission. The Commission's primary function is to develop and monitor sentencing policies and practices for the Federal courts. On Apr. 13, 1987, the Commission submitted initial Sentencing Guidelines and Policy Statements to Congress. The guidelines became effective on Nov. 1, 1987, and apply to all offenses committed on or after that date. These data are derived from the United States Sentencing Commission's fiscal year 1999 Offender Dataset. The Commission collected information on 55,557 cases sentenced under the Sentencing Reform Act (guideline cases) during fiscal year 1999 (Oct. 1, 1998 through Sept. 30, 1999). Given the nature of the data file and reporting requirements, the following types of cases are not included in the data presented here: cases initiated but for which no convictions were obtained, defendants convicted for whom no sentences were yet issued, defendants sentenced but for whom no data were submitted to the Commission, and cases not sentenced under the Sentencing Reform Act (non-guideline cases).

A case or defendant is defined as a single sentencing event for a single defendant (even if multiple indictments or multiple convictions are consolidated for sentencing).

Multiple defendants in a single sentencing event are treated as separate cases. If an individual defendant is sentenced more than once during the fiscal year, each sentencing event is identified as a separate case. (Source, p. A-4.)

Of the 55,557 guideline cases, some were excluded due to missing information. For sex, 169 cases were excluded due to one or both of the following conditions: missing primary offense category, 149; and missing gender information, 48. For race and ethnicity, 1,163 cases were excluded due to one or both of the following conditions: missing primary offense category, 149; and missing race or ethnicity information, 1,124.

Under drug offenses, "communication facility" refers to the use of a device, such as a telephone, in a drug trafficking offense.

[a] Includes both black and white Hispanics.

[b] Includes Native Americans, Alaska Natives, Asians, and Pacific Islanders.

Source: U.S. Sentencing Commission, *1999 Sourcebook of Federal Sentencing Statistics* (Washington, DC: U.S. Sentencing Commission, 2000), pp. 14, 15. Table adapted by SOURCEBOOK staff.

G. Handle Survey Evidence Correctly

1. What do surveys measure?

Survey evidence is often indispensable, and can be fairly reliable. But many surveys are conducted badly, and even well-conducted surveys are often misinterpreted as measuring things that they don't in fact measure. To avoid relying on bad surveys and misrepresenting good ones, we need to ask: What exactly do surveys measure?

Most precisely, surveys measure only what (1) the survey-takers recorded (2) these particular respondents (3) were willing to say (4) in response to the particular questions they were asked—not very useful. But it also turns out that surveys of a small group can reveal to us the likely answers of a larger group, if (and only if) the respondents are a large enough *randomly selected sample* of the broader group; and this can be far more useful, if it's done right. Understanding these limitations of surveys should help us identify several ways that one can err in using surveys, and thus help us figure out how to avoid such errors.

2. Errors in generalizing from the respondents to a broader group

a. Why proper sampling can yield generalizable survey results

Surveying a randomly selected sample of a group gives us results that are pretty generalizable to the whole group. And the survey's accuracy is closely related to the absolute number of people who are asked, not to what percentage of the broader group is surveyed.

That's why you can get a good sense of the views of 280 million Americans by asking even as few as 1000 people. With a randomly selected group of 1000 people, and results ranging from 50%–50% to 80%–20%, you generally get a "margin of error" of ±3%, which means that there's a 95% chance that the actual views of the population at large are within ±3% above or below the result you get from the survey: If the survey says that 42% of respondents say they believe something, there's a 95% chance that the actual number of people who would say they believed that is between 39% and 45%.* The margin of error ends up being

---

* Actually, the margin of error is $196\% \times \sqrt{r \times (1-r)/n}$, where r is the fraction of

roughly 100% divided by the square root of the sample size, so at 100 people the margin is ±10%, and at 2500, it's ±2%.

But—and here's the single most important thing you should remember about surveys—this only works if the respondents *are a randomly selected sample of the whole group*. If the respondents are not a randomly selected sample, or very close to it, then it is mathematically *impossible* to draw an inference from their responses to the likely responses of the whole group.

Unfortunately, several common sample selection techniques violate this assumption.

b. Bad samples: Biased samples

One of the great cautionary tales of survey-taking comes from the 1936 presidential election. The election was won in a 61%–37% landslide by Franklin Roosevelt over Alf Landon, but a vast (2-million-person) *Literary Digest* poll conducted in the weeks before the election showed Landon getting 55% of the vote and Roosevelt 41%.

Part of the problem was simple: The Literary Digest pollsters found people's addresses primarily from telephone books and automobile registration records—which means they disproportionately polled richer people. The views of these richer voters may have been quite unrepresentative of the views of all voters.[46]

c. Bad samples: convenience samples

A special case of the biased sample problem is the so-called "convenience sample"—a group of people chosen because they're convenient, such as a professor's freshman psychology students, or a group of pedestrians who pass by the street corner on which a survey-taker is standing. These samples are likewise wildly unrepresentative of the population as a whole: The respondents have a different level of education, they have jobs or interests that lead them to be in a particular place, they come disproportionately from a certain geographical area, and so on.

---

respondents who lean one way, and n is the number of respondents. Thus, if the split is 50–50, the result is $98\%/\sqrt{n}$; if it's 20–80, the result is $78.4\%/\sqrt{n}$ (because $196\% \times \sqrt{.2 \times .8} = .784$); if it's 10–90, the result is $58.8\%/\sqrt{n}$; and so on.

d. Bad samples: self-selected samples

The media often publish so-called "self-selected" surveys: For instance, *USA Weekend* once ran a reader poll which asked whether readers thought the nation would be safer if all law-abiding adults were entitled to get a license to carry a concealed weapon. It got 34,000 responses, of which 82% said "yes," a stunning majority in favor of gun decontrol.[47]

But this number is meaningless. First, this sample is obviously biased in one way: It measures only the views of USA Weekend readers. Beyond this, though, the survey doesn't even tell us what the average USA Weekend reader thought, because only a small and likely unrepresentative fraction of those readers responded. Who takes the time, effort, or money to answer one of these surveys? Likely the people who feel most strongly about the survey topic, and not just average newspaper readers. What's more, many activists tend to e-mail their friends about these polls, so groups that are particularly well-organized on the Internet can quickly swamp the poll results.

Note, incidentally, that the large size of the sample was irrelevant. If you get 34,000 self-selected responses, the result tells you nothing about the views of the larger group. But, if you select even 1000 people randomly from the country at large, you can get results that are accurate within a range of ±3% (if you do other things right).

e. Bad samples: mail-in samples or Internet samples

Most mail-in polls and virtually all Internet polls involve self-selected samples, since so few people tend to respond to them. This was another problem with the *Literary Digest* poll: Only 25% of the people who were sent surveys responded, and the respondents' views ended up being quite unrepresentative even of all those who got the surveys.[48]

A mail survey might be made valid, if the survey-takers follow up with all the people who didn't respond, and ultimately get a fairly high response rate. But it's virtually impossible to make a Web-based survey be valid.

f. What makes a sample sound

So which surveys are indeed valid? First, the survey-takers must try to reach a random sample of a broader group. Second, they must get responses from a majority of the people whom they're trying to reach, to avoid self-selection bias; the best surveys usually have response rates of 70% or above.* Third, they must have a large enough number of respondents to yield a fairly small margin of error: Remember that you'd need 1000 respondents for a ±3% margin, and having a mere 100 respondents will yield a ±10% margin, which is rarely accurate enough.

Most useful surveys involve either random-digit dialing of phone numbers or exit polls (though even exit polls have had serious problems). As I mentioned, the phrases "online survey" and "Internet poll" are almost sure signs of invalidity.

Note that it's especially hard to do surveys of relatively small subgroups of the population, such as Jews or Asians. There's no master list of Jews from which one can draw a random sample, so the best way to poll Jews is to choose a random sample of the population at large, ask respondents whether they are Jewish, and record the answers of the Jews separately from those of the non-Jews. But Jews only make up about 2% of the population, so to get a sample of even 400 people (enough for a ±5% margin of error) you'd need to call 20,000 people—an expensive undertaking.

Some sophisticated polling techniques might make the task more manageable, but it still wouldn't be easy; and, in addition, some respondents might not want to reveal their religion or ethnicity to a stranger. So most polls that purport to measure the views of small subgroups tend to have very high margins of error for those subgroups, even if they have a lower margin of error for the population as a whole.

3. Errors in generalizing from the question being asked

a. Surveys that ask a different question

A survey can *at best* measure people's views on the particular question that was asked; to accurately use a survey, you must therefore properly identify that question. Consider, for instance, how several newspaper and magazine articles summarized the First Amendment Center's *State of the First Amendment 2002* report; I quote one in particu-

---

* Technically, any response rate below 100% may skew the survey's results, since it may be that the nonrespondents have systematically different views from the respondents; but response rates of 70% are thought to be generally good enough, and ones of as low as 50% are often seen as passable.

lar:

> The First Amendment goes too far in guaranteeing free speech, say 49 percent of people polled by the First Amendment Center. The percentage of people who think speech protections are too robust is up some 10 points from 2001.

Seems pretty striking, no? But here's the question that the survey asked:

> The First Amendment became part of the U.S. Constitution more than 200 years ago. This is what it says: "Congress shall make no law respecting an establishment of religion or prohibiting the free exercise thereof; or abridging the freedom of speech, or of the press; or the right of the people peaceably to assemble, and to petition the government for a redress of grievances." Based on your own feelings about the First Amendment, please tell me whether you agree or disagree with the following statement: The First Amendment goes too far in the rights it guarantees.

This question thus did *not* measure people's attitudes towards "guaranteeing free speech," but rather people's attitudes towards the First Amendment as a whole, including the Religion Clauses. It's impossible to tell from this question how many of the 49% thought the speech protections went too far, and how many only thought this about one of the other protections.

And there's good reason to think that much less than 49% of respondents really thought that "speech protections are too robust." A later question in the survey asked people "Overall, do you think Americans have too much freedom to speak freely, too little freedom to speak freely, or is the amount of freedom to speak freely about right?"; only 10% said "too much" (67% said "about right," 21% said "too little," and 1% said they didn't know, or refused to answer). Moreover, some of the respondents were questioned in the days after a Ninth Circuit panel interpreted the Establishment Clause as forbidding schools from using the words "under God" in the Pledge of Allegiance, so it's likely that many respondents were more focused on the establishment of religion than on the freedom of speech. But even setting these speculations aside, saying that 49% of respondents believe that "[t]he First Amendment goes too far in guaranteeing free speech" is just a misreading of what the survey actually asked.

b. Surveys that ask ambiguous questions

If a survey asks questions that different people are likely to interpret differently, then it can't really measure anything in particular.

The *State of the First Amendment* survey, for instance, also asked the following:

> The U.S. Constitution protects certain rights, but not everyone considers each right important. I am going to read you some rights guaranteed by the U.S. Constitution. For each, please tell me how important it is that you have that right .... [H]ow important is it that you have the right to privacy?

81% of the respondents said this was essential, and 18% more said it was important; only 1% said it was not important.

Unfortunately, this tells us little about people's actual views. The hottest debates about the right to privacy are, of course, about abortion; but obviously many respondents did *not* interpret the right to privacy as covering abortion rights, since far more than 1% of the public believes that the Constitution should not be read as protecting abortion.

Some people must have thought that "the right to privacy" refers to something else—perhaps the right to be free from unreasonable searches and seizures, or the many other things that are sometimes referred to as "the right to privacy" (some of which are *limitations* on the First Amendment rights of the press). And we have no way of knowing how many people used each possible definition. So virtually everyone thinks that *something* called "the right to privacy" is important, but we don't know what they actually mean by that.

"The right to privacy" is a notoriously ill-defined phrase, but the same can happen with other questions. For instance, another question asked people:

> Many college and university professors currently have the academic freedom to take controversial stands in their classrooms and to publish controversial materials in books and journals. Would you favor or oppose restrictions on the academic freedom of professors to criticize government military policy during times of war?

41% favored such restrictions, and 56% opposed them.

Unfortunately, there are two questions combined into one here: whether *what professors say in class* should be restricted and whether *what professors publish outside class* should be restricted. (The courts certainly recognize them as different questions—the First Amendment right of public university professors to speak outside class is well-established, but there's a hot debate about whether they have similar rights inside class, especially when their speech is only tangentially related to the subject matter of the class.[49]) Some respondents may have

166

understood the question as focusing mainly on in-class speech. Others may have understood it as focusing mainly on books and articles. Others may have thought it focused on both, and took the same view as to both. Others may have thought it focused on both, and had no way of expressing their different views about both.

So it is a mistake to report, as some newspapers did, that "41 percent [of respondents] said university professors should be restricted from criticizing U.S. military policy during wartime." We don't know what fraction of the respondents actually thought professors should be restricted from criticizing U.S. military policy altogether, and what fraction thought only that professors should be restricted from using their classrooms to do so—a distinction that judges find significant, and that many readers might, too.

c. Get the text of the questionnaire

To avoid these problems, you should *get the text of the questions* used in any survey on which you want to rely. Many survey organizations release their questionnaires on the Web together with the results (though many media outlets don't fully quote this text); others will give you the questions if you ask them nicely. You should in turn include the text of the relevant question in either the body of the article or the footnotes, where you cite the survey.

If a survey organization refuses to release the questions, then you should be skeptical of the survey's accuracy. You probably shouldn't cite such a survey, and if you do, you should at least alert the reader that the organization refused to release the questions, and that the results of the survey are thus especially hard to evaluate.

4. Errors caused by ignoring information from the same survey

Surveys, especially sophisticated ones, often ask many questions and yield a great deal of information. If you use such a survey, it's your responsibility to make sure that you consider all this information, and not just the parts that seem to support your case. And if you rely on a secondary source that uses such a survey, it's your responsibility to make sure that the source has used the survey properly.

Let me return to the *State of the First Amendment* survey, and an article that summarizes it as follows:

Many Americans, spooked by the Sept. 11, 2001, terrorist attacks on their country, seem inclined to clamp down on First Amendment freedoms, especially freedom of the press ....

Each year, the First Amendment Center in Nashville, Tenn.—an independent affiliate of The Freedom Forum—conducts a survey of Americans' attitudes toward the First Amendment ....

Among the findings:

* About 49 percent said the First Amendment gives us too much freedom, up from 39 percent last year and 22 percent in 2000.

* The least popular First Amendment right is freedom of the press, with 42 percent saying the news media have too much freedom.

* More than 40 percent of those polled said newspapers should not be allowed to freely criticize the U.S. military's strategy and performance.

* About half said the American press has been too aggressive in asking government officials for information about the war on terrorism ....

Freedom of the press exists not only for the news media, but for the very public that it strives to serve. In times when our democratic form of government is under attack, we should fight even harder to preserve our freedoms.

A powerful assertion: People are afraid of terrorism, and they're taking this fear out on the press.

The facts, though, don't fully bear out this story. Here is the fraction of people who think "the press in America has too much freedom to do what it wants" (the 2001 survey was conducted before Sept. 11):

1997	Early 1999	Late 1999	2000	2001	2002
38%	53%	42%	51%	46%	42%

The margin of error is ±3%, so some of the fluctuations may be random, but there's no reason to think that the Sept. 2001 attacks caused *more* people to think the press has too much freedom; in fact, from 2000 to 2002, the fraction of people holding this view *declined* by a statistically significant margin. Likewise, here's the result of another question, which seems to reveal no statistically significant change in attitudes about media freedom from the pre-Sept. 2001 survey to the post-Sept. 2001 survey:

Some people believe that the media has too much freedom to publish whatever it wants. Others believe there is too much government censorship. Which of these beliefs lies closest to your own?

	2001	2002
Too much media freedom	41%	42%
Too much government censorship	36%	32%
Neither (volunteered)	12%	15%
Both (volunteered)	7%	8%
Don't know/refused	4%	4%

On balance, the rest of the survey likewise doesn't seem to show any material change in public attitudes after Sept. 11, 2001—most differences between the 2001 and 2002 numbers are statistically insignificant, and where the difference is significant, the 2002 numbers tend to be similar to numbers from some of the pre–2001 years. It's hard to explain these results as flowing from a fear of terrorism.

But in any event, those who want to make a case for the claim that "Many Americans, spooked by the Sept. 11, 2001, terrorist attacks ... seem inclined to clamp down on ... freedom of the press," need to confront all the data in the survey, and not just cite the few numbers that seem to support the claim.

5. Respondents giving incorrect answers to pollsters

Finally, all this assumes that the respondents answered the questions accurately. This assumption may be wrong for various reasons:

a. If the question asks about past events, some respondents might not have remembered the events well enough.

b. Some respondents might have concealed their past behavior (for instance, drug or gun use) because it's illegal or embarrassing.

c. Some respondents might have concealed their present views, for instance, views that they think might be seen by the survey-taker as racist or otherwise unpopular.

d. Some respondents might have been unwilling to admit their views even to themselves.

e. Some respondents might have misunderstood even carefully designed questions.

f. Some respondents might not have had firmly held views on the subject, but might have said whatever came to their minds just to avoid looking ignorant or apathetic, either to the survey-taker or to themselves.

Unfortunately, it's not easy to deal with these problems, which is why relying on surveys is risky (though sometimes unavoidable). If you think that a particular survey might yield unsound results because of these problems, look at a good textbook on survey evidence for more information on how serious these problems are likely to be.

6. An exercise

Here's an exercise, based on a graphic on the front page of the July 16, 2002 *USA Today*; the question refers to a Ninth Circuit case that concluded that the use of the words "under God" in the Pledge of Allegiance violates the Establishment Clause.

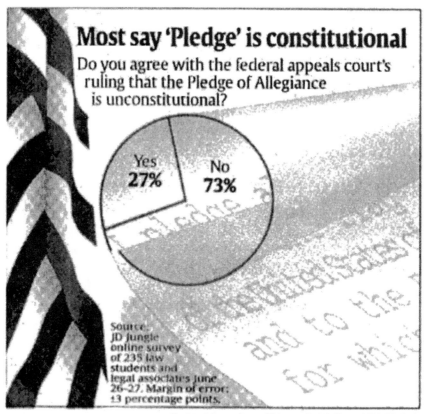

Most say 'Pledge' is constitutional

Do you agree with the federal appeals court's ruling that the Pledge of Allegiance is unconstitutional?

Yes
27%

No
73%

Source:
JD Jungle
online survey
of 235 law
students and
legal associates June
26–27. Margin of error:
±3 percentage points.

By Lori Joseph and Marcy E. Mullins, USA TODAY

There are at least four errors here (not all of them related just to the statistics); what are they? See p. 362 for the answer.

H. Be Explicit About Your Assumptions

Often, your evidence won't precisely match the claim you're making. You might be making a claim about what's happening now, but the available studies might only report what was happening five years ago. You might be making a claim about what's happening throughout the country, but the available studies might focus only on certain regions.

You might be making a claim about the crime rate, but the available studies might measure only the arrest rate. Riskiest of all, you might be arguing that some policy will lead to a certain result, but the studies might only say that when a similar policy was implemented, it was *followed* by that result. Such studies may merely reflect coincidence, rather than causation.

These gaps in the data need not be fatal to your argument. Most policy analysis requires inferring from correlation to causation, or extrapolating from one place, time, group, or variable to another.

But you *must be explicit about the inferences and extrapolations that you make*, and the assumptions on which they rest (for instance, that things haven't changed much from 1998 to 2004). Clearly acknowledge them, at least in the footnotes and, if they're important or controversial enough, in the text. And if it's not obvious that the inference or extrapolation is sound, you need to explain to the reader why it's sound.

There are three reasons why you must do this. First, you need to do this to be honest with your readers. If you say "Studies show that there *are* X contract killings in the country per year," and it turns out that the studies showed only that there *were* X contract killings in the country in 1980, then you're being inaccurate or even dishonest.

Second, you need to do it to maintain your credibility with your readers. Many readers will be savvy enough to notice any unspoken assumptions that you make. They won't be deceived by your silence—but they'll be annoyed, and they'll assume that you're sloppy, dishonest, or oblivious to the logical leaps that you're making.

Third, this explicitness will help you see and therefore correct the potential flaws in your article. When you make clear that you're only inferring or extrapolating something, you might think to yourself: "I wonder why this inference is sound." Perhaps it's not sound, and you need to find a more apt study, or to change or qualify your claim. Or perhaps it is sound, but you realize that you need to explain further why it's sound. In either case, you'll be able to make your article more well-reasoned and more persuasive.

1. Inferring from correlation to causation

"There are more guns in the U.S. than in England; there is also more murder in the U.S. than in England. Therefore, the prevalence of guns causes an increase in murder." This is an argument from *correlation* (the murder rate seems higher where gun ownership is higher) to *causation* (the higher murder rate is caused by higher gun ownership).

Here's another argument from correlation to causation: "There are more guns in rural areas in the United States than in urban areas; there is also less murder in rural areas than in urban areas. Therefore, the prevalence of guns causes a decrease in murder." The premises of both these arguments are true, but the conclusions can't be. This illustrates the danger of inferring causation from correlation.

For another illustration, consider ice cream production and rape in the United States. Within any particular year, the two are highly correlated: In 2000, for instance, the correlation was 0.84, which is very high (1 would be perfect correlation) and statistically significant; look how closely the two coincide on the graph below.[50] Does ice cream production cause rape? Does rape cause ice cream production?

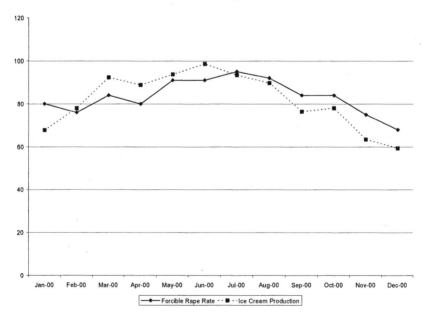

No, it seems more likely that some third factor (often called the "confounding factor") causes both. Here, the third factor is time of year: The rape rate is higher during the summer, probably partly because people are out in public more in the summer. Ice cream sales and therefore ice cream production are also higher during the summer.

We often have to act based on inferences from correlation to causation. Whenever a change in educational policy or policing policy, for instance, is followed by rising test scores or by falling crime, people naturally notice, and think about trying to repeat the experiment elsewhere. When they see the correlation in several places at several times, they reasonably infer that the change is probably good.

The inference may be far from certain, but this is the way practical reasoning necessarily works. It's how we run our daily lives, and it's how we often have to do policymaking as well. If you study statistical methods, you'll learn various ways of drawing such inference more reliably, through multiple regressions or other devices that can eliminate the effects of some obvious confounding factors (such as month, year, location, or other factors).

But for now, the important points are that (1) you must always understand when your sources infer from correlation to causation, and (2) *you must always make clear to your readers when you make such an inference yourself.* When you read a claim that "the tax cut caused economic growth," check: Does the author's data actually show causation, or only correlation (i.e., that the tax cut was followed by economic growth)? If so, then recognize that concluding that the tax cut actually caused growth requires an inference, one which may not be accurate.

And when you make a similar claim yourself, make clear that the tax cut was simply followed by economic growth. This should alert the reader that the data simply shows correlation and not causation. And it should also remind you of the same thing, and prompt you to explain why you think this particular correlation does indeed show that the tax cut did cause economic growth—rather than, for instance, coming when the economy was about to start growing in any event.

2.   Extrapolating across places, times, or populations

a.   Generally

People often draw inferences based on data from a different time, a different place, or a different population subgroup. Consider, for instance, the following table from the 1990 edition of a leading college textbook on sexuality, which reports that the median homosexual man has had 250–499 sexual partners in his lifetime:

TABLE 16–3

Sexual Partnerships Among Homosexuals

	Homosexual Males		Homosexual Females	
	White (N = 574)	Black (N = 111)	White (N = 227)	Black (N = 64)
Lifetime number of homosexual partners				
1	0%	0%	3%	5%
2	0	0	9	5
3–4	1	2	15	14
5–9	2	4	31	30
10–14	3	5	16	9
15–24	3	6	10	16
25–49	8	6	8	11
50–99	9	18	5	8
100–249	15	15	1	2
250–499	17	11	1	2
500–999	15	14	0	0
1000 or more	28	19	0	0
Proportion of partners who were strangers				
None	1%	5%	62%	56%
Half or less	20	43	32	38
More than half	79	51	6	6
Proportion of partners with whom sexual activity occurred only once				
None	1%	4%	38%	41%
Half or less	29	59	51	55
More than half	70	38	12	5

Source: Adapted from Alan P. Bell and Martin S. Weinberg, *Homosexualities*. Copyright © 1978 by Alan P. Bell and Martin S. Weinberg. Reprinted by permission of Simon & Schuster, Inc. and Mitchell Beazley Pub., Ltd., London.

Only if one looks closely at the source citation does one get the sense that the data is pretty old (the copyright date is 1978, though it turns out the study was conducted in 1970). And only if one actually goes to the Bell & Weinberg book does one see that it was conducted in only one city, San Francisco. The number of lifetime sexual partners that the median American homosexual man had in 1990, in the midst of the

AIDS epidemic, might well have been different from the number in 1970. Nor can one reliably generalize from San Francisco to other cities, where both sexual mores and the number of potential partners might be quite different.

As it happens, the most serious problem with the original study is that it was based on a largely self-selected sample, see Part XVII.G.2, p. 161, so it was an unreliable estimate even of the behavior of the median homosexual in 1970 San Francisco. The college textbook noted this limitation three pages before, but still prominently reported the data.

But even had the study been based on a representative sample of homosexual men in 1970 San Francisco, it may not have been representative of all homosexual American men in 1990. And the textbook erred in labeling the data as "Sexual Partnerships Among Homosexuals" generally, rather than "Sexual Partnerships Among a Self-Selected Sample of Homosexuals in 1970 San Francisco."

b. Extrapolating across places

So when you're reading a claim about the behavior of a large group, look closely at the data on which the claim rests. Is the data really about the large group as a whole? Or was it gathered only in one particular area?

Especially when the data is hard to gather—nationwide studies are often much more expensive and time-consuming than local studies—you should expect the data to be limited to one area. It's understandable that researchers would do that, but you should be cautious about generalizing from that one area to the country as a whole, at least unless several studies from several different areas report similar results.

Be similarly cautious when people draw inferences from the general to the specific, as well as from the specific to the general. Just as behavior in San Francisco may not tell you much about behavior in the U.S. as a whole, so behavior in the U.S. may not tell you much about behavior in San Francisco. If the median homosexual male in the U.S. has had 10 sexual partners in his life (that seems to be the best data that I've found, based on surveys conducted from 1991 to 2002*), it doesn't

---

* I derived these numbers from the General Social Survey datasets for 1991-2002. The GSS is generally seen as a well-conducted nationwide study, which isn't limited to one city and which involves a randomly selected sample (see Part XVII.G.2). I treated those respondents who reported having only same-sex partners in the last 5 years as ho-

follow that the median homosexual male in San Francisco has had the same number.

c. Extrapolating across time

Likewise, remember that most of the claims you read are based on data gathered at a particular time, often several years ago. Behavior patterns—sexual behavior patterns, crime rates, accident rates, and more—change over time. Inferring that a population is behaving the same now as it did ten or twenty years ago may be a mistake.

People have sex and commit crimes whatever the decade; but they may do it more in one decade and less in another. You may draw the inference that behavior today isn't materially different from what it was at some time in the past, but *make clear to your readers* that you're drawing this inference, and explain why it's sensible to draw it.

d. Extrapolating across populations

Finally, be especially cautious about inferences drawn from *one*

---

mosexuals, and those having only opposite-sex partners in the last 5 years as heterosexuals. Few respondents had both same-sex and opposite-sex partners in the last 5 years; their median sexual partner count was 12 (again, since age 18). People who reported not having had any sexual partners in the past 5 years were not included in my analysis. (Of course, this analysis is skewed by the likelihood that some respondents weren't entirely candid, but that's a problem with all surveys.)

The study discussed in Edward O. Laumann, John H. Gagnon, Robert T. Michael & Stuart Michaels, *The Social Organization of Sexuality: Sexual Practices in the United States* (1994), also appears to be well-conducted and reliable, but unfortunately the Laumann book gives the average sexual partner counts rather than medians, and averages are less helpful than medians because they can be skewed by the behavior of a small fraction of the population. (Remember that the median is the number for which half the data is above it and half is below, while the average is the sum of the data divided by the number of data points—for instance, the average of 1, 1, 2, 2, 3, 4, 5, 22, and 50 is 10, while the median is 3.)

The Laumann book reports that the average number of sexual partners since age 18 for heterosexual men, defined as those who have had only female sexual partners in the last 5 years, is 17, while the average for homosexual and bisexual men is 27 (with a substantial margin of error). Other definitions of sexual orientation yield results of 16 vs. 43, 16 vs. 44, and 17 vs. 30. *Id.* at 315. So the raw partner counts aren't really comparable to the GSS results, since one can't directly compare averages and medians, but the ratios of homosexuals' partner counts to heterosexuals' partner counts in the two studies are quite consistent: they range from 1.6 to 2.75. And the ratios are not consistent with the claims that the median male homosexual has 250+ lifetime sexual partners, or, as the material quoted in the text a few paragraphs below suggests, 1000+.

subgroup of the population to another, or to the population as a whole. Consider, for instance, this quote from a scholarly-seeming and heavily endnoted book; all the material in the quote, including the ellipses, appears literally in the book, though I've omitted the endnote calls (which refer to citations that appear at the end of the book):

> Research suggests there are qualitative and quantitative differences between patterns of homosexual and heterosexual activity. There is ample evidence homosexuals are likely to have significantly greater numbers of sexual partners than heterosexuals. Examples in the literature include studies showing "homosexual men ... reported a median of 1,160 lifetime sexual partners, compared with ... 40 for male heterosexual intravenous drug users"; "homosexual men had significantly more sexual partners in the preceding one month, six months, and lifetime (median 2, 9, and 200 partners, respectively), than the heterosexual subjects (median 1, 1, and 14 partners)"; and "homosexual patients are likely ... to have more partners ... than heterosexual patients."

It is common in the literature to find homosexuals reporting median lifetime numbers of partners in excess of 1,000. One study reported the "median number of lifetime sexual partners of the [more than] 4,000 [homosexual] respondents was 49.5. Many reported ranges of 300-400, and 272 individuals reported 'over 1,000' different lifetime partners." Another study reported:

> [h]eterosexual patients from all risk groups reported considerably fewer sexual partners than did homosexual men, both for the year before onset of illness and for lifetime.... Homosexuals had a median of 68 partners in the year before entering the study, compared to a median of 2 for heterosexuals.... Homosexuals in the study had a median of 1,160 lifetime partners, compare to a median of 41 for heterosexuals in the study.

In another study of 93 homosexuals, the "mean number of estimated lifetime sexual partners was 1,422 (median, 377, range, 15–7,000)."

Sounds pretty remarkable: More than 1000 sexual partners for the *median* homosexual man—even more than the textbook I quoted above reported—which is to say that half of all homosexual men have had more than 1000 sexual partners. Naturally, one can debate what the legal consequences of this should be. But if it's true, or even if the more modest estimates of 200 or 377 are accurate, then this suggests that most male homosexuals have vastly different sexual behaviors and sexual attitudes than heterosexuals. (This was probably the point the book was trying to make.)

But there's one problem: Every study (except one) that the book cited involved not randomly selected homosexual men, but men who were mostly or entirely drawn from samples of *sexually transmitted disease patients*, mostly patients with HIV. Most of the ellipses in the quote I give above (ellipses that were in the book itself) substitute for text that reveals this limitation in the data. For example, the source that the book quotes as saying "homosexual men ... reported a median of 1,160 lifetime sexual partners" actually said "homosexual men with AIDS reported a median of 1,160 lifetime sexual partners."

Of course, people with sexually transmitted diseases are the very population that's likely to have had disproportionately high numbers of sexual partners, since having many sexual partners dramatically increases one's chances of getting infected. (You can get HIV just from one partner, but you're much likelier to get it if you have had a thousand partners.) Data from this subgroup of people tells us next to nothing about the practices of the median homosexual man generally.

Imagine a study that found that "People who drink alcohol and are dying of liver disease reported drinking a median of 10 drinks a day, compared with 1 drink a day for people with hepatitis who are dying of liver disease." Would it be quite proper to report it as "People who drink alcohol ... reported drinking a median of 10 drinks a day, compared with 1 drink a day for people with hepatitis ...."?

The only cited study that tried to measure the behavior of male homosexuals generally is the one that yielded the lowest number, 49.5. Even this study, though, was conducted in the 1970s, before the AIDS epidemic hit; and it also involved a self-selected sample, which makes its results highly unreliable (see Part XVII.G.2, p. 161 for more on that). As I mentioned above, the best data that I've seen suggests that, as of 1991–2002, the median homosexual man in the U.S. has about 10 lifetime sexual partners, compared to 6 for the median heterosexual man— a nontrivial difference, but nothing like what the excerpt above reports.

So we see the danger of inferring from one population subgroup (American male homosexuals with sexually transmitted diseases) to another (American male homosexuals generally). And in this example the danger was exacerbated by the book's not admitting that it was drawing the inference: The book claimed that it was speaking about the broader group, while it was really speaking about the narrower one.

This shows the importance of what Part XXIII.A stressed—read, quote, and cite the original data, not just the intermediate source that reports on the data, even if the intermediate source looks like a scholarly work. It's tempting to just use the intermediate source's account, without checking the sources: For instance, the original sources cited by the book are in several medical journals that you'd have to get from another library. But if you relied on the book, your article would be badly wrong. You would be letting the book's errors become your errors.

And this again shows the importance of *making clear to your readers the inferences that you're drawing from the data*. Sometimes you do have to infer from one population to another: You can't infer from people with sexually transmitted diseases to people generally, but you might be able to draw inferences when the groups are more similar. But acknowledge to the readers that you are drawing such an inference, and explain why you think this inference is legitimate.

3. Inferring from one variable to another

Arguments often extrapolate from one variable to another. For instance, if you're trying to determine whether ice cream consumption is correlated to some variable, you might look at ice cream *production* data. Production data is apparently easier to get than sales data, and certainly than consumption data, since people don't report to the government every time they eat four ounces of ice cream.

You could try to get consumption data by surveying the public, but people may not know for sure just how much ice cream they've eaten, and might not be entirely candid even if they did know. So if you want to know how much ice cream people are eating, your best bet is probably to look at the production information. It's not perfect, but it probably isn't bad, and it's better than the alternatives.

But some such inferences are more dangerous. For instance, say you read in some article that there were 2.15 million burglaries in the U.S. in 2002. Sounds good, but of course you check the original source, rather than relying on the article—and it turns out the original source is FBI's Uniform Crime Reports, which reports information on burglaries *that were reported to the police*.[51]

Your intermediate source thus took one variable (burglaries reported to the police) and reported it as something else (burglaries actually committed). It seems likely, though, that only about two thirds of all burglaries are reported to the police. The National Crime Victimization Study, which is based on surveys of victims, rather on police data, reports an estimated 3.05 million burglaries in 2002.[52] Surveys, even ones conducted as well as the NCVS is, have their own problems; but they're probably more reliable measures of actual burglaries than the

UCR, which only measures reported burglaries. (The UCR is seen as a fairly reliable measure of *changes in crime rates* over time, because people assume that the underreporting rate will be fairly similar each year, though that may not always be an accurate assumption.)

So, when reading sources, look closely at exactly what variable the original study measured (for instance, ice cream production or reported burglaries), and be skeptical of inferences from that variable to any other variable (ice cream consumption or actual burglaries). Sometimes, you might need to draw that inference—sometimes, the variable you're looking for just isn't measured directly, so you must infer it from other measurements. But recognize that you are drawing that inference.

And again, when making such inferences yourself, *make clear to your readers* what variable the data actually measures, and explain why it's proper to infer that the variable you're interested in is really going to be roughly the same as the variable you're measuring.

4. A summary plus an exercise

A brief summary, through an example: Say you're arguing for a proposed federal law, and you cite a study showing that when a similar state law was enacted in Ohio in 1991, robbery arrests fell by 25% in the following year. When you make this argument, you're implicitly making three assumptions:

a. *The data is generalizable over time and space:* You're assuming that results from Ohio in 1991–92 are generalizable to the whole country in the years after the federal law would take effect. Differences among states and changes over time may make this assumption incorrect.

b. *The data shows causation and not just correlation:* You're assuming that arrests fell as a result of the law. That might be true, but it might be a coincidence: arrest rates might have fallen because crime rates were generally falling, or because some other crime-reducing measure was implemented at the same time.

c. *The data is generalizable from the measured variable to the important variable:* You're assuming that a decline in *arrests* reflects a decline in the crime rate, since presumably the goal of the law is to cut crime (the important variable), and not just to cut arrests (the measured variable). A declining arrest rate doesn't necessarily mean a declining crime rate: maybe there was a surge in some other kind of crime, which caused the police to pay less attention to this crime; maybe police practices changed in some other way; maybe the law discouraged people from reporting the crime. This assumption is easy to miss, because the two terms (arrest rate and crime rate) sound similar, though they're actually quite different.

Relying on such assumptions doesn't make your argument fallacious. You might have evidence that shows your assumptions are plausible; and in any event, we often have to make decisions based on hypotheses that are less than mathematically proven.

But you should make your assumptions explicit, and defend them explicitly, so the reader is persuaded that they're justified. You should certainly never hide them by misstatement—or let such common misstatements in others' articles dupe you.

To see these principles more clearly, try the following exercise: Assume that a study showed that 15% of New York drivers aged 16 to 25 drive drunk at least once a month. The Minnesota legislature is considering new penalties for drunk driving by 16–to–18–year-olds, and a commentator who supports the law writes "Drunk driving has reached epidemic proportion among teenagers, with 15% of driving-age teenagers driving drunk at least once a month." What errors or unstated assumptions can you find in this statement? See p. 363 for the answers.

I. Make Sure Your Comparisons Make Sense

People often use comparisons to draw inferences about causation ("women earn 72.3 percent of what men earn in median annual earnings," so we should infer that this roughly measures the amount of sex discrimination by employers) or about costs and benefits ("a gun in the home is 43 times more likely to kill its owner or a friend than an intruder," so we should infer that the costs of gun ownership for the owners exceed its benefits). Such comparisons are often valid steps in your argument, and can be quite effective rhetorically.

But many comparisons that sound good at first collapse on closer examination, either because they don't consider alternative explanations for the disparities, or because they don't sensibly quantify the costs and the benefits.

1. Consider alternative explanations for disparities

Consider one example, a concurrence in the Supreme Court case *Ring v. Arizona*, which argues that juries, not judges, should decide whether to impose the death penalty (an eminently plausible position, which ultimately got seven votes). The opinion summarizes arguments against the death penalty, and the second-to-last paragraph reads:

> Many communities may have accepted some or all of these claims [that reflect badly on the death penalty], for they do not impose capital sentences. See A Broken System, App. B, Table 11A (more than two-thirds of American counties have never imposed the death penalty since [the death penalty was reaffirmed to be constitutional in 1976] (2,064 out of 3,066), and only 3% of the Nation's counties account for 50% of the Nation's death sentences (92 out of 3,066)). Leaving questions of arbitrariness aside, this diversity argues strongly for procedures that will help assure that, in a particular case, the community indeed believes application of the death penalty is appropriate, not "cruel," "unusual," or otherwise unwarranted.

At the heart of the argument is a comparison—"only 3% of the Nation's counties account for 50% of the Nation's death sentences"—from which the opinion infers that there is a diversity of views about the death penalty.

But one can't simply infer from (1) some counties' imposing more death penalties than other counties to (2) the conclusion that those counties' citizens have different views on the death penalty, because there's an obvious alternative explanation: (3) the counties that impose few death penalties might simply have *few homicides.*

To begin with, many counties have much smaller *populations* than others; there would be few homicides in those counties for that reason alone. Beyond that, many places have lower *per-capita homicide rates* than others, another reason that those places might rarely impose the death penalty.

In fact, in the 3% of American counties that impose the 50% of the death sentences, there were a total of 142,228 homicides in 1973–1995 (according to the table that the opinion itself cites), and according to the Uniform Crime Reports, there were 487,590 total homicides in the U.S. during the same years.[53] Thus, the more accurate way of putting the point was that "The counties that account for 50% of the Nation's death sentences account for 29% [142,228/487,590] of the Nation's homicides"—a much less striking disparity than 50% to 3%.

Curiously, the table that the opinion cites actually lists the county-by-county differences in the death penalty verdicts as a fraction of all homicides. Those differences are indeed huge, ranging, among listed counties with more than 100 homicides, from 3.04/1000 to 128.44/1000, which does suggest that different communities have different views on when the death penalty is proper. (The homicides in the 3.04/1000 county might tend to be less heinous than the ones in the 128.44/1000 county, but that effect isn't likely to be large enough to explain the 40–fold difference in the death penalty imposition rate.)

The opinion's conclusion about the diversity in death penalty views is thus correct. But rather than relying on a comparison that strongly supported its thesis (the county-by-county disparity in death sentences per homicide), the opinion relied on a comparison that didn't support it (the county-by-county disparity in absolute numbers of death sentences).

2. Make sure that cost/benefit comparisons sensibly quantify costs and benefits

When you present a comparison as part of a cost-benefit analysis, make sure that the two sides of the comparison bear some proportion to the activity's true costs and benefits. Consider the statement that "a gun in the home is 43 times more likely to kill its owner or a friend than an intruder," used to support the assertion that "guns in the home, rather than providing protection and safety, actually increase the risk of injury and death to their owners." This claim is a technically fairly accurate summary of a study (albeit one that was limited to five years in one county) that "noted 43 suicides, criminal homicides, or accidental gunshot deaths involving a gun kept in the home for every case of homicide for self-protection."[54]

But while the statement is framed as a cost-benefit comparison, it mischaracterizes the benefit. The primary benefit of guns for "protection and safety" isn't killing intruders, but scaring them away; most defensive gun uses don't even involve the gun being shot, and only a tiny fraction involve an intruder being killed.[55]

The comparison between "likely to kill its owner or a friend" and "likely to kill ... an intruder" is thus unhelpful. It is so far removed from measuring the true benefits of gun ownership as well as the true costs—deaths aren't the only possible cost of gun misuse, and suicides (in the study, 37 of the 43 deaths per self-protective homicide) are, to many people, not equivalent to accidental deaths or criminal homicides—that it adds nearly nothing to the discussion. That it originally seems so telling only makes it more misleading.

3. Say how many cases the comparison is based on, and how small changes in selection may change the result

Imagine someone pointing out that "In the first ninety years of the 20th century, all major American wars began under Democratic presidents." This implicitly compares Democrats and Republicans, and implies that Democratic presidents are more warlike than Republicans.

This assertion (which I have heard in various versions) is potentially misleading in two ways. First, *the claim is based on four data points*: World War I, World War II, the Korean War, and the Vietnam War. It's hard to infer much from four data points, especially since there are so many other factors besides the President's party affiliation that can influence whether a country goes to war. If casual readers aren't explicitly told that the claim is based on just four items, they may miss this important limitation of the comparison.

Second, *if we broadened the sample by a few years* in both directions, we'd get the Spanish–American War (1898) and the Gulf War (1991), both started under Republican Presidents. This doesn't mean that Republicans were somehow more warlike before 1900 and after 1990—but it does show that the seeming pattern may be caused more by the arbitrarily chosen date range than by any genuine difference between the two groups being compared. A conscientious author should tell readers that the result might have been different if only the sample were defined a bit differently, and should explain just why the sample was chosen as it was.

Likewise, say that you're thinking about repeating the following claim (which I've often heard repeated) in your own work:

A BRIEF ASSESSMENT OF THE SUPREME COURT CASES ...

[A] study of the holdings in religion clause cases reveals far fewer victories for religious outgroups than the dominant story would lead one to expect .... As [an earlier article] has trenchantly noted, only Christians ever win free exercise cases. Members of small Christian sects sometimes win and sometimes lose free exercise claims, but non-Christians *never* win ....

By comparing Christians, who sometimes win free exercise claims, and non-Christians, who never do, this book excerpt seemingly implies that the Court or the Court's doctrine is somehow more hostile to non-Christians than to Christians.

As literally written, though, the statement "only Christians ever win free exercise cases" is incorrect. *Cruz v. Beto* (1972) upheld a Buddhist prison inmate's right to sue based on a prison's refusing to give him the same opportunity for religious worship as that given to Christian and Jewish inmates. *Church of the Lukumi Babalu Aye v. City of Hialeah* (1993) struck down a city ordinance that discriminated against practitioners of Santeria (an African religion mixed with "significant elements of Roman Catholicism," but one so distant from traditional American Christianity that it can't properly be called a "Christian sect[]"). *Torcaso v. Watkins* (1961) struck down a law that discriminated against atheists on the grounds that it violated the claimant's "freedom of belief and religion" and "religious freedom"; though the case talks both about the Establishment Clause and the Free Exercise Clause, it was largely a free exercise case, and has been cited as such in other leading free exercise cases.

Referring back to the article that the book cites helps explain matters: The article said "the pattern of the Court's results in *mandatory accommodation* cases is troubling because, put bluntly, the pattern is that sometimes Christians win but non-Christians never do" (emphasis added). Mandatory accommodation claims—claims that the government must exempt a religious observer from a generally applicable law—are· a subset of free exercise claims. The book mistakenly failed to limit its assertion to accommodation claims.

But even if you paraphrase the book's assertions to focus on mandatory accommodations, there would still be three important points that you should tell your readers.

1. *Tell the reader the size of your set of cases:* It turns out that only five Supreme Court mandatory accommodation claims have been won by the claimants, and these cases have involved only three different kinds of claims: (a) entitlement to unemployment benefits when a person was fired for observing his Sabbath (three of the five cases), (b) entitlement to unemployment benefits when a person was fired for a religiously motivated refusal to work in arms manufacturing, and (c) entitlement to an exemption from a compulsory education law.[56]

It's hard to infer much from a set this small—but if one wants readers to draw such an inference, one should acknowledge the size of the set, and explain why it's instructive despite its small size.

2. *Tell the reader how the result would have come out had the in-*

quiry been worded a bit differently: If we ask not who raised the claims in the five cases, but rather who practically benefited from those cases, we see that the holding of three of the five cases substantially (and perhaps primarily) benefited Jews, not just Christians. In 1963, when the first of these cases was decided, there were apparently under 350,000 American Christians who belonged to the prominent Saturday-observer denominations, but over 500,000 Orthodox Jews—the Jews most likely to observe the Sabbath—and 5 million more non-Orthodox Jews, some of whom may also have observed the Sabbath.[57] The exact numbers of likely claimants are unclear, but many Jews doubtless benefited. And the Justices must have realized this: One of the Justices who heard the first case was Jewish (Justice Goldberg), and just a few years earlier, the Court had dealt with a different kind of claim brought by Jewish Sabbatarians.

So it seems that the focus on the religion of these particular litigants is an arbitrary limitation: If we really want to see whether the Court is biased against non-Christians, we should consider which groups practically benefited from the decisions, and not just who the litigants were. But even if there is some justification for focusing on the particular litigants, this choice should be mentioned and defended (as the cited article, though not the citing book, does), and not just made silently.*

3. *More on telling the reader how the result would have come out had the inquiry been worded a bit differently:* Finally, the focus on the accommodation cases is itself an unexplained limitation of the sample. As we saw, to be literally accurate, your assertion would need to be not "only Christians ever win free exercise cases [in the Supreme Court]" but "only Christians ever win mandatory accommodation cases [in the Supreme Court]"—but the new assertion, while literally accurate, becomes accurate only by excluding *Cruz, Lukumi,* and *Torcaso.*

It's not clear that this exclusion is justified: If the Court were biased against non-Christians, one would expect the bias to show up in the non-accommodation cases as well as in the accommodation ones. But again, even if there's a good reason for treating accommodation cases as unusually probative of the Court's biases, the decision to focus on ac-

---

* Some might argue that Jews are an in-group in modern America, and that decisions benefiting them should be viewed the same way as decisions benefiting Christians. But that was certainly not the view of the book's author, as a discussion on the following page in the book made clear; and in any case, if that's your theory, your discussion should make that explicit.

186

commodation cases should be mentioned and defended.

So we can compare the original assertion that you might be tempted to make,

> [O]nly Christians ever win free exercise cases [before the Supreme Court]. Members of small Christian sects sometimes win and sometimes lose free exercise claims, but non-Christians never win.

to the more accurate, more informative, and less likely to mislead version:

> Only Christian claimants have ever won mandatory accommodation cases before the Supreme Court—five cases total, involving three different religious practices. Some of these cases have also benefited non-Christians who share the same practices (for instance, Jewish Sabbatarians), but the important point is that the particular claimants were Christian, because .... And some non-Christians have won religious freedom cases that didn't involve demands for mandatory accommodation, but the mandatory accommodation cases are the important ones, because ....

The first version is more rhetorically effective, and shorter, than the second. But if you were reading a work to learn about the Court and religious freedom, which of these formulations would you prefer as a reader?

4. Make sure your comparison at least shows correlation, even before you worry about whether it shows causation

Consider this item from a leading online magazine (emphasis added):

> The real obstacle to safety reform is that miners no longer have a powerful union sticking up for them. History shows that when miners have: 1) been organized and angry; and 2) had the strong national leadership of the United Mine Workers of America backing them up, they've been able to push for the legislative changes necessary for lasting advances in safety conditions. Sadly, neither of those two factors exist today. In fact, mining in the United States is only safer today than it has ever been because organized mine workers pushed hard for reforms a generation ago—reforms that are still in effect. Whether those reforms are enough is now in question. *The majority of mining deaths in the past few years have occurred in nonunion mines.*

The implication is pretty clear: the stated fact, "The majority of mining deaths in the past few years have occurred in nonunion mines," can only be relevant to imply causation—lack of unionization decreases safety.

But here's another fact, noted in the same item several paragraphs later: "Today, according to the union's own optimistic estimates, only about 30 percent of all mines are organized." This means nonunion mines make up at least about 70 percent of all mines. *Even if nonunion mines were just as safe as union mines*, it would make sense that 70 percent of all mines would account for "[t]he majority of mining deaths." The article didn't just fail to show that lack of unionization causes a decrease in safety; it even failed to show that lack of unionization is correlated with a decrease in safety.

Now it well may be that both correlation and causation are present. For instance, perhaps the 30% of all union-organized *mines* contain 80% of all *miners*, and yet account only for 25% of all mining deaths. Perhaps the unionization is the reason for the greater safety.

The trouble is that the magazine article did not show this. It gave only two pieces of data: Over 50% of mining deaths were in nonunion mines, and 70% of mines were nonunion mines. That doesn't support the author's conclusion that "The real obstacle to safety reform is that miners no longer have a powerful union sticking up for them."

5. Beware of "10% of all Xs are responsible for 25% of all Ys" comparisons

People commonly report that a few supposed bad actors are responsible for a disproportionate share of bad behavior. One unpublished paper I read, for instance, reported that 10% of all police officers in a department accounted for 25% of all abuse complaints, and used that as evidence that some police officers are especially prone to misbehavior.

But this data point, standing alone, *is entirely consistent with all police officers being equally prone to behave badly*. Even if all officers are equally likely to misbehave, and complaints are randomly distributed across all officers, we could easily see the 10%/25% distribution, or many other lopsided distributions.

Consider a boundary case: Say that each police officer has a 10% chance of being the subject of a complaint this year. Then, on average, 10% of all officers will yield 100% of this year's complaints. Yet by hypothesis all the officers are equally prone to having complaints filed against them.

Likewise, say that there is a 1% chance of a complaint against each police officer each year for 10 years, and the probabilities are independent from year to year (because complaints are entirely random, and all the officers are equally prone to them). Then, on average 9.5% ($1-0.99^{10}$) of all police officers will have 100% of the complaints over the 10 years, since 90.5% (0.99^{10}) of the officers will have no complaints.

Or say that each police officer has a 10% chance of having a complaint each year, and we're again looking at results over 10 years. Then 7% of all officers will have 3 or more complaints—but those 7% will account for 22.5% of all complaints.[*] Again, this is so even though each officer is equally likely to get a complaint in any year.

We can likewise see this statistical phenomenon in situations where there's no doubt that the distribution is random. Say, for instance, that you have 100 coins, each of which is 50% likely to turn up heads and tails. You toss each coin twice. On average,

    a.   25 of the coins will come up heads twice, accounting for 50 heads.

    b.   50 of the coins will come up heads once and tails once, accounting for 50 heads.

    c.   25 of the coins will come up tails twice, accounting for no heads.

This means that 25% of the coins (the ones in the first group) account for 50% of the heads—but because of randomness, not because some coins are more likely to turn up heads than others. The same would happen if you tossed 10,000 coins; this is not a problem that can be avoided by increasing the sample size.

Now of course some officers will indeed be more prone to complaints than others. And other kinds of data may indeed support the disproportionate-propensity conclusion. For instance, if nearly the same officers lead the complaint tallies each year, that's generally not consistent with a random distribution of complaints. (Though such a pattern wouldn't necessarily mean that those officers are bad, since perhaps they are just on especially complaint-prone beats, it would mean that complaints aren't randomly distributed among officers.)

But you can't just say "10% of all X's account for 25% of all Y's" in order to support the claim that those 10% have a disproportionate propensity to be Y. Such an inference is not sound, because these numbers can easily be reached even if everyone's propensity is equal.

---

[*] $\sum_{i=3}^{10} \binom{10}{i} 0.1^i 0.9^{10-i} = 0.07$, and $\sum_{i=3}^{10} \binom{10}{i} 0.1^i 0.9^{10-i} i = 0.225$.

J. A Source–Checking Exercise

The mistakes described above may seem obvious; but it's remarkably easy to make them. You can learn to avoid these mistakes by trying to spot them in others' articles, for example when you're cite-checking an article for your law journal. Start with the following exercise, drawn entirely from real articles. Do it yourself, and then check your conclusions against the answers on p. 364.

I'll begin with a paragraph from a student article in a Top 5 law review. Critically read it; assume that you are considering relying on it in an article you're writing, and are checking the original sources to make sure you won't embarrass yourself. I first noticed this article when a law professor relied on it in a talk he gave and in an article he wrote.

There are at least seven errors, of varying importance, in this excerpt. Go through the sources—source A and the other sources on which it relies—and try to find these errors.

The student article:

Proponents of manufacturers' liability further argue that handguns are almost useless for self-protection: a handgun is six times more likely to be used to kill a friend or relative than to repel a burglar, and a person who uses a handgun in self-defense is eight times more likely to be killed than one who quietly acquiesces. [Footnote cites source A.]

Source A (which was indeed written by a proponent of manufacturers' liability, so no need to check that), **quoted in relevant part**:

The handgun is of almost no utility in defending one's home against burglars. A Case Western Reserve University study showed that a handgun brought into the home for the purposes of self-protection is six times more likely to kill a relative or acquaintance than to repel a burglar. [Footnote cites source B.] .... The handgun is also of questionable utility in protecting against robbery, mugging or assault .... The element of surprise the robber has over his victim makes handguns ineffective against robbery .... A survey of Chicago robberies in 1975 revealed that, of those victims taking no resistance measures, the probability of death was 7.67 per 1000 robbery incidents, while the death rate among those taking self-protection measures was 64.29 per 1000 robbery incidents. [Footnote cites source C.] The victim was 8 times more likely to be killed when using a self-protective measure than not!

Although handguns possess little or no utility as self-protection devices, some may have a socially acceptable value when properly marketed under restricted guidelines [such as to the police].

Source B (the Case Western study), quoted in relevant part:

During the period surveyed in this study [1958–73 in Cuyahoga County, Ohio], only 23 burglars, robbers or intruders who were not relatives or acquaintances were killed by guns in the hands of persons who were protecting their homes. During this same interval, six times as many fatal firearm accidents occurred in the home.

Source C, the Chicago robbery study, quoted in relevant part:

Of those victims taking no resistance measures, the probability of death was 7.67 per 1000 robbery incidents, while the death rate among those taking self-protection measures was 64.29 per 1000 robbery incidents.

[accompanying table, with some percentages omitted for clarity:]

Method of Victim Self-Protection	Extent of Injury to Victim			
	Death	Injured	None	TOTAL
Physical force	7 (6.1%)	66	41	114
With Weapon Not a gun	0	1	4	5
Handgun	0	2	4	6
Verbal Denial of goods	2 (4.5%)	17	25	44
Verbal Shouting	2 (3.7%)	20	32	54
Flight	7 (18.9%)	10	20	37
Verbal or Phys. Resis. & Flight	0	7	13	20
Unknown	23 (79.3%)	3	3	29
None	7 (0.8%)	132	774	913
TOTAL	48 (3.9%)	258	916	1222

K. Summary

1. Find the original sources, rather than trusting what intermediate sources say about them. Don't rely on what a case, an article, or a reference work says about another case.

2. Be cautious about relying on what lawyers say about history, economics, and other disciplines (or on what nonlawyers say about law). Look at what the authors who work in those disciplines say.

3. Particularly distrust newspapers, and, in large measure, radio and television transcripts.

4. Use words and phrases carefully, making sure you use the precise term instead of false synonyms: Homicide doesn't equal murder, and foreign-born doesn't equal noncitizen.

5. Include the necessary qualifiers: There's a difference between shouting "fire" and falsely shouting "fire."

6. Use precise terms rather than vague ones: "Child" means different things to different people.

7. Carefully check any studies you use.

8. Be explicit about assumptions you make, such as assumptions of:

  a. *generalizability over time and space* (does a one-year study from one city generalize to the whole country today?),

  b. *causation* (did the study find that A caused B, or only that the two were correlated?), and

  c. generalizability from the measured variable to the important variable (do falling arrest rates really mean falling crime rates?).

9. Avoid language that seems likely to mislead some readers.

XVIII. Writing and Researching: Timeline and Summary

A. Budgeting Your Time

Students often find themselves running late on their papers, and as a result having to cut corners at the end of the semester. Try to avoid this by focusing up front on what you need to do, and when you need to finish it by.

Here's a sample plan and time-chart that you can use. (Some date boxes correspond to several steps, because those steps need to be done together.) Note that you should budget a *lot* of time—many weeks—for writing, and less time for research. The bulk of the work is always in the writing.

Step	Target Completion Date
Identify a problem to be solved	
Create the test suite that you can use to test your claim	
Research: Read the articles that bear on the problem, to get an idea of what your claim should be, and to make sure that there's still something novel left for you to say	
Research: Read the cases, statutes, studies, and other original materials that bear on the problem	
Update the test suite to reflect new aspects of the problem that you found in your research	
Come up with a tentative claim	
Apply the claim to the cases in your test suite	
Refine the claim in light of the test suite	
Repeat the preceding three steps until you're satisfied	
Write the introduction	
Write the short summary of the background law; if you prefer, save this until after you write the proof of your claim	

Write the section that proves your claim, starting with a zeroth draft	
Keep refining your claim as you write	
Write the conclusion	
Polish the writing and the structure (many editing passes)	
Rewrite the introduction to reflect the changes in your thinking, both about your claim and about how best to present it	
Hand in the first draft to your professor or to your law review Notes Department editor, and to any friends who have agreed to help you with it	
Wait for readers' comments; while you're waiting, polish the writing, structure, and substance on your own	
Fix the substantive problems identified by readers (likely to be many)	
Polish the writing and structure in response to the readers' comments (several editing passes)	
Hand in the second draft	
Wait for the readers' comments; while you're waiting, polish the writing, structure, and substance on your own	
Fix the substantive problems identified by readers	
Fix the footnotes, fill in the citations that you originally omitted, find sources that you haven't yet found, and generally fill in all the blanks that you saved for later	
Polish the writing and the structure in response to the readers' comments (several editing passes)	
Update the introduction to reflect further changes in your thinking	
Hand in the final draft	

B. Summary

1. Choose a topic

Choose an area that you find interesting, and that your faculty advisor thinks is a fertile ground for novel, nonobvious, and useful ideas. Find a problem in that area. Do research to learn more about the problem, and to figure out the possible solutions. Be open to switching to another problem if your research leads you to something more interesting or productive.

2. Make a claim

Figure out what claim you want to make—what you think is the best solution to your problem. Formulate it in one or two sentences. If your claim is prescriptive, design a test suite based on the factual scenarios that you've identified in your preliminary thinking, and refine the claim in light of what you learn from applying it to your test cases. Use the pointers in Part I to make the claim more novel, nonobvious, and useful.

Do your research (see Part VIII). Modify your claim in light of your research. Try to make your revised claim still more novel, nonobvious, and useful.

3. Write a first draft

Write an introduction. If you can't do that, you're probably not ready to write the draft—you're probably not yet sure what you want to say or how you want to say it. Look over Part III.A, p. 47, for some pointers.

When you're done with the introduction, write the rest of the article. In this phase, don't stop when you find yourself blocked on one section. Just get a draft out, even if it's rough and incomplete in spots. As you write, be open to revising your claim further.

Rewrite your introduction in light of what you've learned while writing the draft. Try to enrich your article by discussing connections to related issues.

4. Edit

Go through as many drafts as you can, polishing each paragraph, each sentence, and each word. Look over Parts XI through XV for some pointers.

Also go back over Parts I and V.F. Can you make the piece more novel, more nonobvious, and more useful? Can you tighten up its organization? Can you sell it better in your introduction? Can you add further interesting connections?

At some point in the editing process—preferably as early in the semester as possible—give a draft to your faculty advisor for comments. Also ask for comments from some friends whose judgment you trust. Don't wait on this until it's too late.

5. Publish and publicize

See Part XXIII.

6. Think about your next article

See Part XXIII.G.

XIX. A SAMPLE HIGHLY SUCCESSFUL STUDENT ARTICLE

In this Part, we'll spend some time looking at an excellent example of a student article, and seeing what makes it excellent. You are of course already overloaded with reading. But time spent closely examining someone else's successful project is likely to help you succeed with your own project.

The article I chose, *Smith and the Religious Freedom Restoration Act: An Iconoclastic Assessment*, 78 Va. L. Rev. 1407 (1992), has been exceptionally successful. It has been cited in other articles over 120 times. (Probably over 99.5% of all articles written by full-time law professors get fewer than 100 citations.) It has an excellent reputation among religious freedom scholars. And it likely helped its author, Jim Ryan, get a teaching job at the University of Virginia—when he was hired, this article plus one co-written article were Ryan's only published pieces.

The article's success also shows that a student note can be very influential even if it isn't published in Harvard, Yale, or Stanford. The *Virginia Law Review* is a great journal, in which I would always be happy to publish, but it is not seen as being at the very pinnacle of the law review hierarchy. The list of other student articles with more than 100 citations includes articles in the lead journals at Missouri, Hastings, Fordham, Minnesota, Vanderbilt, USC, UCLA, Penn, Michigan, and Columbia.

And the article offers lessons for all student articles, not just the extraordinarily successful ones. I chose Ryan's piece partly because of its stunning citation count. But a student work can be a great success even if it's only cited a few times, or if it's never cited but impresses those who might hire the author. The same things that make some works extraordinarily successful can make many more works highly successful.

So here's the article. The Ryan material—marked with a vertical bar in the left-hand margin—includes all the text, but to shorten the material I've removed the appendices, most of the footnotes, and some of the citations in the remaining footnotes. (This Part is not meant to teach proper footnoting; as you read the material, you can assume that all the assertions are well supported in the original.) I've also numbered the paragraphs, to make it easier to discuss them.

The material without the vertical bar is my running commentary on what makes various sections and passages effective, and (occasionally) how they might have been made still better. Despite my occasional criticisms, keep in mind that this is an excellent work, offered as a sample that you might want to emulate.

Let's start by reading the entire Introduction:

Smith and The Religious Freedom Restoration Act:
An Iconoclastic Assessment

James E. Ryan

INTRODUCTION

[¶ 1] As perhaps befits the subject, the nature of the academic discussion surrounding the Free Exercise Clause is largely just that: academic. Erudite and often esoteric, the discussion contains numerous theoretical expositions on the proper approach to the Free Exercise Clause, either alone or in tandem with the Establishment Clause. There are arguments on the proper relationship between government and religion, theories on how best to define religion, expositions of the history of the clause, and a recognition of the inability of courts and society to deal properly with adherents of minority religions. For all the discussion, however, very little attention is paid to the actual cases, save those that are decided in the United States Supreme Court. Even these cases often receive only scant recognition—the author pausing long enough to explain how and why the Court erred—on the way toward yet another theory of free exercise. Lower court cases, at either the appellate or trial level, are hardly mentioned at all.

[¶ 2] This inattention to how courts have actually been treating the free exercise claimant may explain why the reaction to *Employment Division v. Smith* has been so vehement. In that case the U.S. Supreme Court denied an exemption from Oregon's drug laws for the religious use of peyote by two members of the Native American Church. In so doing, the Court also altered the language of free exercise jurisprudence. Prior to that decision, the Court purported to grant extensive protection to religious liberty. The government could not pass or enforce a law that burdened the exercise of religion unless the law was the least restrictive means of attaining a compelling societal interest.

[¶ 3] In *Smith,* however, the Court abandoned the compelling interest test. By a 5-4 vote, (Justice Sandra Day O'Connor concurred on different grounds), the Court held that "the right of free exercise does not relieve an individual of the obligation to comply with a 'valid and neutral law of general applicability on the ground that the law proscribes (or prescribes) conduct that his religion prescribes (or proscribes)." Writing for four members of the majority, Justice Antonin Scalia made it clear that no longer can an "individual's religious beliefs excuse him from compliance with an otherwise valid law prohibiting conduct that the State is free to regulate."

[¶ 4] Members of the media, academics, members of Congress, and religious interest groups greeted the decision with condemnation and despair. A lead editorial in the *Los Angeles Times* denounced the decision as an exercise of "pure legal adventurism." Of the sixteen law review articles and notes written on the case, all but one condemned the result. Professors Edward M. Gaffney, Douglas Laycock and Michael W. McConnell described the decision as a "sweeping disaster for religious liberty." Congressman Stephen J. Solarz' reaction was even more dramatic: "With the stroke of a pen, the Supreme Court has virtually removed religious freedom from the Bill of Rights." Kim Yelton, director of government relations of Americans United for Separation of Church and State, concurred with Solarz' description: "There's really no such thing as free exercise (of religion) anymore ...." Finally, Rabbi David N. Saperstein called the decision "the most dangerous attack on our civil rights in this country since the Dred Scott decision in the 1850s declared that blacks were not fully human beings."

[¶ 5] Part of the hostility generated by *Smith* is attributable to the decision's poor craftsmanship. In its reliance on certain precedents[20] and its distinguishing of others,[21] the decision seems intellectually disingenuous. Indeed, even those who agree with the outcome in *Smith*

---

[20] For example, the Court relied upon *Minersville School Dist. v. Gobitis*, 310 U.S. 586, 595 (1940), which allowed the criminal prosecution of school children who refused to pledge allegiance to the flag. It failed to mention, however, that *Gobitis* was overturned three years after it was decided, by *West Virginia State Bd. of Educ. v. Barnette*, 319 U.S. 624 (1943). As one commentator noted, "[r]elying on *Gobitis* without mentioning *Barnette* is like relying on *Plessy v. Ferguson* without mentioning *Brown v. Board of Education*."

[21] The Court claimed that the seminal free exercise case of *Wisconsin v. Yoder*, 406 U.S. 205 (1972), which granted an exemption to Amish students from compulsory school laws, was decided not on free exercise grounds alone but in combination with the right of parents to direct their children's education. In the words of one who supported the outcome in *Smith*, the claim that *Yoder* "was decided on the basis of a 'hybrid' constitutional right ... is particularly illustrative of poetic license." Marshall, *supra* note 15, at 309 n.3. *See also* McConnell, *supra* note 15, at 1121 ("[T]he opinion in *Yoder* expressly stated that parents do *not* have the right to violate the compulsory education laws for nonreligious reasons.").

recognize that the Court's opinion "exhibits only a shallow understanding of free exercise jurisprudence and its use of precedent borders on fiction." The opinion is also a classic example of judicial overreaching: the holding goes beyond the facts of the case and the lower court's disposition of the issues involved. In the words, again, of one who supports the outcome, "it appears that the Court framed the free exercise issue in virtually the broadest terms possible in order to allow it to reach its landmark result."

[¶ 6] The Court's aggressiveness in reaching its result and its manipulation of precedent, although significant in themselves, only added salt to the serious wound apparently inflicted by the outcome of the case.[24] The fundamental problem of *Smith*, to most observers, is that the Court appears to have abandoned its traditional protection of religious liberty. In response to this perceived crisis, a large coalition of academics and religious groups petitioned the Court for a rehearing.

[¶ 7] When that effort failed, members in both the House of Representatives and the Senate introduced a Bill, entitled the Religious Freedom Restoration Act of 1990 (RFRA), designed essentially to reestablish the compelling interest test. The Bill is supported by a large bipartisan group within Congress, and by a diverse coalition of religious groups outside of Congress. Introduced last fall, the Bill initially seemed assured of quick passage. More pressing issues, however, have intervened and caused the Bill to stall in committee.

[¶ 8] This Note will depart from the traditional, theoretical approach to the Free Exercise Clause, and examine the lower court cases as well as the Supreme Court cases in which the clause has been invoked. In so doing, it will argue that enacting the RFRA in order to reestablish the compelling interest test is a largely futile endeavor. To be sure, the vehement reaction to *Smith* among academics and interest groups is understandable and justifiable. The decision is a regrettable departure from a doctrine that at least purported to value and protect religious liberty. Nevertheless, the current efforts to overturn that decision through passage of the RFRA are misguided. Despite the obvious change *Smith* brought to the language of free exercise doctrine, the impact of the decision on the outcome of free exercise cases will likely be insignificant.

---

[24] As Professor McConnell observed, the problems caused by the opinion's poor use of legal sources "are of lesser interest, for they might have been overcome (or at least mitigated) by writing the opinion in a different way."

[¶ 9] There are three reasons why this is so. The first and most obvious is the decision itself: it contains several caveats that can readily be used to limit the scope of the holding.[32] The second is that the free exercise claimant, both in the Supreme Court and the courts of appeals, rarely succeeded under the compelling interest test, despite some powerful claims. A survey of the decisions in the United States courts of appeals over the ten years preceding *Smith* reveals that, despite the apparent protection afforded claimants by the language of the compelling interest test, courts overwhelmingly sided with the government when applying that test.[33]

[¶ 10] Finally, *Smith* may have little lasting impact because religious groups experience relative success in the political arena. Exemptions for religious groups already exist in numerous state and federal statutes. Numerous religious antidiscrimination statutes are also already in place. Indeed, many of the "free exercise" cases in the courts of appeals involved determining whether a particular individual or religious group fit within an extant statutory exemption. To the extent that religious groups are able to form coalitions,[37] there is little reason to think that they will not continue to achieve political victories.

[¶ 11] In short, the evidence demonstrates that faith in the courts in this area is misplaced, and that religious groups and individuals fared better in the legislatures than in the courts before the *Smith* decision. Indeed, perhaps the most lasting and helpful legacy of the case will be that it finally dispelled the mistaken notion that courts were the leading institutional protectors of religious liberty.

[¶ 12] This Note will begin by briefly examining the rise and fall of the compelling interest test in the Supreme Court, and will demon-

---

[32] The majority opinion, for example, suggests that "hybrid" claims (such as a free exercise claim coupled with a free speech claim) will still be subject to the compelling interest test. For discussion of hybrid claims and further ways to limit the holding, see *infra* Part III.C.1.

[33] See Appendix B for a list of these cases, and see *infra* part II for a discussion. A ten year period was chosen, somewhat arbitrarily, in an attempt to ensure a significant and representative sample of cases. Although there have been federal appellate court decisions since *Smith*, this Note focuses on those prior to *Smith* in an effort to assess the importance of the compelling interest test. It would be impossible to make this assessment by looking at cases subsequent to *Smith* simply because that test is, in most cases, no longer being applied.

[37] The fact that such a diverse group coalesced in petitioning the Court for rehearing and in support of the RFRA suggests that religious groups can indeed bond together for political gain. For further discussion of this point, see *infra* Part III.C.4.

strate that the Court had begun to dismantle and disable that test almost immediately after it was established. Part II will discuss the free exercise claims brought in the U.S. courts of appeals in the ten years that preceded *Smith*. Dividing the cases into three categories—losing cases, winning cases, and prisoners' cases—this Section will attempt to discern why most cases were decided against claimants, and whether the few that were decided in their favor would be decided differently after *Smith*. Part III will discuss the Religious Freedom Restoration Act in the larger context of possible responses to *Smith* by those interested in preserving religious liberty. It will be suggested that of the various options available, ignoring the decision to the (not insignificant) extent that it can be ignored, while simultaneously focusing on the legislative arena to secure statutory protections, is the most promising. This Note will conclude by suggesting that religious groups pursue a strategy to secure broadly based exemptions within pending legislation and to then rely on the courts to recognize the inclusion of a particular individual or religious group within those exemptions. This strategy should ensure, to the maximum extent possible, the protection of minority as well as majority religious groups.

The most important component of any law review article is its claim. Ryan's article has been cited so often because his claim was novel, nonobvious, useful, and sound, and because it was seen that way by readers. Here is the claim, which appears in ¶ 8 through ¶ 10:

1. "A survey of the decisions in the United States courts of appeals over the ten years preceding *Smith* reveals that ... courts overwhelmingly sided with the government when applying that test."

2. "[E]nacting the RFRA in order to reestablish the compelling interest test is [therefore] a largely futile endeavor," especially given the limits on *Smith*'s holding set forth in *Smith* itself.

3. While religious claimants often lose in court, they "experience relative success in the political arena," especially through their ability "to form coalitions," so asking legislatures for specific statutory exemptions is likely to be a much more effective tactic than relying on a judicially enforced compelling interest test.

Why was this claim so effective? First, it ran contrary to established wisdom, and was therefore novel and nonobvious. This is what ¶ 1 to ¶ 7 of the Introduction aim to show.

Second, it was ambitious in scope: It dealt with an entire constitutional clause, the Free Exercise Clause, not just (say) the Free Exercise Clause analysis of drug laws or of some similar corner of the law.

Third, it dealt with an enduring problem: As the debate over *Smith* and RFRA illustrated at the time, the argument about the merits of judicially defined religious exemptions wasn't likely to go away. And the years since have shown that the debate indeed hasn't gone away.

Fourth, the article offered an answer based on a comprehensive dataset: not just a couple of court decisions picked because the author thought they were erroneous or otherwise especially interesting, but all 97 federal appellate decisions decided during the decade before *Smith*. This helped persuade readers that the author has really discovered something about the way federal courts generally behave in religious freedom cases, and not just about how a few courts have behaved.

Fifth, the answer was striking, as we'll see in more detail below: The results weren't just mixed, or less protective of religious freedom than one might expect, but extraordinarily unfavorable to religious exemption claims. As the article points out later, exactly *one* federal appellate decision would likely have come out differently under the *Smith* regime than it did under the pre-*Smith* regime. (This might have been worth mentioning in the Introduction.)

Sixth, the Introduction and the rest of the article set forth the claim in an effective style and tone. The writing is clear. It is light on rhetoric, and on abstract generalities, and heavy on the specific and concrete (whether it's talking about the cases, or giving examples of the position that it is rejecting).

It also has a confident scholarly tone. It sounds like something written by an expert on the field. In fact, it was written by an expert in the field: Even a second-year law student will become an expert on his chosen topic when he writes a law review article. But some student writers are unduly diffident, either in tone or in substance. This article, by contrast, is neither too aggressive nor too deferential—note, for instance, how it's willing to calmly and politely take on some of the giants in the field (see ¶ 4).

The Introduction might have been better still if it stated the claim near the front, perhaps along these lines:

> The Supreme Court's decision in *Employment Division v. Smith* has been sharply criticized by scholars, members of Congress, journalists, and religious interest groups. Professors Edward M. Gaffney, Douglas Laycock, and Michael W. McConnell, for instance, described the decision as a "sweeping disaster for religious liberty." Congressman

Stephen J. Solarz said that, "With the stroke of a pen, the Supreme Court has virtually removed religious freedom from the Bill of Rights."

And indeed *Smith* seemed to sharply reduce the scope of the Free Exercise Clause. The pre-*Smith* Court purported to grant extensive protection to religious liberty: The government could not pass or enforce a law that burdened the exercise of religion unless the law was the least restrictive means of attaining a compelling societal interest. But in *Smith*, the Court rejected that approach, holding that "the right of free exercise does not relieve an individual of the obligation to comply with a 'valid and neutral law of general applicability on the ground that the law proscribes (or prescribes) conduct that his religion prescribes (or proscribes).'"

This apparent shift led, among other things, to the introduction of the Religious Freedom Restoration Act of 1990 (RFRA), designed essentially to reestablish the compelling interest test. The Bill is supported by a large bipartisan group within Congress, and by a diverse coalition of religious groups outside of Congress.

This Note, though, will argue that enacting the RFRA in order to reestablish the compelling interest test is a largely futile endeavor. Despite the obvious change *Smith* brought to the language of free exercise doctrine, the impact of the decision on the outcome of free exercise cases will likely be insignificant.

First, free exercise claimants, both in the Supreme Court and the courts of appeals, rarely succeeded under the compelling interest test, despite some powerful claims. A survey of the decisions in the United States courts of appeals over the ten years preceding *Smith* reveals that, despite the apparent protection afforded claimants by the language of the compelling interest test, courts overwhelmingly sided with the government when applying that test. And all these victories except one came in cases that would have probably come out in the claimant's favor under *Smith*, because of the several caveats contained in *Smith* itself that can readily be used to limit the scope of its holding.

Second, religious groups experience relative success in the political arena. Exemptions for religious groups already exist in numerous state and federal statutes. Numerous religious antidiscrimination statutes are also already in place. Indeed, many of the "free exercise" cases in the courts of appeals involved determining whether a particular individual or religious group fit within an extant statutory exemption. To the extent that religious groups are able to form coalitions, there is little reason to think that they will not continue to achieve political victories....

In this version, the claim would begin in paragraph four, not paragraph eight. Readers would thus more quickly see the value added by the article; if the claim begins in paragraph eight, some busy readers might stop reading before then.

Still, the article's success shows that plenty of readers did stay until paragraph eight. And the way the author framed the Introduction does have a good deal going for it. The article mixed the "start with an argument or conventional wisdom you want to rebut" mode (see p. 58) and the "start with an explanation of the controversy" mode (see p. 55)—a good way to show the reader the importance of the issue, and the likely value of the future claim. And by showing that the article was arguing against the weight of conventional wisdom, the Introduction helped persuade the reader that reading the article would yield novel, nonobvious, and useful information.

I. Free Exercise Claims in the Supreme Court: A Brief Review

[¶ 13] It is widely recognized in academic literature that free exercise claimants, even prior to *Smith,* did not fare well in the Supreme Court. A sharp divergence existed between the apparent protection afforded by the compelling interest test and the actual success of the free exercise claimant.[39] In fact, since establishing the test in *Sherbert v. Verner*[40] in 1963, the Court rejected thirteen of the seventeen free exercise claims it heard. Moreover, three of the four victories involved unemployment compensation and thus were governed by the explicit precedent of *Sherbert.* In a sense, only one of the four winning cases, *Wisconsin v. Yoder,* can be considered a significant victory for religious liberty. Yet even the holding in *Yoder,* exempting Amish children from compulsory school attendance laws, seems limited to the facts of that case and the adherents of the Amish order.[44]

---

[39] *See, e.g.,* McConnell, *supra* note 15, at 1110. McConnell asserts that the "free exercise doctrine was more talk than substance. In its language, it was highly protective of religious liberty.... In practice, however, the Supreme Court only rarely sided with the free exercise claimant, despite some very powerful claims." *See also* Ira C. Lupu, *Where Rights Begin: The Problem of Burdens on the Free Exercise of Religion,* 102 Harv. L. Rev. 933 (1989). Lupu notes in this article that although the "constitutional standard can be quite protective of religion ... courts have not always employed the standard with full rigor."

[40] 374 U.S. 398 (1963). The case involved a free exercise claim brought by a Seventh-Day Adventist, who challenged South Carolina's refusal to grant her unemployment compensation after she was terminated from her job for refusing to work on Saturday, the day of her Sabbath.

[44] Justice Burger suggested as much when he remarked that "probably few other religious groups or sects could make" such a "convincing showing" that they were entitled to an exemption from compulsory school laws.

[¶ 14] In rejecting the majority of the free exercise claims it heard, the Court found either that the government had a compelling interest or that the free exercise right had not been burdened. In so finding, the Court simultaneously expanded what it considered to be a "compelling" governmental interest and narrowed what it considered to be a free exercise burden. While claiming that only interests of the "highest order" could justify a burden on religious liberty, the Court upheld state regulations that were justified by such interests as the uniform application of laws or administrative convenience. As commentators and federal judges have noted, and as Justice John Paul Stevens intimated in his concurrence in *United States v. Lee,* the Court's acceptance of such flimsy state rationales indicates that it was not applying a genuine "compelling" interest test.

[¶ 15] While relaxing its definition of "compelling," the Court restricted its definition of burden. Justice O'Connor, in *Lyng v. Northwest Indian Cemetery Protective Association,* provided the Court's most recent, and strictest, formulation of the term "burden." The case involved a challenge brought by Native Americans to the construction by the government of a road in a National Park through lands long used by several tribes for religious rituals. Despite noting that the "logging and road-building projects at issue in this case could have devastating effects on traditional Indian religious practices," Justice O'Connor concluded that the Indian's free exercise rights were not burdened. A burden on religion can only exist, she continued, if the government action has a "tendency to coerce individuals into acting contrary to their religious beliefs ...." As Professor Ira C. Lupu describes, this coercion theory of burdens creates a threshold requirement that few free exercise claimants could overcome.

[¶ 16] Thus, even prior to *Smith,* the free exercise claimant faced something of a Catch-22. In order to demonstrate a burden, the government involvement or interference with the adherent's religious practices had to be significant enough that it could potentially "coerce" the adherent to abandon her faith. Yet such extensive involvement or interference would almost always signify that the government had a compelling interest in the law or practice in question, particularly considering what constituted "compelling" in the Court's eyes. In other words, to show a burden was often to present simultaneously the government's compelling interest. Conversely, if the government's involvement or interference was not strong, i.e., its interest was not compelling, it was unlikely that a burden could be demonstrated.

[¶ 17] Seen in this light, *Smith,* in tandem with *Lyng,* simply made this Catch-22 explicit. After *Lyng* it seemed the only sure way of demonstrating a burden would be to show that the particular religious practice in question was criminally prohibited. *Smith,* however, holds that such prohibitions are, at least in some instances, immune from exemptions. Thus, at present the only certain way of proving a burden is also the surest way of ensuring that the free exercise claim will fail. In making this Catch-22 obvious, *Smith* in one sense achieved wholesale what the Court had already been doing retail.

[¶ 18] The *Smith* decision undoubtedly completed the Court's gutting of the Free Exercise clause, but it seems clear that the clause had already been hollowed by the Court before *Smith.* One wonders, then, why so many reacted with such alarm to the decision. The answer, at least in part, stems from a belief—shared by several scholars—that the clause was applied with more vitality in the lower courts.[56] This belief, however, at least with regard to the courts of appeals, is simply misplaced.

This section comes where a "background" section would often appear. And it does explain legal doctrines necessary to understanding the problem.

But it also starts the process of proving the claim: of showing that Free Exercise Clause claimants almost never won even before *Smith.* That's good; you should start proving your claim as quickly as you can. One way to do that is to work your claim into your discussion of the background facts and legal doctrines—of course, while still having your discussion be fair-minded and credible.

Note that this section is short, especially compared to the next one. That's also good: While the Supreme Court cases are important to the article's claim, the article's observations about them aren't that novel, at least to readers who are familiar with pre-*Smith* Free Exercise Clause law. The real value added by the article comes in the analysis of the appellate decisions; and that's where the article rightly spends most

---

[56] *See, e.g.,* McConnell, *supra* note 15, at 1110. Professor McConnell recognizes that the Supreme Court, after 1972, "rejected every claim requesting exemption from burdensome laws or policies to come before it except for those claims involving unemployment compensation, which were governed by clear precedent." Yet he argues that "[t]his did not mean that the compelling interest test was dead, however. There were many more applications of the doctrine in the state and lower federal courts ...." It is unclear whether McConnell equates applications with victories, and it is unfortunate that he fails to cite even one case in support of his assertion.

of its time.

II. Free Exercise Claims in the U.S. Courts of Appeals, 1980-1990

[¶ 19] The win-loss ratio of free exercise claims brought in the federal courts of appeals in the ten years preceding *Smith* is even more lopsided than that in Supreme Court cases. Of the ninety-seven claims brought, the courts of appeals rejected eighty-five. Although twelve successful claims out of ninety-seven is not an insignificant percentage, it will be demonstrated below that no more than one or two of these cases would likely come out differently after *Smith*. Five of the twelve would certainly come out the same, as these five were brought by prisoners, and the compelling interest test has rarely been applied in that context. Among the remaining seven, three involved intra-religious disputes, one involved a case of intentional discrimination, one involved an issue of whether a particular religious group fit within an existing statutory exemption, and one involved an issue of free speech as well as free exercise. None of these types of cases should be affected by the *Smith* ruling. In short, the evidence examined here suggests that the impact of *Smith* on the lower courts will be slight.[63]

The article is moving on to the federal appellate cases. This is a novel dataset, and an especially important one: Many readers know that religious exemption claims had mostly lost at the Supreme Court, but few readers had tracked such claims in the courts of appeals. This paragraph quickly summarizes the findings that are then discussed in detail in the rest of the section.

This is also where the article describes the scope of its dataset: Free Exercise Clause cases decided by the federal courts of appeals from 1980 to 1990. Many readers rightly want to know exactly how the dataset was chosen, and they'll be comforted to know that it was a broad set of cases, not a small subset cherry-picked for one or another likely result.

The dataset is also visibly limited: It excludes pre-1980 cases,

---

[63] Evidence gathered elsewhere demonstrates that the pattern of wins and losses described in this Note is replicated in cases brought in courts of appeals between 1944 and 1981. *See* E.E.O.C. v. Townley Eng'g & Mfg. Co., 859 F.2d 610, 625-29 (9th Cir. 1988) (Noonan, J., dissenting).

though footnote 63 points to an earlier source that does cover the earlier cases, and footnote 33 in the Introduction briefly explains that "A ten year period was chosen, somewhat arbitrarily, in an attempt to ensure a significant and representative sample of cases." The dataset excludes district court cases. And the dataset also excludes state cases.

These two latter exclusions in some measure undermine the article's claim that "the impact of [*Smith*] on the outcome of free exercise cases will likely be insignificant." True, district court decisions are less important than court of appeals decisions: District court decisions don't create binding precedent, and they don't have as much weight as appellate decisions do even as a matter of persuasive precedent. But district court decisions are of some importance, both as persuasive precedent and as a warning to prospective defendants. If a district court somewhere has held that there's a constitutional obligation to grant an exemption request, even faraway cities or states might conclude that it's safer to grant a similar exemption request, rather than to litigate and possibly lose.

State appellate decisions are even more significant: They are indeed binding precedent within the state, and are potentially quite persuasive outside it. And it turns out that religious exemption claims did better in state appellate courts than in federal appellate courts. Consider the claims that would be affected by *Smith*, because they didn't involve discriminatory laws, unemployment claims, hybrid rights, or prisoners: The article finds just one federal appellate victory from 1980 to 1990 among such claims (and, according to the footnote 63 source, none before 1980). But in state appellate courts, there were four victories from 1980 to 1990, plus eight before 1980.[58]

As it happens, religious claimants still had many more state-level defeats than state-level victories. And there may be good reason to treat state decisions differently. Among other things, state courts are free to grant exemptions under the Free Exercise Clauses of their own constitutions, even if such exemptions aren't required under the federal Free Exercise Clause; so *Smith*'s redefinition of the federal Free Exercise Clause may indeed have only a limited effect on state courts.* Nonethe-

---

* Consider, for instance, the eleven states in which state courts had accepted religious exemption claims under the Free Exercise Clause (see p. 382 n.58 in this book). In the years after *Smith* was decided, five of these states read their state constitutions' religious freedom provisions as applying something like pre-*Smith* strict scrutiny. Two more of the states might do so in the future, but have yet to consider the question post-*Smith*. Three more might have done so, but such a result became unnecessary when the state leg-

less, it would have been helpful for the article to include the state appellate cases, or to explicitly discuss and justify its decision not to mention those cases.

Yet again this is a suggestion for how an already excellent article could have been made even more useful. The article remains a great success despite this limitation.

A. The Losing Cases

[¶ 20] As described above, the Supreme Court rejected free exercise claims by fudging what it considered to be a "compelling interest" and what it considered to be a burden. So too did the courts of appeals, when confronted with serious claims. Courts of appeals readily accepted less than compelling government interests and were reluctant to consider some significant state intrusions as burdens on religious practices. The language of the compelling interest test, in other words, proved to be an easily surmountable obstacle to courts intent on rejecting free exercise claims, and the courts' application of that test often presented the claimant with the same Catch-22 described above.

1. Less Than Compelling Interests

[¶ 21] That courts were willing to accept government interests that hardly seemed compelling is well illustrated by the case of *United States v. Slabaugh*. A member of the Amish faith, who was indicted on one count of bribing a public official, objected to having his photograph taken on the ground that it violated his free exercise rights. The court accepted his belief as sincere, but nonetheless rejected his claim, stating that the photograph serves the "compelling" government interests of, first, protecting the public safety "by aiding law enforcement agencies in the identification and apprehension of fugitives" and, second, insuring "the proper supervision of individuals on probation."

[¶ 22] Although this holding appears reasonable on its face, the claimant in this case dressed and wore a beard in a manner unique to the Amish. The court acknowledged this fact, but dismissed it: "Al-

islatures enacted RFRA-like statutes. And only one of the eleven has expressly followed *Smith* as to its state constitution.

though Slabaugh's appearance is distinctive when he is compared with one who is not Amish, if Slabaugh were to surround himself with other Amish people, he would not stand out in the eye of a law enforcement official." Even this argument, though strained, seems plausible.

[¶ 23] But Mr. Slabaugh had only one arm! The government thus had to contend that a photograph of Mr. Slabaugh was the most effective way of identifying him, and that without it law enforcement officials would not be able to pick him out of a crowd. The court ostensibly ignored the fact that this argument was being made about a one-armed Amish man and accepted the government's contention completely: "A photograph of Slabaugh is the most effective solution to this problem," the court wrote, "especially if it becomes necessary for people who are not acquainted with him personally to search for him."

As Part IV.B suggested, you should usually *synthesize* the precedents, rather than summarizing each one; and when you do need to discuss the key precedents in more detail, you should use as little detail as possible. Avoid unnecessary procedural elements (for instance, who won at trial, if the key question is what legal rule was created on appeal). Avoid unnecessary facts. The reader wants to know what original contribution you're making, and what the existing legal rules are. The precedents are important only to the extent they are needed for the reader to grasp those things.

In this article, some discussion of the individual cases is necessary, because the article's original contribution lies precisely in the findings about the cases: The cases came out against the claimants, something that is relevant even now that the cases no longer illustrate the current legal rule (since *Smith* has rejected the cases' underlying analytical framework). Nonetheless, it's important to keep the case discussion tight.

The article does a good job of that. There's no unneeded procedural background. There's little superfluous factual background. (The article doesn't strictly need to mention that the Amish man was indicted for bribery, but the mention is short, and helps make the discussion more vivid.)

Instead, the article sets forth the essential facts of the case; the result; the relevant legal analysis; and then a concrete factual explanation of why the analysis is mistaken (¶¶ 22-23). As usual, it's the concrete factual explanation—such as the weakness of the government's "must have photograph" argument when the claimant has only one arm—that is especially vivid, memorable, and persuasive. (It might also have helped to point out that "has only one arm," while not a perfectly unique identifier, is probably more reliable than a photograph, given that many people look similar and that people's appearance often changes.)

[¶ 24] Although not as comical, a Tenth Circuit case illustrates a common tendency of courts to accept with little discussion or reasoning the government's apparently compelling interest. *In re Grand Jury Proceedings of Doe* involved a fifteen-year old Mormon boy who objected on religious grounds to testifying against his mother at a grand jury proceeding. After acknowledging that the child's belief was sincere, and that forcing him to testify would run "against the command of his deeply held religious beliefs," the court turned to the government's interest:

> [¶ 25] After an individual demonstrates that certain government action places a substantial burden on his religious practice, that burden must be balanced or weighed against the importance of the government's interest. In the instant case, the government has demonstrated a compelling interest in investigating offenses against the criminal laws of the United States. We hold that claimed First Amendment privileges asserted here are outweighed by the government's interest in investigating crimes and enforcing the criminal laws of the United States.

[¶ 26] The court's acceptance of the government's proferred interest in this case is instructive, and representative of a number of cases, in two ways. First, it is illustrative of how little some courts questioned the government's interest, and how quick they were to assume that such an interest existed and was compelling. Second, it demonstrates how courts in some cases did not even consider whether disallowing an exception to a government law or regulation was actually necessary to achieve the state's avowedly important interest. In other words, courts often failed to inquire whether denying an exemption was the least restrictive means of achieving the government's interest. Instead they simply focused on whether the particular law or policy, in general, represented a compelling government interest. Not surprisingly, they often found that it did.[74]

---

[74] Professor Marshall offers an explanation of why courts, in general, may be reluctant to confront whether denying a particular claimant an exemption is the least restrictive means. Marshall, *supra* note 15, at 312. He observes that the exemption balancing process, if undertaken, will normally underestimate the state's interest. "The state inter-

[¶ 27] For some courts the mere fact that a law or regulation existed sufficed to demonstrate a compelling state interest. In *Potter v. Murray City,* for example, the court revisited the issue of religiously motivated polygamy, decided first in the 1878 Supreme Court case of *Reynolds v. United States.* Assuring the claimant that *Reynolds* is still good law, the court rejected his claim that he should not be fired as a police officer for practicing polygamy, a practice that the court conceded was motivated by sincere religious convictions. Admitting that neither the Utah State Legislature nor the state defendants in the case had presented any empirical or sociological evidence that polygamy is harmful or that monogamy is superior, the court relied on the mere fact that the state prohibited it and that a number of civil laws in Utah assume a monogamous marriage. The court held that "beyond the declaration of policy and public interest implicit in the prohibition of polygamy under criminal sanction," the State of Utah had "established a vast and convoluted network of other laws clearly establishing its compelling state interest in and commitment to a system of domestic relations based exclusively upon the practice of monogamy as opposed to plural marriage." Needless to say, the court did not inquire whether forbidding an exemption to this particular claimant was crucial or even necessary to accomplishing the state's interest.[78]

Again the article mentions cases, but focuses just on what is necessary to support the article's claim, and then ties it directly to the claim. That's important: The cases aren't mentioned for their own sake, or

---

est in a challenged regulation will seldom be seriously threatened if only a few persons seek exemption from it. A legitimate state interest is often 'compelling' only in relation to cumulative concerns .... Weighing the state interest against a narrow class seeking exemption is similar to asking whether this particular straw is the one that breaks the camel's back." Courts of appeals in turn typically responded to this difficulty by not asking the question or by providing a brief, conclusory assertion that the state could achieve its compelling interest if an exemption were given.

[78] It is interesting in this respect to note the particular facts of this case. The plaintiff "made an undisputed showing that his two wives consented to the plural marriage, and that the wives and five children of the marriages receive love and adequate care and attention and do not want for any necessity of life." *Potter,* 760 F.2d at 1069. Granting an exemption to this plaintiff would necessarily open the courts to similar claims, but it would not necessarily result in further exemptions being granted. Future claimants may be unable to make the same showing as this plaintiff, namely, that his family is a caring and functional one, and courts could reject claims based on such a distinction. Denying an exemption to the plaintiff in *Potter* thus may be better understood as helpful to judicial economy and administration rather than as necessary to accomplish the state's general interest in preventing polygamy.

with an eye towards having readers draw their own conclusions from the cases. Rather, the cases are the evidence that supports the article's assertions.

Here the main assertion is the article's broader claim about how courts behave. In many other articles, the assertion is something about the scope of a background legal principle that the article will go on to critique, defend, explain, or otherwise use. But both kinds of articles need to be explicit about how the cases support the article's assertion.

2. Unbearable Burdens

[¶ 28] Before a claimant could have her free exercise claim examined under a "compelling interest" test, she had to demonstrate that her religious beliefs or practices had been burdened. As several cases illustrate, this was no easy task. Courts often required claimants, as did Justice O'Connor in *Lyng,* to prove that the state law or policy threatened to coerce them into abandoning their beliefs. Laws or policies that made religion more expensive, or more inconvenient,[83] under this approach, simply did not constitute burdens. Similarly, laws or policies that did not force the claimant to forego an "important" benefit in order to follow her religious dictates, were also not often considered burdens.

[¶ 29] In some cases, namely those involving Native American claims to particular religious sites, courts added an additional element to the burden inquiry: the claimants had to prove that the particular site was "central" or "indispensable" to their religious practices. Thus in *Wilson v. Block,* the court rejected an attempt by Navajo and Hopi tribes to halt the private development (into a ski resort) of government owned land. The court held that the tribes had failed to "demonstrate that the government land at issue is indispensable to some religious practice," and thus it did not even inquire into whether the government had a compelling interest in allowing the land to be developed privately. The court reached this conclusion despite the testimony of the then-chairman of the Hopi tribe, who stated that the contemplated development would "destroy our present way of life and culture," and that it

---

[83] *See, e.g.,* Smith v. Board of Educ., 844 F.2d 90 (2d Cir. 1988). In this case an orthodox Jewish student objected to his school's holding graduation ceremonies on Saturday, his Sabbath day. In rejecting his claim, the court held that "we believe that the burden being placed on David Smith's free exercise of his religious beliefs simply makes the practice of his religion more difficult than the practice of other religions but that it is not the type of burden on core religious freedom rising to the level of a violation of the free exercise clause."

would render "the basis of our existence as a society ... a mere fairy tale to our people."

[¶ 30] Regardless of one's opinion about how cases such as *Block* should ultimately be decided, the court's manipulation of the burden concept to reach its desired result is unmistakable. It suggests, as do the cases discussed in the previous section, that the apparent protection afforded by the free exercise clause was often only apparent. Again, the Catch-22 is clear. When faced with a meritorious claim in which the government's interest was not very compelling, courts often found that no burden existed. And when the burden was obvious, as when the practice was criminally prohibited, courts often relied on the cause of the burden itself to demonstrate the state's compelling interest.[89]

3. Possible Explanations

[¶ 31] Although their rejection of particular claims is sometimes difficult to justify, the courts' general reluctance to grant exemptions is somewhat understandable. One difficulty facing courts is that the constitutional balancing in the free exercise area is unlike that undertaken in other contexts. Often the law from which free exercise claimants seek exemption has a legitimate and compelling governmental purpose— unlike laws, for example, that intentionally discriminate against a particular class.

The most effective arguments tend to combine data with a theoretical explanation. The theoretical explanation helps persuade people that

---

[89] A brief comparison of two cases further illustrates this point. The first is the polygamy case, *Potter v. Murray City*, 760 F.2d 1065 (10th Cir. 1985), discussed *supra* notes 75-78 and accompanying text. As may be recalled, the state's compelling interest in that case was supplied primarily by the existence of criminal laws prohibiting polygamy. The second case is *Messiah Baptist Church v. County of Jefferson*, 859 F.2d 820 (10th Cir. 1988). In that case, members of the Baptist Church challenged the county zoning laws that forbade their building a church on a piece of land they owned. After making the questionable assertion that "the record contains no evidence that building a church or building a church on the particular site is intimately related to the religious tenets of the church," the court held that the claimants had failed to demonstrate how the zoning laws burdened their religious practices. This was not a case, after all "where the church must choose between *criminal penalties* ... and its religious benefits." One presumes that had it been such a case, the claimants would have succeeded in demonstrating a burden. Yet *Potter* demonstrates that the claimants would have also succeeded in demonstrating the state's compelling interest.

the pattern revealed by the data is likely to continue—here, that the pre-*Smith* results would likely endure even if *Smith* were reversed. And, rightly or wrongly, some lawyers and legal academics tend to be more impressed by authors who don't just rely on factual observations but also couple them with theoretical observations.

Here, and in the following paragraphs, the article begins to offer the theoretical explanation. The preceding sections weren't pure data; they provided some analysis of why the courts might have reached the results that they did, and such running analysis is helpful. But standing back and providing a broader analysis is helpful, too.

[¶ 32] The specific exemptions sought, moreover, present the court with a difficult dilemma. Although one or two exemptions to a law will rarely threaten the state's ability to achieve the legitimate purpose represented by that law, a large number of exemptions may very well pose such a threat. The state may thus simultaneously not have even a reasonable interest in denying a particular exemption to a certain law or regulation *and* a compelling interest in denying a large number of exemptions to that same law or regulation. To compensate for this latter possibility, courts seem to eschew the part of the compelling interest test that admonishes them to consider whether the denial of a particular exemption is the least restrictive means by which the state can achieve its interest. Instead they seem to consider the potential harm to the state's interest that would occur if a large number of exemptions to a law or regulation were granted.[91] Although it is understandable that courts consider the future ramifications of particular exemptions and particular decisions, in this context such a consideration nonetheless prevents a proper balancing of interests because it is often done sub rosa[92] and is based necessarily on conjecture rather than facts.

A quibble: Latin phrases such as "sub rosa" are probably best

---

[91] This is evidenced by the courts' weighing the state's interest in the entire law or regulation in question rather than weighing merely the state's interest in denying a particular exemption from that law. See *supra* notes 73-78 and accompanying text for examples of cases in which courts characterized the state's interest in the manner described here.

[92] This skewed balancing is done implicitly in the manner described in the preceding footnote. Why courts are not more forthright in their consideration of future claims when deciding particular cases may be due to the fact that the language of the compelling interest test seems to forbid such a consideration.

avoided, unless you're sure that nearly all your readers will understand them. (The article generally doesn't use such phrases; I suspect the phrase was just so familiar to the author that he didn't even realize that some people might not be familiar with it.)

[¶ 33] A second, related difficulty is illustrated by those claims that were of little merit. Of the federal appellate cases surveyed, some were simply obvious losers. Not included in this grouping, it should be noted, are cases involving religious beliefs that were somewhat incredible. This characterization includes only those cases in which, even assuming the claimant's beliefs were both sincere and valid, the claims presented were only remotely and tangentially related to religious beliefs.

[¶ 34] *Rushton v. Nebraska Public Power District* provides a good illustration of this tangential relationship. In that case, two public employees at a nuclear power plant, who refused to comply with the plant's drug-testing scheme and were therefore fired, brought a free exercise claim challenging their dismissal. The employees did not object to urinalysis per se, but rather to a policy statement concerning the drug-testing that described alcoholism as an "illness for which there is effective treatment and rehabilitation." Conservative Christians who believe alcohol is a sin rather than a disease, the employees argued that by submitting to drug-testing they would be giving tacit support to an heretical idea, and that they thus must be given an exemption from the program to preserve their right of free exercise. Although they recognized that the government has a compelling interest in ensuring that nuclear power plant workers are not under the influence of drugs, the employees argued that granting an exemption to them only would not present much of a safety risk. They argued that "there are numerous backup systems to prevent a release of radiation, so that it would be exceedingly difficult for a drug-impaired person to cause an accident."

[¶ 35] Not surprisingly, the *Rushton* court rejected this "novel" claim, in part because the government's interest was so strong and in part because the burden on the claimant's religion was so slight. Similarly, other courts of appeals have rejected equally spurious claims. Indeed, of the ninety-eight cases examined, at least fifteen were easy losers. Some of those cases, like *Rushton*, involved government actions or policies that imposed de minimis burdens on the claimant's religious practices. Others involved claims in which the particular activity the claimant wished to engage in could not be said to be motivated—or even encouraged—by the claimant's religious beliefs. Still others, finally, involved attempts by religious leaders to rely on the Free Exercise Clause as a shield against government investigations into their allegedly fraudulent activities. These religious leaders typically argued either that the investigation itself infringed on their religious rights, or that the dictates of their religion rendered their personal use of church finances legitimate. Both arguments failed.

[¶ 36] Although it is not particularly insightful to observe that some cases lost because they deserved to, it is an observation that is difficult to make in this context without appearing hostile to either the religious beliefs involved in the cases or to religion in general. This may explain why so little attention is focused on these cases, but it does not justify that inattention. These cases deserve to be discussed because they may help explain the general reluctance of courts to carve out exemptions from statutes based on the Free Exercise Clause.

[¶ 37] In this context, the slippery slope, or parade of potential horribles[105] argument is not raised out of desperation; it is an apparent and realistic possibility. As Professor Lupu notes: "Behind every free exercise claim is a spectral march; grant this one, a voice whispers to each judge, and you will be confronted with an endless chain of exemption demands from religious deviants of every stripe." Professor Lupu's sarcasm notwithstanding, the "spectral march" to which he refers is conjured up by the cases alluded to above. The mere existence of such cases may make courts hesitant to grant seemingly justified exemptions, for fear that they will be unable to limit those exemptions to sincere religious adherents or confine them to situations in which one's beliefs or religious exercise is seriously burdened.[107]

[¶ 38] In addition, these cases highlight a difficulty that seems to inhere in the Free Exercise Clause itself: it admits of no principled way to distinguish the meritorious claims from the fraudulent claims without questioning not only the sincerity but the validity of a claimant's religious beliefs.[108] If an exemption is granted to one religious group, for

---

[105] Justice O'Connor, in *Smith,* uses this phrase to describe the majority's litany of the potential consequences attending unlimited exemptions.

[107] This is not to say that the fear is justified. Whether it is or not, the point is that it may nonetheless exist.

[108] As Justice Scalia stated, in response to Justice O'Connor's "parade of horribles" comment, the purpose of his parade was:

> not to suggest that courts would necessarily permit harmful exemptions from these laws (though they might), but to suggest that courts would constantly be in the business of determining whether the "severe impact" of various laws on

example, it would be difficult to deny it to others who profess similar religious beliefs, without calling those beliefs directly into question. Courts are understandably reluctant to do this.[109] Granting very few exemptions, or none, can thus be seen as one easy way for courts to avoid even the possibility of having to undertake such a task.

[¶ 39] Finally, these cases support the assertion made below that many significant battles over the accommodation of religious beliefs have already been won, and won in the legislatures rather than the courts. The issues presented in these fifteen cases, as well as those presented in a substantial number of others, did not generally represent questions of fundamental importance either to the religion involved or to society in general. The claims were often tangentially related to the doctrines of the religion involved. Consider the religious interests represented in these cases: the claim of a Jewish policeman to arrest those who denigrate his religion; the right of a minister to be free from investigation into his alleged fraudulent television and radio fund drives; the right of draft-exempt theological students not to indicate that they are in fact exempt on financial aid forms; and the right of Conservative Christians not to submit to drug-testing for fear that their participation will offer tacit support to the idea that alcoholism is a disease rather than a sin. It would be difficult to characterize any of these

---

religious practice (to use Justice Blackmun's terminology) or the "constitutiona[l] significan[ce]" of the "burden on the particular plaintiffs" (to use Justice O'Connor's terminology) suffices to permit us to confer an exemption.

Justice Scalia's point seems to be that one reason courts should not be in the business of granting exemptions is because they would then constantly have to consider the merits not only of claims but of religious beliefs. Although Justice Scalia exaggerates the likely frequency of such claims, his recognition is a valid one: there is no principled way of determining ex ante whether a particular religion should be exempted from a particular statute. Considering the rather unprincipled and ad hoc nature of the cases already, one can understand a court's reluctance to create a precedent that could be used in a case of little or no merit. For in those cases, the holding would likely have to turn on the sincerity, centrality, or even validity of the beliefs in question.

[109] Justice Stevens, concurring in *Goldman v. Weinberger*, 475 U.S. 503 (1986), expressed this very concern in explaining why he did not rule in favor of Captain Goldman, who desired an exemption from Air Force dress regulations in order to wear his yarmulke:

The very strength of Captain Goldman's claim creates the danger that a similar claim on behalf of a Sikh or a Rastafarian might readily be dismissed as 'so extreme, so unusual, or so faddish an image that public confidence in his ability to perform his duties will be destroyed.' If exceptions from dress code regulations are to be granted ... inevitably the decisionmaker's evaluation of the character and the sincerity of the requester's faith—as well as the probable reaction of the majority to the favored treatment of a member of that faith—will play a critical part in the decision.

as important or far-reaching issues of religious liberty.

[¶ 40] This is not to say that the issues presented by these cases were not significant to those involved. But the fact that these were the issues being litigated—and not ones of more obvious and central importance to religious adherents—provides some insight into the adequacy of already existing protections afforded to religious belief and practice. Courts may have been presented with weak claims simply because the more important protections for religious adherents had already been secured elsewhere, namely in the legislature. Courts in turn may have rejected a significant number of free exercise cases not out of hostility toward particular religions or religion in general, but rather because a large number of these cases were of little merit and deserved to be rejected.[112]

Observe the tone of this passage (and of the article as a whole), and the messages it sends about the author and the author's credibility.

First, the article is willing to criticize influential people—judges, commentators, and legislators—without getting insulting or one-sided. The article is not friendly to the logic of *Smith*, for instance (see the Introduction), and in footnote 108 it notes that Justice Scalia's argument "exaggerates." But the article also points out the merits of Justice Scalia's argument as well as the weaknesses.

Second, the article makes clear that the author doubts the value of a broad reading of the Free Exercise Clause, but also that the author is not hostile to religion or to the claims of religious adherents: The article makes clear that there are serious arguments for religious exemptions, as well as serious arguments against having courts decide which exemptions should be mandated under the Free Exercise Clause. This makes it possible even for people who passionately support religious accommodations to be persuaded by the article's criticisms, and by the article's view that religious accommodations are best created through legislative decisionmaking about each proposed accommodation.

If an author thinks that religious accommodations are always unconstitutional or unwise, or that religious belief is harmful and should be accommodated as little as possible, the author should say so. Those

---

[112] As the prison cases demonstrate, courts are willing to protect religious liberty when necessary, i.e., when the political process does not. Thus, the argument being made is that courts do not appear protective of religious liberty because many of the most important protections have already been granted through legislation.

are perfectly legitimate positions to take.

But that's not what this author thinks, so it's important that readers (including readers who feel so strongly about such matters that they naturally fall into an us-vs.-them religious-rights-vs.-secularism mode) don't mistake the author's intentions. By having a measured tone, and by substantively acknowledging the value of religious exemptions while expressing skepticism of the value of broad Free Exercise Clause rights, the author maximizes the effectiveness of his argument.

B. The Winning Cases

[¶ 41] The losing claims just discussed demonstrate, implicitly, that the bulk of free exercise cases would come out no differently after *Smith*. They illustrate the courts' ability to manipulate the factors of the compelling interest test, and suggest some reasons why courts use that ability. In a sense, however, the most important cases to examine are those twelve in which the free exercise claimant won, for these are the cases that could potentially come out differently under a post-*Smith* analysis. These claims must be examined in order to assess the importance of the compelling interest test to the free exercise claimant and the dangers of abandoning such a test. The discussion of these twelve claims will be divided between those brought by non-prisoners and those brought by prisoners.

This section is especially important because it involves seeming counterexamples to the article's thesis. The article has to explain why the thesis is valid despite the counterexamples, while still dealing with the counterexamples accurately and fairly, and without appearing defensive. Observe closely how the article does this.

[¶ 42] Of the seven claims that won, and that were not brought by prisoners, three seem least likely to be affected by *Smith*. The first involved an instance of intentional and fairly blatant discrimination against a particular religion. In *Islamic Center of Mississippi, Inc. v. City of Starkville*, the Islamic Center challenged the City Board's refusal to grant it an exception to a zoning ordinance. The ordinance prohibited the use of buildings as churches on property located near the University of Mississippi. Twenty-five churches, all Christian, already occupied sites in the restricted area. The Islamic Center was the only church ever denied an exception, and the Board denied their request even though the building on property immediately adjacent to theirs was being used as a church.

[¶ 43] While recognizing the general validity of zoning ordinances as applied to churches, the court held that the City had failed to "act in a religiously neutral manner when it rejected an exception for the Islamic Center." In essence, the case involved the unfair and discriminatory treatment by a city government of a particular religion, and thus differed from a simple request for an exception to a generally applicable law. Even after *Smith,* as the Supreme Court intimated in that case, this type of claim would still be subject to strict scrutiny.

[¶ 44] The second case, *International Society for Krishna Consciousness, Inc. v. Barber,* involved a hybrid claim of free speech and free exercise. As already mentioned, such claims would still be subject to the compelling interest test after *Smith.* In *Smith,* the Court asserted that the only decisions in which it had held that the First Amendment required an exemption to a general law involved the Free Exercise Clause "in conjunction with other constitutional protections, such as freedom of speech and of the press." Whether one agrees with the accuracy of this characterization of precedent, it is nonetheless a clear statement that "hybrid" claims, such as the one in *Barber,* would still be analyzed under a compelling interest test.

[¶ 45] The third case involved a question of statutory interpretation, namely, whether a union member was entitled to withhold union dues because of his religious beliefs. Title VII of the Civil Rights Act of 1964 requires employers and labor organizations to "reasonably accommodate" employees' religious observances or practices, unless such accommodation would cause the employer or union undue hardship. The question in *Nottelson v. Smith Steel Workers D.A.L.U. 19806* was thus whether allowing the claimant to withhold dues would subject the union to undue hardship, and the court held that it would not. Although the claimant's argument was ultimately grounded in the Free Exercise Clause, the case turned primarily on an already existing statutory exemption. There is no indication in the language of *Smith* that the analysis of such questions should or will be any different after *Smith.*

[¶ 46] Another three of the seven cases stand a greater chance of being affected by *Smith,* although this possibility remains slight. Each of these cases involved intra-religious disputes. The first case involved a Jehovah's Witness who wished to bring a tort suit for emotional harm against members of her congregation, who "shunned" her in accordance with a religious practice akin to excommunication. The court held that the plaintiff's congregation could not be subject to suit for following the dictates of their religious beliefs, even if she had been emotionally harmed.

[¶ 47] The two other intra-religious dispute cases involved claims brought by potential pastors, both of whom were denied positions within their respective churches. The first was brought by a 63-year-old Methodist minister who alleged that he had been denied a "promotion" to a congregation more suited to his training and skills because of his age. He claimed that this denial violated the Age Discrimination in Employment Act (ADEA). The second case was brought by a woman denied a pastoral position in the Seventh-Day Adventist Church. She claimed that the denial constituted sexual discrimination, in violation of Title VII. The courts in each case refused to apply the relevant federal laws to these situations, stating that neither the courts nor the government should interfere with such church decisions. In essence, the courts exempted these personnel decisions from generally applicable federal employment laws.

[¶ 48] In the wake of *Smith,* it is possible that such exemptions would be disallowed, as that seems in keeping with the central holding of the case. There is language in *Smith,* however, that suggests otherwise. In listing what the Free Exercise Clause "obviously excludes," the Court recognized that the government may not "lend its power to one or the other side in controversies over religious authority or dogma." The Court essentially reaffirmed a general tradition, pointed to in these three cases, of abstaining from becoming embroiled in churches' internal decisions. Even if courts were to abandon this tradition, however, it is possible that the religious groups in these cases could present a hybrid claim, combining their free exercise rights with a freedom of association claim. That this particular hybrid would be subject to a compelling interest test is specifically suggested by Justice Scalia in *Smith.*

[¶ 49] The last of these seven cases seems most likely in danger of coming out differently under a post-*Smith* analysis. In *Quaring v. Peterson,* the court held that Nebraska could not deny Ms. Quaring an exemption to its requirement that all driver's licenses contain a photograph of the driver. Such a requirement, the court held, unduly burdened Ms. Quaring's sincere religious beliefs, and was not justified by a compelling state interest. Based on the analysis of the application of the strict scrutiny test in the losing cases, the outcome of this case, which was affirmed by an equally divided Supreme Court without opinion,[145] using the *Smith* rational basis test, would most likely be different.

[¶ 50] It is important to note, however, that a state court heard the same claim in a different case and reached a different result, holding that the state had a compelling interest in preventing such exemptions. Interestingly, one of the judges in *Quaring* dissented along grounds similar to those expressed in this state case. These differing results illustrate that the one case that could come out differently after *Smith,* could—and did—come out differently before *Smith,* depending solely on the court in which the case was brought. Finally, these differing results reinforce the assertion that the compelling interest test, at best, offered the religious claimant unreliable protection.

As I mentioned above, this subsection and the following one are especially important, because they deal with what seem like counterexamples to the article's claim. Observe how the subsection operates.

In ¶ 42 to ¶ 45, the article deals with cases that fit squarely within those zones that *Smith* itself said should still be judged under strict scrutiny. The subsection explains why this is so, why therefore these cases wouldn't actually be affected by *Smith,* and why the article's claim (*Smith* doesn't really change much) isn't undermined by these cases.

In ¶ 46 to ¶ 48, the article deals with the religious organization cases, which less clearly fit within the exceptions set forth by *Smith*; but it points to specific language in *Smith* that could be read—and, the article argues, likely would be read—as covering such cases. At the same time, the article doesn't overstate its argument: It acknowledges that these cases "stand a greater chance of being affected by *Smith,*" though "this possibility remains slight." The caution about these assertions makes the article more credible when it makes more confident assertions. (My sense, by the way, is that this prediction by the article has been proved correct: Religious organizations have generally been winning such claims since *Smith,* for reasons similar to those the article suggests.)

Finally, ¶ 49 and ¶ 50 deal with a case that clearly would come out differently under *Smith*. But even there, the article gives concrete factual details that suggest *Smith* might not change much: 4 out of 8 Jus-

---

[145] Jensen v. Quaring, 472 U.S. 478 (1985) (per curiam). That four Justices were willing to deny even this claim speaks volumes of the weak protection afforded by the compelling interest test.

tices deciding the case at the Supreme Court level, 1 one out of 3 judges deciding the case at the Court of Appeals level, and 1 one out of the 2 courts deciding this issue would have decided against the claimant even before *Smith*.

C. The Prisoners' Cases

[¶ 51] The five successful free exercise claims brought by prisoners were, save one, all judged under a less exacting standard than the compelling interest test. Moreover, the one case judged under a compelling interest test involved a claim similar to one successfully made by another prisoner in a case analyzed under a "reasonableness" test. Other tests applied by the courts varied from rational basis to intermediate scrutiny.[154] The immediate significance of these cases lies in the fact that prisoner claims had always been, and still are, adjudged under a distinct standard, and thus will not be affected by *Smith*. The larger significance of these cases lies in the irony that of the few successful free exercise claims brought, nearly half were decided under a standard offering apparently less protection to the religious adherent than the compelling interest test. These cases suggest that it may be the claim itself, rather than the test applied, that is most determinative of success or failure.

[¶ 52] The claims brought by prisoners involved fairly fundamental civil liberties. Two involved the right to govern one's appearance (specif-

---

[154] ... Prior to the 1987 case of *O'Lone v. Estate of Shabazz*, 482 U.S. 342 (1987), courts of appeals varied in the standards they applied to prisoners' free exercise claims, as is apparent from the six cases discussed here. See Matthew P. Blischak, Note, *O'Lone v. Estate of Shabazz: The State of Prisoners' Religious Free Exercise Rights*, 37 Am. U. L. Rev. 453, 467-70 (1988), for a general discussion of the different standards employed. In *O'Lone*, the Supreme Court dispelled the confusion among the lower courts and held that valid prison regulations that infringe upon inmates' free exercise of religion must "reasonably relate[] to legitimate penological interests." Thus a rational basis test is now to be applied, by all courts, in assessing such claims.

One prisoner case was originally decided prior to *O'Lone* and applied strict scrutiny to uphold an inmate's free exercise claim challenging the prison's hair length requirement. The Supreme Court vacated and remanded the case in light of *O'Lone*, and the Second Circuit reheard the case, now applying the prison context equivalent of the rational basis test. Upon rehearing, the court struck down the inmate's claim, finding that the prison had many legitimate penological goals in regulating beard length. This case demonstrates the fact that even in the prison context free exercise claims are not strongly protected by the courts.

ically hair length) in accordance with one's religious dictates. Two involved the right to receive religious literature, and one involved the right to legal recognition of a name changed because of religious conversion. It is instructive to contrast the nature of these claims with the nature of those brought outside of the prison context. It seems fairly clear that claims brought by prisoners, on the whole, concern rights and infringements of a more basic and fundamental nature than those brought by non-prisoners.[160]

[¶ 53] It is difficult, if not impossible, to imagine a legislature ever attempting to limit the public's religious rights in the same manner that the prisoners' rights in these cases were limited. The greater restrictions placed on prisoners are, no doubt, in part due to the unique nature of prisons and the greater need for control in such a setting. But the restrictions may also be due to the fact that prisoners cannot rely on the political process for protection of their rights and liberties, whereas those outside of prison can. Prisoners' liberties are subject to the control of persons over whom they have no influence or control. If this distinction is a significant one, which it seems to be, the prisoner cases help demonstrate—by contrast—how much protection the public receives from the political process. In other words, one reason those outside of prison are not litigating issues involving restrictions on such basic liberties may be because they do not have to—their basic liberties, unlike the prisoners', have already been secured.

[¶ 54] These cases also demonstrate that courts are willing and able, regardless of the standard being employed, to protect the basic religious freedoms of those utterly unable to rely on the political process for redress and protection. By contrast, the courts seem much more reluctant—as the eighty-five losing cases demonstrate—to assist those who can participate in the political process. Whether such a reluctance is justified or is detrimental depends, to a large degree, on how well the political process protects religious liberty, particularly the liberty of those adhering to minority faiths. It is to this general subject that this Note now turns.

---

[160] All of the prisoners' cases, for instance, involved outright prohibitions of the practices sought to be followed. Although some non-prisoner cases involved religious practices that had been criminally proscribed, these were certainly the exception. Although it is difficult to compare the "fundamentalness" of civil liberties, it seems fair to say that even those cases that did involve criminal prohibitions did not involve the deprivation of basic personal liberties to the degree evident in the prisoners' cases.

Dealing with potential counterexamples is such an important topic that it's worth discussing again here. Five of the successful Free Exercise Clause claims involved prisoners' rights. The reader might well assume that, if anything, this means the courts would have provided even stronger Free Exercise Clause protection for claims brought by law-abiding citizens. The five cases therefore look at first like an important rebuttal to the article's thesis.

The article responds in three ways.

1. The article points out that, doctrinally, prisoner Free Exercise Clause cases have been treated differently from nonprisoner cases (at least since *O'Lone*). That's potentially helpful: If the Court treats the two categories of cases radically differently, this treatment suggests that the categories are indeed importantly different, and that therefore it makes sense for scholars to treat the categories differently.

But standing alone, the doctrinal argument is limited. As noted above, the reader might infer that the difference cuts in the direction of concluding that the courts are interpreting the Free Exercise Clause quite forcefully—if even prisoners win their religious freedom claims, the reader might think, then surely ordinary citizens would, too.

2. So to dispel this possible impression, the article points to the facts of the cases: The prisoner victories involved restrictions that are much more serious than the restrictions under which free citizens labor. It may well be, then, that the prisoner victories shouldn't be counted alongside the nonprisoner victories (or perhaps just the one nonprisoner victory) in evaluating the protectiveness of the pre-*Smith* regime for ordinary citizens. Rather, the prisoner cases would be properly treated the way the doctrine treats them—as entirely separate matters.

3. The article then offers more theoretical support for why the courts indeed treat prisoner cases differently (beyond the extra magnitude of the restrictions on prisoners): Law-abiding citizens have much more access to the political process than prisoners do, and therefore courts have felt less need to protect law-abiding citizens' religious freedom claims.

Such combinations of doctrinal, practical, and theoretical arguments or explanations tend to be much more effective than doctrinal, practical, or theoretical arguments standing alone.

III. Possible Responses to *Smith*

There's much value in just laying out the facts about what has happened. But many readers want news they can use: They want to know how the newly uncovered facts about pre-*Smith* strict scrutiny might affect what people should do in the future. That's what the article turns to now.

A. The Religious Freedom Restoration Act

[¶ 55] Initially introduced in the summer of 1990 and reintroduced the next June, the RFRA seeks to reestablish the compelling interest test. The Bill states that the "Government shall not burden a person's exercise of religion even if the burden results from a rule of general applicability," unless the government "demonstrates that application of the burden to the person—(1) is essential to further a compelling governmental interest; and (2) is the least restrictive means of furthering that compelling governmental interest." The Bill is to apply to federal, state, and municipal governments, and to statutes adopted before and after the passage of this Bill. It places the burdens of going forward with the evidence and of persuasion on the government, and provides for the award of attorney's fees to the successful claimant.

[¶ 56] Support for the RFRA within Congress is strong—there are currently 193 cosponsors in the House of Representatives—and spans the political spectrum. Equally strong and diverse are the supporters outside of Congress. The Coalition for the Free Exercise of Religion, formed explicitly to support the Bill, harbors more than thirty-five organizations representing a wide array of religious and political viewpoints. These organizations, in turn, represent extremely large constituencies.[175] Action on the Bill has been slow-there have been only two hearings thus far. From the amount and strength of support already behind the Bill, however, it appears to have an excellent chance of being enacted. If enacted, there will likely be a challenge as to whether the Bill is constitutional, but given Supreme Court precedent, it appears it would be able to withstand such a challenge.[177]

---

[175] To cite only two examples: the National Council of Churches represents 32 national religious bodies that have an aggregate constituency of 40,000,000. The National Association of Evangelicals is an association of 50,000 churches from 78 denominations that serves a constituency of 15,000,000.

[177] In enacting this bill, Congress would be acting under Section 5 of the 14th Amendment, which provides that "The Congress shall have power to enforce, by appropri-

When the article was published in 1992, it seemed likely that RFRA would be enacted, and would be held to be within Congress's constitutional powers. RFRA was indeed enacted in 1993, but in 1997 it was struck down as unconstitutional when applied to the states: The Court concluded that Congress lacked the enumerated power to bind states this way. RFRA remains the law with regard to the federal government, since Congress does have the power to limit the scope of its own laws and of federal government actions.

But the author rightly recognized that the question of RFRA's constitutionality was tangential to his article, and resisted the temptation to add many more pages discussing this issue. Any such discussion would have required the author to learn a good deal of constitutional doctrine that was unrelated to his newly gained Free Exercise Clause expertise. The discussion would have substantially lengthened an already fairly long article. And the discussion would have distracted readers from the core value added by the article—value unrelated to whether a legislative response to *Smith* was constitutional.

So the author (1) said that RFRA would probably be constitutional, which was indeed the conventional wisdom among scholars at the time, and a reasonable prediction, even if one that ultimately proved to be mistaken. He (2) wrote a footnote that briefly supported his prediction, for the benefit of readers who wanted to know why he was saying what

---

ate legislation, the provisions of this article." In *Cantwell v. Connecticut*, 310 U.S. 296 (1940), the Supreme Court incorporated the Free Exercise Clause into the Fourteenth Amendment, and thus made it subject to the legislative protection allowed under Section 5 of that amendment. In *Katzenbach v. Morgan*, 384 U.S. 641, (1966), the Court held that this section gives congress "the same broad powers expressed in the Necessary and Proper Clause." It is this case that probably would be relied upon to uphold the legislation.

Debate exists, however, over whether *Katzenbach* would be applied to validate this legislation, which essentially works to overturn a Supreme Court decision. Professor Laurence H. Tribe believes that the bill is too confrontational with respect to the Supreme Court's authority, and could run into trouble because of it. Constitutional Law Conference, 59 U.S.L.W. 2272, 2279 (1990) (remarks of Laurence H. Tribe). Indeed, one could argue that it violates the principle of *Marbury v. Madison*, 5 U.S. (1 Cranch) 137, 176 (1803), that "[i]t is, emphatically, the province and duty of the judicial department, to say what the law is." Espousing a contrary view, Professor Douglas Laycock submitted a letter to the Chair of the Subcommittee on Civil and Constitutional Rights, in which he stated that it was his "judgment that Congress has power to enact such a law under section 5 of the fourteenth amendment." The complexities of this debate, as well as its likely outcome, though fascinating, are beyond the scope of this Note. They are also, in a sense, extraneous, as this Note argues that the Bill—constitutional or not—is unnecessary and unwise.

he was saying, and briefly quoted the arguments in both directions. And then he (3) clearly said that this is beyond the scope of the article, and explained why this is so (because "this Note argues that the Bill—constitutional or not—is unnecessary and unwise"). All this saved him a lot of research and writing, and readers a lot of unnecessary reading.

[¶ 57] The reaction of disappointment and outrage to the *Smith* decision is well expressed by the movement to enact the RFRA. It is a reaction that is understandable and justifiable, given the Court's handling of the case and its symbolic evisceration of the Free Exercise Clause. Passage of the RFRA, however, would be little more than a symbolic victory for religious liberty. In actuality, it would be ineffectual and perhaps even detrimental to the protection of free exercise rights.

[¶ 58] As currently written, the bill mimics the Supreme Court's pre-*Smith* formulation of the compelling interest test. The previous sections of this Note demonstrated the inability of this test, as applied by the Supreme Court and the courts of appeals, to protect the free exercise claimant. There is nothing to suggest that courts would become more protective under a reestablished compelling interest test.[181] Indeed, as far as the Native American Church is concerned, it does not appear that passage of the RFRA would help in the least. As Senator Biden explained when introducing the RFRA in the Senate:

> [¶ 59] [A]s I see it, Oregon could still keep native Americans from using peyote during religious ceremonies. In my view, Oregon has a significant interest in preventing the physical harm caused by using drugs like peyote. Oregon could show that it had a compelling State interest in regulating peyote use and that creating an exception for native Americans would interfere too much with that interest.

[¶ 60] In a statement that captures perfectly the hollowness of the protection afforded by a compelling interest test, and the contradiction between the avowed purpose of the RFRA and its likely effect, Senator Biden claimed that the RFRA would simultaneously "protect religious

---

[181] In his statement in support of the RFRA, Reverend [Dean M. Kelley of the National Council of Churches] recognized that "[p]assage of the Religious Freedom Restoration Act does not guarantee how any of those cases would come out." But, he asserted, "[t]hat is not the point. The Act would guarantee only that the free exercise claimants would have their 'day in court." What Reverend Kelley, and other supporters of the RFRA present at the hearing, failed to recognize is that for the free exercise claimant, a day in court almost always ends in defeat.

freedom and still prevent the use of peyote."[183]

[¶ 61] Although accomplishing little, passage of the RFRA could also affirmatively hamper attempts to secure protection for religious exercise. It seems possible that after passing this legislation, Congress—and state legislatures—could be content to allow courts to determine when exemptions should be granted. Rather than drafting exemptions into pending legislation, legislatures may wish to avoid such issues altogether, particularly if they are controversial. That legislatures, when possible, dodge controversial issues and in effect delegate such issues to the courts for resolution, is hardly a novel observation.

[¶ 62] It is plausible that such a phenomenon could occur in the area of free exercise exemptions. Content that they had done their part in passing the RFRA, Congress might then turn a deaf ear to future requests for specific statutory exemptions.[185] If this were to occur, the religious adherent would have only the courts to rely upon for protection. But courts, as already documented, are not very reliable. To make matters worse, it seems particularly unlikely that a legislature would override a court decision that applied a compelling interest test in denying a specific exemption. To do so would embroil the legislature in the very controversy they, by hypothesis, wished to avoid in the first place, forcing legislators not only to confront the controversy, but to exacerbate it by overturning the court's resolution of the issue. The free exercise claimant, having had her day in court and probably having lost there, would thus most likely have nowhere else to turn for redress.

Note again that the arguments are concrete and pragmatic. It's perfectly legitimate, of course, to make theoretical arguments about moral

---

[183] Senator Biden claimed that the RFRA is concerned with religious freedom, not with allowing Native Americans to use peyote in religious ceremonies. What he fails to recognize is that for members of the Native American Church, religious freedom revolves around the ability to ingest their sacrament, peyote. To suggest that the RFRA protects religious freedom but allows peyote to be prohibited is thus, at least to a member of the Native American Church, a blatant contradiction.

[185] There is, however, another possibility. If legislatures enact statutes with an eye toward how that statute will be interpreted by the courts, it could be argued that the compelling interest test motivates legislatures to consider free exercise exemptions when passing legislation. This may be particularly true of state legislatures, and may be a useful way of ensuring that free exercise exemptions are seriously considered by legislators. As Professor Thayer noted, legislatures often "insensibly fall into a habit of assuming that whatever they can constitutionally do they may do ...." If it is constitutional not even to consider free exercise exemptions, perhaps such a consideration will not be made.

right and wrong. But in practice the more concrete and pragmatic arguments, or concrete and pragmatic arguments that are tied to the theoretical arguments, tend to be more persuasive.

The arguments in this subsection are also speculative: The article talks about what "could" happen, and what "is plausible." But readers recognize that all claims about the outcome of proposed new statutes (or legal doctrines) are necessarily speculative. They just want speculation:

1. that is founded on facts (and Part II gave ample facts to support the speculation that reestablishing strict scrutiny is unlikely to be much help to religious objectors),

2. that is based on well-defended inferences from those facts, and

3. that doesn't overstate its case by claiming that something will certainly happen in the absence of strong evidence that it will indeed certainly happen.

B. Establishing a New Test

[¶ 63] Another possible response to *Smith* is formulating a test that would be more protective of free exercise rights. Such a formulation could restrict what constitutes a compelling state interest and relax what constitutes a burden. Numerous suggestions on how to accomplish the former have already been made. Professor Stephen L. Pepper, for example, suggests that courts determine if there is a "real, tangible (palpable, concrete, measurable), nonspeculative, non-trivial injury to a legitimate, substantial state interest."

[¶ 64] Professor McConnell alone has offered no less than three possibilities. He suggests framing the inquiry as whether the religious practice is repugnant to the "'peace' or 'safety' of the state." Alternatively, when minority religions are involved, he suggests that courts ask: "Is the governmental interest so important that the government would impose a burden of this magnitude on the majority in order to achieve it?" Finally, he and Judge Richard Posner have proposed that burdens on religious practice should "be justified only on the basis of a demonstrable and unavoidable relation to public purposes unrelated to the effects on religion."

[¶ 65] One could also turn to the suggestion of Reverend Dean M. Kelley of the National Council of Churches, and some members of his coalition, who recognize that the Supreme Court has "diluted the compelling State interest threshold in the past 27 years." They have suggested that religious practices be restricted only when they threaten "public health and safety." One could even look back to James Madison, finally, who once suggested that free exercise be protected "in every case where it does not trespass on private rights or the public peace."

[¶ 66] As for the burden side of the free exercise balance, Professor Lupu has suggested adopting a common law test. Under this test, a government action would be burdensome if an analogous act committed by a private party "would be actionable under general principles of law." For instance, application of this test to the Native Americans in *Lyng*, would find their free exercise rights to be burdened. The tribes would have had a strong easement claim against a private land owner, if that land owner—as the government did—tried to exclude the tribes from burial grounds on the land owner's property.

[¶ 67] Although it is difficult to predict how the adoption of any of these reformulations would affect the outcome of free exercise cases, there seem to be two significant difficulties confronting these suggestions. The first is deciding which one to choose. It is unclear whether any particular one could garner enough support in or outside of Congress to secure its adoption. The second, and more debilitating obstacle, is preventing judicial circumvention of the new standard. It is questionable whether the insertion of adverbs before "compelling," such as "truly" or "really," would insure that courts strictly scrutinize proffered state interests. Although certain stricter formulations would certainly make it more difficult for judges to reject as many claims as they do now, based on their past performances it seems that judges are up to the task.

[¶ 68] After all, Justice Burger was fairly clear in *Yoder* when he wrote that only "interests of the *highest* order" could prevail over legitimate free exercise claims. Perhaps providing specific examples of such interests, or inserting "very" before "highest" would lead to more favorable outcomes for free exercise claimants, but the cases examined suggest that courts, for various reasons, are extremely reluctant to side with them. As long as that reluctance continues, it seems difficult to imagine a test of general applicability that would prevent courts from reaching the outcomes they desire.

C. Limiting Smith and Focusing on the Legislature

1. Avoiding the Holding in Smith

[¶ 69] As alluded to earlier, the *Smith* decision itself suggests how its holding may be limited. First, the Court states that "hybrid" claims will still be subject to the compelling interest test. Such claims could potentially limit this holding quite substantially. For there appear to be numerous free exercise claims that also involve (or could involve) a free speech, freedom of association, or parental rights claim, to name the three "constitutional" protections the Court cites. Taken together, these hybrid cases may offer protection in a wide array of contexts in which free exercise claims arise.[203]

[¶ 70] Second, the Court reaffirmed its tradition of remaining neutral in intra-religious disputes. The Court evidenced no intention of becoming involved in controversies within churches over religious authority or dogma. Third, *Smith* does not apply to laws that directly target religion, or to actions that intentionally discriminate against religions. Fourth, it appears that free exercise claims brought in the unemployment context will still be judged under a compelling interest test. Fifth, *Smith* does not alter the analysis of already existing statutory exemptions. Finally, it is possible that courts could limit *Smith* to criminal prohibitions, as Justice Scalia's opinion emphasizes in several places that the statute at issue in *Smith* was a criminal one.

[¶ 71] Courts interested in circumventing the *Smith* decision, therefore, appear to have ample means to do so. In fact, several courts of appeals have done just that in cases arising after *Smith*. In *Ferguson v. Commissioner,* for example, the court did not even cite *Smith* in upholding a free exercise claim against a requirement that those in a federal tax court swear or affirm before testifying. In another example, *Salvation Army v. Department of Community Affairs,* the court remanded a free exercise claim specifically to allow the claimants to raise a "hybrid" claim involving freedom of association. Thus, for courts intent on granting a free exercise exemption, *Smith* may not be as big an obstacle as it appears.

2. Focus on the Legislature

---

[203] Free speech hybrid claims, for example, could cover proselytizing and worship services. Parental right hybrids could cover educational issues. And freedom of association claims could potentially protect all group ceremonies, gatherings, or concerted efforts.

[¶ 72] Because few courts evidence such an intention, however, those interested in protecting their religious liberty should turn their attention to the legislature. There exists much evidence to suggest that legislatures will be receptive to their claims. Indeed, a search through all the existing statutes, both state and federal, reveals that the terms "religion" or "religious" appear over 14,000 times. Religious exemptions, in turn, exist in over 2,000 statutes. Although the probative value of these numbers is obviously limited, a closer look at federal statutes and those of four states[216] suggests that the political process has been fairly protective of religious freedom.

[¶ 73] In the United States Code, for example, exemptions exist in food inspection laws for the ritual slaughter of animals, and for the preparation of food in accordance with religious practices. The tax laws contain numerous exemptions for religious groups and allow deductions for contributions to religious organizations. Federal copyright laws contain an exemption for materials that are to be used for religious purposes. Antidiscrimination laws, including Title VII, the Fair Housing Act, and the Aid to the Disabled Act, contain exemptions for religious organizations. Ministers are automatically exempt from compulsory military training and service. Aliens seeking asylum can do so on the grounds that they will suffer religious persecution if returned to their home countries and gambling laws contain an exemption for religious organizations. Those in the military may wear religious apparel while wearing their uniforms, subject to limitations imposed by the Secretary of Defense. And last, but certainly not least for purposes of this Note, federal drug laws contain an exemption for the religious use of peyote by members of the Native American Church.

[¶ 74] At the same time that religious organizations are exempted from several antidiscrimination laws, numerous statutes prohibit other organizations from discriminating on the basis of religion. Although these statutes are based on equal protection grounds, rather than on free exercise grounds, they illustrate the protection granted to religion by legislatures. An example of such statutes is the provision prohibiting the selection of civil service employees on the basis of religion. Further, federally assisted institutions of higher education are forbidden to discriminate on the basis of religion, whereas the same type of institutions

---

[216] Those states are Alabama, Minnesota, California, and Connecticut. They were chosen with an eye toward assembling a group that represented states of different sizes and in different parts of the country.

run by religious groups are free to discriminate on the basis of sex, if their religion so dictates. Title VII prohibits employers and labor organizations from discriminating on the basis of religion, and requires both groups to reasonably accommodate workers' religious practices. Organizations receiving federal money under the National and Community Services Act are prohibited from engaging in religious discrimination. Finally, Organizations receiving federal assistance under the Public Works Act are forbidden to practice religious discrimination.

[¶ 75] The legislatures of the four states studied were equally beneficent toward religious adherents, although the number and type of exemptions did vary from state to state. All four states exempt churches and religious organizations from a wide array of tax obligations; from property taxes to franchise taxes to sales taxes on church restaurants and dining rooms. All four also allow tax deductions for contributions to religious organizations. All four exempt from militia service ordained ministers and divinity students as well as those who object to such service on religious grounds. In some states, children whose parents object to their being taught certain subjects are excused from those classes. And children whose parents object to their being immunized may also be excused from such obligations. Religious schools, in turn, receive various exemptions and protections, ranging from an exemption from antidiscrimination laws to an exemption from registration and approval requirements.

[¶ 76] All four states also have various antidiscrimination laws that forbid discrimination on the basis of religion in such contexts as public employment and educational benefits. Gambling regulations in two of the states contain exemptions for religious organizations. Two states also exempt religious organizations from solicitation regulations and reporting requirements. Religious corporations, in each of the states, are free from many state corporate rules and regulations. Employees in two of the states are excused from physical examination requirements if they object to such exams for religious reasons. Child care facilities and preschools that are run by religious organizations are free, in one state, from licensing requirements and other state regulations.

[¶ 77] Finally, each of the states grants some unique exemptions to religious groups. Alabama, for example, exempts church buses from state inspection requirements, and exempts income earned by foreign missionaries from its income tax laws. California allows religious exemptions from mandated autopsies (to be claimed by members of the decedent's family), and provides various exemptions from health and insurance regulations to those who rely on prayer for healing. Connecticut allows churches and religious organizations to ignore the state prohibition on Sunday work, and allows religious groups to show movies without obtaining a license. And Minnesota allows an exemption from its prohibition against corporate farming for farms run by religious groups; exempts the religious use of peyote from its drug laws; and exempts funeral directors who belong to religious organizations that object to embalming from the requirement of obtaining an embalming license.

[¶ 78] The exemptions mentioned are not exhaustive of those contained in the federal and state statutes, nor are they meant to be. They are included only to provide a sense of the degree to which religion and religious practices are accommodated and protected by legislatures. Although these protections vary somewhat from state to state, the statutory exemptions nonetheless serve to contrast the treatment of religious practice in the legislatures to that in the courts. In numerical terms, at least at the federal level (state court decisions were not studied), it is clear that religious groups have received significantly more exemptions from legislatures than they have from federal courts.

[¶ 79] The results of this brief survey of federal and state statutes, though illuminating, are not very surprising. That legislatures are helpful to "majority" religions[261] is generally recognized and rarely questioned. Indeed, the very existence of so many Establishment Clause cases suggests that legislatures tend, at least in the eyes of plaintiffs, to be too helpful to (majority) religious groups. If such religious groups are

---

[261] The term "majority" appears in quotations because, although the distinction between majority and minority religions is made regularly in academic literature, it is difficult to discern precisely which religion or religions comprise the majority. A recent Gallup Poll revealed that 56% of those surveyed consider themselves Protestant, while 25% consider themselves Catholic, 2% Jewish, 6% "other" (a group that includes Eastern Orthodox, Mormons, and Muslims), and 11% expressed no preference or affiliation. Protestants alone, or together with Catholics, are normally considered the "majority" religion or religions, but this characterization—although numerically correct—overlooks the different denominations within these groups. Southern Baptists, Fundamentalists, Evangelicals, and Methodists are all Protestants, for example, but harbor different religious and, at times, political beliefs. If one views religious groups in terms of denominations, there is simply no numerical majority religion. *See* Yearbook of American & Canadian Churches 1987 (Constant H. Jaquet, Jr. ed., 1987) (listing 128 distinct religious bodies and 345,961 churches in the United States). Although defining the term "majority" more precisely is beyond the scope of this Note, and as used here "majority" religion will connote those religions generally considered within the mainstream of American society (i.e., Protestants and Catholics), it should at least be recognized that this is an inherently inaccurate term as applied to religious groups. There is simply no religious majority, for example, akin to the white majority.

forced to rely on the political process rather than the courts for protection, therefore, one would expect their success in that process to continue.[263]

Here again we see the value of more data. Rather than just speculating that the legislature might provide religious exemptions, the article reports what is actually happening, and therefore what is likely to keep happening.

The data here is less complete: The article doesn't purport to catalog all the statutory exemptions, even in the five jurisdictions that it covers—federal law and the law of Alabama, Minnesota, California, and Connecticut—the way that it catalogued all the federal appellate Free Exercise Clause cases from 1980 to 1990. Still, the article gives a lot of specific examples that help show that religious groups do often get specific statutory exemptions.

And the data is persuasive in part because it shows these effects to be broad, rather than just limited to a few narrow areas. As footnote 216 points out, the states were chosen to cover different parts of the country; the article's evidence can't be dismissed as just the practice of the especially religious and Protestant Southern states, or of the especially religiously mixed states such as California. The laws cover many different legal rules and religious practices. And, as we'll see below, the laws benefit minority religions and not just the most common denominations.

3. Minority Religions

[¶ 80] Many argue, however, that religious minorities would suffer if left to rely solely on the political process. As Professor McConnell asserts:

> [¶ 81] In a world in which some beliefs are more prominent than others, the political branches will inevitably be selectively sensitive to-

---

[263] It is interesting in this regard to consider Representative Solarz' statement that our nation has always accommodated religion, citing as an example "the use of wine in religious ceremonies during Prohibition." His clear implication is that the Court historically has been responsible for such accommodations, and that they are now in jeopardy as a result of *Smith*. Yet the exemption for sacramental wine during Prohibition was created by Congress, not the Court.

ward religious injuries. Laws that impinge upon the religious practices of larger or more prominent faiths will be noticed and remedied. When the laws impinge upon the practice of smaller groups, legislators will not even notice, and may not care even if they do notice.

[¶ 82] That minorities of any kind fare worse in the political arena than majorities almost goes without saying. Even Justice Scalia, writing for the *Smith* majority, recognized "that leaving accommodation to the political process will place at a relative disadvantage those religious practices that are not widely engaged in ...." Thus, religious minorities have the most to lose by the decision in *Smith,* the argument continues, for they apparently lost in that case the protection of the one institution—the courts—upon which they could rely.

[¶ 83] Despite the logical force of this argument, however, there are reasons to question whether religious minorities are better off relying on the courts rather than the political process for protection. First, one must consider the number of political concerns that all religions inevitably share, despite their theological differences. In conjunction one should consider the number of protections that legislatures already offer to religious groups that benefit all religions. Indeed, the majority of extant statutory protections and exemptions are available and useful to all religious adherents. Laws that prohibit religious discrimination, for example, prohibit discrimination against minority as well as majority religions. Tax exemptions are available to all religions, both small and large. Laws that allow religious groups to discriminate in employing or housing members of their own faith allow all religious groups to discriminate. Even the statutory exemptions that may not be useful to some faiths—because their religious tenets do not require a particular exemption—such as immunization exemptions or physical examination exemptions, are nonetheless written generally and apply to any and all whose religious beliefs mandate such exemptions. The existing statutory exemptions, in other words, reveal almost no instances where an exemption or a protection is coupled with a particular religion.

[¶ 84] Second, even those exemptions that are not universally useful to all religions do not necessarily favor majority religions, nor do they demonstrate any bias against minority religions. As Professor Mark Tushnet has argued, religious groups tend to form shifting coalitions in the political arena, simply because there is not one monolithic religious majority and different religions will have different issues in common. In addition, those who are members of religious groups are also members of other types of groups, such as those based on geography, age, politics, gender or race. Thus, the concern that legislative accommodations will disproportionately benefit majority religions should not be overstated:

> [¶ 85] Every statute, including an accommodation one, is only one of many laws that a legislature enacts. In a pluralistic society with crosscutting group memberships, the overall distribution of benefits and burdens is likely to be reasonably fair. Otherwise the disadvantaged minority can offer its support to some coalition that is just short of a majority, in exchange for relief from the disproportionate burdens it is bearing.

[¶ 86] The final reason why even minority religions may fare better in the political process than in the courts is simple: they could not do much worse in that process than they already have in the courts. As [one scholar] observed in reviewing the Supreme Court's disposition of free exercise cases: "[P]ut bluntly, the pattern is that sometimes Christians win but non-Christians never do."[270] Although minority religions fared marginally better in the federal courts of appeals,[271] the overall pattern was still one of defeat, for minority as well as mainstream religions.

As Part XVII.I.3 (p. 184) argued, the "sometimes Christians win but non-Christians never do" argument is not sound. Moreover, the relative success rates of Christians and non-Christians don't much bear on the subject of the subsection as a whole, and in particular of the first and last sentences of the paragraph—the relative success rates of "minority

---

[270] [The scholar] reviewed a series of Supreme Court cases rejecting free exercise claims brought by non-Christians, and observed that although "[e]ach of these cases can be explained away, ... to one who pays attention to bottom line results, the pattern is troubling."

Professor McConnell takes issue with [this] argument. Although he shares [the scholar's] "pessimistic assessment" of the Supreme Court's handling of free exercise claims, he argues that judges are more likely to accept free exercise claims brought by "non-mainstream" groups than mainstream ones, because they are less likely to question the latter groups' claims about religious necessity. Professor McConnell's argument appears to be that the more bizarre the sect, the more likely the judge will accept their religious claims. Whatever the merits of this argument may be, Professor McConnell nonetheless admits that "non-Christians never win, and Christians almost never win, either." For the purposes of this Note, it is this observation that is most important.

[271] Members of the Muslim faith won one free exercise claim. Islamic Ctr. v. City of Starkville, 840 F.2d 293 (5th Cir. 1988). Jehovah's Witnesses won another. Paul v. Watchtower Bible & Tract Soc'y, 819 F.2d 875 (9th Cir. 1987). And a third was won by a woman who though an avowed Christian was not affiliated with an organized religion. Quaring v. Peterson, 728 F.2d 1121 (8th Cir. 1984), *aff'd sub nom.* Jensen v. Quaring, 472 U.S. 478 (1985). It is interesting to note that whereas all three claimants could be fairly said to belong to minority religions, only *Islamic Center* involved a non-Christian religion.

religions" and "mainstream religions." As footnote 271 points out, the "minority religions" category includes small Christian denominations such as the Jehovah's Witnesses, as well as individual Christians who aren't affiliated with any denomination. Under that definition, *all* of the five Supreme Court victories for religious accommodation claims involved "minority religions": One involved a Jehovah's Witness; two involved Seventh-Day Adventists; one involved the Amish; and one involved a nondenominational Christian.

But again these are modest disagreements on my part with this one part of the article. And even given these disagreements, this section's bottom-line claim is persuasively defended: Minority religions as well as mainstream religions have had little success in court under the rules overturned by *Smith*, and substantial success in the legislative process.

[¶ 87] Finally, that minority religions may have less to fear from the political process than they do from the courts is well-illustrated by the experience of the Native American Church (NAC). Whereas theirs may be a well-recognized church, those in the NAC would certainly classify as members of a minority religion. One would thus expect them to fare poorly in the political process. Yet prior to the *Smith* case, twenty-three states and the federal government provided NAC members an exemption from their drug laws for the religious use of peyote. The Supreme Court in *Smith,* on the other hand, denied such an exemption. That NAC members fared worse in court than they did in the legislative process is not only obvious, it is also typical of the disparate treatment of tribal religions by the courts and legislatures.

4. Building Coalitions

[¶ 88] Whether religious groups, minority or majority, are successful in the political process may ultimately depend on how well they can coalesce. As a coalition, religious groups have the potential to be incredibly powerful politically. Indeed, religious adherents as a single, undifferentiated group probably represent the single largest group-larger than whites, males, females, or those in a particular age group-in the country.[275] This fact alone suggests that statutory protections that ben-

---

[275] Eighty-nine percent of Americans claim to be affiliated with a religious group. There is simply no other single group in the country that could boast such a membership.

efit religion in general should face almost no political opposition.

[¶ 89] The Religious Freedom Restoration Act supports this suggestion. In restoring the compelling interest test, all religions would apparently benefit; certainly no religions would be disproportionately disadvantaged. The coalition that supports the Act represents an enormous and enormously diverse constituency. Not surprisingly, to this date no religious groups have expressed opposition to the Act. The same should be true for all pieces of legislation that provide benefits or protection to all religions.

[¶ 90] The real question, then, is whether religious groups will coalesce when only one or two religions within the coalition stand to lose or benefit. Can or will religions band together to protect just one religion, particularly a minority one? The answer to this question turns on such considerations as how often minority and majority religions will have issues in common, the degree to which religious groups will see in each exemption struggle a common issue of religious liberty in which they feel a vested interest, or the degree to which religious groups will lend support to others out of altruism. Although a full exploration of these considerations is beyond the scope of this Note, there is one piece of evidence that suggests that religious groups will coalesce, and will do so for a variety of reasons.

[¶ 91] That evidence lies in the amicus curiae briefs filed in Supreme Court free exercise cases and in several of the appellate cases. These briefs demonstrate that religious groups of different faiths and different denominations do in fact lend support to each other. Sometimes the reason for the support is obvious, as in *Sherbert v. Verner,* when the Jewish Committee wrote a brief for the Seventh-Day Adventist claimant, who sought relief when denied unemployment compensation because she would not work on Saturday, the day of her Sabbath. In other cases, however, the only apparent connection between the groups is their general interest in religious liberty.[279] Although hardly

---

[279] For example, briefs were filed in *Wisconsin v. Yoder,* 406 U.S. 205 (1972), by the General Conference of Seventh-Day Adventists, the National Council of the Churches of Christ, the National Jewish Commission on Law and Public Affairs, and the Synagogue Council of America. None of these religions require exemption from school attendance in the way the Amish do. Another example is *Bowen v. Roy,* 476 U.S. 693 (1986), a case in which Native Americans objected to obtaining a social security number for their two-year-old daughter, claiming that it would violate their religious beliefs. Amicus briefs were filed by the Catholic League for Religious and Civil Rights and the Rutherford Institute (a conservative religious and antiabortion group). It is arguable that in both cases, those groups filing amicus briefs believed a favorable outcome for the religious group involved

conclusive, these briefs reveal that religious groups will unite in the courtroom, even when only one religion can gain directly from a favorable judgment.[280] If they are willing to coalesce in that context, there appears to be no reason why they would not do so in the political process.

[¶ 92] In addition, religious exemptions do not present a zero-sum scenario, such as affirmative action seems to (in the eyes of some) for blacks and whites. One church's gain, in the form of an exemption, is not another's loss. Thus even if they do not band together, there is little political incentive among churches to oppose exemptions. There also seems to be little religious incentive to oppose exemptions, unless one religion is intent on eviscerating the others. Regardless of differences in theology or belief, therefore, there seem to be more incentives than disincentives for religious groups to form political coalitions for the purpose of securing statutory protection and exemptions.

[¶ 93] That religious groups may be forced or encouraged by *Smith* to coalesce more than ever may ultimately benefit not only those groups but society as a whole. Rather than sequestering themselves in their own private court rooms, perhaps religious groups will come together to wage political battles in the halls of Congress, in state legislatures and in town halls, and in so doing lower the walls of prejudice and ignorance that often separate adherents of different religions. To the degree that this increased contact will increase understanding and toleration, members of differing faiths can only gain. Their gain, in turn, can translate into a society more tolerant and accepting of diverse religious faiths.

This section, like the section on RFRA (Part III.A), offers a good example of persuasive speculation. The article can't prove that religious groups, including minority religions, will often be able to prevail in the legislative process by building coalitions. But it offers concrete evidence that such coalitions have been common, and that we should therefore expect them to remain common. That's probably the best that can be done here, and the article does it effectively.

---

could somehow apply to them. Even so, this does not detract from the fact that they offered their support.

[280] An illustrative appellate case is *In re The Bible Speaks*, 869 F.2d 628 (1st Cir. 1989), in which members of The Bible Speaks church challenged a bankruptcy court's finding that a former member of their congregation had fraudulently procured gifts for the church. The Council on Religious Freedom and the National Council of the Churches of Christ filed amicus briefs in the case.

IV. Conclusion

[¶ 94] Scholars have begun recently to debunk the myth that the courts, and particularly the Supreme Court, have been the great institutional protectors and promoters of civil liberties. In the context of free speech cases, for example, Professor Robert Nagel has argued that "at a minimum, the systemic utility of judicial review in free speech cases has been a matter characterized far too much by convenient assumptions and cheery faith."[284] The federal appellate cases surveyed demonstrate that the same can be said of the court's role in free exercise cases. In this sense, *Smith* can be seen as providing the final proof that cheery faith in the courts, in this context as in others, is misplaced. *Smith* simply made obvious what was true all along: courts have done little to aid or protect the religious adherent, and certainly have done less than legislatures.[285]

[¶ 95] Unfortunately, the support generated by the RFRA illustrates that the real lesson of *Smith* has not yet been widely learned. It is therefore ironic that this lesson is only made more apparent by the progression thus far of the RFRA. After losing (once again) in the courts, this time losing big, religious groups coalesced and approached Congress for redress. Faced with such a powerful coalition, Congress re-

---

[284] See also Michael J. Klarman, *The Puzzling Resistance to Political Process Theory,* 77 Va. L. Rev. 747 (1991). Professor Klarman points out that the Court has rarely taken a leading role in protecting such civil liberties as freedom of speech and suffrage, and concludes that "we should not kid ourselves into believing that our cherished civil liberties tradition depends as much on judicial review as many lawyers would have us believe."

[285] This lesson of *Smith* lends support to the more general critique of the importance of judicial review. In what has become a famous statement of this critique, Learned Hand remarked:

> I often wonder whether we do not rest our hopes too much upon constitutions, upon laws and upon courts. These are false hopes; believe me, these are false hopes. Liberty lies in the hearts of men and women; when it dies there, no constitution, no law, no court can save it; no constitution, no law, no court can even do much to help it. While it lies there it needs no constitution, no law, no court to save it.

Learned Hand, The Spirit of Liberty 189-90 (3d ed. 1960). If one believes that the legislatures represent, to some degree, what lies in the hearts of men and women, Learned Hand's assertion seems correct at least as regards freedom of religion. For it has been the legislatures, not the courts or the Constitution, that have provided the real protections of religious liberty.

sponded quickly. Their response, however, is schizophrenic. While professing their deep respect for religious freedom, in reestablishing the compelling interest test members of Congress are tossing the issue of free exercise back into the courts, and in a sense saying that they do not trust the political process (i.e., themselves) to protect religion. Yet once in the courts, the free exercise claimant, as documented, is not likely to succeed.

[¶ 96] If the real lesson of *Smith* is to be useful, those religious groups that have banded together to support the RFRA should drop that effort but remain together to wage other campaigns. They should continue to seek broad based exemptions in specific pieces of legislation, and force legislatures to confront and discuss such exemptions. If the courts need to be relied upon at all, they can serve as useful forums for determining whether a particular religion or religious adherent fits within a statutory exemption. The pursuit of such a strategy, one that entails open discussion of how religion and religious groups should fit within society, holds potential rewards not only for religious adherents but for democratic government as well.

Here, the article tries to connect to broader theoretical debates about the value of courts as protectors of civil liberties (see Part V.F for more on drawing such connections to broader debates). But it does this only in passing.

This is probably a sound approach. It's helpful to explain how the specific findings in this article can be relevant to a more general discussion. And some reference to broader theoretical debates can be impressive to some readers, if it seems well-connected to the article's thesis (as the reference here is).

At the same time, a more elaborate discussion of the theoretical points might be largely repetitive of what the theorists have written (though it might be able to avoid that by focusing closely on the particular findings of this particular article). It would have probably required much more time and effort. And even if it was done well, it probably would not have added as much value as the article itself: A good but probably not terribly novel portion on grand theory would have diluted the strikingly useful and original material on actual religious accommodation decisions. So the Conclusion here is a good example of the author's rightly deciding what to set aside (see Part VI.C for more on this) with just a brief discussion.

* * *

XIX. A SAMPLE HIGHLY SUCCESSFUL STUDENT ARTICLE

We have spent a good deal of time with this article, but for good reason: Seeing how something is done well can help you do your task well, too. Whatever you're writing about, and however many citations your article is eventually likely to get, you would do well to emulate the innovativeness, organization, clarity, and tone of student Notes such as this one.

APPENDIX A

UNITED STATES SUPREME COURT

1963-1990

I. Free Exercise Claims That Lost
[Citations.]
II. Free Exercise Claims That Won
[Citations.]

APPENDIX B

UNITED STATES COURTS OF APPEALS

1963-1990

I. Free Exercise Claims That Lost
[Citations.]
II. Free Exercise Claims That Won
[Citations.]

XX. Turning Practical Work into Articles

A. *The Big Picture*

Writing an article from scratch can be daunting. Fortunately, you can often save time and effort by adapting work you originally wrote for another purpose—for instance, for a summer law firm job or a judicial externship.

Not all such work can be turned into a good article; some lacks novelty or nonobviousness, the stress in the real world being largely on utility. But much practical work does focus on largely unexplored questions, as you might have found if you searched for relevant law review articles before starting to write. And though memos and motions are generally shorter and shallower than a good law review article, that can be remedied.

The trick is to ruthlessly strip away those things that are unsuitable for law review articles, and to add the material that you never included because it was unsuitable for practical work. I recommend a four-step approach: Extract, deepen, broaden, and connect.

1. Practical work often covers issues that were important to the case on which you were working, but that aren't new or academically interesting. *Extract* those portions that would be a valuable addition to the literature, and throw out the rest.

2. Practical work often glosses over counterarguments and omits significant steps in the analysis. *Deepen* the work by confronting the hard questions that the original work avoided.

3. Practical work is generally tied to particular facts, a particular jurisdiction, or a particular procedural posture. Make it more useful by *broadening* your discussion.

4. Practical work tends to ignore (for good reasons) broader academic debates. Make your article more academically impressive and perhaps more useful to later scholars by *connecting* what you've written to these debates.

Ethical note: Before turning a law firm memo into an article, get permission from the firm. Most firms will want to make sure that you aren't inadvertently including confidential client material, but some might also not want you to share work that they paid for (and in which they own the copyright). Few articles are worth ruining your relationship with a prospective employer, or with a likely reference for future employment. Likewise with work you've done as a judicial extern or a law clerk.

If you're getting class credit for your work, you should also disclose to your advisor or seminar teacher that you want to base your paper on some material that you had written before. Some professors might balk at that, because they may think that you should only get credit for work that you've done specifically for school. That's the professor's prerogative, and you'll be glad that you checked with the professor up front, rather than having him learn this later, and accuse you of chicanery and of violating academic standards.

But other professors might recognize that turning a practical piece into an academic one itself requires a lot of work, and they would thus have no objection to your proposal—especially if you show them the original memo, with a brief but impressive discussion of the many things that you plan to do to it.

B. Extract

Find the material in your work that's novel and nonobvious. (Don't worry so much about utility; if the work was useful in one case, it will probably be useful in others like it.) Many cases involve some issues that have rather simple or at least not very interesting answers, and other issues that are more worthy of academic treatment.

Cut mercilessly. Remove any subtopics for which you think you can't really add any academic value. Don't worry if the result looks too short; you'll solve that problem in the next three steps. The important point is that your paper should contain maximum value added, and minimum repetition of what others have already said.

Some memos contain several interesting issues that arose in the same case but aren't inherently connected—for instance, a jurisdictional question and a largely unrelated substantive question. Split them up. Better to have several short articles, each with a coherent internal structure, than one long article that contains several essentially unrelated matters.

C. Deepen

Practical work encourages you to take certain shortcuts. Replacing these shortcuts with more thorough analysis will make your article deeper, more valuable, and more impressive.

1. Question existing law

If the case law in your state or your federal circuit is settled, your law firm memo or judicial externship bench memo generally isn't supposed to analyze whether the decisions are sound; it's supposed to work within the existing framework.

Not so for law review articles. Articles are generally addressed to a national audience, and other states or other circuits may be free to adopt a different rule. And an article may also argue that the Supreme Court, state supreme courts, or federal circuits sitting en banc should change even a settled rule—an argument that most practical memos rarely make.

So don't just say, "this result is right because *X v. Y* and *Z v. W* have so held." Instead say, "this result is right because it fits with these general principles (whether doctrinal principles or policy principles), and courts have indeed seen it this way (citing *X v. Y* and *Z v. W*)." Or feel free to say, "this result is right because it fits with these general principles; some courts have disagreed, but here is why they're wrong."

2. Take counterarguments seriously

Briefs often gloss over some counterarguments, whether because the counterarguments are so weak that they aren't worth discussing given the page limit, because they're so strong that the supervising lawyer prefers not to stress them, or because you think that this particular judge won't care much about them. Law review articles, on the other hand, are generally strengthened by a full discussion of the counterarguments.

Go through your work carefully and look for all the fudging. When you say, "because X is true, Y is true," is there a missing step? Is there a counterargument that you haven't confronted? Are you entirely persuaded by your own writing?

Resist the temptation to take the easy way out. Your article should aim to impress readers with your thoughtfulness and fair-mindedness; the best way to do that is to confront the hard counterarguments, not ignore them.

3. Reflect on your initial goal

Practical work is often constrained by its procedural posture. What should a prudent client do to avoid any chance of liability under a vague rule? What's the best place to file a particular case?

Ask yourself whether it's good that lawyers are asking these questions. For instance, maybe the legal rules shouldn't be so vague that they pressure people into taking the most conservative path; you could use the suggestions from your memo as illustrations of the rule's vagueness. Maybe the legal system should discourage forum-shopping in this context; you could use the discussion from your memo to show how the choice of forum makes a big difference.

Remember: You're no longer locked into the particular assignment you were given. You should take advantage of the time and effort you've invested in your work, but build on the work by thinking beyond the specific problem you were originally trying to solve.

D. Broaden

Practical work usually focuses on a particular fact pattern and a particular jurisdiction. While you want your article to be narrow enough to be manageable, you also want to make it more useful, and that means making it applicable to as many cases as possible.

You can often generalize your analysis with fairly little extra effort. Say your work dealt with only one state's law; usually the law in many other states will be similar. Turn your article into something that focuses on general U.S. law, or at least the majority (or even minority) rule.

You can still use the cases from your state as illustrations and as support for your argument. You'll need to do some more research on just how similar the law in the other states really is, but that tends to be considerably easier than researching a new subject from scratch.

Similarly, see to what extent you can easily generalize your fact pattern. Say your memo was about the remedies for unauthorized publication of the fact that someone is HIV-positive. You can probably broaden the work to cover unauthorized publication of the fact that someone has any medical condition that would lead some to shun him.

You might have to add a bit more analysis—there may be legally significant differences between HIV status and other medical conditions—but this may mean only a bit of extra work. Broadening the subject to "remedies for any unauthorized publication of private facts," however, would likely be much harder (and might therefore not be worth doing) because so much of your original analysis was likely to have been tied to your focus on a medical condition.

E. Connect

Finally, your work may profit from connections to debates in related areas (see Part V.F, p. 70), and these connections may even shed light on the proper outcome of those debates. Briefly but cogently discussing such connections can make your piece more useful and more impressive.

XXI. WRITING SEMINAR TERM PAPERS

A. *Introduction: Comparing Seminar Term Papers and Academic Articles*

Seminar term papers are often much like law review articles, though the rules vary from instructor to instructor.

1. Nonobviousness

Seminar term papers should be nonobvious. Your goal is to impress the professor with your smarts and your creative thinking. Papers that apply settled law or well-established arguments to slightly new fact patterns generally won't serve this goal, and won't get a good grade.

2. Soundness

Seminar term papers should of course be sound; and your instructor, who specializes in the seminar topic, will be a much more critical judge of the quality of your arguments than a casual reader of an article would be.

3. Writing and structure

Seminar term papers should be well-written and well-organized. True, you have a captive audience, and needn't worry that a boring introduction will lose the reader. But most instructors see the seminar paper as a way of teaching you how to write better, and they will therefore prefer that your paper be as engaging as possible. Likewise, though some professors might let you omit some sections—such as the discussion of the background legal rules—others might see the paper as an opportunity for you to practice writing sections like this, and will therefore insist that they be done well.

4. Utility

Utility may be less necessary, depending on what your professor prefers. As Part I.E pointed out, utility is relative: The goal is to make the work as useful as possible given your area of interest. Not every work needs to appeal to thousands of lawyers, but once you choose a topic, you should do what it takes to make your work appeal to as many readers as possible.

In a seminar paper, the instructor may relax this constraint, since the work will have exactly one reader. Still, some instructors may insist on utility even there, because they want you to use this opportunity to learn the skill of making articles more useful.

5. Novelty

Novelty may also be less necessary, depending on what your professor prefers. Because the paper isn't meant to be published, your teacher might conclude that your paper doesn't have to say something that's genuinely new to those who work in the field. It may be enough that it say something that is new *to you*, and that shows that you've thought about the matter yourself.

Many instructors, though, prefer that seminar papers be novel. First, seminars are supposed to teach you to think creatively and originally—to come up with ideas that others haven't had.

Second, if your paper does say something that someone else has already said, the instructor might suspect that you didn't really do that much work on it yourself, but just relied, consciously or not, on the arguments of others. He might not think you were plagiarizing; you might have properly given credit to people, and cast everything in your own words. But he might feel that your work may not have involved as much hard thinking as a more novel proposal would require.

Finally, novel work is just more impressive—it better shows off your abilities. Even people who say they don't require novelty will often value a novel paper (all other things being equal) more than a paper that says what many others have said before.

B. Figuring Out What Your Instructor Expects

As you see, while most seminar papers have the same general requirements, different instructors do things differently. Your first task, then, is to ask about what your instructor expects. Does the instructor want the work to be novel (again, in the sense of novel to scholars, as opposed to just novel to you)? Does the instructor expect it to summarize the background legal principles, as well as setting forth a new proposal? Does the instructor prefer that you spend more time describing the law (to show that you've learned the subject matter well), instead of setting forth any suggested changes? Will the instructor give more credit for a topic that's designed to be as useful as possible to its fictional readers?

Many instructors will quickly give you and your classmates clear guidance on this. A few, though, might not have thought fully about the matter, which is why asking them for specifics can be helpful.

You're writing *for an audience of one*. Start by figuring out what that one person expects.

C. Finding a Topic

Topics for seminar papers are generally limited to the seminar's subject matter. Sometimes this limitation can be helpful: I suspect that many students struggle a long time to find a topic for a publishable article precisely because there are so many fields to choose from.

Here are a few ways you could find a topic.

1. Ask the teacher

Ask your professor to recommend some possible topics. Some teachers don't like to provide paper topics, since they think that finding a topic is part of the student's task; but others are more accommodating. Professors usually teach seminars in subjects that they like, that they write about, and that they read about. They therefore often have many topic ideas.

2. Pay attention to the readings

In most seminars, you end up reading recent academic papers. See what topics are flagged as unresolved by the readings, or are glossed over with only a shallow analysis. Don't frame your paper as a response to the particular article (see Part I.I.5, p. 37) unless your instructor tells you that this is fine. Organize it instead around the issue that you've identified from the readings.

3. Pay attention to the discussions

Listen carefully during class discussions. If classmates are debating a particular question and you see there's no clear answer, the question might be worth exploring further. Check with the instructor when you've identified such a topic, since you might end up using some insights that were first raised by classmates; but generally the instructor won't mind, because your written analysis of the subject will require vastly more thinking than the classmates' off-the-cuff statements did.

4. Pay attention to the news

Many seminar readings and class discussions mention recent events, which often contain the seed of an interesting article. What's more, immersing yourself in the class can lead you to notice interesting events in the news, or remember events that you heard about a few months before.

Don't feel constrained by the circumstances of a particular event, which may raise only a very narrow question, or have some unusual aspects. Use the event as a concrete example that helps you identify and confront a broader problem.

D. Budgeting Your Time

Students often have less time to write a seminar paper than a student article. Student article topics, and especially law review Note topics, tend to be chosen during the summer or at the start of the semester. In a seminar, though, you may have to wait until mid-semester, after you've gotten into the material and perhaps gained a better sense of what you want to write about.

This makes it especially important to manage your time wisely. You need to have the time to select a topic, do your research, write several drafts, and (if the instructor allows it) have your instructor read and comment on at least one draft. So look at the timeline on pp. 104–104, adjust it to your seminar's timetable, and stick to it.

E. Turning the Paper into a Publishable Article

Once you've written a seminar term paper, publish it. You've done the work; why not get an extra credential out of it?

Don't worry if you aren't on law review. If your paper is any good, you can get it published in some outside journal (see Part XXIII.A, p. 260). You might not get into the top law reviews, but a publication in a specialty journal or a second-tier journal is better than no publication.

You'll probably need to do some extra work to make the paper publishable. For instance, if your instructor let you skip explaining the legal background, you might need to fill in that section. But generally this isn't hard, since you've already thought through the problem, done the research, and written the paper. Even a law firm memo can be turned into a law review article (see Part XX), though the two are very different genres. A seminar paper is much closer to an article already.

Obviously, if you're planning to do this, ask your professor for advice: He might have suggestions that he never mentioned when the discussion was focused only on your writing a student paper. Better still, if you plan from the beginning to turn the seminar paper into an article, talk to your professor about this up front. He may have ideas about your choice of a claim and your organization that he won't bring up unless he thinks about the paper eventually becoming publishable.

XXII. CITE–CHECKING OTHERS' ARTICLES

A. Recommendations for Cite–Checkers

Part XVII applies not just to your own work, but also to articles that you're cite-checking for a law journal.

Cite-checking is important, and should be done thoroughly and thoughtfully. Checking authors' sources is part of what law journals *owe the legal profession*. Lawyers, judges, academics, and students rely on the accuracy of journal articles. (Scholars writing their own articles might check the original sources cited by the articles they read, but most readers don't have the time to do that.) Your journal's name attached to the article is an assurance by the journal that the article has been thoroughly checked.

Checking the sources is part of what you *owe the author*. Most authors count on cite-checkers to help catch their errors before the errors appear in print and become public embarrassments.

Checking the sources is part of what you *owe your fellow journal members* (past, present, and future), because embarrassing errors reflect badly on the journal as well as on the author.

Checking the sources is part of your *legal education*, since it helps you develop a careful and skeptical perspective that will help you in your own legal research and writing. It's easier to find errors in others' work than in your own; checking someone else's work is the best practice you can have for your own article and your future memos or briefs.

Finally, catching an author, especially some respected academic, in an error, and then (politely) suggesting that he correct the error can be *rewarding*—you can justly feel good about preventing embarrassment and misinformation.

So when you're cite-checking, you should look out for the same problems that I outline above:

1. If an article cites an intermediate source, find the original source, check the article's assertion against the original source, and suggest that the author cite the original source as well as the intermediate one.

2. Particularly carefully check articles citing newspaper summaries of court decisions, court filings, or empirical studies, or citing law review descriptions of historical, economic, or social science work.

3. Make sure that the article describes facts accurately, without using false synonyms, omitting important qualifiers, or relying on vague terms.

4. To the extent possible, investigate the soundness of the studies on which the article relies. If you see a weakness in the study, or find seemingly cogent criticisms of the study, urge the author to correct or clarify the article, or at least to briefly respond to the objection.

5. Look closely for unstated assumptions that the article makes when it draws inferences from the evidence, and suggest that the author make these assumptions explicit.

6. Think about how readers might misinterpret the article's assertions, and suggest that the author clarify the assertions to avoid such misinterpretations.

Of course, you'll need to use your judgment about how far you should go on all these points—how much effort you should invest in source-checking, how many suggestions you feel comfortable making to the author, and how many of those suggestions you insist on. My recommendations are:

a. Cite-check thoroughly, since that's part of your duty.

b. Err on the side of making more suggestions rather than fewer; the author will generally appreciate your input (especially since it represents an objective outside judgment), and, at worst, will just decline some of your proposed changes.

c. Insist only on those suggestions that you think are needed to prevent genuine errors or very probable reader misunderstandings.

d. Present your case politely, and leave room for compromise language.

e. *Never* make corrections without informing the author and giving the author a chance to reject or modify them, even if you think that the corrections are obviously necessary.

Fairly thorough cite-checking is one advantage that law has over other disciplines. In most other fields, editors don't systematically check the article's use of sources, though they might check the overall logic of the argument, and might object to factual claims that they themselves know to be false.

Some of the cautionary examples in Part XVII came from publications that don't do cite-checking; *Crime and Justice* is a faculty-edited journal that relies on authors to check their own sources, and some of the other sources were books, which generally aren't cite-checked by the publishers. Law review cite-checking isn't perfect (consider the student note that I gave as an example in Part XVII.J, p. 190), but it's better than nothing. And you can make it better still.

B. Recommendations for Law Review Editors

Few people come to law school as good cite-checkers. Critically checking sources is a skill that incoming law review members need to learn, and law review editorial boards are the ones who must teach it.

The material in Part XVII and XXII.A should be helpful for that. I recommend that you tell all new staffers to read these parts *and to do the exercises in Part XVII*, on pp. 158, 170, 181, and 190 (and perhaps also the editing exercises in Part XVI). You might tell them to first do the exercises without looking at the answers in Appendix II, and then to compare their results against the answers when they're done.

You might also organize a talk in which an editor orally walks the students through those exercises, and explains to them the errors that they were supposed to spot. The site *http://volokh.com/writing* contains some PowerPoint presentations that might be useful for such a talk.

XXIII. PUBLISHING AND PUBLICIZING

You've written your law review article; what now? (If you're no longer a student, skip the next two subsections and go straight to Part XXIII.A.3, p. 262.)

A. *Consider Publishing Outside Your School*

1. You can

If the journals at your school decide not to publish your work, submit it to other journals at other schools. Many journals hesitate to publish work by students from other schools, but many will seriously consider it. And many journals are starving for good material. To give an example from my own school, in the 2006-07 school year twelve UCLA students had their work accepted for publication in non-UCLA journals.

I've seen the same with other students I've known. One Harvard student whom I advised circulated his article, got offers from two top 20 main journals, and published it in the *Northwestern Law Review*, a journal that's pretty clearly in the top 15. One of my UCLA students circulated two of her articles to the main journals at the top 50 law schools, and to specialty journals at the top 20. On the first, she got three offers from primary journals and three from specialty ones; she accepted an offer from a specialty journal at Harvard. On the second, she got six offers from primary journals and nine from specialty ones, and accepted the one from the *U.C. Davis Law Review*.

Another UCLA student got offers for her article from the *Georgetown Immigration Law Journal* and the *Columbia Human Rights Law Review*, both well-respected publications at top 15 law schools. (Note that "law journal" and "law review" are essentially synonyms.) My brother had an article published in the *University of Pennsylvania Law Review* before he even started law school.

Remember, you've invested a lot of effort in your article. If you publish it, you'll get a valuable credential, and you might actually help improve the law a little bit. Don't let the opportunity slip away.

2. You should

What if you do have a chance to publish your article as a student Note at your own school? You might still prefer to send the piece out to be competitively considered by other journals.

This requires some effort, but I think it gives you a better credential, unless your own journal is a primary journal at a Top 20 or so school (e.g., the *Northwestern Law Review*), or perhaps a specialty journal at a Top 5 or so school (e.g., the *Harvard Journal on Legislation*). People who see a home-school Note publication on a resume may assume the student was on the journal, and discount the publication because journals tend to publish their own students' work with less quality screening than they use for outside work. But when people see a publication in a journal at a different school, they'll realize that the article was competitively selected, and might think more highly of it.

Before sending out your article to other journals, you should think about how this will look to your fellow journal members. If they see such behavior as disloyal, then ruining your relationship with them might not be worth the extra credential value of an outside publication. And you certainly should not look for an outside placement *after* you've already agreed to publish in your journal, or even after you've submitted it for consideration by your journal (since such submissions to your own journal usually carry an implicit promise that you'll accept an offer of publication).

But journals ought to *welcome* their members' publishing their work elsewhere—and if they don't see it that way, you should be able to persuade them. First, it's no harm to the journal: A journal's reputation turns on the school's reputation and on the quality of the articles from outside authors, not on the quality of its own students' Notes.

Second, it's good for other students on the journal. If a journal has room for, say, 12 student Notes per year, and 20 people want to publish their pieces, then your placing your good article in another journal means one more open slot for the other students. And third, it's good for the school and for student authors when the students' work is published in outside journals rather than inside ones.

In fact, I think journals (other than the primaries at the top 20 schools and specialty journals at the top 5 schools) should adopt a *policy* of advising their students to send their article out for competitive publication. Not all students will follow this advice; some people won't think that the extra credential is worth the trouble. But students should be encouraged to think that outside publication is better for them, for the school, and for their classmates than publishing in their own journal.

It may be too bad that the world is so credential-conscious; if everyone had enough time, they would actually read people's articles rather than just looking at where they were published. Still, the reality is that the place where a piece was published—and whether it was published at an outside journal, through competitive screening—matters, and both student authors and journal editors should recognize this.

3. Here's how

Here's what you do:

1. *Timing:* Figure out the right time to send the article. The best times are mid-February to March, and mid- to late August. April and September are a little worse but generally fine, May through early August are so-so, and October through early February are particularly bad.

Most journals' editorial boards serve from mid-February to mid-February, and many well-regarded journals fill up for the year by the end of October, which is why you should avoid October through early February. Most journals operate more slowly during the summer, or don't operate at all, which is why May through early August aren't very good. And because manuscripts might stay in journals' inboxes for several weeks before they're read, April and September submissions may run into problems similar to those of May and October submissions.

On the other hand, if the article is especially time-sensitive, send it out as soon as possible. Ask your faculty advisor for guidance on this.

2. *Cover letter:* Write a one-page cover letter that briefly, clearly, and effectively shows that your article is novel, nonobvious, and useful; see Appendix III.A, p. 371, for an example. You're trying to get journal editors to think, "This is a thoughtful, well-written article on an important topic, and if we publish it, many people will read it and cite it. We should be the ones who snag it, rather than letting it go to our rival journals." (Of course, be more subtle and more concrete than that.)

This may sound like mere salesmanship rather than Serious, Dignified Scholarship. But much of life requires good salesmanship. If you have a good idea, you should invest some effort into making sure that people see how good it is.

3. *Re-proofreading:* Give the article (and its abstract, see Part XXIII.C) one more editing and proofreading pass, to make sure that it looks as polished as possible. Ask your faculty advisor to suggest more improvements to the article. Sometimes seeing your willingness to actually publish the piece will persuade the professor to give you some

tips that he might have otherwise thought were moot.

4. *Re-bluebooking:* While you're proofreading, make sure that the footnotes are in Bluebook format. Rightly or wrongly, many journal editors see good bluebooking as a sign of professionalism; accommodate their prejudices. Not all law journals follow the Bluebook, but the great majority do, so it makes sense to follow the dominant convention. And journals that don't follow the Bluebook probably get 90% of their pieces in Bluebook form anyway, so they won't resent you for being part of that 90%.

5. *Your status as a student:* Do not say that you're a student in your cover letter or in the article, though of course do not lie or make misleading statements about your status. Many journals will realize you're still a law student, but no need to rub their noses in this fact.

6. a. *Finding specialty journals:* Find any specialty journals (for instance, the *UCLA Entertainment Law Review* or the *Yale Journal of Law & the Humanities*) that focus on your area. You'll want to submit the article to all these journals.

Some articles may fit into multiple categories: For instance, a historical article about constitutional challenges to statutes that discriminate based on sex might be of interest to constitutional law journals, journals on women and the law, and history journals. To find out which specialty journals are best for you, check the list of law review addresses linked to at *http://volokh.com/writing/submitting*; the list is nicely organized by category. Also ask your faculty advisor whether there are any other specialty journals that he can recommend.

b. *Faculty-edited specialty journals:* Most specialty journals are student-edited, but some are faculty-edited, and many faculty-edited journals insist that you not submit to anyone else while they're considering your work; call them to check whether they indeed have this policy. You should generally avoid journals that forbid simultaneous submissions, since they might not get back to you for months, and during those months you won't be able to send the article anywhere else.

On the other hand, sometimes you might have the time to wait (for instance, if you finish the article in December, when many student journals aren't accepting submissions). Then you should submit to faculty-edited journals, which are often quite prestigious—but politely ask them how quickly they'll give you an answer.

7. *Finding the best generalist journals:* Look up the latest *U.S. News & World Report* rankings of law schools; this list is not a great indicator

of schools' quality, but it does give a good sense of their reputations, which is what matters to you here. You'll want to send the article to the general journals at all the schools ranked 60 to 21, or possibly 100 to 21.

If you are a recent graduate, you should also submit to general journals at the top 20 schools. If you're a current student, you might do the same (especially if someone else is paying for the submission), but your odds with those journals as a current student are quite low.

This whole process may sound unpleasantly class-conscious, but there's a pecking order out there, and ignoring it is costly, for two reasons. First, the higher-ranked the journal, the better the publication will look in your resume, precisely because the higher-ranked journals tend to be more selective.

Second, consider the likely thinking of potential readers (law professors, lawyers, students, judges, or clerks) who do a Westlaw or Lexis search, and find fifty articles, all with relevant-sounding titles and written by people whom they don't know. How will they choose which articles to read? In large part by the prestige of the journal in which they're published. They'll realize that this is an imperfect way of selecting articles, but it's the only way they can afford to use, since they probably won't have the time to read or even skim each one.

There are other journal ranking systems out there—for instance, ones based on how often articles in the journal have been cited—and you might prefer to use them instead. But my sense is that the *U.S. News* rankings best reflect (and shape) schools' reputations, and journals' reputations generally track their schools' reputations.

8. *Formatting:* Format your article to look like an already published article: use a proportionally spaced font, nicely formatted footnotes, single spacing, running page heads, a justified right margin, hyphenation, and so on. This makes your work more readable and more professional-looking. (I've put a sample document template on the Web at *http://volokh.com/writing*.) Some journals claim that they want submissions in other formats—for instance, double-spaced—but I've never gotten any complaints about my method, and I suspect that most editors actually find it easier to read articles formatted the way I describe.

9. *Submitting:* There are three ways to submit your article.

a. *ExpressO:* Berkeley Electronic Press's ExpressO service lets you automatically submit your article to nearly all the journals you want. (A few journals don't accept ExpressO submissions, but very few.) I link to it at *http://volokh.com/writing/submitting*.

ExpressO asks you to indicate the journals to which you want to send the article, and prompts you for the names of the files that contain your article and cover letter. It then picks up the documents from your computer, prints and sends them to the few journals that insist on print copies, and e-mails them to the many journals that take electronic submissions. This can save you a lot of effort, and it costs—as of the time I write this—a reasonable $6.50 per journal for print copies and $2 per journal for electronic copies.

Some schools have a school-wide license for ExpressO (an "Institutional ExpressO Account"), under which anyone with an e-mail address at the school, including students, can submit without paying anything extra. If your school has such an account, then ExpressO simply won't ask you for payment information before making the deliveries; so just try submitting your article, and see if you can do it for free.

b. *SSRN:* The Social Science Research Network also lets you submit your article to many journals just by filling out a few Web forms; and, as of the time I write this, SSRN is free. I also link to it at *http://volokh.com/writing/submitting*.

SSRN doesn't handle as many journals as ExpressO does: It doesn't submit to journals that only take print copies, and it omits even some of the journals that take electronic copies via ExpressO. But in the meantime, if you want to save money, you should use SSRN to submit to those journals that SSRN covers, and then use ExpressO to submit to the remainder.

All this may change over time: SSRN may cover more, some journals that take only paper submissions may start accepting electronic submissions, ExpressO rates may fall, or SSRN may start charging. I hope to summarize the current ExpressO vs. SSRN tradeoff at *http://volokh.com/writing/submitting*, and to update the summary as things change.

c. *Manually sending:* You can also print and copy the article yourself, and then mail it; *http://volokh.com/writing/submitting* links to a list of journal mailing addresses. Some journals also let you submit by e-mail directly—a list of their e-mail addresses is also linked to by *http://volokh.com/writing/submitting*—but many do not.

If you do submit by e-mail, keep in mind that e-mail addresses change more often than postal addresses. If an e-mail address looks like a personal address, call the journal or visit its Web site to confirm that the address is still current. Also, regardless of whether the address looks official, watch for "unknown address" messages that you might get in response to your e-mails, and resubmit the materials to a better e-mail address, or by sending a paper copy.

Sending the article manually, though, is a huge hassle, and I much recommend using ExpressO or SSRN instead. Among other things, if you don't use the electronic services, you'll be tempted to save effort by submitting to fewer journals—a mistake, because then you'll be less likely to get a good offer, which means you won't get the most out of the much greater effort that you've expended on writing your article.

10. *Saving money:* As I mentioned, if your school has an Institutional ExpressO Account, you can submit via those services for free. But if those services cost money, see if your school (1) is willing to reimburse all or part of your ExpressO submission costs, or of your copying and mailing costs, or (2) is willing to let you use its copying machines for free, or to send your article for free through its mailroom. Option 2 may be bureaucratically easier, since it might be doable without getting the accounting department involved.

Ask your dean's office. If your school has a faculty member or administrator in charge of helping students get jobs as law clerks or professors, ask that person. Or ask your faculty advisor to ask on your behalf (or perhaps just to let you use his copying and mailing account, if the faculty are allowed to do that).

Don't be bashful: It's in the school's interest for their students and graduates to get valuable credentials, and it's hardly a vast expense. Many schools are willing to do this; and even if the administration isn't already committed to helping this way, a sympathetic faculty member may be able to pull the right strings with little effort.

Whether you're spending your own money or trying to persuade the school to spend its money, you might want to use the "Media mail" (also known as "book rate") postage rate, which is available for manuscripts as well as published works. A package that weighs less than a pound costs only about $1.50 if you use media mail, but may cost, depending on the weight, $3 or more if you use first-class mail or priority mail. (Weigh the package and then compare the prices on the USPS Web site.) Note, though, that media mail tends to take about a week longer to deliver, so plan your mailing schedule accordingly.

11. *Sending the second wave of submissions:* Then, if you haven't gotten any offers by two or three weeks later, send your article to the next 50 general journals, or even to more than that. How long you wait should depend on the timing of your initial submission, see item 1; if you submitted late in the cycle, then don't wait long until sending the

second batch. Definitely do not wait until all the journals in your first wave reject you—many of the journals won't send you a rejection notice for many months, and some will never send it.

12. Wait for an offer.

13. *Getting the offer's expiration date:* If you get an offer, ask how long you have to decide whether to accept it. The journals usually give you from twenty-four hours to two weeks, though they'll sometimes give more. If they don't give you a deadline, ask for two weeks—that's not unreasonable, and other journals are usually well-equipped to consider your shop-up requests (see item 15) within two weeks. You generally don't have to accept the offer on the spot, though if the journal does insist on an immediate answer, you may want to say yes if the journal is good enough that you doubt you'll do much better.

14. *Getting the offer's terms:* Listen closely to the offer to hear whether they're offering you publication as a student Note, as opposed to as a full-fledged article. Such student Note offers are not as good, though they're better than nothing. If the journal is just offering to publish your piece as a student Note, call other journals to see if you can get an article offer from a comparably ranked or even slightly lower-ranked journal.

If you'd like, you might ask the journal to send you an e-mail confirming the expiration date. It's good to have for future reference, just so there's no misunderstanding; and such an e-mail will likely also indicate whether the offer of publication is as an article or as a Note.

15. *Shopping up:* a. E-mail all the journals on your list that are ranked substantially higher, and tell them that you have an offer from the first journal and that you'd like an expedited review. ExpressO lets you do this very easily, and also keeps a record of whom you've e-mailed this way.

Such shopping up can often get you an offer from a more prestigious place. It's considered ethically permissible. It's expected (though of course not relished) by the journals. And it's done all the time. If the other journals need more time than the original journal gave you, you might be able to persuade the original journal's editors to give you an extension, especially if you give them something in return (for instance, a promise that you'll shop up the article only to a small set of journals, and withdraw it from the others).

This process may seem tacky, and many people have argued that this system, where authors submit articles to many places and then shop up offers to higher-ranked journals, unfairly wastes student editors' time. This may be a good argument, and it might be good if people could come up with another system for doing this.

Still, I feel obligated to give you the advice that's best for you as an author. As a journal editor, you might understandably resent the current system—but until it's changed, as an author you ought to know the most effective way of operating within it. Professors know these rules. You're entitled to know them, too.

b. Unless your original offer was merely for publication as a student Note (see point 14 above) or has a short deadline, you should probably call only those journals that are substantially higher-ranked. There's no real difference between a primary journal at school 30 on the list and the one at school 25, so if #30 gives you an offer first, and gives you plenty of time before the offer expires (at least a week or two), you may want to reward the editors' good taste.

On the other hand, there probably is a real difference in reputation between #30 and #15. (For advice on where to draw the line, talk to your faculty advisor.) Moreover, if #30 gives you a short deadline, you might want to call #29 and better (or even #31–35), hoping to get an offer which can give you more time for higher-ranked journals to consider your piece.

c. Don't feel embarrassed about trying to shop an offer from a #75 journal to a #1. True, it would be more impressive to #1 if you were calling to shop up an offer from #10—but any offer is a signal that some readers think well of the article, and in any event there's no real harm to you if the #1 people aren't impressed by your call.

d. Which is higher-ranked: A primary journal at a school that's ranked #50, or a specialty journal at a school that's ranked #15? (Assume that neither journal is faculty-edited.) It's hard to answer this recurring question in the abstract, partly because evaluating reputation is hard, and partly because the answer varies from discipline to discipline. Specialty international law journals, for instance, seem to be especially well-regarded among international law scholars.

The best advice I can give is to ask a professor who specializes in the field, and to check the Washington & Lee law library's citation counts (linked to at *http://volokh.com/writing/submitting*; check the "Comb." box and then click on "Submit").

16. *Abiding by the deal:* Do not renege once you've accepted an offer: It's unethical and bad for your reputation, and with the Internet, word

can get around quickly. "Bust a deal," Auntie Entity tells us, "face the wheel"—all the contract law you need to know.*

Also, once you've accepted an offer, call, write, or e-mail the other journals to withdraw your piece from them; that's the kind thing to do, because it saves them the substantial effort of considering your article further. There's an incomplete but still helpful list of journal e-mail addresses linked to by *http://volokh.com/writing/submitting*; other journals' e-mail addresses should be available from their Web sites; and the list of phone numbers and postal addresses is also linked to by *http://volokh.com/writing/submitting*.

17. *Editing some more:* If you get no offer, give your article a few more good editing passes; you'll be amazed how many improvements you can make after a month or two away from the piece. Send the revised version to the next twenty or thirty lower-ranked journals.

If you're resubmitting in the next editorial board year (editorial board years usually run March to March), also send the revised version to the same journals to which you sent the earlier version—a new editorial board may be willing to publish an article that the old board rejected. Repeat until you have an offer. There are over 400 law journals in the U.S. If your article is at all worthwhile, you'll get it published somewhere.

18. *Checking for updates:* All this is the best advice I have as of the time this book is being published; but check *http://volokh.com/writing/submitting* for updates—if there are important changes in the articles market, I will post new recommendations there.

* * *

Finally, a word about an inevitable part of this process—*rejection*. Even experienced law professors at top schools generally get rejected by over 90% of the journals to which they submit. I've written nearly 50 law review articles, half of which were published in top 20 journals, but my submissions still get rejected by the great majority of the places to which I send them.

Rejection is part of the process, and the only way to deal with it is to try to ignore it. Remember that all you need is one acceptance. Remember also that rejections happen for many reasons, and might have noth-

---

* *Mad Max 3: Beyond Thunderdome.* The civil procedure aspects of the Thunderdome judicial system—especially the trial by combat, where the mantra is "Two men enter, one man leaves"—are more controversial.

ing to do with the merit of your piece—for instance, the articles editors might prefer other topics, or might be prejudiced against work written by students or even by law clerks or practicing lawyers.

The *worst* thing you can do is let your fear of rejection keep you from circulating the article as widely as possible, or recirculating it if it wasn't picked up the first time around. Remember: It's not personal. It's not about you. It happens to your professors all the time. And no one will know.

B. *Choosing a Title*

1. The three functions of a title

A title should do three things. Most importantly, the title should *persuade people to read the article*. When busy people do a Westlaw or Lexis search that yields fifty items, how do they choose what to read? They look at the authors' names and at the titles. If the title looks helpful—not necessarily exciting, but helpful—they'll read further. The title is your opportunity to get people to devote time to at least reading the Introduction.

Second, the title can *frame people's thinking* once they start reading your piece. If a title focuses the reader on a concept, the reader is more likely to keep that concept in mind.

Third, the title can *help readers remember your article*. Remember, though, that a memorable title is of little use to you if it wasn't attractive enough to get people to read the piece in the first place.

So how should you choose your title? Let me suggest the following approach.

2. Start with a descriptive title

Start with a descriptive title, which summarizes the general question that your article is answering (though not necessarily your specific answer). If a person's query comes up with an article called "Freedom of Speech and Workplace Harassment," the person will have a good sense of the article's substance. Naturally, the title can capture only a small part of your point, but it can capture enough to give readers some idea of whether the article is relevant to their interests. Purely descriptive titles might not be that memorable, and might not much help frame readers' thinking, but they're good at getting people to read the piece.

Of course, it's not enough that your title be comprehensible to you; *make it comprehensible to your readers*. I named one of my articles "Test Suites," but late in the publication process realized that few readers would know what that means. Renaming the piece "Test Suites: A Tool for Improving Student Articles" made the purpose and value of the article clearer (though I think the title could have been made better still).

It's acceptable for an article to have *a subtitle as well as a title*. This can let you communicate two ideas, one general and one more specific. For instance, "Freedom of Speech and Information Privacy: The Troubling Implications of a Right to Stop Others from Speaking About You" conveys both a general point (the article is about the First Amendment problems with information privacy laws) and a specific one (the problems arise because "information privacy" really refers to a supposed right to stop others from speaking about you). The combination is long—perhaps too long—but it takes advantage of its length. Likewise, "Academic Legal Writing: Student Notes, Law Review Articles, Seminar Papers, and Getting on Law Review" gives people a short summary (the book is about academic legal writing) but also tells them that it's useful for four different purposes.

3. Try including your key innovative concept in the title

If your article focuses on a particular concept—and especially if it pioneers the concept—try to include the concept in your title. Say you're writing an article about laws requiring passersby to help strangers whom they see to be in peril. Your main thesis is that these laws might have the perverse effect of *discouraging* some people from cooperating with the police; but you also think this broader idea of anticooperative effects of law deserves more attention in other contexts as well.

"Duties to Rescue and Anticooperative Effects of Law" may be a good title: It tells potential readers that your article is both about duties to rescue and about the general problem of law discouraging cooperation with the authorities; it focuses readers' attention on the concept of "anticooperative effects"; and it gives them a phrase that they can remember the article by. My colleague Ken Karst, for instance, pioneered the term "The Freedom of Intimate Association" in a *Yale Law Journal* article with that title, and now the phrase is a well-established part of constitutional jurisprudence.

4. If you want to make the title witty, consider that only after you've made it descriptive

If you have a witty play on words that you'd like to include in the title, the time to consider it is now—after you've come up with a descriptive title.

I try to avoid witty titles in my own work, but I concede that a little wit can make the article seem more appealing, can put the reader in a good mood, and can help the reader remember the article later. I still remember an article title I saw in the early 1990s, "One Hundred Years of Privacy"; this both communicated the article's essence (a look back on the privacy tort a century after Warren and Brandeis first proposed it), and humorously alluded to the novel "One Hundred Years of Solitude."

Another article was called "A RFRA Runs Through It," echoing the title of the movie "A River Runs Through It." People who are familiar with religious freedom law know that RFRA is the Religious Freedom Restoration Act, commonly pronounced "riff-rah," not that different from "river." The article's thesis was that after the enactment of the federal RFRA, the entire U.S. Code should be read as if RFRA had amended each statute, and changed the policy balance struck by the drafters of each statute—hence RFRA runs through the entire Code, so the joke is apt. Plus the article was published in a symposium conducted by the *Montana Law Review*, and the movie was set in Montana. Cute.

But be careful. First, amateur comedians notoriously overestimate how funny their jokes are.

Second, with some topics (abortion, the death penalty, and the like), some readers will find any humor to be jarring. For instance, "Creole and Unusual Punishment: A Tenth Anniversary Examination of Louisiana's Capital Rape Statute"—a real title—contains a pun that's amusing in the abstract; but, when applied to the death penalty, the joke might alienate more readers than it amuses. It's hard to know for sure, but you should at least consider the risk.

Third, even an amusing gag distracts the reader from your main point. To be effective, the joke must be interesting and memorable enough that its value overcomes the distraction.

Fourth, some writers find a joke so appealing that they use it even when it doesn't quite capture the point they are trying to make, or when it is surplus that doesn't add anything valuable. Better use serious words that mean exactly what you need to say, no more and no less, than a joke that means something slightly different, or that takes up words that could be used for something substantive. Humorous subtitles are common offenders here: They often add nothing besides the joke, and the joke's place can often be effectively taken by a subtitle that actually communicates something useful about the piece.

So reread the title on several occasions to make sure that the gag really works, and ask friends whether they agree. If you're in doubt, err on the side of having a purely substantive title.

5. Edit the title especially carefully

Edit the title even more carefully than you edit the rest of your work. Clarity, proper word choice, and liveliness are especially important in a title, both to make people more interested in reading the piece, and to set the right tone for their reading—if the title sounds clunky or abstract, people will expect the rest of the article to be the same.

Thus, for instance, "Considering the Advantages and Disadvantages of Prohibitions on Concealable Firearms" isn't as good as "The Costs and Benefits of Handgun Prohibition." The "considering the" is surplus; "costs and benefits" is shorter and simpler-sounding than "advantages and disadvantages"; and "handgun prohibition" cuts out an unnecessary prepositional phrase, and recasts the abstract "concealable firearms" as the concrete "handguns."

6. Avoid case names

Generally, avoid case names. Just as the article should usually be about a topic and not just a particular case (see Part I.I.2, p. 35), so should the title. First, the case name might not be familiar to some readers, unless the case is extremely famous; a reader might be interested in the general subject, but might not connect the case to the subject. Second, stressing a particular case makes your claim seem narrower and less useful.

Sometimes, a case may be so important and controversial that many readers will want to read articles about it—referring to the case name will then draw more readers than it will repel. But generally speaking, titles should be about concepts, not cases.

7. Avoid jargon, little-known terms, and statutory citations

Readers may be put off by titles with little-known legal terms, statutory citations (unless they're extremely well-known, such as "Title VII" or "42 U.S.C. § 1983"), and jargon, whether it's drawn from economics, literary criticism, feminist studies, libertarian philosophy, or what have you.

Many readers will be interested in the general topic, but will not fully understand the terms; and when the query gives them those fifty titles, they'll choose the ones they understand rather than the ones they don't. Again, there may be exceptions, for instance if the substance of your article will only appeal to those people who know the jargon—then, the technical terms may attract exactly the readers you want. But usually, stick with plain English.

8. Choose your role models wisely

That other articles have silly or mystifying titles doesn't mean yours should, too. Well-known authors can get away with less descriptive titles, since people will read their pieces because of the author's name, not the article's name. You don't have that luxury.

9. An example

Here's an example. You decide to write an article about whether compulsory licensing of copyrighted musical compositions makes sense, using the recently decided *Allman v. Capricorn Records* as a starting point. Don't start with "Compulsion or Anti–Monopoly?" or "Licensing Fair and Foul," or, heaven forbid, "Copyright and § 115: Is *Capricorn* a Sign of the Times?"

Rather, (1) start with a descriptive title, such as "Copyright and Compulsory Licenses" or "Compulsory Licenses in Copyrighted Musical Compositions." These aren't exciting, but people who see the title will know whether the piece is likely to help them.

Then, (2) see if there are any other basic concepts around which your article is oriented. For instance, if you argue that compulsory licenses make copyright a form of "intellectual quasi-property," rather than true property, mention that concept in the title: "Compulsory Licenses in Copyrighted Musical Compositions: Intellectual Quasi–Property as a Remedy for Transaction Costs." This is especially so if you're trying to pioneer the concept of intellectual quasi-property.

If you do want to rework the title to (3) include some pun or witticism, now is the time to do it. This way, you have the descriptive title in front of you, and can compare it with the amusing alternative. If the amusing version is clearly better, go with it. But if it's not better—and it probably won't be better—then stick with the purely substantive title.

Now (4) see if you can make your title shorter, clearer, and more forceful. Does the subtitle really add enough value to the title? Do you really need the word "Compositions," or will the title be clear enough (and less technical-sounding) without it? Do you really need the word "Copyrighted," or will that be obvious, since virtually all musical compositions are protected by copyright? (I think "copyrighted" is probably helpful, because it makes it clearer to the casual reader that the article is about copyright law.) Can you make the title sound more active, perhaps "Compulsory Licenses in Copyrighted Music: Fighting Transaction Costs Through Intellectual Quasi–Property"? I'm not sure what the best title would be, but I am sure that you should spend some time editing it.

You don't have (5) any case names here, and you probably don't need them. "Transaction costs" is a bit of (6) economics jargon, but it's so well-known that it's probably worth keeping, especially since there's no really good synonym. You don't have any technical legal terms or statutory cites, which is good: If your title had been "17 U.S.C. § 115: Fighting Transaction Costs Through Intellectual Quasi–Property," you should have changed it to our working title ("Compulsory Licenses ...")—many readers, even ones who know something about copyright law, might not be sure what § 115 covers.

So you now have a pretty good title. It's not exciting, but it should get the job done. Someone who is interested in compulsory licenses and who comes across a piece labeled "Compulsory Licenses in Copyrighted Music: Fighting Transaction Costs Through Intellectual Quasi–Property" will probably think it's worth looking at—and that's the title's main function.

C. *Writing an Abstract*

An abstract is a short summary of an article. You should write it before submitting it to the journal, and include it at the start of the article, perhaps in a format such as this:

MY ARTICLE TITLE

My Name

ABSTRACT

[Abstract goes here. Abstract goes here. Abstract goes here. Abstract goes here. Abstract goes here. Abstract goes here. Abstract goes here.]

[The rest of the article goes here. The rest of the article goes here. The rest of the article goes here. The rest of the article goes here.]

Some journals print abstracts in italics, but I recommend against formatting the abstract that way. Big blocks of italicized text are harder to read than the same text set in a normal font.

There are four places an abstract might be distributed and read:

1. Some journals publish it at the start of the article, on the issue's table of contents, or on the journal's Web site.

2. Whether or not the journal publishes an abstract, services such as the Social Science Research Network (see p. 286) maintain e-mail distribution lists through which hundreds of subscribers get abstracts of forthcoming articles. These distribution lists are valuable tools to get readers for your work.

3. Some researchers search the Social Science Research Network abstract database to find articles, including forthcoming articles that aren't yet on Lexis, Westlaw, or HeinOnline.

4. Some law review editors look at the abstract when the article is submitted, and forward it to other editors when they recommend that the article be accepted.

So it's worth taking some care with the abstract. Don't view it as an afterthought, to be cobbled together a few minutes before you circulate the article. Write it at least several days beforehand, and edit it several times, just like you edited the rest of the article several times. Take special care with editing the abstract, since for many readers the abstract will be the first part they read—and maybe the only part they read. And take special pains to tighten the wording as much as possible, to make it as terse (but readable) as possible.

The abstract is an advertisement for your article: It tries to persuade readers to invest their scarce time and attention into reading your article, or at least the Introduction. A good abstract might persuade some to read the article right away. But it could also help others remember the article (even if just vaguely) for the future, so that when the underlying issue becomes important to them, they can find and read the article then.

And the audience for your advertisement is quite demanding. They've generally found the abstract just through a quick skim of an SSRN e-mail or a law review table of contents, so they aren't sure the article will be of any value to them.

You need to quickly show them this value, by clearly and tersely telling readers (1) what problem the article is trying to solve, and (2) what valuable original observations the article offers. Naturally, the abstract can't go into much detail. But it has to at least give a general idea of what the article contributes.

Here, for instance, is an adequate abstract, adequate because it quickly captures the essence of the value added by the article:

> People often argue that symbolic expression—especially flag burning—isn't really "speech" or "press," and that the Court's decisions protecting symbolic expression are thus illegitimate.
>
> But it turns out that the original meaning of the First Amendment likely includes symbolic expression. Speech restrictions of the Framing era routinely treated symbolic expression the same as literal "speech" and "press." Constitutional speech protections of that era did so as well, though the evidence on this is slimmer. And the drafting history of the phrase "the freedom of speech, or of the press," coupled with the views of leading commentators from the early 1800s, suggests that the First Amendment's text was understood as protecting "publishing," a term that at the time covered communication of symbolic expression and not just printing. Though the Court has never relied on this evidence, even originalists ought to accept the Court's bottom line conclusion that the First Amendment covers symbolic expression.

The first sentence does three things. First, it notes the general topic of the article—the First Amendment and symbolic expression generally. Second, the sentence identifies the specific focus of the article, which is whether the text of the First Amendment must be read as protecting only "speech" and "press" and not symbolic expression. Third, the sentence quickly provides a concrete illustration (flag burning) of the abstraction (symbolic expression).

277

The second sentence explains the article's claim: The original meaning of the First Amendment likely covers symbolic expression. Readers who stop reading there will at least remember something like "There's an article that says that even originalists should approve of the Court's flag-burning decisions."

That would be an oversimplification of the article's claim, but that's fine—any one-sentence summary that lingers in people's minds will inevitably oversimplify. The important thing is that if the issue comes up for readers in the future, they might well search for the article, find it, read it, and use it. And, if the author is lucky, maybe some readers will be interested enough to actually read the article right away, or at least move from reading the abstract to reading the Introduction.

The next three sentences quickly summarize the main arguments that the article uses to support its claim. These arguments—here, historical assertions, though for another article they might be normative arguments or empirical findings—are part of the contribution that the article offers. Again, the summary is an oversimplification, and as a result may not be entirely clear to all readers. But it should at least give the reader a glimpse of the observations that the article makes.

Finally, the last sentence ties the argument to the caselaw: The sentence explains that this is an article that offers historical support for the Court's precedents, rather than an article that argues against the Court's precedents.

Many authors try to fit an abstract into one paragraph, and some journals seem to prefer that. I advise against this, unless the abstract has to be very short. Shorter paragraphs tend to be more readable, and longer paragraphs tend to be alienating to many readers. And the reader of the abstract will likely be the sort of reader who is especially unmotivated to read further. The more you can do to make the abstract appealing, within the space constraints you're given, the better.

Likewise, I like including numbering, for instance in this abstract:

> How should state and federal constitutional rights to keep and bear arms be turned into workable constitutional doctrine? I argue that unitary tests such as "strict scrutiny," "intermediate scrutiny," "undue burden," and the like don't make sense here, just as they don't fully describe the rules applied to most other constitutional rights.
>
> Rather, courts should separately consider four different categories of justifications for restricting rights: (1) Scope justifications, which derive from constitutional text, original meaning, tradition, or background principles; (2) burden justifications, which rest on the claim

that a particular law doesn't impose a substantial burden on the right, and thus doesn't unconstitutionally infringe it; (3) danger reduction justifications, which rest on the claim that some particular exercise of the right is so unusually dangerous that it might justify restricting the right; and (4) government as proprietor justifications, which rest on the government's special role as property owner, employer, or subsidizer.

I suggest where the constitutional thresholds for determining the adequacy of these justifications might be set, and I use this framework to analyze a wide range of restrictions: "what" restrictions (such as bans on machine guns, so-called "assault weapons," or unpersonalized handguns), "who" restrictions (such as bans on possession by felons, misdemeanants, noncitizens, or 18-to-20-year-olds), "where" restrictions (such as bans on carrying in public, in places that serve alcohol, or in parks, or bans on possessing in public housing projects), "how" restrictions (such as storage regulations), "when" restrictions (such as waiting periods), "who knows" regulations (such as licensing or registration requirements), and taxes and other expenses.

Though it's unusual to number individual clauses in normal prose, here the numbering quickly shows the hurried reader how the sentence is structured, and what the four elements of the proposed framework are. It might have even been helpful to number the list in the last paragraph, but too much numbering might have annoyed readers—a bit of departure from standard prose style is fine, but more might have made the abstract look odd. And the quotation marks surrounding the key items in the last paragraph probably provide some internal delimiters that can serve as alternatives to numbering.

Two more tips:

1. Don't just say "this article analyzes problem X"; say, as well as you can given the limited space, what your solution to problem X is. (The second abstract quoted above does violate this rule, but that's probably inevitable given the size of that article and the number of specific restrictions the abstract covers.)

2. Talk about concepts, not case names, statutory citations, or other scholars to whom you're responding, unless the cases, statutes, or people are very important to your topic and nearly certain to be familiar to your likely readers.

D. Working with Law Journal Editors

So your article is accepted for publication, whether at your school or elsewhere. Now, the journal will cite-check it, and work with you to edit it. Here are some tips for getting the most out of this process.

1. Have the right attitude about edits

Editors are law students just like you are (or like you recently were). They have some advantages over you: (1) They are probably more objective about the subject and about your writing than you are, so they can see flaws that you might miss. (2) They probably know less about the subject than you do, so they can more easily read things from the average reader's perspective, and see where the article doesn't explain enough things that the reader would need to know. (3) Some of them are better writers than you are, perhaps because they have more pre-law-school writing experience, or are just more talented.

They also have some disadvantages compared to you: (1) They know less about the subject than you do, so some of their suggested changes may be incorrect. (2) Some of them are worse writers than you are, so their suggested changes may be inelegant or even ungrammatical. (3) They're proposing changes and additions to an existing article, and this new material may clash stylistically with the existing material. (4) The article is *your* article, not theirs, so you are entitled to make your point in your style, not their point in theirs.

These observations lead to some suggestions:

a. *Seriously consider* any claims that something you wrote is unclear, inadequately proven, unpersuasive, wrong, or inelegant. If your first reaction is to say "no, my way is better," that might just be because you've fallen in love with your own words, and don't see the flaws that the more impartial editors see. You might want to adopt a *presumption in favor of accepting proposed edits*—if both your view and the editor's seem reasonable, go with the editor's, which is more objective and closer to the likely view of most readers.

b. *Consider especially seriously* claims that you're mischaracterizing a source or making an unsound argument. If the editor thinks this is so, then some readers might, too. Moreover, journals are entitled to insist that you correct any substantive mistakes—ensuring accuracy is part of their job.

c. *If material needs to be inserted, write it yourself, or at least heavily edit the proposed insertions.* While you should take seriously editors' objections, you should be more skeptical about their proposed solutions, especially suggestions for new wording (new text, new parentheticals for footnotes, a new abstract, and the like). These proposed changes are often good, but they can contain errors, and they can be inconsistent with your article's style. Feel free to heavily edit the proposed insertions, and other proposed changes, or just reject them and write your own insertions instead.

d. *Look carefully at proposed changes both in the text and in the footnotes.* The footnotes, as well as the text, will be published under your name, and any errors will be your fault. Check the editors' work, just like they will check yours.

e. *Reject proposed changes that you think make matters worse.* This is your right as the author (unless the unchanged text would be incorrect or misleading), and in my experience most journals acknowledge that it's your right. If, after taking seriously the suggestion, you think the current text is fine and the proposed change is worse, reject the change—change it back yourself, or mark it with a "STET" (the editing term for "change back").

f. *Investigate suspicious-seeming claims of erroneous usage.* If you think that some objection is unfounded (for instance, if the editors are saying that it's wrong to put a preposition at the end of a sentence, and you disagree), look it up. Check a usage dictionary—for example, *Merriam-Webster's Dictionary of English Usage, The New Fowler's Modern English Usage,* or Bryan Garner's *A Dictionary of Modern Legal Usage*—or do a Lexis search to see how reputable publications do this. There are many usage myths (such as the myth that you may not end a sentence with a preposition), and editors sometimes believe them. If the sources say that you are correct, and if on reflection you believe your usage is not just correct but also more readable, then STET the change, and, if asked, politely explain to the editors why you believe you're right.

g. *Be skeptical about claims of "journal policy."* Generally, when you're making a reasonable request, and the journal responds just with "no, that's against journal policy," that very response is often evidence that the journal doesn't have a better reason for its objection. (It may also be evidence, however, that your request is unreasonable, and the editors are understandably tired of arguing with you about it.) Claims that "we need to maintain consistency within the volume" are also weak. Very few people will read several articles within one volume (or even one issue) of the journal and say "this article contains split infinitives and that one doesn't—how inconsistent."

Obviously, you and the editors might eventually reach an impasse, and you might be the one who has to give in. But don't give in too quickly. If you feel strongly about the issue, say so to the editors, explain why your position is sensible, and explain that the article will be primarily seen as your work, not the journal's. Often, the editors will be persuaded.

h. *But remember that your article should be readable, not just correct.* If your usage is technically correct, but the editors' proposal is indeed more readable, go along with it. Tip (a)—take proposed changes seriously—is still the most important one, though sometimes, after taking the proposal seriously, you might find yourself rejecting it.

2. Insist on seeing all changes

All the above presupposes that you are aware of all the changes that are being made—as you should be. Politely but firmly ask the editors to mark any changes they make, either on any paper edits that they send you, or through computerized redlining if the edited versions are sent to you electronically. Stress that you'd like to see even tiny changes, and even changes in footnotes.

Most editors are good about showing you all the changes; even if they know they will insist on a change, they know that they should alert you to it and give you a chance to make it the way you want it made. They understand that the article will have your name on it, and that you therefore deserve to sign off on every letter in it.

Unfortunately, editors sometimes neglect this important point, especially when they think that time is short and that some error is particularly glaring. I once got a final round of page proofs a few days before the article was supposed to be sent to the printer, and found that someone had added a whole paragraph to the introduction, without warning me. Had I not been rereading the whole piece carefully, I would have missed the change, and would have had my name attached to some text that I never wrote and never checked. And on top of that, the new paragraph was grammatically incorrect, and was written in a style that jarringly differed from mine.

So politely tell the journal that you need to see all the changes, no matter how minor; and if you see any unannounced changes being made, raise a fuss (again, politely) so that this doesn't happen again.

3. Always keep a copy of any marked–up draft you mail

First, imagine how rotten you'd feel if you spent days marking up a draft, and then the only existing copy of the mark-up got lost in the mail. Second, keeping the copy lets you do what the next subsection suggests.

4. Make sure your earlier changes were properly entered

Whenever you get a new draft, make sure that any changes that were marked on the previous draft were properly entered. Even the best editors make mistakes when they enter changes—and you and the editors are jointly responsible for catching these mistakes.

5. Use the opportunity to edit more yourself

When a law journal publishes an article, it usually sends you two rounds of edits, and then one or two rounds of page proofs.

This is a great opportunity for you to go through some more editing passes yourself. You should have edited the article thoroughly before handing it in to your professor and before sending it out to the journals. But now you've had a few months away from the piece, so it will be easier for you to read it with new eyes; you may have learned more about the subject since then; and you're now incorporating edits from someone else, and these edits might cause new problems. So reread the whole piece thoroughly each time you get it, and mark it up just as you did in your earlier edits—correct substantive errors, clarify vague points, remove redundancy, and improve the wording.

In some very late editing passes, for instance in the last round of page proofs, the journal may reasonably demand that you limit your changes to the strictly necessary. That's fine; but make sure that even then you reread the piece and find all those strictly necessary changes—it's amazing how many errors can persist undiscovered until the last moment, or be added in the editing process. I know this from personal experience, since one of my published articles contains a footnote that refers to the "freedom of speach."

6. Keep the copyright, but grant nonexclusive rights

Your goal as an author is to have your piece be as widely read as possible. This means that:

a. You want to be able to put it on your Web site, either one you have now or one you'll have when your law firm decides that it wants to publicize its associates' written work.

b. You want to be able to make copies in case you run out of reprints.

c. You want to be able to e-mail the paper to people who prefer to get it electronically.

d. You want to be able to reuse your words and your article's structure in future articles on the same theme, or future works based on the article. (This book, for instance, is based on an article I wrote earlier.)

e. You want to be able to let people photocopy the article for a law school class or a Continuing Legal Education event, and to let them reprint it in practitioner journals or excerpt it in textbooks.

f. You want to be able to make presentations based on your article, and create handouts, overhead transparencies, or PowerPoint displays to go with the presentations.

If you transfer the copyright to the law journal, you may lose these rights. True, in practice, you might still be able to do what you want, since law journals aren't assiduous at enforcing their copyrights. But if you want to be honest, you'll have to ask the law journal's permission to do some of these things; and some people, such as publishers of textbooks that might include an excerpted version of your article, might insist on that. Who needs the hassle, and the possible expense?

The law journal, of course, does need to get some rights from you. But there's no reason that it needs *exclusive* rights: Student-edited journals are generally heavily subsidized by their schools, and get the rest of their money from subscriptions and issue sales, so they don't really rely on charging people for permission to reprint articles. Even if they do want to charge for this permission, you should fight them, because such charges are against authors' and readers' best interests—and because permission fees are such a small matter to most journals, you usually won't need to fight much.

Here's some sample language that should give both you and the journal what you both need:

> The author conveys to the journal perpetual, unlimited, nonexclusive rights to reproduce, distribute, and display the article, and to authorize others to do the same. The author conveys to the journal the exclusive right to be the first to publish the article in a law journal. The author promises to clearly state in each copy or presentation that the article was originally published in the journal.

This lets the journal (a) print the piece without fear of copyright liability, (b) put the piece on its own Web site, (c) let Lexis and Westlaw put the piece online, and (d) respond to requests for permission to copy or reprint the article, if the request is sent to the journal (as such requests often are). It also assures the journal that you won't scoop it by publishing the article elsewhere first. But it leaves you free to distribute the article broadly, and to reuse your words later.

If the journal for some reason insists on getting the copyright, offer the following compromise:

> The author conveys to the journal perpetual, unlimited, exclusive rights to reproduce, distribute, and display the article, and to authorize others to do the same. The author, however, retains the perpetual non-exclusive right to reproduce, distribute, perform, display, and adapt the article, and to authorize others to do the same (so long as the author clearly states in each copy or presentation that the article was originally published in the journal), except that the journal retains the exclusive right to be the first to publish the article in a law journal.

This will have the same effect that I describe above, but will technically let the journal own the copyright, subject to your rights to use the article.

If the journal resists, point out the various ways that you might want to reuse the article—for instance, the ways mentioned at the start of this subsection—and ask the editors why they would want to bar you from such reuses. My guess is that most editors will realize that they don't want to stop you from doing these things, and will agree to let you keep at least unlimited nonexclusive rights.

If, however, the editors refuse to leave you with unlimited nonexclusive rights to do what you like to the piece, at least try to persuade them to give you the specific rights you need, for instance:

> The author conveys to the journal perpetual, unlimited, exclusive rights to reproduce, distribute, and display the article, and to authorize others to do the same. The author, however, retains the perpetual, unlimited, nonexclusive rights to do the following (so long as the author

clearly states in each copy or presentation that the article was originally published in the journal):

    1. post the article on the Internet and allow others to do the same;

    2. make and distribute photocopies of reprints;

    3. distribute copies of the article by e-mail.

    4. create new articles and other works that are based on the origi-
nal article;

    5. allow others to make copies of the article, or of parts of the ar-
ticle, for classroom use, republication in a book, use in Continuing Legal Education programs, or other purposes;

    6. make presentations that are based on the article and that reuse
the article's expression, and to produce audiovisual materials related to
those talks.

In my experience, some journals only ask for nonexclusive rights in
the first place; others ask for exclusive rights, but, if you object, send
you an alternate contract that gives them nonexclusive rights; and most
others let you change their standard contract to one of the forms that I
give above. Only two journals ultimately insisted on denying me the unlimited nonexclusive rights that I wanted, and they eventually agreed
to leave me most of the specific nonexclusive rights that I asked for.

You might also want to add the following to your author's footnote,
to encourage people to copy the article as broadly as possible:

    The author hereby licenses all readers to make unlimited photoco-
    pies of the article. For permission to make other copies, please e-mail
    the author at [if possible, give an e-mail address that you expect will
    work for at least several years].

This will make it easier for people to make photocopies, while still giving you the chance to check any copying that might involve heavier editing and might thus accidentally quote your article out of context.

E. Publicizing the Article Before It's Published

1. Post the article on SSRN

As soon as your article is accepted by a journal, electronically submit the article and the abstract to the Social Science Research Network,
http://www.ssrn.com (just click on the "Submit" button). This way, the
article will be publicized even before it's published, and academics will
be able to immediately read it, cite it, and possibly even give you valua-

ble advice about it. If you haven't yet written the abstract, write it now; Part XXIII.C (p. 275) gives you some tips on that.

Don't wait until your article is published, which could be many months away. If you think your draft needs one more editing pass before you're willing to have people read it, do that extra edit, but don't let it delay you too much: The earlier you promote your ideas, the more influence they'll have, and the more they'll help build your reputation.

You might even want to submit the article before it's accepted by a journal—many scholars do, and label the piece a "Working Paper"—but I generally wouldn't recommend it: The article's acceptance by a journal will serve as a signal that encourages people to read it, even if they don't know the author and even if they know the author is still a student.

2. E-mail bloggers in your field

Find law professors and lawyers who write blogs on subjects to which the article relates—the list at *http://www.lawprofessorblogs.com* is a good place to start, but don't stop there—and e-mail those bloggers a brief message

  a. mentioning that you've written a new article and saying where it will be published,

  b. very briefly and clearly summarizing your claim (for instance, by including in the e-mail text an abstract, if you've written one), and

  c. including the URL at which the article can be found (likely on SSRN, if you've uploaded it there).

No need to say that you'd like them to link to you—they'll understand that this is your goal, and they may be annoyed by the explicit request. Also, don't bug them to ask whether they're going to link to it: They aren't obligated to link to new articles, and many link to only a small fraction of the items that people pitch to them. But there's a decent chance that they will link to it, and will bring you readers as a result.

F. Publicizing the Published Article

1. Reprints

Once your piece is published, you want people to read it, or at least to know that it exists. Ideas that are actively promoted are more likely to be adopted. People who actively (but tastefully) promote themselves are more likely to get jobs, either immediately or down the road.

Order at least 100 reprints, though more is better. Reprints tend to run about 50 cents to one dollar for each extra copy beyond a minimum number, so splurge. Don't just make your own photocopies, unless you have to; nicely bound reprints are generally easier to read and store on a shelf for further reference, and look more professional.

Distribute the reprints, with a brief descriptive cover letter, to:

a. All professors at your school whose work is connected, even remotely, to your area.

b. All professors and lawyers who have helped you. (Did you thank them in your author's note?)

c. All professors and lawyers whom you cite in your footnotes. Mention in your cover letters the precise place that you cite them. We all like to see our names in print, so we're much more likely to look at the article when we know it cites us.

Don't be shy about sending reprints to people whose work you disagree with. If you're worried that the person might be offended, soften the blow with a nice note, saying something like "I found your viewpoint very provocative, and while I ended up disagreeing with it, it was very useful in helping me sharpen my own point of view." (Thanks to Hazel Glenn Beh for suggesting this wording.)

d. All lawyers you know who work in the field, including those you met while working as a law clerk, summer associate, or intern.

e. All law teachers who write treatises and casebooks in the field. Their addresses are in the *AALS Directory of Law Teachers,* which you can find in your law library, and which you can search online in Westlaw's WLD-AALS database.

f. The offices of any legislators, lobbyists, or ideological groups that are interested in any legislation to which your article is relevant.

g. Anyone else who might be in a position to help you spread your ideas.

h. Anyone else whom you want to impress.

It also helps to personalize the cover letter as much as possible. When you're sending something to law professors, try to connect it (if possible) to each professor's scholarship. When you're sending it to lawyers, stress how your piece can be practically useful to each of them. See Appendix III.B–C (pp. 372–374) for some examples.

2. Distributing the article electronically

When the article is ready to be published, you should get the file containing the final version. Then put it up on SSRN (see Part XXIII.E.1) instead of the original draft version that you posted.

Some law reviews may be reluctant to let you post the final version on SSRN, because such posting competes with their own distribution of the article on their sites, or because it is supposedly inconsistent with their agreements with Westlaw, Lexis, or HeinOnline. I don't endorse this reluctance; I think law reviews should be eager to help their authors distribute their articles. That way the articles can better help the profession and the academy, and can get more citations, which every law review wants.

But if the law review insists on not letting you post the final version on SSRN, offer a compromise: Ask the law review for a version without the final pagination, for instance with the pages starting at p. 1 rather than the proper page number within the volume, and with a page size that's a little different from the page size in the published version. This pagination change means readers won't be able to tell the published page number from the page number in the document—so if they want to cite the article, they'll need to look up the final version on Westlaw, Lexis, HeinOnline, or the law review Web site. But the pagination change won't stop readers from reading the article for free on SSRN, and that means more readers will want to cite the article.

Even if the law review doesn't let you put up the final version of the article on SSRN, you should ask for an electronic version that you can e-mail to people. Sometimes lawyers and professors in other disciplines, who don't have Westlaw, Lexis, or HeinOnline access, see a citation to an article, or see it mentioned in an online discussion, and e-mail the author asking for a copy. You want to be ready for that.

G. Planning the Next Article

After you've published your piece, you might never want to write another law review article again. But if you do want to write more, look back over your article to see where it can lead you.

To begin with, while writing the article you've probably several times thought, "that's an interesting related question, but it's too much for me to take on." For instance, if you wrote an article about religious freedom provisions and drug laws, you might have focused only on the government acting as sovereign (banning all drug possession by everyone) and set aside the government acting as employer (firing employees for consuming drugs) or as proprietor (barring drug use on government property, such as public parks). Dealing with the other areas would have made an already tough project unmanageable.

Consider writing a separate article about one of these questions, especially since you've already educated yourself on the basic field (here, religious freedom). Better yet, consider returning to these questions but at a broader level. Don't just write on the government as employer and religious drug use, which some might see as too close to your previous work and thus less impressive. Instead, try writing on the government as employer and religious freedom more generally, perhaps using drug use as a prominent test case.

Likewise, as you were developing your approach to one area, you might have seen connections to other areas (see Part V.F, p. 70): For instance, if you were writing on how waiting periods for gun purchases should be evaluated under state constitutional rights to keep and bear arms, you might have also noticed that your general reasoning could be applied to waiting periods for abortions under state constitutional rights to privacy. This may have been too tangential a point to cover thoroughly in your earlier piece, but why not use your thinking as the basis for a new article, perhaps one on waiting periods and constitutional rights more generally?

So build on what you learned while writing your old work; but make sure that you say something new.

XXIV.   ENTERING WRITING COMPETITIONS

A. Why You Should Do This

Many organizations run legal writing competitions, usually on a particular subject—admiralty law, health law, Second Amendment law, and other subjects. These competitions offer three benefits:

1. *Money*: The prizes range from a few hundred dollars to $5000 or more.

2. A *credential*: You can note the award on your resume, in cover letters, and in job interviews. People who work in the field will probably be fairly impressed that a professional organization—to which they themselves might belong—has given an award to your article.

3. *Publication*: Some of the organizations arrange to publish the winning entries, either in a practitioner journal or in a law review.

Several Web sites list many competitions, often sorted by topic, deadline, and award size; *http://volokh.com/writing//competitions* links to those sites.

If you've already written a paper for publication, it makes sense to also submit it to one or more of these writing competitions. (If you're submitting to more than one, call them first to see whether they allow such simultaneous submissions; I suspect some do and some don't.) A few of the competitions require students to answer a fixed question, so you can't enter your article in them unless you've chosen to write on that very question. But many other competitions will consider papers on any topic within, say, business law or copyright law. Why not let your business law or copyright law paper do double duty?

B. Competitions That Don't Offer Publication

If the competition doesn't offer to publish the winner, your goal should be (a) to submit the article both to the competition and to the law reviews, and (b) to use success in one field to get success in another.

The perfect scenario would be if you finish the paper during a month when many law reviews aren't considering submissions, such as November (see Part XXIII.A.3, p. 262); the competition deadline is in that month; and the organizers promise to announce the results before the next law review submission window (here, March). That way, if you win the competition, you can mention your success in the cover letter to the law review.

I suspect that many law reviews will be impressed by the seal of approval that the competition gives: The law review editors may realize that the competition was judged by experts in the field, who probably know more about the topic than the editors do. The editors will still evaluate the article for themselves—to make sure, for instance, that the paper isn't just a good piece for practitioners, but also fits the academic format that the law review prefers. But they'll probably be influenced by your success.

If the competition doesn't get back to you until April, after you've already submitted the article, no problem. Many journals will still be considering your piece; you should send them a follow-up letter noting that the article you sent them has won the award. This may seem like bragging, but professional manners aren't quite the same as social manners—some amount of subtle boasting is quite proper.

You shouldn't, however, delay submitting to the law reviews until the competition results are announced. Even if your paper is very good, it's impossible to predict whether you'll win the competition; you might end up delaying your submission for nothing. And the longer you delay submitting your article for publication, the likelier it will be that it will be preempted by someone else's work, or by some new case or statute.

What if the competition deadline is after the best time to submit to the journals? For instance, what if your article is ready for the March submission window, but the competition deadline is in June? Submit the article to the law reviews in March, and then if the article is accepted by June, mention this in the cover letter to the competition.

I doubt that this mention will help, since the people who run the competition probably think (and rightly so) that they know much more about the field than does the typical law review student editor. The competition judges might also feel that, since this is a formal competition, they should ignore anything other than the quality of the paper. But the mention probably won't hurt, since people are often influenced by credentials even when they try not to be.

C. Competitions That Guarantee Publication

If the competition promises to publish the winner, you should ask yourself a few questions:

a. *"Is this the sort of publication in which I want this article to be published?"* If, for instance, you're writing your article because you eventually want to get into law teaching, you probably want it published in a traditional law review, and not a practitioner journal. If the competition comes with a promise that the winner will be published in a practitioner journal (such as the *California Lawyer*, a well-regarded publication but one that's not a traditional law review), then it might not be right for you, even if there's, say, $1000 being offered as a prize. Practitioner journals also generally want shorter pieces than law reviews do, so your article might not fit their announced page limits in any event.

If you're in doubt about the nature of the publication, go to the library and skim a few copies. If after that you're still in doubt about whether you want your piece published there, talk to a professor who works in the field.

b. *"Do I think I can do better by circulating the article to the law reviews?"* In my experience, some law students circulating a very good article can get it into a primary journal at a Top 50 school, or into a specialty journal at a Top 20 school. If they can't make that, then they tend to be able to get it into a primary at a Top 100, or a specialty journal at a Top 50. They almost always get it published somewhere—but the goal is to publish it in as prestigious a place as possible.

If the competition offers to publish the winner in a journal of roughly that stature (such as the *Cardozo Law Review* or the *Michigan Journal of Race & Law*), or at some other journal that's at the top of its specialty (such as the *American Indian Law Review*), then you should be pleased by the opportunity. On the other hand, if the journal seems likely to be less well-regarded, then you might prefer to take your chances with the higher-ranked law reviews, unless the prize is really too good to resist.

c. *"Am I willing to delay submitting the piece to the other journals while I wait to hear from the competition?"* If the organization promises to publish the winner, then it doubtless expects that the winner will be available to be published. If they call to tell you that you've won, and you say "Thanks, but I can't let you publish the article, because it's already being published elsewhere," they probably won't give you the award, and might be annoyed that you've wasted their time. Don't expect to be able to publish the piece in both places—you'd need the permission of both, and at least one of them will almost certainly refuse.

You should therefore wait to hear the results of the competition before you submit the article to other journals. Or, if you don't want to wait, and don't mind losing the chance for an award if you get a good publication offer, then you could submit simultaneously both to the competition and to the journals (unless the competition's rules forbid this) and just withdraw the article from the competition if a journal accepts it first.

If your article seems time-sensitive—if, for instance, you expect there to be new court decisions, statutes, or regulations that may preempt your piece in the next year or two—then you might not want to wait to publish it. The same is true if you're writing in a hot field, and you expect that lots of other people will be writing on the subject. This is especially so if the organization is planning on taking a while to judge the competition; you might call or e-mail them to check how long they'll take to decide.

On the other hand, say you don't think that a delay will hurt much, the competition promises to give an answer quickly, or you actually want a delay (for instance, if you want to circulate the article right after you graduate, rather than a few months before you graduate, to counteract some law reviews' prejudice against publishing articles that are submitted by law students). Then you might want to send the article to the competition, hope for the best, and if they say "no," then circulate it to the law journals.

D. Competitions That Offer a Chance for Publication

Some competitions that say the winning piece will be merely *considered* for publication might not mind your publishing the piece elsewhere, and may give you the prize in any event. They may, for instance, take the view that the offer of publication is just a benefit they offer to competitors, and that it's no loss to the organization or its journal if the competitor isn't interested. In that case, you may want to treat them like the competitions that don't offer publication (see Part XXIV.B, p. 291), unless their journal is so prestigious that you do want the chance to publish there.

On the other hand, many might feel that if they give you the money, they're entitled to first crack at the article. If that's so, then you should treat them like the competitions that do offer publication (see Part XXIV.C, p. 292 above).

To figure this out, just call or e-mail the competition up front and ask: "I'd like to submit my essay to you, but I also think I should submit it to the law reviews for publication, especially since your competition doesn't guarantee that the winner will be published. Would that disqualify me, or do you not mind it?"

E. Competitions That Solicit Published Pieces

Some competitions are described as open only to articles that have already been published. (Obviously, these competitions don't offer publication, unless for some unusual reason they want to republish an article that has already run elsewhere.)

If a competition is indeed described this way, call the organization and see whether it will also consider articles that have been accepted for publication, but not yet printed. Some competitions might in fact take this view: If they consider only published pieces because they want someone else to prescreen the works for quality, then it might not matter to them whether the article has already been printed, so long as it has been accepted.

In any event, if you're submitting to some such competition, just circulate the article to the law reviews, and once it's accepted or once it's published (whichever the competition requires) send it in to the competition.

F. Competitions That Solicit Unpublished Pieces

Some competitions are described as open only to pieces that have not already been published, even though the competitions don't themselves offer to publish the winner. Call them and check whether they mind pieces that have not yet been published, but that have been accepted for publication.

If a competition only rejects pieces that are already in print, then keep in mind that articles are generally published only nine months or more after they are circulated. So if, for instance, your article is done in January, the best time to submit the article to law journals is in March (see Part XXIII.A.3, p. 262), the competition deadline is in April, and the competition announces its results in July, don't delay the journal submission because of the competition—the article will remain unpublished for many months after the competition is done.

On the other hand, if the competition insists on articles that are neither published nor accepted for publication, then either skip the competition, or submit to it first and then submit to the law reviews only after the competition's results are announced. It's the honest thing to do, and it will avoid making possibly influential enemies.

XXV. GETTING ON LAW REVIEW

A. What Is a Law Review?

Academic legal articles are mostly published in student-edited journals. Students not only proofread, revise, and cite-check the articles in these journals, but also select which articles are published. This is a rare power by the standards of the academy—in nearly all other disciplines the journals are edited by professors—and it's a power that students should cherish.

There are some faculty-edited journals in law, and many are highly regarded: the *Supreme Court Review* and the *Journal of Legal Studies* are two examples. But these are the exception. Even among the most prestigious law journals, most are student-edited. ("Law review" and "law journal" are generally synonyms; there is no inherent difference between the two.)

Nearly every law school has a *general-purpose journal*, which generally bears the name of the school followed by "Law Review" or "Law Journal," for instance the *Hastings Law Journal* at U.C. (Hastings) School of Law. Such journals publish articles on many legal topics. Many schools also have several *specialty journals* that focus on a particular topic, such as the *UCLA Entertainment Law Review*.

Students usually work on a law review for about two years, starting some time from the middle of their first year (more likely for specialty journals) to the start of their second year, depending on the school. Many journals are divided into "staff," generally students in their first year on the journal, and "editors," generally students in their second year.

The staff mostly cite-check and proofread, and write their student Notes. The editors tend to be divided into groups: The article editors mostly select articles; the notes or comments editors mostly help staffers with their student Notes; another group mostly supervises the cite-checking and proofreading process; and other editors edit the substance and the wording of the articles. The jobs, though, tend to overlap: On many journals, for instance, all editors occasionally help out with the wording and substantive edits. And remember that these are generalizations—different journals do things differently.

B. *Why Be on a Law Review?*

Being on a law review takes a lot of effort, often many hours a week that you'd rather spend studying for other classes or having fun. Why do it?

1. The credential

Law review is a valuable credential on your resume. It's especially valuable if you want to get a judicial clerkship or a teaching job, but it's also helpful for other jobs, too. Employers assume that if you've been on law review, you've had more practice editing, proofreading, and writing. Also, because many law reviews (especially general-purpose journals) have selective admissions procedures, having "made law review" is seen as evidence of good grades or of writing skill.

What's more, unlike grades, law review is a credential that's socially acceptable to talk about. It's hard to politely work your grades into casual conversation with potential employers. The grades will be on your resume, but not everyone at your prospective new job will have seen the resume, and those who have seen it may well have forgotten it.

But law review is a project that you've been involved in, so you can safely discuss it (of course, so long as you aren't too blatant about it). "What are you doing at school this year?" "Oh, law review is taking up a lot of my time." "Oh, really? What do you on the law review?" "I'm the chief articles editor." Polite but impressive.

2. Editing, proofreading, and source-checking training

The key to good legal writing is the ability to edit and proofread your own work, and care in using sources. The key to these things is practice, both with your work and with others' work. Law review will give you plenty of such practice—and in the process will teach you to pay attention to detail, another important skill lawyers must have.

3. An incentive to write and an opportunity to publish

Many law journals require you to write a student Note, as a condition of being promoted from a staffer to an editor. Some of these Notes (the number varies from journal to journal) end up being published.

As I mention in Part XXIII.A, you can indeed write a Note and get it published even if you're not on law review. But writing is hard, and if you don't have an obligation and a deadline, it's easy to keep putting it off. Being on a law review commits you to making that effort, and makes it easier for you to get a publication out of your work.

4. An opportunity to do cooperative and valuable work

Most things you do in law school—read, study, take exams—you do by yourself. Even those things that are cooperative, such as study groups or moot court, tend to be exercises, pedagogically valuable but with little effect on the outside world.

Law review lets you work as part of a team that produces something that matters: The articles you edit may end up being cited by courts and by scholars, and might actually make some difference to the development of the law and legal thinking. This sort of team effort can be exciting and rewarding.

5. Exposure to ideas

Working on the law review will lead you to read quite a few law review articles—and if you're in the articles department, it will lead you to read very many. Many of the articles aren't going to be very interesting or helpful to you, but some will be.

This exposure to ideas can be both exciting for its own sake, and valuable for your future work, either scholarly or practical. Naturally, you could just decide to expose yourself to ideas by reading articles on your own. But few people have the discipline to do that unless law review forces them to.

C. *Which Law Review?*

A school's general-purpose journal (sometimes called the "main law review" or just "law review") usually tends to be more prestigious than the specialty journals; being a staffer or editor on the general-purpose journal is thus usually the better credential for getting clerkships, practice jobs, and teaching jobs. The general-purpose journal will also tend to get better articles submitted to it, because authors would prefer to be published in the more prestigious place. I'm not sure this self-reinforcing pecking order is fair, but that's the way things are.

Nonetheless, there are advantages to being on a specialty journal, if you're interested in the particular specialty—for instance, working on the school's intellectual property journal, entertainment law journal, or media law journal if you're interested in intellectual property law. First, working with material that excites you can be more fun than working with whatever comes in the general-purpose journal's door. Second, focusing on one topic can help you better learn that field. Third, working on a specialty journal may be seen as a good credential by employers who are looking for people who are knowledgeable in the field, and committed to the field. Fourth, working on the specialty journal can give you more to talk about with those employers, and thus help you show off your brilliance to them.

D. "Making Law Review"

There are several basic ways that journals select their staffers:

1. "Walk-on": If you're willing to put in the work, you're welcome as a member. Some, though not all, specialty journals operate this way; few general-purpose ones do.

2. "Grade-on": You get on the law review if you are near the top of your class, for instance in the top 10%.

3. "Write-on": The law review conducts a writing competition, which usually requires you to write a short Note-like paper on a fixed topic in a fixed time (say, over Spring vacation) using a fixed set of materials. The people who write the best papers are selected.

4. Mixed grade-on and write-on: Some law reviews select a percentage (say, half) of their staff through grade-on and the rest through write-on. Others merge the students' classroom grades and writing competition scores into one number, and select the students who received the highest combined result. Often the write-on competition happens *before* people know who got the highest classroom grades, so even if you think that you'll grade on, you need to participate in the competition just in case.

5. One of 2, 3, and 4 plus "note-on": Some law reviews provide one extra shot to students who didn't make it through their standard method—the journals let students write a full-fledged student Note, usually over the students' first summer, and then select the students who have written the best such Notes. A typical timetable might be this:

After finals of first year	Write-on competition

October of second year	Student Notes due from people who didn't write on, and who are therefore participating in the note-on competition
February of second year	Student Notes due from the regular staffers who wrote on normally

E. Writing On: Background

In Spring 2006, I participated anonymously (and, fortunately, successfully) in the *UCLA Law Review* write-on competition. I had written onto the law review 16 years before, when I was a student; but I thought it would be helpful to have some more recent experience so that I could offer better advice.

What follows is based partly on that week, partly based on my general writing experience, and partly on reactions I've gotten from law students who successfully used earlier editions of this book in their competitions.

F. What the Competitions Are Like

So you're trying to write on to the law review. How do you succeed? Law review competitions vary from school to school and year to year, but here are some general guidelines that should help you in most situations.

Consider a typical write-on assignment. (I stress again that different law reviews do things differently; this is only an example.) You are given a *main assignment*, which may require you to write a short student Note.

You are given a task that your assignment should accomplish. It might, for instance, be "Express and defend your views on whether alcohol manufacturers should be held strictly liable in tort for crimes committed by people who have gotten drunk on the manufacturer's product," or "Analyze and critique the recent *Doe v. Roe* case." This is different from a real student Note, where you choose your own topic.

You are given a prepared set of research materials. You are generally not allowed to cite any authority that is not part of those materials. (Some competitions may give you a set of materials but not give you a specific question. In those competitions, you would have to come up with an interesting issue to write about, but of course one that's raised by what the materials cover.)

You are given a length limit and a time limit: For instance, over Spring vacation (say, from Friday evening before Spring vacation to Monday morning after it), you must produce at most 10 pages of text and 15 pages of endnotes, with particular margins and in a particular font.

You are given detailed instructions, which tell you all about the required formatting, structure, and so on. *Follow them to the letter*, no matter what anyone (including this book) tells you.

Finally, you may be required to do a *proofreading, bluebooking, or editing assignment*—a few pages that are separate from the main assignment, and that contain dozens of intentionally planted errors. You must find those errors and properly correct them, generally using the particular proofreading symbols that you'll be instructed to use. Again, use those symbols exactly as you're given them, and follow the rules of English and of the Bluebook (or whatever citation manual you're assigned) to the smallest detail.

Your job is to write the best-written, best-reasoned, best-proofread, and best-bluebooked Note that you can; to proofread and bluebook the editing assignment as well as you can; and to scrupulously follow all the rules you are given.

G. Begin Before the Competition Starts

You should start preparing for the competition weeks before it starts. Yes, it's extra work, at a time when you're already swamped with work. But just as an athlete needs to prepare well before the competition, so do you. The write-on competition will require specialized bluebooking and writing knowledge that you probably haven't fully learned. Use the time before you compete to acquire that knowledge.

1. Do background reading

In the several weeks or even months before the competition:

a. Ask your law review which citation style manual it uses, and whether it has any supplemental instructions explaining how its style deviates from the standard manual.

b. Ask your law review which writing style manual it uses.

c. Read the citation style manual *several times*.

d. Read the writing style manual *several times.*

e. Read a good general writing manual, such as Strunk & White's *The Elements of Style,* at least once.

f. Read the Editing and Writing chapters of this book (Parts IX through XVI) at least once.

Citation manuals tell you how cases, statutes, law review articles, and other materials should be cited. Writing style manuals tell you how to resolve contestable writing issues—for instance, when to put a hyphen after the prefix "non," or whether to start sentences with conjunctions. Much of the editing assignment, if there is one, will require you to know the citation manual very well. Even if there is no editing assignment, you'll be expected to use the proper citation form in your own citations, and to follow the writing style manual in your text.

Most law reviews use a citation style manual called the Bluebook; for convenience, I will talk about "the Bluebook" and "bluebooking" throughout this section, meaning "whatever citation style manual your law review uses." Many law reviews use the Texas Manual of Style as their writing style manual.

2. Especially focus on the Bluebook

Once you've figured out what citation and writing style manuals you need to use, make them your bus reading, your exercise bike reading, your bathroom reading. The manuals contain many rules, and many of them are not intuitive—and this is especially true of the Bluebook. Even the existence of the Bluebook rules might not be intuitive; for instance, would you have guessed that the Bluebook has special citation formats for *The Federalist* and *Shakespeare?*

The only way you can master the Bluebook is by reading it carefully and repeatedly, and by marking (with post-its, for example) those items that you found most surprising, and that you think you'll most need to be reminded of during the competition. You will then (a) have a good sense of the rules; (b) understand the general logic behind the rules (not all the rules are explicable using a general logical principle, but some are); and (c) have seen enough of the examples in the Bluebook that you might more easily notice when something departs from the Bluebook rules.

Pay particularly close attention to the bluebooking rules related to (1) cases, (2) statutes and constitutions, (3) articles, (4) books, (5) short forms, and (6) citation signals. If you can read the Bluebook cover to cover once, and then read these especially important rules again, you'll be in good shape. If you can't do that much, but can at least skim most of the Bluebook and pay close attention to the especially important parts, that's a lot better than nothing.

Students I've corresponded with agree: "I found particularly helpful ... the advice about thoroughly reading the Bluebook. My familiarity with it by the time the competition started made the cite-checking MUCH easier for me." "The most helpful advice [in this chapter] is on the Bluebook—reviewing the Bluebook BEFORE the competition begins and tabbing the book."

Your bluebooking skills will likely be a big part of your grade, both on your editing assignment and your main assignment. (Many of the law reviews that have separate editing assignments count them for 20-30% of the final grade.) The law review, after all, is looking for people who'll be good cite-checkers, and part of a cite-checker's job is bluebooking.

The law review is also looking for people who are diligent, and who are attentive to detail. If you weren't willing or able to put in the effort to properly bluebook your own work, when the result affects your professional future, the editors will reasonably assume that you probably won't do a good job bluebooking others' work, when you're on the law review and have no personal stake in getting things right.

Bluebooking is also the part of the competition where success is most within your control. Evaluations of the substance are subjective, so a difference of perspective between you and the editors can lose you a lot of points (even though the editors are trying hard to be fair). But care and precision in following the bluebooking rules is much more objective; if you bluebook well, you'll get a good grade on that part of the assignment.

I have my quarrels with the Bluebook. I think it's often helpful to depart from some of the rules, and I've had fights with law review editors about that. You may have similar objections.

Save them for when you're an editor or an author. During the competition, follow the Bluebook word for word. And before the competition, read it again and again.

3. Check past competitions

A couple of weeks before the competition, *see whether past competitions are available.* Read them, just to get a feel for what's going on. If some model answers are available, pay particularly close attention to them. (A student reports: "I found [this suggestion] incredibly helpful, because [reading past submissions] gave me a sense of what [editors] were looking for, yet ... also made [me] realize that there was not one 'right' way to organize it.")

If no model answers are available, see whether friends of yours who wrote on to the law review in past years can give you copies of their old competition papers. They may want to check with their Notes Department to make sure that there's no rule against this, but I suspect that it should be fine: They aren't helping you with any details of your own assignment.

Some people suggest that you read some law review articles to get a sense of how these articles are written. I'm not sure whether this is a great idea; some articles aren't very well-written, and some professors—especially the great writers—can get away with things that others can't get away with. But if you'd like to do a bit of extra reading, you might read a few pieces from the most recent issues of the law review.

If the past competitions include practice editing and proofreading tests, do as many of the tests as you can; compare your results against the answer keys, if those are given. If there are no answer keys, compare your answers against those of some friends of yours who are also doing the practice competitions. (You can't work together with people on the actual competition, but there's no problem with cooperating on practice projects.)

You might also check *http://volokh.com/writing/bluebooking*, which contains some pointers to bluebooking exercises.

4. Talk to people about what to expect

If you know some people who are now law review editors at your school, or who were law review editors a few years before, ask them for tips. They will know the process at your school, and can give you more specific advice than this chapter can. You can also ask them for advice tailored to your own study skills, if they know you well enough or you explain to them how you work.

Finally, talking about the process can help make it less mysterious and intimidating. Being prepared is important, but feeling prepared is helpful too.

5. Review your professors' comments on your written work

Go over any comments that you've gotten on your past written work, such as the papers in your first year legal writing course. Most writers make the same mistakes repeatedly. Figure out what your weaknesses are, so you can avoid them while doing the write-on.

Your writing instructor will likely be happy to help you with this. Writing teachers like it when you come to them out of a sincere desire to improve your writing; and they often have specific advice that they'll be glad to pass along.

6. Clear your calendar

Try to make sure you have no other obligations during your write-on competition. If it's during Spring vacation, try not to do your class outlines that week—do them before, or save them for later. If you're working part-time, see if you can take the week off, and make up the lost time before or after. If you have children, do what you can to get the other parent or someone else to spend more time with them during the competition.

Try to avoid leaving town to see friends or family, even if it is Spring vacation. You might intend to do lots of work when you're on the trip, but it's hard to work when you're around people you haven't seen in months, and who understandably want your company. Going out to dinner with friends is fine; everyone needs a study break. But try to avoid more demanding commitments. (A student reports: "This is essential.")

The writing competition requires you to do something that's new to you, under considerable psychological pressure, in a limited time. As I'll mention shortly, you'll want to finish your draft as early as possible, so you can edit it as many times as you can. You really might need most of your waking hours to do this. Even if you've found that the first year of law school hasn't been as time-consuming as you were initially told, this week will be quite a burden.

If, however, you can't get out of your other obligations for the week, don't use that as an excuse to just sit out the competition. It's possible for you to do well even if you also have to travel, work, study, or mind the kids that week—it's just easier if you can focus solely on the competition.

7. Figure out how your friends can help (including by staying quiet)

Your friends can't help you write or edit your paper, but they can help put you and keep you in the right mindset. One student, for instance, reports that "I found helpful ... having another student keep me accountable for the number of hours I was working. A close friend and I would exchange phone calls, playfully teasing each other to work a bit harder. Toward the end we would sit in coffee shops together [but at separate tables], each one's presence ensuring the other wouldn't turn in early and ignore some responsibility....

"[I]f it weren't for my buddy's consistently applying social pressure to be better than I would if no one were looking, I would have put in fewer hours and (presumably) performed more poorly." If you're the sort of person who responds well to such friendly peer pressure, take advantage of it.

On the other hand, other people react differently. One student, for instance, suggested: "[Don't] talk to people doing the law review about the law review because others can contribute to your ... mid-competition blues .... It can be discouraging when another person says, 'Just revising my draft,' [when] you are not done [with the first draft] yet." If you're the sort of person who responds this way, make a deal with your friends that you won't talk to each other about how far you've gotten.

The important thing is to know yourself, and to set things up so you and your friends help each other rather than inadvertently depressing each other. Humans are social creatures, and our mood and efficiency can change dramatically depending on our social environment. For this especially important, high-pressure task, take a few pains up front to arrange your environment so it helps you.

8. The really good and fortunate friends can help by lending you their apartments

If you live with a roommate, and a friend of yours is going out of town for the duration of the competition—not unlikely, since the competitions are usually during vacations—see if the friend will lend you his apartment. For most people, solitude and lack of distractions are a great help (even if occasional company can be a help, too).

9. Oh, no! I'm reading this chapter the day before the competition is to start

Don't panic. I stand by the advice I gave you, but preparation is helpful, not mandatory. Even if you couldn't prepare beforehand, just do the best you can during the competition. Likewise, even if you do less preparation than you hoped you could (you just skimmed the Bluebook chapters instead of reading them a couple of times), don't worry.

As one student reports, "A good friend of mine was in a section that had their huge memo due the day the competition started. As a result, he didn't prepare at all, and he still made it. I'm sure he's happy he tried, despite the [lack of] preparation."

H. A Timeline for After You Start

1. Start quickly

Start quickly. Everything will take longer than you think, and you don't want to delay, no matter how much you dread the process.

Also, fatigue will be your enemy. If you get the materials in the morning or afternoon, but put off starting until the evening, you'll quickly get tired and inefficient, and therefore dispirited.

2. Read the instructions

Read the instructions carefully. You will have to follow them precisely. The instructions may tell you

    a. how to format your document, for instance

        i. which font to use,

        ii. what margins to use,

        iii. how many lines to have per page,

        iv. how to organize the footnotes,

        v. whether to use footnotes or endnotes,

        vi. which of several possible citation styles to use (for instance, the Bluebook style for briefs or the Bluebook style for law review articles),

    b. how to structure your paper,

    c. what topics to cover or not to cover,

    d. what research you may or may not do,

    e. how many copies of your paper you should submit,

    f. when exactly the paper is due, and more.

Obey these instructions, no matter how much you may disagree with them, or how unimportant you may think they are. If they tell you to underline the period in "<u>Id.</u>," then always underline the period. The law review editors are looking for people who are willing and able to follow directions.

Also, try to follow your editors' advice about how to manage your time. They've probably thought hard about how much time each section would require, and you should take advantage of their thinking.

3. Photocopy

Make five copies of the editing/bluebooking/proofreading test, if there is one, and two copies of the rest of the packet. You'll want to have a clean copy of the editing test onto which you can eventually make your final markings, plus several clean copies that you can use as rough drafts. ("[E]xtremely helpful" tip, one student responds. "Although I didn't use all the copies I made, it was extremely convenient to have several extra copies of the test during the competition.")

4. Read the assignment and the source materials

Read the assignment and the source materials that you're given, and read them *completely* before you start writing. Read the sources (i) actively, and (ii) constantly thinking about how they're relevant to your problem.

a. As you read, highlight and mark the sources, and write on a separate notepad (or in a separate computer file) any thoughts that you have. Pay particularly close attention to quotes that seem to capture the key point of the source, or that seem especially important to the problem. You're going to be stressed, busy, and excited, which makes it easy to forget some of the ideas that come to your mind. Don't rely on your memory—write things down.

b. If you have voice recognition software on your computer, consider taking audio notes. This can be quicker and less tiring than writing notes, and can lead you to take more notes than you otherwise would.

c. As you read every source, and every section of each source, ask yourself: How is this relevant to my problem? How can it be used as an argument for or against some possible solutions? What similarities are there between this case and my fact pattern, and what differences? Constantly asking these questions can make it easier for you to come up with ideas that will be helpful to your paper.

If some section of a source doesn't seem relevant, though, don't just skip it. Still read it carefully, and see if you can find some connection that might not be obvious at first.

The readings will likely be a tough slog. During your first year, most of your readings were probably in casebooks; and while many casebooks have flaws, they at least tend to edit the material down, and tend to choose cases that are as readable and instructive as possible. Your packet of readings may have many entire sources, whether cases or law review articles, and they won't be easy to get through. Don't despair: Your competitors will likely find them as difficult and tedious as you will.

5. Choose a claim

Most law review write-ons require you to give your own solution to the problem you were posed. For instance, if the problem is "Does the Fourth Amendment allow laws that require people to submit their DNA to a nationwide database?," you'll be expected to decide for yourself whether the answer is yes, no, or it depends. You'll also be expected to come up with the principle underlying this answer, for instance, "yes, because it's reasonable to have such a policy, if it applies to everyone equally, even in the absence of probable cause." The answer coupled with the basic justification is what I call your "claim." The law review generally chooses the problem so that the source materials are compatible with several possible answers.

This is probably different from what you've done before in your writing class. Most first-year writing assignments are objective memoranda, where you're supposed to ask yourself "What are courts likely to decide here?," and persuasive briefs, where you're supposed to ask yourself "How do I argue for the position I'm assigned to argue?" The law review write-on typically requires you to ask "What should I suggest as the right result, and how should I defend my proposal?"

For an actual student Note, the claim has to be pretty ambitious: It has to be something genuinely new, and it generally has to deal with a topic that you yourself chose. (See Part I.C.) But the write-on assignment is only an exercise. You don't have to say anything really novel. You just have to choose a claim that you think you can defend, usually on a topic that you're given, and then explain the claim clearly and defend it persuasively.

What are the ingredients of a good claim for a write-on assignment?

1. Most importantly, it should be *as legally defensible as possible.* Your argument's soundness is much more important than its creativity.

2. Most well-designed write-on topics will have several plausible answers. When you choose among them, try to choose *a politically inoffensive one.* You'll probably have a good sense of your classmates' political views—choose something that is unlikely to strongly conflict with those views. If most of your classmates are pro-choice, for instance, then chances are that most of the law review editors are, too; don't risk alienating them by taking a strong pro-life position.

Even if the editors try hard to avoid being influenced by a write-on note's political slant, some such influence is almost inevitable. The editors are looking for well-reasoned pieces, and they think their own views are better reasoned than the other side's (or else they wouldn't have adopted those views). So, all else being equal, a piece that's close to the editors' views is more likely to seem well-reasoned to them.

You needn't, and can't, match the editors' views precisely. But try to avoid claims that are very far from your best guess of the average law review editor's perspective.

When you're writing a real article for publication, you should express your own views, even if most law review editors may disagree with them. Such candor is your duty as a scholar—and it's also likely to make you happier, since spending months writing an article that you don't believe in is likely to be an awful experience.

But your write-on, once read and graded, will never be read by anyone else. It can't persuade anyone to accept your ideas. Its *only* purpose is to get you a spot on the law review. Focus on that goal.

3. If you have several plausible and politically inoffensive proposals, try to choose *one of the more creative ones.* If you think you have a good answer besides the obvious "yes" and "no"—for instance, "the DNA submission requirement would be constitutional, but only if the DNA data

311

is usable only for identification and not for analyzing people's genetic traits"—then use it. Likewise if you have a good justification that you think is different from the standard ones.

Don't try too hard here: In the write-on, it's more important for your position to be defensible than creative. (In your real student Note, which you'll write for publication, both originality and soundness are very important, but not in the write-on.) Also remember the page limit—if you don't have much space to develop and defend your claim, don't choose one that's too complex.

But if you think your creative solution is just as sound as the obvious ones, use it. And keep in mind that sometimes the more nuanced solution is actually more sound than the yes-or-no one.

6. If you can't find the perfect claim, go with what you have

In all these steps—choosing a claim, writing, editing, and so on— you may find yourself being uncertain. Is this exactly the right claim? Is this subsection really persuasive? Is this quite the right way to read this case? Often you may have good reason for uncertainty: You may rightly sense that there's something wrong, though you might not know how to fix it.

When that happens, the best bet is usually to *move on*. Your time is limited; you can't afford to spend it worrying about one item, even an important one. Just do the best you can, and go on to the next step. Even if you're not sure whether you have the right claim, go with it. If you're not sure that you wrote a section right, go on to the next section.

After you do the next step or two, come back to the part that you're not sure about. Sometimes, the work that you've done in the meantime will help you solve your problem. Sometimes, just the time away from the difficulty will give you a fresh perspective.

Occasionally, this will mean that you'll have to redo a considerable amount of work. If, for instance, you realize that your original claim was mistaken, but you've already written a lot in defense of that claim, you might find yourself having to do some rewriting. But in my experience, such rewriting is much quicker than writing the first draft.

7. Do the editing/proofreading/bluebooking test (if there is one)

After you've chosen the claim for your paper, write down your claim and any ideas you have related to the claim. Then set the paper aside, and do your editing test, *before* starting to write the paper.

First, you'll probably need a break from reading and thinking about your paper topic. Alternating working on the paper and doing the test can help freshen your thinking about both.

Second, editing tests are hard. They tend to contain lots of errors for you to find, and many of the errors (especially the bluebooking ones) are carefully hidden. One good way to find such errors is to do the test from scratch several times and then merge the results. If you miss something or miscorrect something one time, you might not make the same mistake the next time.

As one student reported to me, "Every time you put down your bluebooking test and pick it up again after some time has passed, you'll find new mistakes." I found the same when I was competing; even though I'd written and bluebooked about 50 law review articles, every time I redid the test I found things I'd missed.

For this to work, you have to have several unmarked copies of the test—that's why I suggested that you photocopy the test right after you get it. But you also have to have forgotten as much as possible about what you did the last time you did the test, or else you'll end up making the same mistakes all over again. This means you'll have to space your efforts: For instance, you might do the test once the first day, once the third day, once the fifth, and once the seventh. So don't leave the test until the very end. Begin right after you've identified your claim.

Many law reviews give you a list of correction symbols (symbols that mean "delete," "insert," "capitalize," "italicize," and the like) that you should use for marking up the editing test. The list usually contains examples of how each symbol is used. Look over the list carefully, and use the symbols precisely as you're instructed to.

A few tips for doing the editing test:

a. If the editing test consists of a bunch of footnotes that you have to check, assume that each footnote has at least one error. If you haven't found any errors in a footnote, check again. (It's possible that some footnotes in the test will be perfect; but for any particular footnote, chances are that there'll be at least one mistake.)

b. Once you've found one error, or one set of errors, don't relax. Devious test designers will often throw in some errors that fall into one genre (for instance, citation format errors) and others that fall into another (for instance, grammatical errors in the citation parenthetical). It's easy to get distracted by the first set of errors you find, and stop thinking about other kinds of errors.

Don't let that happen to you: For every footnote you check, don't stop until you've thought of all the ways that the material might be wrong. Keep a mental checklist of the various things that you need to check for each footnote—such as the signal, the case name format, the format of the rest of each citation, the accuracy of the citation, the grammar and spelling in the parentheticals, the accuracy of the parentheticals, the rules for short forms, and so on—and make sure that you check each item for each citation in each footnote.

c. Don't just check citation format, unless you are explicitly told to limit yourself to that. Also check the accuracy of each citation, the accuracy of any quotes, and the accuracy of any paraphrases of sources (for instance, in parentheticals following citations).

d. Compare the various citations you're asked to check to see if you can spot any inconsistencies. Seeing "U. S." written with a space might not make you think there's anything wrong; but seeing it written with a space in one place and without a space in another should remind you that at least one of the citations is incorrect.

e. Go over (i) any bluebooking exercises you might have done in your first-year legal writing class, (ii) any bluebooking exercises you might have done while preparing for the competition, and (iii) any citation format corrections that your legal writing instructor might have made in your first-year writing papers, and see if there are bluebooking rules that you've consistently ignored or erred on. If there are, chances are that you'll have made the same mistakes again in the editing test; go over the test to correct any such mistakes.

f. Take advantage of the Bluebook's Index, which is pretty comprehensive (though don't rely on it exclusively—it's also important for you to have read the relevant chapters from beginning to end). If you have any uncertainty about a citation, look it up.

g. Expect the editing test to be time-consuming. Even one sentence in one footnote could take you a long time, as you check all the rules that may apply to it. That's another reason to do one pass of the editing test early.

8. Write a rough draft of the paper, quickly

a. Follow the law review's instructions about the structure

The law review will likely give you instructions about how to structure your paper—for instance, whether you should include a separate section describing the facts of the problem, whether you should include one for a summary of the background law, and so on. Follow these rules precisely. As one former law review editor told me, "If you can't even follow the basic directions on format put in front of you, in writing, why should we think you'll be better on substance?"

b. Get something done

Try to finish a first draft quickly. Skip over sections on which you're blocked. Don't spend time proofreading as you write (except when you're too tired to write more, and proofreading what you've written is the best use of your time—see Part XXV.H.8.m, p. 320). Don't worry too much about citation format. Just get something done.

The result will be badly structured and clumsy. (My first draft certainly was.) It may be full of misspellings, grammatical errors, and unnecessary words. Your argument may change as you write. Don't worry: Just get something down on paper, flawed as it may be.

In my experience, it's much easier to edit a draft that you've already written than to get a rough draft finished; and I've heard many others say the same thing. You'll need to spend lots of time editing in any event, so you need to finish the first draft as quickly as possible. You'll also need a bit of time to rest after the mind-frying experience of reading the sources, coming up with a thesis, and writing the first draft. Give yourself this time by getting the first draft done as fast as you can.

Students I've talked to agree: "Get a draft done as soon as possible. For me, leaving significant time to edit not only helped me edit for sentence structure, usage, grammar and spelling, but also helped me think about the topic and choose the most compelling arguments and counterrarguments."

If you're afraid that your paper will have serious flaws even at the end of the competition, don't despair. You don't have to have a perfect paper, or even the best paper. It just needs to be good enough compared to the rest of the competition: In many competitions, the top third or more of the competitors will be accepted. That's not reason to slack off. But it is reason not to give up.

c. Don't worry about the page limit for the first draft

When writing the first draft, or even the second or third draft, don't worry about the page limit. A typical first draft is probably at least one-third flab. There are always redundancies, surplus phrases, long-winded explanations, and unnecessary digressions that you can cut.

For the first draft, focus on getting your thoughts down on paper. Then trim it down during the editing.

d. Deal with the counterarguments

Deal with the most important counterarguments. The write-on problem is usually a close case, with good arguments to be made on both sides. There will almost always be something in the sources that supports the other side as well as yours. Understand the arguments against your position, treat them with respect, and explain why they don't defeat your position.

Don't overstate the strength of your position. For instance, if the statute you're interpreting is ambiguous, don't try to deny the ambiguity; admit that the law is ambiguous and explain why it's better read the way you want to read it. The write-on is a test of scholarly writing, and intellectual honesty is a hallmark of good scholarly writing. You should have an opinion, but you should defend it fairly, without overstatement.

e. Use the facts—but don't focus too much on them

Some competitions will give you a fact-rich scenario: For instance, you may be asked to write about whether a particular statute is constitutional; the relevant constitutional test (for instance, strict scrutiny) may turn on a factual inquiry (for instance, whether some alternative proposal would be less restrictive but as effective at serving a government interest); and you may be given some facts, either in studies that are excerpted or summarized for you, or in findings from the lower court.

Try to use as many of those facts as possible. See which parts of the legal test the facts might be relevant to, and explain that relevance. Much of the lawyer's art, and the legal scholar's art, comes in applying the law to the facts. And the graders may well be looking to see how skilled you are in that art.

At the same time, pay close attention to the call of the problem. If your assignment calls on you to deal with a general issue (for instance, if it asks you to propose how the Compulsory Process Clause should be interpreted in certain situations), don't spend too much space on the facts of the case that you're presented. Focus on the issue, and use the particular case in which it arises as an illustration.

f. Use headings for each subsection

Use headings for each subsection. They'll help organize your thinking, help you make sure that each subsection stays focused on its key point, and help you see what the key points of each section are. And the law review editors will probably appreciate the headings, because the headings will help them understand the structure of your paper.

After you're done, automatically generate a table of contents from the headings. That will give you a quick outline of the paper, and give you a sense of whether some important parts are missing, whether some sections are redundant, and whether the sections don't fit well together. The table of contents will also let you make sure that the section headings are consistently capitalized and grammatically parallel.

After you check the table of contents, though, delete it, unless the law review wants you to include one. Its purpose was to help you visualize the article's structure; the editors will probably want to read the paper and visualize the structure for themselves.

g. Follow the advice in the Writing chapter and in your writing style manual

As you write, try to follow the advice in Parts XI through XVI, and in whatever writing style manual you've read (such as Strunk & White). Much of your grade will depend on the quality of your writing rather than of your legal reasoning—and even your legal reasoning will be more impressive if you don't obscure it with bad writing.

317

h. Keep it clear and simple

The single most important writing principle is: Keep it clear and simple. That means:

1. Use short, simple words.

2. Use short sentences.

3. Use short paragraphs.

4. Use direct, unaffected prose; avoid the flowery and the pompous. (A tip I once got: "If you're not sure whether something you've written sounds pompous, it probably does.")

5. Use the active voice except where the passive really seems more apt.

6. Avoid redundancy—it makes your writing less clear and forceful, and of course it's especially bad when you're facing a strict page limit.

7. Avoid jargon, whether law-and-economics jargon, literary criticism jargon, critical legal studies jargon, or whatever else. Some readers won't understand it. Many will understand it, but will have to work hard to understand it, and will resent you for it. And some might understand it better than you do, and conclude that you've used it incorrectly.

8. Explain what is literally going on; avoid metaphors and other figurative usages unless they seem really helpful.

9. Don't make up your own abbreviations. If you're writing about the California Plum Marketing Act, don't call it the CPMA, even if you define the new abbreviation for the reader. Call it the Act, or the California Act, or something like that. Unfamiliar abbreviations make articles seem less accessible and interesting.

Remember that each of your graders will be reading a couple of dozen papers, all on the same topic. That's a boring, unpleasant job, and it makes people grumpy. When the readers see something unclear in your paper, they won't take the time and effort to figure out exactly what you're saying, and they won't give you the benefit of the doubt. They'll just mark you down. Conversely, the easier you make things for them, the more they'll like you.

i. Follow your legal writing instructors' advice

Follow the advice that your instructors gave you in your legal writing class, even if you don't fully agree with it. The graders were probably taught by the same instructors, and will likely follow the rules that those instructors taught.

j. Don't alienate the reader

Avoid (1) sarcasm, (2) snideness, (3) ad hominem attacks, and (4) political labels that some might see as unfair. If you're writing about a gun control issue, don't talk about "gun nuts" or "gun-grabbers." If you're writing about abortion, it doesn't matter that you sincerely believe that pro-choice forces are baby-killers, or that pro-life forces are sexist theocrats. Put that out of your mind, and be scrupulously polite to both sides. Some of the people grading you will be pro-choice, and some will be pro-life. You can't afford to alienate either group.

Also, to the extent that you can, avoid making politically controversial substantive assertions. Don't shy away from those assertions that you need in order to support your claim. But don't pick any unnecessary political fights, for instance on tangential issues.

If you do have to make such a controversial statement, be sure to carefully support it, and to confront the counterarguments against it. Again, remember that some of the people grading your paper will strongly disagree with you. Even if you can't persuade them that you're right, you should at least show them that you're taking their side's arguments seriously.

You want to sound thoughtful, respectful, and careful, not self-righteous, contemptuous, or blinded by your moral passions. If you think some argument is too harsh or over-the-top, it probably is. The substance of your argument should be hard-hitting; but your tone should be mild.

k. Be modest

You also want to sound modest, though not noncommittal or too deferential. Be careful about emulating the style of accomplished and respected scholars—it might seem good when coming from them, but too arrogant when coming from a first-year law student.

"Only a deep philosophical understanding of the matter can help us avoid the errors that the Court makes" suggests that you are a deep philosopher, and that the Justices are shallow fools. Even if that's what you think, it's not what you should say.

Likewise, "This article will conclusively demonstrate that Professor X's views are flat wrong" sounds arrogant enough that it invites skeptical readers to look for ways in which your demonstration isn't conclusive, and X's views are possibly right. Better just to substantively support your position, and rebut the other side's, without praising yourself.

l. Avoid humor

Being funny in print is hard. Being funny under stress and time pressure is harder still. Better to stay serious.

Don't worry about making an impression, standing out, or being remembered: Your goal is to come across as smart, careful, and clear, not scintillating. As one former law review editor told me, "The simplest way to stand out is to write well."

Especially avoid sarcasm. Another editor's comment: "Some people can write well, but far fewer people can write wittily and well; and even fewer can write sarcastically and well. A serious and respectful tone will generally get a better response from a reader of a write-on submission; moreover, they are more likely not to be angered if they happen to disagree with your political stance."

m. When you get tired

When you get too tired to write, you may still have some energy for other things. Alternate between (1) doing another pass of the editing test (see p. 313) and (2) proofreading whatever you've written of your piece. A student reports: "alternating between writing and doing the Bluebook test helped me be as productive as possible."

Doing the editing test as you write your piece will also help keep the bluebooking rules fresh in your mind, and thus help you bluebook your own piece well.

n. Add the footnotes/endnotes as you write, but don't let the formatting distract you too much

When you use a source, add the footnote or endnote right away. If you plan to add it at the end, you might find at the end that you didn't leave enough time for that, or that you've forgotten where to give credit or what source to credit. And a good chunk of your grade will be based on the completeness, accuracy, and formatting of the footnotes. Checking and editing footnotes is a big part of the law review's job, so the editors are looking for people who are good with footnotes.

At the same time, don't let the details of the footnotes distract you too much as you write. If you're on a roll with your writing, keep writing, and don't take time off to make the formatting perfect. Then, when you're tired of writing, and need a distraction—later in the day, not at the very end of the competition—go over the footnotes and fix them up.

Also, if you know some assertion is right but don't remember where you read it, just add a blank footnote. You can then fill it in when you go over the passages you highlighted as you read the sources (see p. 324 below).

o. Avoid putting text in the endnotes

If you want the graders to read something, put it in the text. They probably won't read the endnotes until they're done with the rest of the paper; they thus won't see any important text that you put in the endnote until it's too late. On the other hand, if you don't care whether the graders read the material, then why include it anywhere, even in the endnotes?

There is at least one exception to this rule: If you cite a case in an endnote, and think there might be some controversy about whether it applies, you might want to clarify this in the endnote. Also, if you're told to use footnotes rather than endnotes, you might have more flexibility, because a reader is likelier to notice footnote text than endnote text. But be careful even then; some readers will be distracted and annoyed by what they see as a digression.

p. Avoid strange formatting features

Don't use fancy formatting features that you aren't asked to use (for instance, line numbers on the left-hand side of the page, strange fonts, and the like). Grading is a tedious process, and graders tend to be easily annoyed. Don't try to distinguish your paper through its look. Distinguish it through its clarity and persuasiveness.

9. Use the sources effectively

a. Use all the endnote space that you're allowed

If you are asked to put your sources in endnotes, and are given limited space for them, try to use all the space that you're given. Otherwise, the piece may look shallow and quickly patched together. Of course, don't just throw in irrelevant filler: Find citations that are relevant to your argument—there will almost certainly be plenty.

A former chief notes editor at a leading law school echoes this. "Make sure you use all of the endnote space you are given. It's not really fair (or reflective of literary merit), but I remember that people who used, say, only 5 pages of endnote space out of the 15 they were given were regarded as not having worked very hard at their submissions. Every bit counts, and even the appearance of lack of effort can be fatal."

b. Try to use all the sources

If you haven't used some of the sources that you're given, look over them again to make sure that you haven't missed anything.

Sometimes, editors may intentionally give you sources that you don't really need. Sometimes, your argument may legitimately take you in a direction that makes certain sources irrelevant.

But those situations should be rare. Generally, if the editors give you some sources, each one of the sources is likely to be helpful. Read them, cite them, but most importantly, *use* them: Don't just cite them for the sake of having cited each source, but figure out what the value of the source is to your argument (or to some counterargument).

c. Don't just describe the authorities

Don't just describe the authorities, for instance, "In *X v. Y*, this happened. The Court ruled this way. In *A v. B*, this happened. The Court ruled that way.... Therefore, in this case, the Court should rule this way." Rather, synthesize the authorities into a rule, and then cite them to support your synthesis. See Part IV.B, p. 64 for examples.

d. Pay attention to the weight of authorities

If the law review editors give you a packet of source materials, the packet may contain statutes, U.S. Supreme Court cases, lower appellate court cases, trial court cases, law review articles, and excerpts from treatises. If they ask you to do your own research, then the results of that research will contain a similarly mixed set of materials.

Keep in mind that some of the authorities are more important than others. A U.S. Supreme Court case is more important than a district court case; the U.S. Supreme Court case is binding throughout the nation, while the district court case isn't even binding in that very district. Don't overstate the value of lower court precedents.

"*X v. Y* held that *Z*," where *X v. Y* is a district court case or even a court of appeals case, is not itself a conclusive argument that *Z* is the law, or that other courts will reach the same result. Definitely use the lower court cases where they seem relevant—but keep in mind that if you rely on a lower court case, you must also explain why that decision should be followed, rather than just assuming that it would be followed (even if the lower court case seems very close to your facts).

You should also rely on the real authorities—such as cases, statutes, constitutions, and regulations—more than on any law review articles that you might have been given. Articles are just opinions; "Professor Schmoe says this-and-such" is not by itself a good argument that courts would or should accept this-and-such.

Certainly cite the articles when you borrow arguments from them; and do take advantage of whatever enlightenment they can provide, and whatever support they can give your thesis. But the main support for your argument should be the legal authorities, linked together by your own logic.

e. Cite everything you rely on

The law review editors will likely be on the lookout for inadequate attribution, which they may well see as plagiarism that would categorically disqualify you. What's more, because they're familiar with all the sources, they can easily spot any unattributed copying, paraphrasing, or even reuse of a general idea. You should read Part XXVI.A for more on what constitutes plagiarism, and how you can avoid it; but the brief summary is *cite everything you rely on*, including sources that you rely on for ideas as well as for literal words. A few tips:

i. Include footnotes or endnotes as you write, rather than just waiting for later. Later, it will be too easy to forget.

ii. If you run out of footnote space, edit the footnotes down—for instance, by tightening the parentheticals—rather than just deleting enough of the footnotes to get within the limit.

iii. Don't worry about having your work look too derivative if everything is footnoted. Footnotes generally make the work look well-supported, not unoriginal.

iv. When you use an idea or an argument that you borrow from a source—even if you didn't use any of the literal text from the source—give credit in a footnote.

v. Even when you come up with an idea on your own, and then see it in a source, give credit. The academic tradition is to credit people who came up with an argument before you did, even if you arrived at it independently. What's more, your readers won't know that you found the argument independently: They might just assume the worst, and think that you deliberately borrowed it, and refused to acknowledge the borrowing.

10. After the first draft is done, go over what you've highlighted in the sources

After you're done with the first draft, look again at the material you've highlighted in the sources. Much of that will be worth citing in the endnotes.

I found this particularly helpful when doing the competition myself. As I was writing the draft, I had to make many assertions that I knew were supported by the sources, but for which I didn't remember the right citation. So I just left the endnotes blank instead of wasting time tracking down each one separately. Then, after the first draft was done, I went over the highlighted material in the sources. This let me fill in nearly every blank footnote.

11. Ignore the mid-competition blues

About halfway through the competition, you're likely to panic, get depressed, or both. You're going slower than you thought you would. You don't like what you've written. You're not sure you can finish. You're sure that even if you finish, the editors will hate your paper.

Ignore this. Almost everyone goes through it. The other competitors are going through it, too.

The write-on is a genuinely difficult, high-pressure task, and it's hard to keep up your enthusiasm throughout it. But a large fraction of those who actually make it through the project, and turn in the paper, are indeed selected. Your chances are quite good. There's no cause for panic, and nothing to be gained by panicking. Just keep going.

12. When you have a moment, reread the instructions

Misreading the instructions is shockingly easy. When I did my anonymous write-on experiment, I read the instructions and saw that I was allowed to use 80 characters per line. Then, after I wrote the first draft at 80 characters per line, I reread the instructions, and saw that they really allowed only 70 characters per line. Whoops.

Resetting the format and then cutting the extra pages proved to be pretty easy. But if I hadn't noticed the error and therefore went nearly 15% over the space limit, I'd have been heavily penalized—or perhaps disqualified outright.

So when you have a chance, reread the instructions that came with the paper. Did you miss some important substantive detail? Are you following the formatting instructions to the letter? Are you positive about when the paper is due, and how you're supposed to submit it?

13. Edit

a. Edit, edit, edit

The key to clear, persuasive, and error-free writing is going over the draft again and again. Never ever ever plan on handing in a first draft, or even a second or third draft. Every time you proofread, you'll find more problems to correct. The more proofreading passes you can make, the better.

If you've planned your time well, you'll have a first draft done with plenty of time to edit it. But if you're running out of time, make sure that when you take a break from writing, you spend the break time editing what you've written. (You might want to avoid editing while you're actually writing—it will probably slow you down too much.) That way you'll be able to polish at least a good chunk of the article, and do it several times.

b. Cut

Whether or not you need to cut to save space, edit with an eye towards trimming away the usual flab described in Part XIII. Check for unnecessary introductory clauses ("To analyze this problem, we must bring to bear the relevant Supreme Court precedents," or "The First Amendment is of fundamental importance to our nation's system of civil liberty"). Check for unnecessary words more generally. Check for redundancy.

Nearly all first drafts include redundancy—the same idea needlessly repeated, often in consecutive paragraphs or even consecutive sentences. As you're thinking about some theory you like, you'll naturally express it in two or more similar ways. But mercilessly cut such redundancy, and the other kinds of flab (see Parts XIII.A–XIII.C, pp. 119–120 for more details on that). They take up valuable space, they add nothing to the analysis, and they make your paper look vacuous and cliché.

So the good news: Because there's always fat to be trimmed, you don't have to panic when the first draft is too long. The bad news: If you don't trim the fat, you'll be marked down for bad writing even if your draft is not too long.

Also keep alert for facts and legal principles that seemed relevant when you first read through the materials, but that ultimately end up not being important to your particular proposal. This material will bore or distract the reader, and will take up space you can use for arguments that are much more closely tied to your claim.

c. As you cut the fat, watch to preserve the meat

Many write-on competitions dramatically limit the length of your submission, both to keep you focused and to save work for the graders. This format necessarily prevents you from going into things very deeply. Don't worry too much about this lack of depth. But at the same time, make sure that you cut wisely, and that the remainder includes at least the core of your argument, the core support for that argument, a discussion of the counterarguments, and some concrete examples.

d. Take particular care in editing the Introduction

The Introduction will set the tone for the rest of your grader's experience with your paper. If it's readable and organized, it will put your grader in a good (and perhaps even forgiving) mood.

Also check the Introduction to make sure that it reflects your final thinking on the subject. Often your claim will have changed from the time you start your draft to the time you finish it. Change the Introduction accordingly.

e. Check the substance and the structure as well as the form

Both your logic and your language should be perfect. Think "solid": You want the reader to think "Well, that's a solid argument." In a write-on competition, it's better to aim for "solid" than to aim for "that's a brilliant argument."

This means that there shouldn't be any loose ends: no holes in the logic, no important arguments omitted or unanswered, no unsupported assertions. For every significant assertion you make, ask yourself "why?"—why is this assertion accurate? If your text doesn't answer that, then it's not solid. Likewise, for every significant assertion you make, ask yourself "why not?"—what counterarguments might there be to this assertion?

To be solid, your piece should also be well-structured: It shouldn't meander from one subject to another and then back to the first, or deal with unrelated points in the same subsection.

f. Check for consistency

As you edit the article, make sure that all parts are consistent with each other. If you propose a new test, or synthesize a test from the precedents, do you always articulate the test the same way? If you criticize a court for doing something—for instance, for departing from the statutory text—are you sure that you aren't guilty of that yourself?

g. Proofread the footnotes or endnotes as well as the text

Make sure the prose in the footnotes is correct, and the citations are properly bluebooked.

Do *not* rely on citation formats that are used in the sources that you're given to read. Court opinions generally don't follow law review citation style. Law review articles may have been published in journals that use a different citation manual, or that used a different edition of the citation manual. And some sources might have made errors. Follow the citation manual you're told to use, not what others may have followed.

h. Check the quotes

If you quote a source, make sure that you quote it correctly, down to the punctuation and the capitalization. Also make sure that any omissions or changes are noted using the proper Bluebook style, for instance using the proper bracketing or ellipses.

i. Look it up

If you're unsure about spelling, grammar, usage, punctuation, or bluebooking, look it up, in the dictionary, the writing style manual, or the citation style manual (such as the Bluebook). Look at the bright side: Unlike with law, there are right answers to those questions; you have no excuse for not finding those right answers. And these details count, often for a lot.

j. Use your ears

Read the piece out loud to yourself. You might hear errors that you didn't see.

k. Have others proofread your work, if you're allowed to do this

Most law reviews forbid competitors from letting anyone else—law student or not—proofread or comment on your work. But if your law review lets you have a friend proofread your work, take advantage of this as much as you can. Other readers will always be able to catch errors that you didn't catch.

14. If you have time, reread this section and the Writing sections

This section (Part XXV.H) and the Writing sections (Parts XI through XVI) contain a lot of advice, likely more than you can absorb in one sitting. If you have some spare time during the competition—time when you're too sick of writing, proofreading, editing, and bluebooking to do any of that, but too worried or industrious to relax—reread these sections. You might find some tips that you initially missed, or didn't properly understand before you started the competition. Or you might realize that you made certain mistakes that you ought to correct.

15. What to do if you're over the page limit

As I mentioned before, when you're writing, don't worry about the page limit. Write what comes to mind, and then cut it down to size later.

But now "later" has come, and you're several pages over. What to do?

a. Use the editing advice in the previous subsection

First, edit the paper. As you edit, you'll find words, sentences, and even whole paragraphs that are redundant or unnecessary. Reread Parts XII–XIV for tips on how to recognize these. Cutting them will both save space and make the paper more effective.

b. Trim the background / fact summary / case summary section

Most student writers spend too many pages on the sections that restate the facts or the law—the sections that explain the background legal principles, the fact pattern, or, in a case note, what the case held—and too few on their original analysis. If you need to trim, trim down the background section first. A paper that's mostly a summary of the background law, with little original analysis, will not get a good score.

Naturally, some of the background section is necessary, but much of it probably won't be. Look over each paragraph and each sentence, and ask yourself: Does this really help make the paper accurate, readable, and persuasive? If it does help, can it nonetheless be put more succinctly? Is the discussion of some particular leading cases really needed, or can you just explain the rule that can be drawn from those cases, citing them as needed in footnotes? Are certain procedural details really important, or can they be omitted? See also Part IV for more about this.

c. Decide which digressions and counterarguments are important

Some of the things you say may be less important to the argument than others. It's always hard to tell which are which, but sometimes you have to do it. A few tips:

i.   Focus on the counterarguments that seem most familiar, rather than the ones that seem the most creative. Often, your proposal will be at least reminiscent of ones you've heard before, and you would have heard the standard counterarguments against those proposals as well. Chances are that the graders have heard the same counterarguments, and will expect you to deal with them.

ii. Focus on the counterarguments that are made somewhere in the materials you've been given, in preference to the counterarguments you think up yourself. Again, these are the ones the graders are most likely to be looking for.

iii. Focus on those twists to your argument for which there is some relevant authority. Say that you're writing about pornography law, and all your sources have to do with the tests for whether the material is obscene (the substantive question) rather than with the tests for when an obscenity regulation is a prior restraint (a procedural question). You probably don't need to discuss the prior restraint issue: Chances are that the graders aren't expecting a prior restraint discussion, and won't give you any points for it.

d. Maintain an "outtakes" file

When you decide that something is worth deleting, don't just delete it; move it to a separate file, so you can bring it back if you change your mind. This will help you undo deletions that you later realize were mistakes. And more importantly, this will embolden you to delete things that you really do need to delete, but that you might at first be afraid of deleting.

16. Near the end

You're near the end. You have only a day left. If all has gone well, you've finished the first draft of the paper days ago, and you've edited both the text and the footnotes several times. You've also done the production test several times from scratch, and merged the results into your final answer. What do you do?

a. Leave time for the final procedural details

Remember that there are a few things you need to do at the very end: You need to print the paper, make the proper number of copies, and drive to school or to the post office. These things take longer than you think; make sure you leave time for them.

b. Reread the Introduction

You've probably learned a lot, and perhaps even changed your mind on some issues, since you started the paper. Reread the Introduction and make sure that you still agree with everything you said there.

In particular, make sure that the Introduction and the Conclusion are compatible. For instance, if both state your basic thesis, make sure there aren't subtle but important differences in the way they state it.

c. Reread the materials you were given

What you've learned while writing the paper may also affect how you understand the materials—cases, statutes, and articles—that you were given as part of your competition packet (or that you found on your own, if the competition requires to do your own research). If you reread the materials, you may catch details that you missed when you first read them, that seemed irrelevant or mysterious at the time, or that you forgot shortly after reading. Look in particular for:

    i.   Quotes or arguments that seemed unimportant when you first read them, but that you now realize directly support your proposal.

    ii.   Materials that show the author (whether a judge or a commentator) would likely disagree with your proposal—you might need to deal with these as possible counterarguments.

    iii.   Provisos that limit the scope of a principle on which you're relying, such as when a court announces a rule but then explicitly or implicitly notes that the rule only applies in certain situations.

    iv.   Factual details that make some case especially similar to the scenario you're discussing, or that make it importantly different from your scenario.

d. Do the editing/proofreading/bluebooking test one more time

If your assignment includes an editing/proofreading/bluebooking test, and you have some spare time, do it once more. As p. 313 explained, each new pass can let you find errors that you'd missed before.

I. *Special Suggestions for Case Notes*

If your law review competition requires you to write a case note—something that's focused on one particular case, rather than on a more general issue—read Part I.J, p. 38, which may give you some ideas about the kinds of things that you could say about the case. (Remember, though: If the instructions require you to focus only on certain things, such as criticisms of the opinions, then *follow the instructions* rather than the suggestions given in this book.)

J. *The Personal Statement*

Some law reviews ask you to write a personal statement, and consider it as a factor in deciding whom to let on. A few tips for writing one.

1. Write well and proofread carefully

The personal statement is part of your competition packet. You will be graded on it. Even if there's no official procedure by which errors in the personal statement are counted together with errors in the other material, they'll still count against you indirectly: The point of the personal statement is to make people like you—and law review editors don't like people who can't write, or who don't take the time to make their writing look good.

So proofread the statement carefully. Look for all the problems you look for in your academic writing:

  a. Grammatical errors.

  b. Spelling errors.

  c. Punctuation and capitalization errors.

  d. Usage or word choice errors.

  e. Unnecessary redundancy.

  f. Unnecessarily complex words, sentences, or paragraphs.

g.   Pomposity.

2. Pay attention to the instructions

As with all the other parts of your competition, pay attention to the instructions. If you're asked to stress why you want to be on the law review, explain that. If you're asked to describe your ambitions as a lawyer, explain that.

The instructions probably won't require you to limit yourself only to one topic, so feel free to include other items. But do make sure that you focus on what the instructions tell you to focus on.

3. Make yourself sound interesting, but politically unthreatening

In a perfect world, everyone would be tolerant of all political views. In our world, even people who are trying hard to avoid political bias tend to prefer those with whom they agree, or at least with whom they don't strongly disagree.

Avoid dwelling on especially controversial groups to which you belong. Avoid explaining your most ideological ambitions or experiences. Don't make yourself seem completely bland, but don't make yourself seem too spicy, either.

4. If you're applying to a specialty journal, stress your interest or experience in the specialty

Some specialty journals are looking for people who are particularly enthusiastic about the specialty, rather than just random students who want journal experience to put on their resume. So if you're applying to the specialty journal, stress your interest or experience in the specialty.

Naturally, be honest; and if you're writing personal statements for several journals, don't say inconsistent things in those statements. But honestly explain why you find the field interesting—if you're applying to the specialty journal, you probably find at least something interesting about the field. And honestly explain what things in your past, both before law school and during, would make you a particular good staffer for this particular journal.

XXVI.   ACADEMIC ETHICS

Academic ethics sounds like a dreary topic, and instruction in academic ethics risks sounding preachy. Plus why should you need to read about the rules, if you're an ethical person already?

But complying with the ethical rules is important pragmatically, and not just ethically: You certainly don't want people to even suspect that you've behaved improperly. And the rules are sometimes not entirely intuitive—even honest people may inadvertently violate the rules unless they've focused on them. Reading a quick summary of the ethical rules can help avoid some nasty and unnecessary problems.

There may be some controversies about such rules, and some people might have plausible arguments for why the rules are too broad or too demanding. But I assume that you'd rather err on the side of caution, so I try to recommend the safest course.

A. Avoiding Plagiarism

1. The two harms of plagiarism

Everyone knows you shouldn't plagiarize—but what exactly does that mean? For instance, are you safe if you just include a footnote citing the original source, or if you paraphrase instead of directly quoting?

Scholars condemn plagiarism for two reasons. First, it *deceives the reader*. When you write as a scholar, you are implicitly vouching for your claims' originality, as well as their accuracy. You expect your reputation—and your grade—to be built partly on your creativity.

Naturally, you're expected to also build on the work of others; but if you don't explicitly give credit when making some important assertion, then you'll be seen as implicitly claiming that you came up with the idea yourself. And if you lead the reader to believe that some words or ideas are yours when they really aren't, you're duping the reader into giving you more credit than you deserve.

Second, it *wrongly denies credit to the people whose work you're copying*. Just as you're trying to impress your reader with your creativity, so other authors were trying to impress the public with theirs. If you take their words without acknowledgment, you're failing to give them the credit they deserve.

Each of these two points is an independent reason why you must give adequate credit. For instance, paraphrasing without attribution a

Supreme Court opinion from 1813 does no great injury to its author. Even borrowing ideas or text from last year's opinions may not much harm the Justices who wrote them; Justices probably care little about getting credit in law review articles. But if you don't give proper credit, you're wronging your readers by misleading them into thinking that your work is original when it really isn't.

This also explains why the rules for legal practice differ from those for scholarly work. "Law," the old saying goes, "is the only discipline where 'That's an original idea!' is a pejorative." There's nothing wrong with a lawyer's copying language from an earlier brief written by other lawyers at the same firm—the judge expects accuracy, not originality, and the other lawyers know that their work is the firm's to use as it likes. But the *rules in scholarly writing are more demanding.*

2. Your obligations

What exactly are these more demanding rules? You should check any specific policies that your law school or university might have, but here are some general guidelines:

a. *If you use someone else's idea, whether or not you use that source's literal words, give credit for the idea in the footnotes.* Acknowledge:

i. any source (law review article, case, or what have you) that you're quoting or paraphrasing;

ii. any source from which you got an idea, even if no one can tell that you got the idea from it;

iii. any source that you know has expressed the idea first, even if you came up with the idea independently (since the academic convention is that people are entitled to credit for being the first to say something).

This is the fair thing to do. It makes your work seem more scholarly, because it shows that you've done your research. And it greatly decreases your chances of being accused of plagiarism.

Don't worry that giving too many people credit will make your work look derivative. First, readers know that even truly original work necessarily rests on some preexisting material. And, second, if proper attribution would show that your work *is* too derivative, the honest and effective solution is to make your work more original, not to try to hide its lack of originality.

People sometime ask whether it's proper to cite blogs in a law review article. Not only is it proper, but it's mandatory, if your observation was borrowed from someone else's blog post, or even anticipated by a blog post—that's the same rule as when you borrow from a law review article, an op-ed, or even a personal conversation.

b. *If you use someone else's words, acknowledge this by using quotation marks (and by giving credit in the footnotes).* Besides giving credit in footnotes for the *ideas* you borrow, you must also make sure that the *words* you use are either your own, or marked with quotes to indicate the borrowing.

c. *Don't use close paraphrases as a way of avoiding direct quotes.* Really close paraphrasing can also constitute plagiarism. For instance, if instead of quoting the preceding paragraph, you write in your paper

> *When you copy another person's text, indicate this via the use of quotes (and through providing acknowledgments in the citations).* In addition to providing acknowledgments in citations for the concepts you use, you should likewise ensure that the language you use is either written by you, or indicated with quotation marks to identify the copying.

you've likely plagiarized the paragraph, even though you've only literally copied a few words: You've taken so much of the structure and choice of concepts that you're still passing off someone else's writing as your own. Rewrite the sentence instead of paraphrasing—it's more honest, and the result will likely be simpler and better tailored to your claim than a close paraphrase would be. And then of course give credit to the original source, since even the rewrite has drawn from that source's ideas.

So either quote using quotation marks or, if that seems inelegant, rewrite the material in your own words. Then, your words will either be original or properly marked as unoriginal by the quotes; and the idea will be properly attributed by the footnote.

d. *Include the proper attribution in the first draft, rather than waiting for the final draft.* First, your school may well treat unattributed quotes or excessive paraphrases as plagiarism even in early drafts, not just in final ones; don't take that risk.[59] Second, even if the law school rules only cover final drafts, the instructor might view unattributed material in a first draft as an early warning sign of an attempt to plagiarize—and even if you do everything right in the end, you don't want to be graded by someone who suspects your ethics. Third, including the attribution at the outset prevents your forgetting to do it later; and "I was going to properly attribute the material, but I forgot" is rarely a persuasive defense.

e. *What you needn't do.* You don't have to give people credit in the text; thorough citation in the footnotes is enough to discharge your intellectual debts. What's more, repeatedly saying "Professor X says this, but that's wrong because" can distract from your affirmative point (see Part V.D, p. 68). You need to deal with the counterarguments, but you don't have to make the other commentators the protagonists of your article.

The goal of the text is to convey your ideas to the reader, and the text should be focused on that goal. In legal writing, we can acknowledge our sources in footnotes. There's no need to use the text for that.

f. *Other media.* Note that these rules apply to academic legal writing, where footnotes are indeed an option. Some have argued that the rules can't be quite the same for works in which footnotes are forbidden or strictly limited (such as op-eds, most magazine articles, or unfootnoted books aimed at laypeople). That's a complex debate; it's clear that some borrowing has to be attributed even in those media, but I suspect the requirements have to be somewhat less demanding. Nonetheless, when you can give credit in footnotes—for instance, when you're writing law review articles, student notes, seminar papers, or write-on competition papers—you have an obligation to do so.

3. Copying from yourself

If you're seeking *law school credit* for a project, and you're reusing work that you did before, you need to clear this with your instructor. Most law schools will probably not let you reuse substantial parts of a project for which you've already gotten school credit; but they might let you reuse parts of an outside project, if your instructor agrees. Get permission up front.

Also, if you're going to rely heavily in *one published work* on *another of your published works,* then you should let your readers know, with a footnote such as "Portions of the discussion in this section are adapted from ...." When law review editors are deciding whether to accept the piece, the footnote warns them that part of the new work isn't novel, and gives them a chance to check how much overlap there is. If the overlap is small, they won't mind it—they'll understand that one often needs to repeat part of an old argument while making a new one. But they'll appreciate knowing about this up front; and if you hadn't warned them up front, they might be justifiably upset with you for not having warned them.

Such a footnote is also a matter of politeness and self-interest as well as honesty: You don't want readers to notice a familiar passage and assume that you've copied someone else's work, or to become annoyed that they've been led to reread something they've already read before. Alerting them at the outset is better for them and for you.

B. Being Candid

It's unethical to characterize sources in a way that you know is wrong or misleading (for instance, by quoting out of context, by omitting important qualifiers, or by portraying some source as dispositive when you know that there are contrary sources that you aren't citing). You would feel betrayed if a supposedly scholarly source deceived you, and you'd condemn the source's author. You should likewise make sure that your work is never open to this sort of criticism.

Candor is also practically useful as well as ethically necessary. Explaining and responding to the weaknesses in the evidence tends to make your work more impressive and ultimately more persuasive. Trying to hide the problems or, worse, mischaracterizing the facts (even by omission or misleading description) will on balance make your work less effective and less worthy of respect.

And if your faculty advisor suspects you—even without solid proof—of knowing misstatements or omissions of important details, your grade will suffer. At best, the advisor will give you the benefit of the doubt and conclude that you've been merely sloppy rather than deceitful; and who wants that as a best case scenario? This, after all, is the person who will be grading your work, and whom potential employers may call when they want a candid evaluation of your qualities (whether or not you list the advisor as a possible reference).

The same is true of potential employers who read your work because it's listed on your resume. Some of them will only skim your work casually, and not see the problems; but others will know more about the field than you do, especially if you're looking for a job in the field in which you've been writing. They'll be tolerant of occasional errors—but if they see a pattern of errors that is suggestive of dishonesty, the results can be devastating for you. If you're one of several applicants for a job, even a hint of possible misconduct might be enough to get you rejected.

C. Being Fair and Polite to Your Adversaries

As Parts XV.A (p. 138), XV.B (p. 139), and XX.C.2 (p. 249) mentioned, it's better to be polite and impersonal in your criticisms of your adversaries, and to be candid, fair, and thorough in responding to their arguments. It's the right thing to do. It makes your article more persuasive. It makes you look better. And it avoids turning your adversaries into your enemies.

D. Being Fair to the Law Review Editors Who Publish Your Article

You'll be working closely with your law review editors, and you may run into them unexpectedly in your future career. Everything will go much more smoothly if both sides treat the other fairly. Some particular points:

1. If you borrow from an old article of yours in a new article, mention this in the footnotes (p. 337).

2. Never renege once you've accepted an offer (see p. 268).

3. Don't lie about your credentials.

4. When you're shopping up an offer (see p. 267), be clear and honest about who gave you the offer and what the offer's terms are.

5. After you've accepted an offer, call or e-mail the other journals to withdraw your piece (see p. 267).

6. Comply with the law review's publication schedule, and if you need to be a few days late with some step, let the editors know as soon as possible.

E. Preserving Confidentiality

Make sure that nothing you write violates any of your obligations of confidentiality.

1. If you're borrowing from a memo you wrote while working at a law firm or in a judge's chambers (see Part XX), make sure that (a) you get your past employer's permission (since the entire work may be confidential work product), and that (b) your article doesn't include any client confidences.

2. If you interview anyone for the article, make sure that you clearly

339

tell them that their words—or the information they reveal—may end up in print.

3. If you want to quote an e-mail, fax, or letter that was sent to you personally, ask the author for permission; such messages are presumptively confidential, both as a matter of copyright law and as a matter of people's expectations.

This is true even if the message contains nothing terribly secret. People are often less careful in what they write in a casual e-mail than they would be if they had known their message would be published. They may speak less clearly, precisely, or temperately than they otherwise might, and then be understandably upset if what they thought was a personal e-mail becomes public knowledge. Give them a chance to re-think and clarify their words.

There are some possible exceptions, especially if there's reason to fault the sender for sending the message that he did: For instance, if someone sends you an e-mail trying to stop you from writing about something by threatening you with a frivolous lawsuit, you may generally legitimately quote the e-mail in the process of explaining why the threat is unsound. (Of course, if you think the threat is serious, quoting the letter may increase the chances of litigation, and might thus be imprudent even if not unethical.) But as a general matter you shouldn't quote personal messages unless you first get the sender's permission.

It's best to also check with the author if you want to quote a message that was e-mailed to an Internet discussion list. There may be a plausible argument that the message was voluntarily made public; but the matter isn't completely clear, so you're better off erring on the side of checking with the author.

F. Treating Sources Fairly

1. Make sure that any sources that you quote *agree to be quoted* (see above).

2. *Check the quotes* with the sources to make sure that you're not misquoting them, that you aren't quoting them out of context, and that they didn't inadvertently misspeak.

3. Use of surveys and interviews is often covered by *university rules related to protection of human subjects*. These rules apply not just to medical experiments, but also—much to the surprise of many law professors—potentially to a much broader range of research that relies

even partly on surveys and interviews.

Perhaps the rules shouldn't apply so broadly, and perhaps under a sound interpretation of the rules, they won't be interpreted apply so broadly. But the safe course is to assume that they do apply. Fortunately, the committees tend to be willing to give exemptions for most surveys that gather nonconfidential information; but you do need to ask for the exemption beforehand. If you run into trouble with the committee, ask your faculty advisor to intercede on your behalf.

The rules are quite complex, so you should check with your university's Human Subjects Protection Committee or Institutional Review Board (or a similarly named institution) before starting any research that involves surveys or interviews. Don't just check with your faculty advisor, unless you have reason to think that he's very knowledgeable about such committees. Many law professors know little about this subject, and sometimes innocently violate the rules themselves.

G. Making Data Available

If you rely on unpublished data, especially on data that you gathered yourself, be prepared to make it available to other researchers who are trying to check or repeat your work. This isn't strictly an ethical requirement; but if you don't share your data, many people will assume that you have something to hide. Telling people "you don't need to check my data, just trust me" is a good way to lead them not to trust you.

The best approach is for you or the law review to put the data—both any tables that you might already have computerized and scanned versions of any important documents you have uncovered—on a Web page, and for you to then cite the Web page in your footnotes. That way, even readers who don't actually check your data will know that you're making it available to be checked, and will trust you a bit more as a result.

Putting the material on the Web can also save you time and trouble later, especially since it will decrease the chances that you'll lose the data. Even if no one else will ever check the data, the law review cite-checkers probably will, so you'll in any case need to format it in a way that others can read it. You might as well use a medium—the Web— that will let you do it once, and not have to worry about repeating it each time someone asks you for the information.

Whether or not you put your data on the Web, make multiple copies or printouts of your materials, and keep them in a safe place. Don't just rely on your computer, or you might lose everything to a disk drive crash. And don't rely on the journal's filing system, even if you sent in the unpublished material and the journal labeled it in the footnotes as being "on file with the law review." I haven't investigated the matter closely, but I highly doubt that such files are well-organized and well-maintained.

CONCLUSION

This book has tried to provide a short but comprehensive guide to academic legal writing, from choosing a topic to publishing and publicizing the finished work. I hope it helps you make your article better, and encourages you to write still more.

Writing and publishing can help you become a better writer, and thus a better lawyer. It can help you become a more successful lawyer, by getting you a good grade, a good board position on your law review, a publication credit, and the clerkships, lawyer jobs, or teaching jobs that these credentials can yield. And it can, even if only slightly, influence the law for the better.

APPENDIX I: CLUMSY WORDS AND PHRASES*

Here are some common clunkers, and their simpler, more readable replacements. Naturally, there's some subjectivity in any such list—other writers will doubtless disagree with me about some of these items. Moreover, the replacements aren't always perfect synonyms: Sometimes, for instance, you need to use the clunker as part of a legal term of art (e.g., "a cease and desist letter").

Still, I suspect that nine times out of ten the replacements will be better than the original, and that you should at least consider making the change. Of course, some of these changes also require some grammatical adjustment of other parts of the sentence.

A. *Needlessly Formal Words*

> "Short words are best, and the old words when
> short are the best of all."
>
> —attributed to Winston Churchill

Some words are fancy synonyms for simpler words. Your readers will know these complex words—but such words take more time and effort to process than simple ones. Switching to simpler words will make your work more pleasant to read, and will make it less likely that readers will set it aside.

1. Verbs

Avoid	Use instead
acquire	get
advert to	mention
afford	give *(when used in this sense)*
ascertain	find out
assist	help
attempt	try

* Sources: much e-mail from many people; Joseph Stevens, *Legal Language, Plain and Simple*, Mo. B. Bull., Mar. 1993, at 4. For an even more thorough list, see Bruce Ross–Larson, *Edit Yourself: A Manual for Everyone Who Works with Words* (1996).

cease	stop
commence	start
demonstrate	show
desire	want
elucidate	explain *or* clarify
endeavor	try
enquire	ask
evince	show
exit	leave
expend	spend *(when referring to money)*
facilitate	help
indicate	show *or* say *or* mean
inquire	ask
locate	find
negative	negate *or* reject
notify	tell
observe	see *or* watch
obtain	get
opine	say *or* write *(usually)*
permit	let *or* allow
possess	have
procure	get
provide	give
purchase	buy
request	ask
retain	keep
state	say *or* write *(often, but not always)*
substantiate	prove *or* support
utilize	use

2. Nouns

ambit	reach *or* scope
consequence	result *or* effect
echelon	level
individual	person *(except when counterposed to a group or a corporation)*
individuals	people
objective	goal
personnel	people
portion	part
remainder	rest *(usually)*

3. Adjectives, adverbs, conjunctions, and prepositions

additional	another *or* more
additionally	also *or* another
adjacent to	next to *or* near
approximately	about
contiguous to	next to
exclusively	only
firstly, secondly, etc.	first, second, *etc.*
forthwith	immediately
frequently	often
inter alia	among others *or* among other things
notwithstanding	despite
numerous	many
prior to	before
provided that	if *or* but *or* so long as
said	the *or* this *(e.g., in "said contract")*
subsequent	later

subsequent to	after
subsequently	after *or* later *or* then
sufficient	enough
very	*consider omitting*

B. Circumlocutions

These are phrases that talk around the subject instead of getting to the point. They often add unneeded prepositional phrases or other grammatical complexities that make the sentence harder to parse and its substance harder to see.

1. Generally

a bad thing	bad
a good thing	good
a large number of	many
a number of	some *or* several *or* many *or* *something more precise*
at present	now
at the place that	where
at the present time	now
at this point in time	now *or* currently *or* at this point *(rarely)* *or some such*
at this time	now *or* currently *or some such*
concerning the matter of	about
does not operate to	does not
during the course of	during
during the time that	while
excessive number of	too many
for the duration of	during *or* while
for the reason that	because

had occasion to	*omit*
I would argue that	*omit*
in a case in which	when *or* where
in accordance with	by *or* under
in an *X* manner	*X*ly, *e.g.*, "hastily" *instead of* "in a hasty manner"
in circumstances in which	when *or* where
in close proximity	near
in point of fact	in fact (*or omit altogether*)
in reference to	about
in regard to	about
in the course of	during
in the event that	if
is able to	can
is cognizant of	knows *or* is aware of
is lacking in	lacks
is unable to	cannot
it could be argued that	*replace with an explanation for why the argument is sound (if that's what you mean)*
it has been determined that	*omit*
it is apparent that	clearly *or omit*
it is arguable that	*replace with an explanation for why the argument is sound (if that's what you mean)*
it is clear that	clearly *or omit*
it should be noted that	*omit*
most of the time	usually
negatively affect	hurt *or* harm *or* decrease *or some such*
on a number of occa-	often *or* sometimes

sions	
on the part of	by
piece of legislation	law *or* statute *or* bill
referred to as	called
serves to *X*	*X*s (*e.g., change* "this only serves to strengthen the opposition" *to* "this only strengthens the opposition")
sufficient number of	enough
the case at bar	this case
the instant case	this case
the manner in which	how
this case is distinguishable	*all cases are distinguishable; you probably mean* "this case is different"
to the effect that	that
under circumstances in which	when *or* where
with regard to	about

2. Verbs turned into nouns or adjectives

accord respect to	respect
during the pendency of *X*	while *X* was pending
for the purpose of doing	to do
has a deleterious effect on	hurts *or* harms
has a negative impact on	hurts *or* harms
is aware that	knows
is binding on	binds
is desirous of	wants
is dispositive of	disposes of

made negative refer-ence to	criticized *or* disagreed with
render assistance	help
was aware that	knew
with regard to	about

3. "The fact that"

The phrase "the fact that" adds an extra conceptual level; you're not just talking about an event or condition ("John sold the land to Mary"), but rather about the fact that the event or condition occurred ("the fact that John sold the land to Mary"). Sometimes this extra complexity is necessary—but rarely. The phrase can usually be omitted entirely (perhaps with some grammatical adjustment of the following clause, e.g., "John's selling the land to Mary"), or replaced with "that."

because of the fact that	because
despite the fact that	despite *or* though
due to the fact that	because
in light of the fact that	because *or* given that
owing to the fact that	because *or* since
the fact that	that

C. *Redundancies*

These are phrases in which one word simply repeats what is already embodied in another; this is sometimes worth doing for emphasis, but only rarely. If you replace the phrases with their simpler equivalents, you'll find that the result is usually clearer, and no less emphatic.

any and all	all
cease and desist	stop (*except in* "cease and desist order" *or* "cease and desist letter")

APPENDIX I: CLUMSY WORDS AND PHRASES

consensus of opinion	consensus
each and every	every
null and void	void
period of time	time *or* period
point in time	time *or* point
provision of law	law
rate of speed	speed
still remains	remains
until such time as	until

APPENDIX II: ANSWERS TO EXERCISES

A. *Editing Exercises*

1. Basic Editing, p. 141

Let's start by rewriting the opening paragraph of the first paper:

The Child Firearms Safety Act as currently written is a well intentioned piece of legislation which will likely have little effect on the incidence of minors accidentally killed by handguns. However, with some critical modifications the act could play a significant role in lowering the number of minors lost to handgun accidents each year. These modifications should include: compelling either that the gun be kept in a locked container *or* unloaded; the inclusion of long guns in the Act; and making violation of the Act a felony offense.

1. Consider the first sentence:

The Child Firearms Safety Act as currently written is a well intentioned piece of legislation which will likely have little effect on the incidence of minors accidentally killed by handguns.

What information does it convey to the reader?

a. The Act is well-intentioned.

b. It won't protect minors much from accidental handgun deaths.

Comparing this brief summary with the full sentence shows two areas of flab. First, we see *unnecessary words*. The summary says "the Act" instead of "the Act as currently written," with no loss of clarity: The phrase "as currently written" restates the obvious—mentioning some law generally refers to the law as currently written, unless there's some reason to think otherwise. The author probably wanted to distinguish the current version from the proposed change, but this distinction is clear enough even without the "as currently written." Likewise, "piece of legislation" is a long way to say "law" or "bill."

Second, we see *an unhelpful idea*. The first sentence in our summary—"the Act is well-intentioned"—doesn't convey much valuable information. Whether the law is well-intentioned is probably as clear to the reader as it is to the writer, and it in any event doesn't much matter, given the terms of the assignment ("write a short memo advising the Senator whether she should vote for the law").

The author probably wanted to acknowledge the drafters' good intentions as a polite gesture, before criticizing their handiwork; but such a gesture is unneeded in a memo to one's boss. Cut these phrases, which leaves us with:

> The Child Firearms Safety Act will likely have little effect on the incidence of minors accidentally killed by handguns.

2. *Do normal people talk* about things "having little effect on the incidence of" other things? Say instead

> The Child Firearms Safety Act probably will not significantly protect minors against fatal handgun accidents.

or

> The Child Firearms Safety Act probably will not significantly reduce fatal handgun accidents involving minors.

or

> The Child Firearms Safety Act will probably do little to protect minors from fatal handgun accidents.

The bureaucratese noun phrase "incidence of" is cut, and the noun phrase "little effect on"—which doesn't explicitly say what kind of effect you're looking for—is replaced with the verb phrases "will not significantly protect [or reduce]" or "will do little to protect." None of these is perfect, but all are clearer, more concrete, and more active than the original.

3. Consider the second sentence together with the revised first one:

> The Child Firearms Safety Act will probably do little to protect minors from fatal handgun accidents. However, with some critical modifications the act could play a significant role in lowering the number of minors lost to handgun accidents each year.

Note the *redundancy*: The first sentence talks about "protect[ing] minors against fatal handgun accidents" (or, in the original version, "hav[ing an] effect on the incidence of ... fatal handgun accidents"). The second talks about "play[ing] a significant role in lowering the number of minors lost to handgun accidents"—pretty much the same thing.

How about merging the two sentences? True, shorter sentences are usually better than long ones, but eliminating redundancy is generally better still. If we merge the two sentences, we get:

> The Child Firearms Safety Act will probably do little to protect minors from fatal handgun accidents unless some critical modifications are made.

The result is shorter, and still communicates the same message: The word "unless" concisely indicates that there's a problem (a lack of "significant protect[ion of] minors," which is the same as a high "number of minors lost to handgun accidents") that will remain until something is done ("some critical modifications are made").

We can improve the sentence still further by changing the *bureaucratese* "unless some critical modifications are made" to the clearer and more colloquial "unless it is modified":

> The Child Firearms Safety Act will probably do little to protect minors from fatal handgun accidents unless it is modified.

4. Let's now look at the new first sentence together with the old third sentence:

> The Child Firearms Safety Act will probably do little to protect minors from fatal handgun accidents unless it is modified. These modifications should include: compelling either that the gun be kept in a locked container or unloaded; the inclusion of long guns in the Act; and making violation of the Act a felony offense.

One sentence now ends with "unless it is modified" (originally, it called for "some critical modifications"), and the other begins with "These modifications should include." If we merge them and cut *the repetition*, we get:

> The Child Firearms Safety Act will probably do little to protect minors from fatal handgun accidents unless it is modified to compelling either that the gun be kept in a locked container or unloaded; the inclusion of long guns in the Act; and making violation of the Act a felony offense.

The new sentence is shorter than the original two put together, and still not unreadably long.

5. We now need to fix the grammar to match the changes in sentence structure ("it is modified to compel*ling*" is wrong), but in the process we see that the *original grammar was itself flawed*: The three proposed modifications—"compelling" / "inclusion of" / "making"—weren't grammatically parallel. (Editing often exposes logical and grammatical errors that had been obscured by the excess words.) Tidying up the grammar and trimming yet further, we get:

> The Child Firearms Safety Act will probably do little to protect minors from fatal handgun accidents unless it is modified to cover long guns, to treat violations as felonies, and to allow guns to be kept in a locked container or unloaded.

Before: 88 words, 454 characters.

After: 42 words, 198 characters.

All the information, fewer than half the words.

Now, on to the second paper's opening paragraph:

The proposed Child Firearms Safety Act (the "bill") is an inconsequential piece of legislation. Aside from the significant political impact of the bill, it carries little weight and makes little difference. Despite public misconceptions, the few benefits of the bill, notably the probable slight decrease in the number of childhood gun accidents, do not exceed the drawbacks, such as the inaccessibility of guns during a home invasion and loss of civil liberties. Therefore, unless some strong amendments are made to the bill, I recommend that you oppose the bill.

Here's a quick mark-up of all the word- and phrase-level problems:

The proposed Child Firearms Safety Act [(the "bill")] *[obvious]* is an [inconsequential] *[word choice]* [piece of legislation] *[legalese]*. [Aside from the significant political impact of the bill,] *[throat-clearing/obvious]* it [carries little weight] *[word choice]* and [makes little difference] *[redundant]*. [Despite public misconceptions,] *[throat-clearing]* the few benefits of the bill, notably the probable slight decrease in [the number of] *[not really necessary]* childhood gun accidents, do not exceed the drawbacks, such as the inaccessibility of guns during a home invasion and [loss of civil liberties] *[vague/possibly redundant]*. Therefore, unless some [strong] *[word choice]* amendments are made to [the bill], I recommend that you oppose [the bill] *[repeated phrase]*.*

---

* For those who want a detailed explanation:

The parenthetical "(the 'bill')" adds nothing new; in a memo that discusses one bill, it's clear what you're referring to when you say "the Act" or "the bill."

"Inconsequential" isn't quite idiomatic; one can have inconsequential arguments, but one rarely hears of an "inconsequential law."

"Piece of legislation" is usually legalese for "law," "bill," or some such.

"Aside from the significant political impact of the bill" doesn't add anything. The Senator can easily tell what the bill's political impact would be; you have no specialized knowledge on this subject beyond what she has.

Arguments can "carry little weight," but laws are generally not described this way.

"Carries little weight" and "makes little difference" seem, in context, to mean the same thing.

"Despite public misconceptions" doesn't add anything. Sometimes it might, for instance if you were asked to research what the public thinks about the law. But in this problem, you probably don't know anything more about public attitudes than the Senator does.

"Loss of civil liberties" is vague: Does this refer to Second Amendment rights? To Fourth Amendment rights? To a general right to self-defense? If it's either of the first two, it should be made clearer. If it's the third, then the sentence is redundant. I inferred that it was indeed the third, because the paper didn't say anything later about the Second or the Fourth Amendments.

"Strong" is the wrong word to describe amendments.

And here's the text with those problems corrected:

> The proposed Child Firearms Safety Act would be ineffective. It will do little good. The few benefits of the bill, notably the probable slight decrease in childhood gun accidents, do not exceed the drawbacks, such as the inaccessibility of guns during a home invasion. Therefore, unless some amendments are made to the bill, I recommend that you oppose it.

The revised version is already shorter, but the revisions expose something deeper: The four sentences overlap considerably.

1. The first sentence says the law is ineffective (the original first sentence called it "inconsequential").

2. The second sentence says the same thing, originally by saying that the law "carries little weight" and "makes little difference."

3. The third sentence explains why the law is ineffective, and makes the first two sentences superfluous: Explaining that the law's benefits don't exceed the drawbacks also communicates that the law would on balance be ineffective.

4. The fourth sentence says that the Senator should oppose the law as it is now written, which adds little to the first three sentences.

Here's the text with the fat (the first, second, and most of the fourth sentence) trimmed away:

> I recommend that you oppose the proposed Child Firearms Safety Act. Its few benefits, notably the probable slight decrease in childhood gun accidents, do not exceed the drawbacks, such as the inaccessibility of guns during a home invasion.

This is shorter, and says pretty much all that the original says, but it still lacks force—as did the original, but this revision just shows the weakness more clearly. And this weakness comes from the second sentence's primarily focusing on abstractions ("benefits" and "drawbacks") and not the concrete things to which the abstractions refer ("slight decrease in childhood gun accidents" and "the inaccessibility of guns during a home invasion"). What's more, the second concrete phrase ("the inaccessibility of guns ...") is itself a bit abstract: The real problem isn't "inaccessibility" as such, but the interference with self-defense. While abstractions sometimes work as political rhetoric, intelligent readers

---

The phrase "the bill" is repeated in the last sentence; the second occurrence should be changed to "it." That's what pronouns are for.

are usually more swayed by concrete points.

So here's an alternative:

> I recommend that you oppose the proposed Child Firearms Safety Act. The Act will probably only slightly decrease childhood gun accidents, but will likely make it substantially harder for people to defend themselves and their children against criminals.

This isn't the best possible rewrite, but it's better than the preceding version—and it's much better than what we began with.

Before: 89 words, 477 characters.

After: 38 words, 214 characters.

All the information, fewer than half the words.

2. Editing for Concreteness, p. 141

Here again is the paragraph, with the clauses numbered for convenience:

> [1] The existence of antimask laws poses difficult questions of constitutional law. [2] We know that the freedom of speech is one of our most cherished rights, [3] especially when there is a danger that the free expression of unpopular speakers would be deterred by the fear of negative consequences. [4] And yet the prevention of crime, [5] including crime facilitated by the wearing of masks, [6] must surely be ranked as one of the more compelling of the possible government interests. [7] The public understandably wants to avoid the harm to property, persons, and the social fabric that may flow from such crime.

Sentence 1 says nothing substantive. It does try to persuade readers that the article is important; but the best way to do that is to describe the problem in a way that will make readers come to that conclusion themselves. Simply asserting the difficulty or importance of the problem doesn't help much.

Clause 2 is likewise a platitude, and adds nothing to the analysis. Either the reader already believes freedom of speech is important, or he thinks it's overrated. In either case, the clause is useless.

Clause 3 does add something substantive: It points out that antimask laws can deter some people from speaking. But what "negative consequences" is the clause talking about? Do we usually say "He didn't want to speak out, because of a fear of negative consequences"?

No, we tend to be more concrete about what the negative consequences were—a fear of being fired, of being harassed by the police, of being ostracized by acquaintances, and so on. Such concrete examples are more vivid and more persuasive than a general statement about "negative consequences."

A reader who just sees "negative consequences" might not be sure what that means, or might not imagine those consequences that we want him to think about: For instance, he might think of imprisonment, but conclude that this isn't something to worry about—if the speech is protected, he might reason, First Amendment law will shield people from being imprisoned for the speech, and if it's unprotected, then speakers ought to be deterred from engaging in such speech. And in any case, the reader will have to do extra work to translate the abstraction "negative consequences" into specific examples that he can visualize and evaluate.

Likewise, "unpopular speakers" is more abstract than it should be. Which speakers do we have in mind? Which speakers do we want the reader to have in mind? Even if the statement is true of all or most unpopular speakers, it would help if we can give some concrete examples that will help persuade the reader that this is a real problem that's likely to arise fairly often.

Clauses 4 and 6 likewise add something substantive—they suggest to readers that preventing crime is so important that it might sometimes justify even laws that deter speech. But they don't add much: This point is pretty obvious, and to the extent it's not obvious, it's better made by showing readers some crimes that antimask laws can cause, and leading the readers themselves to conclude that it's important to prevent those crimes. And this is even more true of clause 5 ("including crime facilitated by the wearing of masks"): Of course the paragraph means to include crime facilitated by the wearing of masks, but it ought to do this by actually describing how masks can facilitate crime.

Finally, sentence 7 is almost entirely redundant of clauses 4 and 6.

So here's a possible rewrite, shown alongside the original:

| The existence of anti-mask laws poses difficult questions of constitutional law. We know that the freedom of speech is one of our most cherished rights, especially when there is a danger that the free expression of unpopular speakers would be deterred by the fear of negative consequences. And yet the prevention of crime, including crime facilitated by the wearing of masks, must surely be ranked as one of the more compelling of the possible government interests. The public understandably wants to avoid the harm to property, persons, and the social fabric that may flow from such crime. | Unpopular speakers, whether Klansmen, civil rights advocates, or anti-globalization protesters, often understandably fear retaliation: social ostracism, firing, government harassment, or worse. If they are barred from wearing masks while demonstrating, the risk of retaliation may deter them from speaking.

Wearing a mask, though, can help people get away with crimes. Masked demonstrators may feel that they can break windows, throw stones, or even attack people with relative impunity, because eyewitnesses will find it hard to identify exactly who did what. |

The general and the abstract have been replaced or supplemented by the concrete and the specific:

"unpopular speakers"	becomes "Klansmen, civil rights advocates, or anti-globalization protesters"
"negative consequences"	becomes "social ostracism, firing, government harassment"
"crime facilitated by the wearing of masks" and "harm to property, persons, and the social fabric"	become "break windows, throw stones, or even attack people"

One concrete connection has been added: Instead of making the reader figure out how anti-mask laws lead to speech being "deterred by the fear of negative consequences," the revised version now makes the causation clear—"If they are barred from wearing masks while demonstrating, the risk of retaliation may deter them from speaking." This might not be strictly necessary, since it should be pretty obvious, but I think it's helpful.

At the same time, two generalities have been removed: "the freedom of speech is one of our most cherished rights" and "the prevention of crime ... must surely be ranked as one of the more compelling of the possible government interests." Such platitudes almost never persuade people. It seems to me that most readers will be much more persuaded by the concrete details in the revised version: the examples of unpopular speakers, and the examples of the crimes that they can cause.

B. Understand Your Source, p. 159

1. The quote said "[T]he annual accidental death toll for handgun-related incidents is slightly under 200," and referred to the *Injury Facts* excerpt that I reproduce below. *Injury Facts* lists 187 accidents as involving handguns, 93 as involving shotguns, 50 as involving hunting rifles, and 804 as involving "Other and unspecified firearm missile."*

ALL DEATHS DUE TO INJURY, UNITED STATES, 1995–1997, Cont.

Type of Accident or Manner of Injury	1997ᵃ	1996	1995
Mechanical suffocation, E913	1,145	1,114	1,062
In bed or cradle, E913.0	236	219	207
By plastic bag, E913.1	44	40	37
Due to lack of air (in refrigerator, other enclosed space), E913.2	21	15	14
By falling earth (noncataclysmic cave-in), E913.3	54	57	59
Other and unspecified mechanical suffocation, E913.8, E913.9	790	783	745
Struck by falling object, E916	727	732	656
Struck against or by objects or persons, E917	247	171	198
Caught in or between objects, E918	85	71	90
Machinery, E919	1,055	926	986
Agricultural machines, E919.0	530	496	514
Lifting machines and appliances, E919.2	119	115	141
Earth moving, scraping, and other excavating machines, E919.7	85	73	106
Other, unspecified machinery, E919.1, E919.3–E919.6, E919.8, E919.9	321	242	225
Cutting or piercing instruments or objects, E920	104	97	118
Firearm missile, E922	981	1,134	1,225
Handgun, E922.0	161	187	233
Shotgun (automatic), E922.1	84	93	116
Hunting rifle, E922.2	65	50	64
Other and unspecified firearm missile, E922.3–E922.9	671	804	812
Explosive material, E923	149	130	170
Fireworks, E923.0	8	9	2
Explosive gases, E923.2	57	49	62
Other and unspecified explosive material, E923.1, E923.8, E923.9	84	72	106
Hot substance or object, corrosive material and steam, E924	111	104	97
Electric current, E925	488	482	559
Domestic wiring and appliances, E925.0	53	66	88
Generating plants, distribution stations, transmission lines, E925.1	139	135	158
Industrial wiring, appliances, and electrical machinery, E925.2	27	15	26
Other and unspecified electric current, E925.8, E925.9	269	266	287
Radiation, E926	0	0	0
Other and unspecified, E914, E915, E921, E927, E928	3,007	2,984	2,730
Late effects (deaths more than one year after accident), E929	1,204	1,126	1,091
Adverse effects of drugs in therapeutic use, E930–E949	248	253	206

Thus, for most fatal gun accidents, the type of gun isn't reported, or the report isn't entered into the databases on which *Injury Facts* relies. "Under 200" is just the number of fatal gun accidents *known* to involve handguns. The actual number of fatal handgun accidents doubtless includes many (maybe most) of the 804 fatal gun accidents categorized as "Other and unspecified." *Understand how the line items relate to each other.*

2. The *Sourcebook of Criminal Justice Statistics Online* table (see

---

* The careful reader will have noted that one of the categories is a bit oddly described: There are very few truly automatic shotguns. It turns out that the label is a bit inaccurate; the "shotguns (automatic)" category, a CDC source tells me, includes all shotguns.

below) does say that 69.4% of all sexual abuse offenses in its dataset were committed by "Native Americans, Alaska Natives, Asians, and Pacific Islanders." But the table reports only *federal* prosecutions, as the heading "Offenders sentenced in U.S. District Courts" and the fourth line of the Note reveal.

Table 5.25

Offenders sentenced in U.S. District Courts under the U.S. Sentencing Commission guidelines

By primary offense, sex, race, and ethnicity, fiscal year 1999

Primary offense	Total cases	Sex – Male Number	Male Percent	Female Number	Female Percent	Total cases	White Number	White Percent	Black Number	Black Percent	Hispanic[a] Number	Hispanic Percent	Other[b] Number	Other Percent
Total	55,388	46,841	84.6%	8,547	15.4%	54,394	16,728	30.8%	14,246	26.2%	21,231	39.0%	2,189	4.0%
Murder	108	95	88.0	13	12.0	103	29	28.2	18	17.5	17	16.5	39	37.9
Manslaughter	57	38	66.7	19	33.3	57	10	17.5	6	10.5	8	14.0	33	57.9
Kidnaping, hostage-taking	81	77	95.1	4	4.9	80	19	23.8	19	23.8	22	27.5	20	25.0
Sexual abuse	230	226	98.3	4	1.7	229	42	18.3	17	7.4	11	4.8	159	69.4
Assault	455	404	88.8	51	11.2	437	120	27.5	96	22.0	72	16.5	149	34.1
Robbery	1,790	1,638	91.5	152	8.5	1,771	732	41.3	852	48.1	138	7.8	49	2.8
Arson	82	79	96.3	3	3.7	82	60	73.2	10	12.2	3	3.7	9	11.0
Drug offenses														
Trafficking	21,993	18,992	86.4	3,001	13.6	21,780	5,311	24.4	6,743	31.0	9,345	42.9	381	1.7
Communication facility	397	320	80.6	77	19.4	395	120	30.4	137	34.7	130	32.9	8	2.0
Simple possession	689	565	82.0	124	18.0	612	275	44.9	171	27.9	146	23.9	20	3.3
Firearms	2,679	2,570	95.9	109	4.1	2,647	1,064	40.2	1,179	44.5	328	12.4	76	2.9
Burglary, breaking and entering	54	52	96.3	2	3.7	54	14	25.9	10	18.5	2	3.7	28	51.9
Auto theft	189	178	94.2	11	5.8	184	87	47.3	56	30.4	37	20.1	4	2.2
Larceny	2,082	1,322	63.5	760	36.5	1,977	981	49.6	705	35.7	170	8.6	121	6.1
Fraud	6,196	4,517	72.9	1,679	27.1	6,077	3,127	51.5	1,876	30.9	752	12.4	322	5.3
Embezzlement	959	386	40.3	573	59.8	939	519	55.3	272	29.0	80	8.5	68	7.2
Forgery, counterfeiting	1,295	1,008	77.8	287	22.2	1,287	526	40.9	533	41.4	167	13.0	61	4.7
Bribery	195	177	90.3	19	9.7	194	91	46.9	49	25.3	33	17.0	21	10.8
Tax	728	596	81.9	132	18.1	712	519	72.9	83	11.7	53	7.4	57	8.0
Money laundering	1,001	766	76.5	235	23.5	991	442	44.6	166	16.8	321	32.4	62	6.3
Racketeering, extortion	977	893	91.4	84	8.6	961	344	35.8	291	30.3	200	20.8	126	13.1
Gambling, lottery	136	124	91.2	12	8.8	136	112	82.4	6	4.4	5	3.7	13	9.6
Civil rights	81	73	90.1	8	9.9	78	52	66.7	16	20.5	10	12.8	0	X
Immigration	9,659	9,053	93.7	606	6.3	9,531	363	3.8	339	3.6	8,652	90.8	177	1.9
Pornography, prostitution	414	405	97.8	9	2.2	410	347	84.6	24	5.9	22	5.4	17	4.1
Prison offenses	299	270	90.7	29	9.7	289	101	34.9	107	37.0	75	26.0	6	2.1
Administration of justice offenses	866	631	72.9	235	27.1	840	350	41.7	182	21.7	271	32.3	37	4.4
Environmental, wildlife	211	195	92.4	16	7.6	205	160	78.0	6	2.9	24	11.7	15	7.3
National defense	20	17	85.0	3	15.0	20	15	75.0	0	X	2	10.0	3	15.0
Antitrust	44	42	95.5	2	4.5	43	37	86.0	2	4.7	1	2.3	3	7.0
Food and drug	78	67	85.9	11	14.1	76	48	63.2	12	15.8	9	11.8	7	9.2
Other	1,342	1,065	79.4	277	20.6	1,197	711	59.4	263	22.0	125	10.4	98	8.2

Note: The sentencing reform provisions of the Comprehensive Crime Control Act, Public Law No. 98-473 (1984), created the United States Sentencing Commission. The Commission's primary function is to develop and monitor sentencing policies and practices for the Federal courts. On Apr. 13, 1987, the Commission submitted initial Sentencing Guidelines and Policy Statements to Congress. The guidelines became effective on Nov. 1, 1987, and apply to all offenses committed on or after that date. These data are derived from the United States Sentencing Commiss on's fiscal year 1999 Offender Dataset. The Commission collected information on 55,557 cases sentenced under the Sentencing Reform Act (guideline cases) during fiscal year 1999 (Oct. 1, 1998 through Sept. 30, 1999). Given the nature of the data file and reporting requirements, the following types of cases are not included in the data presented here: cases initiated but for which no convictions were obtained, defendants convicted for whom no sentences were yet issued, defendants sentenced but for whom no data were submitted to the Commission, and cases not sentenced under the Sentencing Reform Act (non-guideline cases).

A case or defendant is defined as a single sentencing event for a single defendant (even if multiple indictments or multiple convictions are consolidated for sentencing).

Multiple defendants in a single sentencing event are treated as separate cases. If an individual defendant is sentenced more than once during the fiscal year, each sentencing event is identified as a separate case. (Source, p. A-4.)

Of the 55,557 guideline cases, some were excluded due to missing information. For sex, 169 cases were excluded due to one or both of the following conditions: missing primary offense category, 149; and missing gender information, 48. For race and ethnicity, 1,163 cases were excluded due to one or both of the following conditions: missing primary offense category, 149; and missing race or ethnicity information, 1,124.

Under drug offenses, "communication facility" refers to the use of a device, such as a telephone, in a drug trafficking offense.

[a]Includes both black and white Hispanics.
[b]Includes Native Americans, Alaska Natives, Asians, and Pacific Islanders.

Source: U.S. Sentencing Commission, *1999 Sourcebook of Federal Sentencing Statistics* (Washington, DC: U.S. Sentencing Commission, 2000), pp. 14, 15. Table adapted by SOURCEBOOK staff.

Nearly all sexual abuse cases are prosecuted in state court; the main federal law covering sexual abuse is the one that applies to Indian reservations. American Indians thus commit a tiny fraction of all sexual abuse nationwide, but they commit a large fraction of the sexual abuse prosecuted by the federal government. *Understand what jurisdiction your data covers.*

C. *USA Today Survey Report, p. 170*

As the problem mentioned, the question in this graphic refers to a Ninth Circuit case that concluded that the use of the words "under God" in the Pledge of Allegiance violates the Establishment Clause.

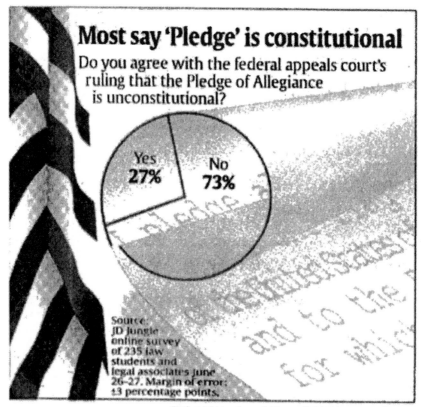

Most say 'Pledge' is constitutional

Do you agree with the federal appeals court's ruling that the Pledge of Allegiance is unconstitutional?

Yes
27%

No
73%

Source:
JD Jungle
online survey
of 235 law
students and
legal associates June
26–27. Margin of error:
±3 percentage points.

By Lori Joseph and Marcy E. Mullins, USA TODAY

1. The first problem isn't with the statistics: The court of appeals didn't rule that "the Pledge ... is unconstitutional"; it ruled that the in-

clusion of "under God" in the Pledge is unconstitutional. This means that though the current text of the Pledge is impermissible, the Pledge could still be said with two words out of about 30 excised. Simply calling the decision a "ruling that the Pledge of Allegiance is unconstitutional" is likely to mislead many readers.

2. From the text of the headline ("Most say 'Pledge' is constitutional"), most *of whom* did you think said this? When a national paper says "most say," most readers will assume "most Americans," "most citizens," or some such. But the tiny type in the bottom of the box says, "Source: JD Jungle online survey of 235 law students and legal associates June 26–27. Margin of error: ±3 percentage points."

So the survey only measured the views of *law students and legal associates* (whatever "legal associates" exactly means), not a representative sample of the public. Is "Most say 'Pledge' is constitutional" / "Yes 27% / No 73%"—in a paper that isn't aimed at lawyers—an accurate way of summarizing a poll of an uncertain subset of the legal profession?

3. Beyond this, the poll isn't even a valid estimate of the views of "law students and legal associates." The poll is an "online survey," so it's not a random sample, but a self-selected one: It registers only the votes of those people who hear about the survey and care about it enough to participate—likely those who are unusually interested in the subject, and not a representative sample of *any* group.*

4. Finally, even a random sample of 235 people couldn't yield a margin of error of ±3% (an assurance that there's a 95% chance that the reported result is within 3% of the true breakdown of people's views). If you divide 100 by the square root of 235, you get a margin of error of roughly ±6.5%, and if you're more precise and follow the instructions in the footnote on p. 161, you'll get roughly ±5.8%.

The margin of error only makes sense for randomly chosen samples, not for self-selected ones—but even if we ignore that problem, the ±3% margin of error is incorrect.

D. Drunk Driving Study, p. 181

Recall the exercise: Assume that a study showed that 15% of New

---

* I called JD Jungle and confirmed that the survey was indeed self-selected, as the words "online survey" in the USA Today description strongly suggest.

York drivers aged 16 to 25 drive drunk at least once a month. The Minnesota legislature is considering new penalties for drunk driving by 16–to–18–year-olds, and a commentator who supports the law writes "Drunk driving has reached epidemic proportion among teenagers, with 15% of driving-age teenagers driving drunk at least once a month." What errors or unstated assumptions can you find in this statement?

1. *Extrapolating from one place and time to another:* The commentator is making a claim about people generally. Listeners will presumably mean that he's referring either to the nation or to Minnesota, and that he's referring to people now. The commentator should make clear that the numbers refer to New York drivers, at the time the study was conducted. The results might be similar for Minnesotans today, but the reader should be told that this is an assumption, not a proven fact.

2. *Inferring from a group's behavior to the behavior of a subset of the group:* The study focused on behavior among drivers aged 16 to 25, but the commentator is inferring that "driving-age teenagers"—which readers might interpret either as 16–to–18–year-olds, which is what the law refers to, or 16–to–19–year-olds, which is what "driving-age teenagers" literally means (assuming the driving age is 16)—will behave the same.

This inference may or may not be correct. It may be that 16–to–18–year-olds drink and drive more than 16–to–25–year-olds generally, because they're less mature—or less than 16–to–25–year-olds generally, because they can't legally buy alcohol, or because they're less likely to own a car. In any event, the commentator should again make clear the assumption that he is making.

3. *Misreporting the study:* Finally, the commentator errs in reporting one aspect of the study—the study reported that 15% of New York *drivers* aged 16 to 25 drove drunk at least once a month, not that 15% of 16–to–25–year-olds drove drunk at least once a month. The commentator's ultimate position may be right: There may be a serious drinking and driving problem among Minnesotan teenagers, and perhaps the law will help fight that. But the errors and omissions in reporting the study need to be corrected.

E. Source–Checking Exercise, p. 190

Let's quickly repeat the sources.

The student article:

Proponents of manufacturers' liability further argue that handguns are almost useless for self-protection: a handgun is six times more likely to be used to kill a friend or relative than to repel a burglar, and a person who uses a handgun in self-defense is eight times more likely to be killed than one who quietly acquiesces. [Footnote cites source A.]

Source A (which was indeed written by a proponent of manufacturers' liability, so no need to check that), **quoted in relevant part**:

The handgun is of almost no utility in defending one's home against burglars. A Case Western Reserve University study showed that a handgun brought into the home for the purposes of self-protection is six times more likely to kill a relative or acquaintance than to repel a burglar. [Footnote cites source B.] .... The handgun is also of questionable utility in protecting against robbery, mugging or assault .... The element of surprise the robber has over his victim makes handguns ineffective against robbery .... A survey of Chicago robberies in 1975 revealed that, of those victims taking no resistance measures, the probability of death was 7.67 per 1000 robbery incidents, while the death rate among those taking self-protection measures was 64.29 per 1000 robbery incidents. [Footnote cites source C.] The victim was 8 times more likely to be killed when using a self-protective measure than not!

Although handguns possess little or no utility as self-protection devices, some may have a socially acceptable value when properly marketed under restricted guidelines [such as to the police].

Source B (the Case Western study), quoted in relevant part:

During the period surveyed in this study [1958–73 in Cuyahoga County, Ohio], only 23 burglars, robbers or intruders who were not relatives or acquaintances were killed by guns in the hands of persons who were protecting their homes. During this same interval, six times as many fatal firearm accidents occurred in the home.

Source C, the Chicago robbery study, quoted in relevant part:

Of those victims taking no resistance measures, the probability of death was 7.67 per 1000 robbery incidents, while the death rate among those taking self-protection measures was 64.29 per 1000 robbery incidents.

Method of Victim Self-Protection	Extent of Injury to Victim			
	Death	Injured	None	TOTAL
Physical force	7 (6.1%)	66	41	114
With Weapon Not a gun	0	1	4	5
Handgun	0	2	4	6
Verbal Denial of goods	2 (4.5%)	17	25	44
Verbal Shouting	2 (3.7%)	20	32	54

Flight	7 (18.9%)	10	20	37
Verbal or Phys. Resis. & Flight	0	7	13	20
Unknown	23 (79.3%)	3	3	29
None	7 (0.8%)	132	774	913
TOTAL	48 (3.9%)	258	916	1222

1. The First Claim

(i) The first error is small—the clause

> a handgun is six times more likely to be used to kill a friend or relative than to repel a burglar

aims to summarize source A ("a handgun brought into the home for the purposes of self-protection is six times more likely to kill a relative or acquaintance than to repel a burglar"), but replaces "acquaintance" with "friend." The two terms are false synonyms; they sound interchangeable, but they're different—members of rival gangs, for instance, may be acquaintances but not friends, and likewise for a drug dealer and his customer, or a prostitute and her client.[*] Not that huge a mistake, but worth avoiding all the same.

The more serious problem is that source A errs in quoting source B, which actually says

> During the period surveyed in this study [1958—73 in Cuyahoga County, Ohio], only 23 burglars, robbers or intruders who were not relatives or acquaintances were killed by guns in the hands of persons who were protecting their homes. During this same interval, six times as many fatal firearm accidents occurred in the home.

Let's compare the student article and the original study (source B), noting the differences (tagged in italics):

Source A (citing source)	Source B (cited source)
a. "a handgun" *(ii)*	a. "guns"
b. "six times more likely"	b. "six times as many"
c. "to kill a friend or relative" *(iii)*	c. "[to be used in a] fatal firearms accident[]"

---

[*] Source A also says "a handgun brought into the home for the purposes of self-protection," rather than just "a handgun," which is how the Harvard article quotes A. But it turns out that the error is in source A, not in the Harvard piece: The original source, B, focused on guns generally, without regard to why they were brought into the home.

d. than "to repel" *(iv)*	d. than to "kill[]"
e. "burglar" *(v)*	e. "burglars, robbers, or intruders who were not relatives or acquaintances"
f. [No place / time specified] *(vi)*	f. Cuyahoga County, Ohio, 1958-73

(ii) The study discusses guns generally, not handguns in particular (item a). Nearly 2/3 of all guns in civilian hands are rifles or shotguns, not handguns.[60] *Make clear when you're inferring from general data* (which covers all guns) *to a specific subset* (handguns).

(iii) The cited study talks about *fatal firearm accidents,* which is not the same as *killings of friends or relatives* (item c). Most uses of firearms to kill a friend or relative are intentional killings, not accidents;[61] and apparently about half of fatal firearm accidents involve the shooter accidentally killing himself, and others involve killings of strangers.[62]

(iv) "Repel[ling] a burglar" is different from "killing" one (item d). One can also repel a burglar with a handgun by visibly pointing it at him, by shooting and missing, or by shooting and wounding—and such uses are probably 50 or more times more common than killings of burglars.[63] *Avoid false synonyms.*

(v) "Burglar" is not the same as "burglars, robbers or intruders who were not relatives or acquaintances" (item e). The difference may not be great, but there is a difference.

(vi) The study is limited to one county and one period (item f). Gun crimes, accidents, and defensive uses vary by place and time; for instance, fatal gun accidents in the U.S. during the study period 1958–73 averaged about 2400/year, while in 2004–2006 they averaged about 700/year.[64] It's therefore hard to tell how generalizable the study's findings are, but the article should certainly have acknowledged (at least in a footnote) that the study was limited to gun use in a particular place and time, and not to gun use generally. *Make clear when you're inferring from a specific subset* (Cuyahoga County, 1958–73) *to general data* (the country generally and at all times) *or to another specific subset* (the country in the year that the article was written).

The article said that "Proponents of manufacturers' liability further argue that handguns are almost useless for self-protection ...." Can the article's assertions be defended on the grounds that the article is only describing what *proponents are arguing,* not what is in fact true? If so, we shouldn't fault the author of the article being cite-checked, though we'd fault the author of source A.

But I don't think this is right. An author must expect that readers will interpret a statement like this as implicitly endorsing the cited statistics—and the article that we're checking has indeed been cited as endorsing the statistics that it describes. If authors want to cite erroneous sources only to show what others believe, they should explicitly state that the cited material is likely in error: This is part of their *responsibility not to mislead their readers.*

2. The Second Claim

The second claim is that "a person who uses a handgun in self-defense is eight times more likely to be killed than one who quietly acquiesces"; and the article cites source A, which says,

> A survey of Chicago robberies in 1975 revealed that, of those victims taking no resistance measures, the probability of death was 7.67 per 1000 robbery incidents, while the death rate among those taking self-protection measures was 64.29 per 1000 robbery incidents. The victim was 8 times more likely to be killed when using a self-protective measure than not!

Here, source A does correctly summarize the original study (source C). But let's compare the student article with source A:

The student article (citing source)	Source A (cited source)
a. [No place / time specified] *(vi ½)*	"A survey of Chicago [events] in 1975"
b. [No crime type specified] *(vi ½)*	"robberies"
c. "a person who uses a handgun in self-defense" *(vii)*	"[a] victim[] ... taking self-protection measures"
d. "is eight times more likely to be killed"	"[is] 8 times more likely to be killed"
e. "than one who quietly acquiesces"	"[than one who] tak[es] no resistance measures"

(vi½) As in error (vi), source A talks about one place, Chicago, one time, 1975, and one crime, robbery; but the student article talks generally about "a person who uses a handgun in self-defense." The reader should be alerted to this limitation, since the specific data may not apply equally to self-defense more broadly (for instance, to self-defense against burglary, assault, rape, or attempted murder), to the country generally, or to the year that the article was written.

(vii) But the big error is the leap from "self-protection measures" to "us[ing] a handgun in self-defense." Neither source A nor the original study, source C, explicitly equates the relative risk of self-protection measures generally with the relative risk of self-protection using a handgun. *The student article falsely claims something about a specific subset when the data only relates to a broader set.*

Look again at the table from source C:

Method of Victim Self-Protection	Extent of Injury to Victim			
	Death	Injured	None	TOTAL
Physical force	7 (6.1%)	66	41	114
With Weapon Not a gun	0	1	4	5
Handgun	**0**	**2**	**4**	**6**
Verbal Denial of goods	2 (4.5%)	17	25	44
Verbal Shouting	2 (3.7%)	20	32	54
Flight	7 (18.9%)	10	20	37
Verbal or Phys. Resis. & Flight	0	7	13	20
Unknown	23 (79.3%)	3	3	29
None	7 (0.8%)	132	774	913
TOTAL	48 (3.9%)	258	916	1222

The study found that when a handgun was used for self-protection, *0 out of 6* robberies led to death—not *18 out of 280* (64.29 per 1000), the ratio on which source A relies, and which covers weaponless self-defense, self-defense with weapons, verbal response, and flight. The study doesn't tell us how effective handguns really are for self-defense, since six cases are far too few to justify any inference. But the study also does not show that "a person who uses a handgun in self-defense is eight times more likely to be killed than one who quietly acquiesces."

So the author of the student article made a bad mistake. But the author of source A also erred because his citation of source C is *likely to mislead readers.* Three sentences shortly before the "8 times more likely" sentence and the one sentence immediately after had to do with self-defense using a handgun:

> A Case Western Reserve University study showed that a handgun brought into the home for the purposes of self-protection is six times more likely to kill a relative or acquaintance than to repel a burglar .... The handgun is also of questionable utility in protecting against robbery, mugging or assault .... The element of surprise the robber has over his victim makes handguns ineffective against robbery .... A survey of Chicago robberies in 1975 revealed that, of those victims taking

no resistance measures, the probability of death was 7.67 per 1000 robbery incidents, while the death rate among those taking self-protection measures was 64.29 per 1000 robbery incidents. The victim was 8 times more likely to be killed when using a self-protective measure than not!

Although handguns possess little or no utility as self-protection devices, some may have a socially acceptable value when properly marketed under restricted guidelines [such as to the police].

The sentences that cite source C are easily misread as focused on defensive *handgun* uses, rather than on what they literally discuss, which is self-protection generally—and the author of the student article seems to have misread these sentences exactly this way. Had source A explicitly said that it was extrapolating from general self-defense data to handgun data, the student article's author might have recognized the limitations of the data, and at least made them clear to his readers.

Appendix III: Sample Cover Letters

A. *For Sending an Article to Law Reviews*

[Your name]
[Your address]
[Your phone number]
[Your e-mail address]

Articles Department
[Law review name and address]

[Date]

Dear Madam or Sir:

In the attached short article,* I aim to make two contributions. First, I argue that laws requiring bystanders to help crime victims—a hot subject in recent years†—may be practically counterproductive.‡ The laws' likely practical effects have been largely ignored by the literature, which has focused almost exclusively on whether the laws are morally justifiable.§ As too often happens, discussion about a law's morality has driven out discussion about its wisdom. Such laws have been recently proposed both on the federal level and in some of the largest states; I

---

* [Note: These footnotes are, of course, explanations for the benefit of this book's readers. You shouldn't include footnotes in your cover letters, or overtly talk about novelty, nonobviousness, or utility—these points should be implicit in your letter, not explicit.]

The piece for which I wrote this letter was unusually short—about 10 pages—and I thought some readers might be troubled by this. I therefore decided to warn readers up front: People's judgments turn in large part on their expectations, so if they are warned to expect something short, they won't mind as much that it's short. Likewise, if there's something unusual about your article, you might want to mention it up front.

The article, incidentally, got picked up by a Top 20 primary journal.

† I'm trying to persuade readers that this is a hot field, and that the article will be useful to academics and will thus get cited.

‡ Saying that a law yields unexpected or counterproductive results tends to highlight that the piece is nonobvious.

§ Suggests that the subject is novel.

371

hope my analysis will help the debate about these proposals.*

Second, I hope to start a broader discussion about what I identify as the potential "anticooperative effect" of criminal law and tort law generally: The tendency of some kinds of government coercion, even when they are in the abstract morally proper, to deter citizens from cooperating with the authorities. Sometimes, I suggest, even a morally justifiable urge to legally compel correct behavior can seriously backfire in this way. I hope the example of duty-to-rescue/report laws can stimulate attention to this practical effect of coercive rules.†

Please let me know if you have any questions about the piece.

Sincerely Yours,

[Signature]

B. For Sending a Reprint to Potential Readers

[Your name]
[Your address]
[Your phone number]
[Your e-mail address]

[Recipient name]
[Recipient address]

[Date]

Dear [salutation]:

In the attached short article, I aim to make two contributions, which I hope will be of some use to criminal law teachers.‡

---

* Aimed at persuading people that this is useful.

† The first paragraph explained the piece's core claim. The second paragraph connects the claim to a broader debate; this is again aimed at persuading readers of the article's academic utility.

‡ I sent this letter to various criminal law professors, including casebook authors. With the casebook authors, part of my goal was to persuade them to cite the article in the casebook; but I thought it was better to suggest this indirectly.

First, I argue that laws requiring bystanders to help crime victims may be practically counterproductive.* The laws' likely practical effects have been largely ignored by the literature, which has focused almost exclusively on whether the laws are morally justifiable. As too often happens, discussion about a law's morality has tended to drive out discussion about its wisdom. I hope my analysis will help broaden both the public, scholarly, and legislative debate about these proposals and class discussions about them.† *[Personalize to the extent possible, e.g., with a sentence such as this:]* Given your work on [subject or article title], which I found to be quite helpful when writing my article and which I cite on p. ___, I thought you might find this topic particularly interesting.

Second, I briefly point to what I call the potential "anticooperative effect" of criminal law and tort law generally: the tendency of some kinds of government coercion, even when they are in the abstract morally proper, to deter citizens from cooperating with the authorities. I freely admit that the precise magnitude of this effect is hard to gauge, but I argue that the effect must be considered, both as to duty-to-rescue/report laws and as to other laws, such as prostitution laws, illegal immigration laws, and bans on carrying concealed weapons (see pp. ___–___).‡

And I hope this discussion may be pedagogically helpful. Students often miss these sorts of indirect practical effects, and discussing the anticooperative effect in this context might help train students to analyze criminal law policy questions more comprehensively.§

I would love to hear any reactions you might have to this piece.

Sincerely Yours,

[Signature]

---

* This is a very brief summary of the article's main claim. You might want to summarize your claim in a bit more detail, but remember that this cover letter's purpose is to persuade readers to read the Introduction. If you think one short sentence will do that, stick with the one sentence.

† These sentences are aimed at quickly communicating to the reader that the piece is novel, nonobvious, and useful.

‡ This connects the main claim to a broader theoretical issue.

§ If you think your article has a teaching payoff as well as a scholarship payoff, mention it.

C. For Sending a Reprint to Potential Readers on Whose Work You Substantially Rely

[Your name]
[Your address]
[Your phone number]
[Your e-mail address]

[Recipient name]
[Recipient address]

[Date]

Dear [salutation]:

I much enjoyed reading your [article name], and found it very helpful in writing my own article, which I enclose; your article is of course cited heavily on pp. ___-___ [or *"cited heavily throughout,"* if it is indeed *cited throughout the piece*]. [*If you disagree with the recipient's article, write:*] As you may notice, my analysis diverges in some measure from yours, but I nonetheless found your work to be very thought-provoking, and useful in helping me sharpen my own viewpoint.

In my article, I argue that laws requiring bystanders to help crime victims may be practically counterproductive. The laws' likely practical effects have been largely ignored by the literature, which has focused almost exclusively on whether the laws are morally justifiable. As too often happens, discussion about a law's morality has tended to drive out discussion about its wisdom. I hope my analysis will help broaden both the public, scholarly, and legislative debate about these proposals and class discussions about them.

I also briefly point to what I call the potential "anticooperative effect" of criminal law and tort law generally: the tendency of some kinds of government coercion, even when they are in the abstract morally proper, to deter citizens from cooperating with the authorities. I freely admit that the precise magnitude of this effect is hard to gauge, but I argue that the effect must be considered, both as to duty-to-rescue/report laws and as to other laws, such as prostitution laws, illegal immigration laws, and bans on carrying concealed weapons (see pp.

__-__).

Finally, I hope this discussion may be pedagogically helpful. Students often miss these sorts of indirect practical effects, and discussing the anticooperative effect in this context might help train students to analyze criminal law policy questions more comprehensively.

I would love to hear any reactions you might have to this piece.

Sincerely Yours,

[Signature]

ENDNOTES

1 "We must think things not words, or at least we must constantly translate our words into the facts for which they stand, if we are to keep to the real and the true." Oliver Wendell Holmes, Jr., *Law in Science and Science in Law,* 12 Harv. L. Rev. 443, 460 (1899).

2 *See Insulted Thai Convicted,* L.A. Times, Mar. 3, 1988, Metro sec., at 2.

3 *See* Militia Act of May 8, 1792, ch. 33, § 1, 1 Stat. 271, 271; United States v. Miller, 307 U.S. 174, 179 (1939).

4 *See* Eugene Volokh, *"Necessary to the Security of a Free State",* 83 Notre Dame L. Rev. 1 (2007).

5 *See* Christopher L. Eisgruber & Lawrence G. Sager, *The Vulnerability of Conscience: The Constitutional Basis for Protecting Religious Conduct,* 61 U. Chi. L. Rev. 1245, 1247 (1994).

6 This discussion builds on Eugene Volokh, *Intermediate Questions of Religious Exemptions—A Research Agenda with Test Suites,* 21 Cardozo L. Rev. 595 (1999); for examples of the incidents on which the test suite is based, *see id.* at 603 n.18, 630 nn.106–109. *Cf.* KDM *ex rel.* WJM v. Reedsport School Dist., 196 F.3d 1046, 1056–57 (9th Cir. 1999) (Kleinfeld, J., dissenting) (also using computer test suites as a model for testing legal claims).

7 *See* Centers for Disease Control & Prevention, *Injury Mortality Reports, 1999–2006,* http://webappa.cdc.gov/sasweb/ncipc/mortrate10_sy .html (query selecting [1] Homicide, [2] Firearm, [3] Year(s) of Report 1999 to 1999).

8 *See* Gary Kleck, *Targeting Guns* 149–62 (1997)

9 Pamela Samuelson, *Good Legal Writing: Of Orwell and Window Panes,* 46 U. Pitt. L. Rev. 149, 158 (1984).

10 Deirdre N. McCloskey, *Economical Writing* 31 (2nd ed. 2000).

11 *See* Samuelson, *supra* note 9, at 165.

12 L.P. Hartley, *The Go-Between* 17 (2002).

13 McCloskey, *supra* note 10, at 33.

14 *See id.* at 50–52.

15 *See* Centers for Disease Control & Prevention, *Injury Mortality Reports, 1999–2006,* http://webappa.cdc.gov/sasweb/ncipc/mortrate10_

sy.html (query selecting [1] Unintentional, [2] Firearm, [3] Year(s) of Report 2006 to 2006, [unlabeled] custom age range <1 to 14); Centers for Disease Control & Prevention, *WISQARS Nonfatal Injury Reports,* http://webappa.cdc.gov/sasweb/ncipc/nfirates2001.html (queries selecting [1] Unintentional, [2] Firearm, [3] Year(s) of Report 2006 to 2006 and Disposition either "Treated and Released" or "Transferred or Hospitalized," [unlabeled] custom age range <1 to 14).

[16] *See* Garry Wills, *Lincoln at Gettysburg: The Words that Remade America* 34, 36 (1992).

[17] I owe this example to *Webster's Dictionary of English Usage* 640 (1989).

[18] *See id.* I have not checked the source myself (Webster's doesn't give a precise cite), but (1) I trust Webster's, and (2) I couldn't bring myself to omit this example.

[19] http://prawfsblawg.blogs.com/prawfsblawg/2006/12/thoughts_on_ the.html.

[20] *Id.*

[21] The Kentucky 1835 source is listed in the bibliography as "Digest of the Statute Laws of Kentucky. Edited by C.S. Morehead and Mason Brown. 2 vols. Frankfort, Ky.: A.G. Hodges." Because the journal is interdisciplinary, it uses social science citation conventions rather than those more common in law reviews.

[22] Ky. Const. art. X, § 23 (1799), *in* 3 Francis N. Thorpe, *The Federal and State Constitutions* 1290 (1909).

[23] *Id.* art. III, §§ 28–30, *in* 3 Thorpe, *supra* note 22, at 1283–84.

[24] *See id.* art. IX, *in* 3 Thorpe, *supra* note 22, at 1288; Legislative Research Comm'n, *A Citizen's Guide to the Kentucky Constitution,* http://www.lrc.state.ky.us/lrcpubs/rr137.pdf, at 159 ("Previous Kentucky Constitutions did not recognize amendments, but required the more elaborate revision process.").

[25] Ky. Const. art. XIII, § 25 (1850) ("That the rights of the citizens to bear arms in defence of themselves and the State shall not be questioned; but the general assembly may pass laws to prevent persons from carrying concealed arms."), *in* 3 Thorpe, *supra* note 22, at 1314.

[26] *See* Henry A. Kelly, *Rule of Thumb and the Folklaw of the Husband's Stick,* 44 J. Legal Educ. 341 (1994).

27 521 U.S. 844, 877 (1997).

28 *See* Virginia State Bd. of Pharmacy v. Virginia Citizens Consumer Council, Inc., 425 U.S. 748, 761 (1976).

29 *See In re* Application of Pacifica Found., 50 F.C.C.2d 1025 (1975) (describing Pacifica as "the licensee of noncommercial educational FM Stations" including "WBAI, New York"); *In re* Citizen's Complaint Against Pacifica Foundation Station WBAI (FM), 56 F.C.C.2d 94 (1975), *eventually aff'd sub nom.* FCC v. Pacifica Found., 438 U.S. 726 (1978) (confirming that the broadcast was indeed on WBAI).

30 *Marina Wants to Send Too–Salty Sailboat Back to Sea*, Ventura County Star, Apr. 4, 2002, at B01.

31 *Compare Neighborliness Between Trying Neighbors,* Boston Globe, Apr. 27, 1997, at E2 ("During a swing through Latin America, another vice president, Dan Quayle, remarked that he wished he had studied Latin so that he could communicate.") *with A Dan Quayle Joke,* Wash. Post, June 1, 1989, at A24 (describing the story's origins).

32 *See* http://www.c-span.org/search/basic.asp?BasicQueryText=dc+ rally+against.

33 *All Things Considered: Important Supreme Court Decisions From This Past Term,* Nat'l Pub. Radio, July 3, 2002.

34 Corrections, N.Y. Times, Apr. 7, 1995, at A2.

35 *See* Bureau of the Census, *Historical Statistics of the United States: Colonial Times to 1970* at 116 (1976).

36 433 U.S. 562, 573 n.10, 576 (1978) (stressing that the Court was dealing only with the narrow version and not the broad one).

37 *See, e.g.,* Comedy III Prods., Inc. v. Gary Saderup, Inc., 80 Cal. Rptr. 2d 464, 471 (Ct. App. 1998) (concluding, in a name-or-likeness case, that *Zacchini* "considered, and rejected, a First Amendment defense to liability for infringement of the right of publicity"), *aff'd,* 25 Cal. 4th 387 (2001); Landham v. William Galoob Toys, Inc., 227 F.3d 619, 622 (6th Cir. 2000) ("The right of publicity [speaking of a right to control one's name or likeness] is a creature of state common law and statute and originated as part of the common-law right of privacy. The Supreme Court has recognized its consistency with federal intellectual property laws and the First Amendment, *see generally Zacchini* ...."). Some law review articles make the same mistake.

[38] Schenck v. United States, 249 U.S. 47, 52 (1919) (emphasis added).

[39] A Lexis search in the NEWS;US file for "(shouting fire in a theatre or shouting fire in a theater or shouting fire in a crowded theatre or shouting fire in a crowded theater) and date(< 1/1/2002)" yielded 333 results. The same query with "falsely" before the "shouting" yielded only 72. Some of these results were false positives (e.g., stories that used the metaphor more broadly than just in a free speech context, and the occasional story discussing the common omission of "falsely"), but only relatively few.

[40] *Cf.* Editorial, *Misjudgment of "Nuremberg,"* Omaha World–Herald, Mar. 30, 2001, at 16 (acknowledging that the Holmes quote was limited to "falsehood," but arguing that it should also apply to speech that implicitly urges the killing of abortion providers).

[41] *See, e.g.,* National Safety Council, *Injury Facts* 9 (2000).

[42] The article cites National Safety Council, *Accident Facts* (1980), without giving a page number, but the fatal firearms accidents broken down by age range appear on p. 7 of *Accident Facts*, where the accidents for children under 5 are given as 60, for age 5 to 14 as 300, and for 15 to 24 as 600. The 1000 figure must thus refer to ages 0 to 24.

[43] *See* Centers for Disease Control & Prevention, *Injury Mortality Reports, 1999–2006,* http://webappa.cdc.gov/sasweb/ncipc/mortrate10_sy .html (queries selecting [1] Unintentional, [2] Firearm, [3] Year(s) of Report 2004 to 2006, [unlabeled] custom age range <1 to 17).

[44] *See* Centers for Disease Control & Prevention, *Injury Mortality Reports, 1981–1998,* http://webapp.cdc.gov/sasweb/ncipc/mortrate9.html (queries selecting [1] All Intents, [2] Firearm, [3] Year(s) of Report 1995 to 1995, and [1] Suicide, [2] Firearm, [3] Year(s) of Report 1995 to 1995).

[45] U.S. Census Bureau, *Table 3: Annual Estimates of the Resident Population by Sex, Race, and Hispanic Origin for the United States,* http://www.census.gov/popest/national/asrh/NC-EST2008/NC-EST2008-03.xls (Nov. 1, 2000 estimates).

[46] *See* Peverill Squire, *Why the 1936 Literary Digest Poll Failed,* 52 Pub. Opin. Q. 125, 128–30 (1988).

[47] *Vote Now,* USA Weekend, Dec. 29–31, 1995, at 5; *Call-in Results,* USA Weekend, Feb. 2–4, 1996, at 10.

48 Squire, *supra* note 46, at 130–31.

49 *See, e.g.,* Levin v. Harleston, 966 F.2d 85 (2nd Cir. 1992) (holding that a professor's writings outside the class are presumptively constitutionally protected); *compare* Dambrot v. Central Mich. Univ., 55 F.3d 1177, 1190 (6th Cir. 1995) ("An instructor's choice of teaching methods does not rise to the level of protected expression."), *and* Cohen v. San Bernardino Valley College, 92 F.3d 968, 971 (9th Cir. 1996) ("Neither the Supreme Court nor this Circuit has determined what scope of First Amendment protection is to be given a public college professor's classroom speech. We decline to define today the precise contours of the protection the First Amendment provides the classroom speech of college professors ...."), *with* Hardy v. Jefferson Community College, 260 F.3d 671, 679 (6th Cir. 2001) ("Because the essence of a teacher's role is to prepare students for their place in society as responsible citizens, classroom instruction will often fall within the Supreme Court's broad conception of 'public concern.'").

50 The data is from International Dairy Foods Ass'n, *Dairy Facts* 45 (2003), and FBI, *Uniform Crime Reports—Crime in the United States, 2000*, tbl. 2.18 (2002), http://www.fbi.gov/ucr/cius_00/00crime2_4.pdf. The graph plots ice cream production, in millions of gallons, against 10 times the monthly rape numbers (as a percentage of total rapes in 2000). The multiplier of 10 is used simply to get the two lines to the same vertical location, so the correlation is more visible.

51 FBI, *Uniform Crime Reports—Crime in the United States, 2002*, at 45 (2003), http://www.fbi.gov/ucr/cius_02/pdf/02crime2.pdf.

52 U.S. Department of Justice, Bureau of Justice Statistics, *Criminal Victimization, 2002*, tbl. 1, http://bjs.ojp.usdoj.gov/content/pub/pdf/cvus02.pdf.

53 U.S. Department of Justice, Bureau of Justice Statistics, *Homicide Trends in the U.S.,* http://bjs.ojp.usdoj.gov/content/homicide/tables/totalstab.cfm.

The comparison in the text isn't quite precise. The table cited by the Supreme Court concurrence counts only "homicides ... occurring during years within the 1973–1995 study period when the state in which the county resides had a valid capital-sentencing statute." When we divide the 142,228 number by the total homicide count throughout the country (487,590), we should presumably adjust the denominator to better match the way the numerator is measured, so the percentage may end up being more than 29%. But 29% is in any event just a rough estimate (for instance, we should probably be dividing not the total homicide counts, but rather the counts of the most serious homicides), and the bottom line would in any event remain the same: The disparity between death sentences and homicides is much less than the concurrence suggests.

[54] Arthur L. Kellermann & Donald T. Reay, *Protection or Peril? An Analysis of Firearms–Related Deaths in the Home,* 314 New Eng. J. Med. 1557, 1560 (1986).

[55] *See infra* note 63 and accompanying text.

[56] Sherbert v. Verner, 374 U.S. 398 (1963); Hobbie v. Unemployment Appeals Comm'n, 480 U.S. 136 (1987); Frazee v. Illinois Dep't of Emp. Sec., 489 U.S. 829 (1989); Thomas v. Review Bd., 450 U.S. 707 (1981); Wisconsin v. Yoder, 406 U.S. 205 (1972).

[57] *World Christian Handbook* 99–101 (H. Wakelin Coxill & Sir Kenneth Grubb eds., 1962) (estimating the number of Seventh–Day Adventists, Seventh–Day Baptists, and members of the Seventh–Day Church of God); American Jewish Comm., *American Jewish Year Book* 63 (1961) (estimating the number of Jews); Samuel C. Heilman & Steven M. Cohen, *Cosmopolitans & Parochials: Modern Orthodox Jews in America* 2 (1989) ("As a group, [the Orthodox] have for over a generation remained constant at about 10 percent of the American Jewish population of nearly six million."). Of course, some Christian Sabbatarians might not belong to the leading Sabbatarian denominations, and some Christian Sunday observers (such as Frazee in 1989) might take advantage of the religious exemption (though in 1963, many state laws already protected many Sunday observers, even without need for a mandatory Free Exercise Clause accommodation). Nonetheless, there seems to be reason to think that Jews formed the majority of U.S. Sabbath observers in 1963, and very strong reason to think that they at least formed a large fraction of U.S. Sabbath observers.

[58] *See* First Covenant Church of Seattle v. City of Seattle, 787 P.2d 1352 (Wash. 1990) (exemption from landmark preservation ordinance); State v. Hershberger, 444 N.W.2d 282 (Minn. 1989) (exemption from requirement of displaying orange slow-moving vehicle emblem on horse-drawn carts); People v. Swartzentruber, 429 N.W.2d 225 (Mich. Ct. App. 1988) (same as *Hershberger*); Cabinet for Human Resources Kentucky Health Facilities v. Provincial Convent of the Good Shepherd, Inc., 701 S.W.2d 137 (Ky. Ct. App. 1985) (exemption from certain nurs-

ing home regulations). For pre-1980 cases, see Frank v. State, 604 P.2d 1068 (Alaska 1979) (exemption from moose hunting restriction); Bureau of Motor Vehicles v. Pentecostal House of Prayer, Inc., 380 N.E.2d 1225 (Ind. 1978) (exemption from driver's license photograph requirement); *In re* Palmer, 386 A.2d 1112 (R.I. 1978) (exemption from ban on headgear in courtroom); Whitehorn v. State, 561 P.2d 539 (Okla. Ct. Crim. App. 1977) (exemption from peyote ban); State v. Whittingham, 504 P.2d 950 (Ariz. Ct. App. 1973) (exemption from peyote ban); McMillan v. State, 265 A.2d 453 (Md. 1970) (exemption from ban on headgear in courtroom); People v. Woody, 394 P.2d 813 (Cal. 1964) (exemption from peyote ban); *In re* Jenison, 125 N.W.2d 588 (Minn. 1963) (exemption from jury duty). *First Covenant Church* and *Hershberger* were reversed and remanded by the Supreme Court in light of *Employment Division v. Smith*, but this doesn't matter for the article's purposes.

⁵⁹ *See* Terri LeClercq, *Failure to Teach: Due Process and Law School Plagiarism*, 49 J. Legal. Ed. 236, 254 (1999).

⁶⁰ *See* Gary Kleck, *Targeting Guns* 96–97 (1997).

⁶¹ In recent years, the ratio of intentional gun killings in the U.S. per year to fatal gun accidents has been over 17 to 1 (though this statistic isn't limited to killings in the home). *See* Centers for Disease Control & Prevention, *Injury Mortality Reports, 1999–2006,* http://webappa.cdc.gov/sasweb/ncipc/mortrate10_sy.html (queries selecting [1] Homicide, [2] Firearm, [3] Year(s) of Report 2004 to 2006, yielding 36,767, and selecting [1] Unintentional, [2] Firearm, [3] Year(s) of Report 2004 to 2006, yielding 2,080).

About 15% of the homicides in 2005 were known to be of family members, boyfriends, or girlfriends, and the number seems roughly similar for gun homicides. See U.S. Department of Justice, Bureau of Justice Statistics, *Homicide Trends in the U.S.—Family Homicides,* http://bjs.ojp.usdoj.gov/content/homicide/tables/familytab.cfm (2005 data) (1242 homicides were of family members, not including spouses); U.S. Department of Justice, Bureau of Justice Statistics, *Homicide Trends in the U.S.—Intimate Homicides,* http://bjs.ojp.usdoj.gov/content/homicide/intimates.cfm & http://bjs.ojp.usdoj.gov/content/homicide/tables/intimatestab.cfm (2005 data) (1510 homicides were of spouses, ex-spouses, boyfriends, and girlfriends); Centers for Disease Control & Prevention, *supra* (query selecting [1] Homicide, [2] Year(s) of Report 2005 to 2005, reporting a total of 18,124 homicides). I have no current data about the fraction that involves friends (as opposed to acquaintances).

Note that the numbers may vary across place and time; for instance, fatal gun accidents have been falling more or less steadily since the mid–1970s, while gun homicides rose sharply in the late 1960s and then fell in the late 1990s. Nonetheless, the disparity is great enough that I suspect intentional gun killings are almost always considerably more common than fatal gun accidents.

[62] According to Kleck, *supra* note 60, at 294, "about half of unintentional gunshot woundings are self-inflicted"; I've seen no data specifically limited to *fatal* gun accidents, but I see no reason why the results would be markedly different. I know of no data indicating how many fatal accidents involve a shooter accidentally killing a stranger.

[63] The best study I've seen on this suggests that in over 90% of all defensive gun uses, the assailant isn't even wounded by the defender, much less killed, and another study suggests that only about one in 6.25 gunshot wounds flowing from an assault leads to death. See Gary Kleck & Marc Gertz, *Armed Resistance to Crime: The Prevalence and Nature of Self–Defense With a Gun*, 86 J. Crim. L. & Criminology 150, 185 (1995); Gary Kleck, *Point Blank: Guns and Violence in America* 62 (1991). This data is for assaults generally, not for self-defense shootings specifically, but I know of no reason to think that the ratio for self-defense would be significantly higher.

To take another benchmark, guns are *used* in self-defense from 64,000 to 2.5 million times per year, but are used to *kill* in self-defense from 1400 to 3200 times per year. See Gary Kleck, *Targeting Guns* 151, 152, 163 (1997) (describing the different estimates). If only half of all defensive uses successfully *repel* an attacker, the ratio between repulsions and killings is still from 10 to 1 (64,000/2/3200) to about 900 to 1 (2.5 million/2/1400). These figures are for all crimes, not just burglaries, but the general point should likely largely hold for burglaries, too.

[64] National Safety Council, *supra* note 41, at 42–43; *see* Centers for Disease Control & Prevention, *Injury Mortality Reports, 1999–2006,* http://webappa.cdc.gov/sasweb/ncipc/mortrate10_sy.html (query selecting [1] Unintentional, [2] Firearm, [3] Year(s) of Report 2004 to 2006).

INDEX

References are to pages. Terms in italics are words or phrases that the text discusses.